THE AMIABLE BALTIMOREANS

PUBLISHER'S NOTE

Works published as part of the Maryland Paperback Bookshelf are, we like to think, books that have stood the test of time. They are classics of a kind, so we reprint them today as they appeared when first published many years ago. While some social attitudes have changed and knowledge of our surroundings has increased, we believe that the value of these books as literature, as history, and as timeless perspectives on our region remains undiminished.

Also available in the series:

The Bay
by Gilbert C. Klingel
Tobacco Coast
by Arthur Pierce Middleton

The Amiable
Baltimoreans

FRANCIS F. BEIRNE

The Johns Hopkins
University Press

BALTIMORE, MARYLAND

The Johns Hopkins University Press
Baltimore, Maryland 21218

The paper in this book is acid-free and meets the
guidelines for permanence and durability of the Committee
on Production Guidelines for Book Longevity of the
Council on Library Resources.

Library of Congress Cataloging in Publication Data

Beirne, Francis F., 1890–
  The amiable Baltimoreans.

  (Maryland paperback bookshelf)
  Originally published: New York: E. P. Dutton, 1951.
  Bibliography: p. 380
  Includes index.
    1. Baltimore (Md.)—History.   2. Baltimore (Md.)—
Social life and customs.   I. Title. II. Series.
F189.B157B439   1984   975.2'6   84-47953
ISBN 0-8018-2513-X (pbk.: alk. paper)

To

ALL AMIABLE BALTIMOREANS
PAST AND PRESENT
NATIVE AND ADOPTED
AT HOME AND ABROAD
This Book is Sincerely Dedicated

The Table of Contents

ACKNOWLEDGMENTS

IT IS AN OLD SAYING that every French soldier carries a marshal's baton in his knapsack. It could be said with equal truth that every Baltimorean carries a book about his city under his belt.

So much as mention that you are planning such a book and these potential authors will overwhelm you with advice on how to go about it. But while everybody has an idea as to how it should be done, no two ideas agree. In consequence, excellent though they all are, trying to follow them leads to madness.

The only way to progress is to evolve an idea of your own and, however inept it may be, pursue it relentlessly. Obviously what you write will not satisfy the critics, but at least there is a chance of getting the job done.

The foregoing refers to the bold outline; not to the details. On the latter, others can be of inestimable help in supplying material, suggesting sources, recalling past incidents, reciting anecdotes, correcting errors and the like. First and foremost I am under great obligation to all those writers on Baltimore who have gone before and whose names and works will be found in the Bibliography. I have helped myself generously and unashamedly to their material. If they feel I have been too free with it my defense is that imitation is the sincerest flattery.

Thanks are owing to the staffs of the Enoch Pratt Free Library and of the Maryland Historical Society. Among the personnel of those two institutions Baltimore amiability reaches its peak and virtually begs to be imposed upon. To them no request appears too unreasonable, and none goes unfulfilled.

The files of the Sunpapers have proved a rich source of material. In many instances the unpleasant prospect of long and painstaking research into some essential subject has been relieved by finding it already definitively treated in the "Brown Section" of The Sunday Sun. Such instances are too numerous to mention individually. However, I am especially grateful to the Section's former editor, Mr. Harold Williams, for his sketch of Mrs. Bauernschmidt which I have followed closely.

ACKNOWLEDGMENTS

Above all, I am again indebted to Edith Rossiter Bevan and my wife, Rosamond Randall Beirne, who, as on a former occasion, performed the laborious task of reading manuscript. They made many useful suggestions for alterations.

Finally, it is hardly an exaggeration to say that there is not a single friend, or even casual acquaintance, who has not contributed something to this book in the way of information or suggestion. A number of them have gone to a lot of trouble to do it, too. It would be unfair to mention some of them to the exclusion of others. My profound gratitude and appreciation to these unnamed benefactors.

To those potential authors whose advice it was impossible to follow my suggestion is that they go ahead and get their books out of their systems. There is still a lot left to be said about Baltimore. They can get a good start by noting the sins both of commission and omission in this volume.

FRANCIS F. BEIRNE

Ruxton, Maryland. July 7, 1951

Chapter 1

HOW IT ALL BEGAN

ON THE WALLS of the central hall of the Enoch Pratt Library in Baltimore are the full-length portraits in oil of the six Lords Baltimore for whom the city is named. They are George, Cecil or Cecilius, Charles, Benedict, a second Charles and Frederick, in the order of their succession to the title. Their family name was Calvert.

The spacious central hall of the library, rising from the street level to the roof, is an impressive feature of an exceptionally handsome building. At the time of its construction in the early 1930's the librarian was Mr. Joseph Wheeler, a native of Massachusetts. Who by nature and tradition is better equipped to look after books than a New Englander? Joseph Wheeler, in his eminently practical way, had much to do with planning the details of the construction of the new building.

The portraits of the six Lords Baltimore were imported from England in the 1920's. They had been the property of Sir Timothy Calvert Eden, elder brother of Anthony Eden, the statesman, and a descendant of the Calverts through a female line. Chiefly responsible for the library's acquisition of them was Dr. Hugh Hampton Young. He heard about the sale and offered to buy and present five portraits to the library if the library would itself buy the portrait of the second Lord Baltimore. This the library agreed to do. Dr. Young was of Virginia stock though he came to Baltimore by way of Texas.

Here, then, in the central hall of the Pratt, which hundreds of Baltimoreans visit daily, is visual evidence of a synthesis peculiar to Baltimore and to which it owes its strength, the fruitful collaboration of a Yankee and a Southerner against a British baronial background. This meeting of North and South in the hospitable climate of Baltimore began early and brought into action on the local scene the complementary qualities of these two disparate regions.

George Calvert, the first Lord Baltimore, was the son of Leonard Calvert, a country gentleman of Yorkshire, England, and his wife, Alicia Crossland. He was educated at Trinity College, Oxford, went to London and prospered. He was appointed a Secretary of State to King James I and also was a member of the Privy Council. He was first given a knighthood by his sovereign and for a time was known as Sir George Calvert. He embraced Catholicism which, in 17th-century England, ended his political career. But James elevated him to the Irish peerage, giving him the hereditary title of Baron Baltimore, of Baltimore in Ireland. The name was that of a modest little fishing village on a sheltered bay of the south coast of Ireland, in the "parish nearest America." It is not quite clear why George Calvert took this particular title since his estate was in another part of Ireland.

The Irish pronounce the name of their town *Bal-tee-moor*, the *Bal* having the same sound as the Cal in California. This is one of the few ways the natives of Baltimore, Maryland, do *not* pronounce it. When they are being formal they may give each syllable its full value and say *Bawl-ty-more*. Frequently they abbreviate it to *Bawl-ty-muh* or *Balt-muh*. An even more popular pronunciation is *Bawlermuh*.

But the Irish title was not George Calvert's only reward. After his attempt to plant a colony in Newfoundland had failed he made a trip to Virginia and petitioned King Charles I for a grant to the north of that colony. With the King's sanction he drew up a charter giving him large proprietary rights on both sides of Chesapeake Bay. He died before the gift was consummated but it was carried out in the name of his son, Cecil. On his trip to Virginia George Calvert explored Chesapeake Bay and it is even possible that he visited the spot on which the great city named in his honor was to rise. There is no doubt that Captain John Smith reached the site in the preceding decade when he made a voyage in an open boat up the Bay.

To Cecil Calvert, second Lord Baltimore, fell the distinction of founding the colony and of being the first Lord Proprietary of the Maryland Palatinate. He did not come to Maryland himself but sent his brother Leonard in the autumn of 1633 as head of the expedition in the *Ark* and the *Dove* and first governor of the colony. The only other Lords Baltimore to visit Maryland were Charles, the third Lord Baltimore, and Charles, the fifth Lord Baltimore. The third Lord Baltimore, before succeeding to the title, served as governor. After the death of his father he lived in Maryland as resident proprietor. The fifth Lord Baltimore was in Maryland long enough to discover that, through his ignorance of local geography, he had unwittingly given to the Penns a large slice of territory which now constitutes most of the State of Delaware.

Though for the most part the Lords Baltimore practiced absentee ownership nevertheless the imprint of the family on Maryland was deep and remains so in Baltimore to this day. There are such tangible evidences as the statue of Cecil Calvert before the Courthouse, place names and the State and municipal flags. There are Calvert Street and Baltimore Street. The name Lord Baltimore is memorialized in a hotel, a candy company, a tobacco company, a clothier, a firm of decorators, a chain of filling stations, a florist shop, a barber shop, a laundry, a printing house, a realty company and a theater.

There are almost as many establishments bearing the name "Lord Calvert." Local historians insist that no matter how much the name may be associated with "men of distinction" there never was in real life anybody who was called "Lord Calvert." Cecil Calvert married Lady Anne Arundel, daughter of the Earl of Arundel. The name is sometimes spelled with two "l's." Her name likewise has been given immortality in Baltimore and its environs. The county immediately to the south of the city is Anne Arundel. There is an Arundell Club. There is L'Hirondelle Club, a pun on the name which also is carried out by the swallows on the Arundel coat of arms. Lady Anne's maiden name is attached to a miscellaneous assortment of enterprises and goods running from petroleum and roofing to meat and ice cream .

Having their origin also with the Lords Baltimore are the flag of the State of Maryland and the flag of the municipality. No one is long in Baltimore before becoming acquainted with them. The flag of the municipality boasts the oldest lineage. The field consists of alternating panels of black and gold with a diagonal black and gold strip across it which makes a checkered effect. These are believed to have been the only colors used during the rule of the Lords Proprietary. The flag of the municipality was created by using this black and gold field and superimposing in the center a shield bearing a silhouette of Battle Monument.

During the rebellion of Richard Ingle in 1644 the great seal of Maryland was carried away and never recovered. In 1648 Cecil Calvert sent over another one. On the reverse side were shown the black and gold arms of the Calverts and quartered with them the red and silver arms of Cecil's grandmother Crossland. This is the combination seen on the Maryland flag, white being substituted for silver in the Crossland arms. This picturesque flag is very modern indeed. The first one is believed to have been made in 1889 by the firm of Sisco Brothers which for years supplied the city with flags and banners. But it was not until 1904, in the administration of Governor Edwin Warfield, that the flag was made official by an act of the Legislature. If the flag is of recent origin certainly no other state colors have a more distinguished background or conform more strictly to the meticulous rules of heraldry. When the flag is flown outside the State it never fails to arouse interesting and favorable comment. In Baltimore no official decoration is complete without it.

The Baltimore color scheme of black and gold is delineated also in the Baltimore oriole which has been made the official State bird. Unfortunately for the tradition, in spite of their name, orioles are comparatively rare in the Baltimore area and are no more indigenous to Baltimore than to other parts of the East Coast.

On the other hand the Black-eyed Susan, which is the State's official flower and magnificently combines the Baltimore colors of black and gold, is found in every field of the city's surburbs in season. That season is midsummer, and it has led to a painful predicament. For when the winner of the Preakness, Baltimore's classic horse race, returns for the weighing in and all the ceremony attendant upon victory, what more appropriate than that a horseshoe of Black-eyed Susans be hung about his neck! But the Preakness is run in May. However, the Maryland Jockey Club has not allowed itself to be balked by the obstinacy of nature. Each year it orders a horseshoe of ordinary daisies and hires an artist to use brush and paint converting them into Black-eyed Susans.

In the old days when barber poles throughout most of the country were red, white and blue, Baltimore barbers showed their rugged individuality by painting their poles black and gold. The local custom has been all but forgotten today.

The baronial titles and coats of arms and portraits are all very romantic. But, after all, the Lords Baltimore had to live and the Palatinate was fundamentally a business enterprise. The proprietors derived revenue from the tobacco planters, but farmers are a decidedly inferior source of taxation as compared to prosperous burghers. The Lords Baltimore, being practical men, saw the great advantage of towns to the colony and to themselves.

So in 1683 the Assembly, in a sympathetic mood, passed a law calling for the establishment of towns. Indeed, several towns bearing the name of Baltimore were chartered. There was a Baltimore Town on the Elk River at the head of Chesapeake Bay. There was a Baltimore on the Bush River. But silt filled up its harbor and made it a ghost town. Still another Baltimore Town is said to have existed at one time on the Eastern Shore.

Consequently when, in 1729, a group of planters petitioned the Assembly for a charter for a Baltimore Town on the Patapsco River, nobody expected much to come of it. The site for the town as it was described in the document embraced land owned by one John Moale. Mr. Moale at the time was interested in a vein of iron on his land and he didn't want to be bothered. He was also a member of the Assembly. So he went down to Annapolis and blocked the bill as far as it concerned his land. The petitioners had to change the site of their proposed town to the northwest branch of the Patapsco, adjacent to a decidedly unpromising marsh. The bill as amended by Mr. Moale went through and a charter was granted.

Mr. Moale did not know that, by protesting change, he was establishing a local precedent that was to endure for over two centuries. Let anybody propose a change today and half of Baltimore rises up against it. For years the route through Baltimore on the way from Washington to New York has been a nightmare for motorists. Everybody agrees that something should be done about it. An expressway was designed under the direction of no less an authority than Robert Moses who had no trouble in bending New Yorkers to his will. On the drawings the expressway was made beautiful and inviting with hanging gardens, tennis courts and playgrounds, shade trees and shrubbery.

For a brief moment it looked as though the plan might be

adopted. Then Baltimoreans began to worry because it would cost money. They were concerned over what it might do to Mt. Vernon Place. When it was learned that the project called for the demolition of several ancient houses on Hamilton Street its doom was sealed. One letter to the *Sunpaper* from an elderly subscriber was enough to do the trick. The expressway was pigeon-holed.

There have been proposals for building an elevated highway, for erecting a bridge over the harbor, for tunneling under the harbor. There once was talk of by-passing the city altogether by constructing a highway around it. People in the suburbs at once were up in arms. The route through Baltimore is still a nightmare and promises to remain so for a long time to come.

Another case in point is Lexington Market, an ancient landmark for which General John Eager Howard gave the ground shortly after the American Revolution. For some fifty years it was apparent that Lexington Market had seen its best days. For twenty-five years a new Lexington Market was discussed. It probably would still be a subject of discussion had not a fire a few years ago mercifully destroyed it. Mention change to a Baltimorean and he turns cold to the most inviting proposition. But who knows? Perhaps this quality of proscrastination has saved the city from making costly mistakes.

On the other hand there have been moments of great crisis in its history when Baltimoreans have risen nobly to the occasion. One, as we shall see, was in the founding of a railroad when the town was still young. And it has but lately kept abreast of the times by constructing a modern airport as fine as is to be seen anywhere. Nevertheless the John Moale type continues to be common in Baltimore.

Like the other Baltimores, this one on the Patapsco had a precarious infancy. It was designed as a port of entry, primarily for tobacco. On the tobacco farms in the hills to the west of the new town the tobacco was packed in hogsheads. Then a pole was attached to each hogshead so that it could be drawn, or "rolled," downhill by a team of oxen, to the nearest wharf. These odd highways were known as "rolling roads." One survives to this day and continue to bear its ancient name. But, alas! it took tobacco to Elkridge Landing, a rival port on the Patapsco. In fact,

Baltimore was a failure as a tobacco port in its early days. For some twenty-five years the town languished for want of suitable cargoes.

It was not until 1750 that one John Stevenson, a Presbyterian immigrant from the north of Ireland, exported the first cargo of flour to his homeland as an experiment. The enterprise proved a financial success. From then on Baltimore Town's prosperity was linked with wheat, not with tobacco, and its future was reasonably assured.

With John Stevenson came his brother Henry. Both had studied medicine in England. While John turned to commerce and promotion Henry stuck to his profession. He made a speciality of inoculation against smallpox and very soon patients were coming to him from the neighboring colonies. Thus within a few decades of its founding Baltimore had a doctor of wide reputation, a merchant interested in wheat exports and an iron works nearby. Soon it was to have a thriving shipyard at the adjacent settlement of Fell's Point and a race track. Numbered among its inhabitants were Britons, Irishmen, Jews, Germans and Negroes.

For Dr. Stevenson substitute the Johns Hopkins Hospital, for John Stevenson's wheat exports the grain elevators at the port terminals, for John Moale's iron works the Bethlehem Steel Company at Sparrows Point, for the Fell's Point shipyards the Bethlehem Shipyards, for the race track in Baltimore Town the race track at Pimlico. Add Italians, Czechs, Poles, Lithuanians and Greeks to the original racial stocks and there you have the Baltimore of today. All the principal ingredients of the modern city were there soon after its founding. The chief difference between Baltimore Town and Baltimore City is one of size. The place had bred true to type.

Baltimoreans in these later days have become so accustomed to playing second fiddle to the great metropolises of the North and West that they have to be reminded that in its heyday Baltimore was a place of great consequence. If size and wealth are the true measures of a city's greatness then Baltimore's golden age fell in the first half of the 19th century.

When Baltimore Town was founded in 1729 Annapolis already was the political and cultural center of the Maryland colony. Here the wealthy planters had their town houses and came with their families to disport themselves. The Annapolitans, whose city was spoken of as "the Athens of America," looked down their noses at the upstart merchants of Baltimore. Old Annapolitans and county folk still do. But this does not prevent them from sending their sons to the city to share in the spoils.

Up to the close of the Revolution the growth of the town was gradual. The first census of 1790 gave Baltimore 13,501 inhabitants. It was far outranked by New York, Philadelphia and Boston. Then the French Revolution and the Napoleonic wars disrupted European commerce and immensely stimulated the American merchant marine. Baltimore greatly profited thereby and experienced a phenomenal growth.

In a single decade Baltimore doubled its population, caught up with and passed Boston. Its growth continued. The census of 1830 showed it with a population of 80,620, a few hundred persons ahead of Philadelphia. Baltimore was now second only to New York. This position it held up to 1850. Then Philadelphia reasserted itself and forged ahead. In the Civil War Maryland's most lucrative trading area in Virginia and the Carolinas was well nigh destroyed. On top of that the great new cities began to rise in the Middle West and on the Pacific Coast. In recent years Baltimore has had to be content with sixth place and has battled hard to get even that.

Reference has been made to the happy collaboration of a New Englander and a Southerner in the acquisition of the portraits of the Lords Baltimore and the provision of a suitable hall for the hanging of the same. Very early in the history of the town New Englanders began to find their way to Baltimore. Here they were confronted not only with native sons, but also with Eastern Shoremen and Southern Marylanders steeped in Southern tradition, as well as with exiles from Virginia and the Carolinas. When the Civil War devastated the South the migration to Baltimore to escape the evils of reconstruction was greatly increased. Whether or not it is due to the spirit of toleration fostered by the first Lord Proprietary, New Englanders and Southerners have learned to get along together in Baltimore. They live side by side and their children intermarry. They see good in each other. While New Englanders have excelled in finance and banking the Southerners have taken a prominent part in government and the law. In Ferdinand Ossendowski's book *Beast, Men and Gods* the author described the Siberian forests as a place where north and south meet. Here, he said, the Arctic bear comes face to face with the saber-toothed tiger of the jungle. Such is the situation in Baltimore. Rather than suffer the inconveniences of a state of perpetual warfare there has been a tacit agreement to live and let live. There are monuments paying honor to the North as well as those recognizing the glory of the South even in defeat. It is altogether in keeping with these sentiments that the shoulder insignia of the local National Guard should be a circle in which blue and gray embrace or that the 175th Infantry, recruited in Baltimore, should include in its stand of colors not only the Stars and Stripes and the Maryland State Flag bearing the arms of Lord Baltimore but also the battle flag of the Confederacy.

As time has gone on the picture has become much more complicated by the arrival in the city of new elements. They have come from Europe. More recently there have been heavy injections of new blood from the Middle West. There are acquisitions from Illinois, Michigan and Minnesota, to say nothing of an occasional immigrant from California or such remote places as the Dakotas and Idaho. Baltimore accepts them all quietly and calmly. It is as though Baltimore said that if Yankees from New England can live in peace with Eastern Shoremen, Southern Marylanders, Virginians and Carolinians, then anybody can get along together.

New arrivals from the South are so stimulated by the climate that they imagine they are in New England or Canada. They are seized with a zeal they had not known in their native habitat. On the other hand the immigrants from the North and West exercise their natural endowment of energy. They are full of ideas for making Baltimore over. They have only to look about them to see all the things that need desperately to be done. Often they are frankly critical and faultfinding.

Their first surprise is that, after they have blown off steam, no native Baltimorean utters the stock reply, "Well, if you don't like it here, why don't you go back where you came from?" Native Baltimoreans are much too subtle for that. What they are thinking about is how much work they can get out of the newcomers before they, in their turn, succumb to the native lethargy.

The native Baltimoreans smile tolerantly. Then before the new-comer knows it he has been named general chairman of the Community Chest or put on a slum clearance commission or given some similar thankless job. Nobody asks him to go back home so long as they can turn over to him a laborious task that a native son otherwise would have to do.

That attitude is true of Baltimore's native men. It is not quite true of Baltimore's native women with respect to female immigrants. The native women do not want women from Kalamazoo or Wichita running things. They are glad enough to have them put in good hard work. They may even elect them to boards. But they stop short of making them the chairman or the president. The unwritten law is particularly rigid in social organizations. One lady of great charm and with all the proper social attributes once was proposed for membership on the board of an exclusive "patriotic" society. "But," someone protested, "she is not a Baltimorean." That settled it, though she had been resident in the city more than fifty years.

Baltimore has reached middle age and has all the characteristics of that mature period. It can look back on a career that in some instances has been distinguished. It has had its dramatic moments and its fair share of conquests. It is quite ready to enjoy serenity. It likes its homely comforts and doesn't care to be rushed. It has plenty of life left but no desire to fight it out with younger cities. It is happy merely to hold its own. It is too wise in worldly matters to aspire to being bigger and better. It does not try to ape New York or Chicago. For the most part it likes to go to bed around 10 P.M. It is a very discouraging town for boosters.

Chapter 2

MOSTLY GEOGRAPHICAL

IF YOU take an elevator to the top of the Mathieson Building, which rises some thirty-five stories above Baltimore Street, you will get a good idea of the layout of the city. In broad outlines it is like a saucer. That is to say the city proper, though resting on rolling land and also on some rather steep hills, is rimmed by considerably higher ground to the west, north and northeast. Thus hundreds of thousands of Baltimoreans who live in the suburbs enjoy at home the advantages of the clearer and cooler air that is found at higher elevations.

Two outstanding topographical features of the city are its roads and its streams. While Baltimore is a port it also is a glorified market town. From its center radiates a series of highways over which farmers from the counties used to bring their produce to market. In some instances these highways also connected Baltimore with more distant cities. Thus, beginning on the south at the Annapolis Road and moving clockwise, one runs successively into the Washington Road, the Frederick Road, the Windsor Mill Road, the Liberty Road and the Reisterstown Road. These are the main arteries of communication on the west. Continuing with the hands of the clock one next meets the Falls Road to the north and, in succession the York Road, Harford Road, Belair Road and Philadelphia Road. The Philadelphia Road to the northeast and the Washington Road to the southwest constitute links in the great eastern highway used by the Indians long before the arrival of the white men.

The site of the city also lies on three streams which rise in the hills to the west and northwest and flow in meandering courses into the Patapsco River to the south and east. These, from west to east, are Gwynns Falls, Jones Falls and Herring Run. They in turn have numerous tributaries, many of which now disappear underground in the city limits but are still found in the suburbs. Among them are streams bearing such picturesque names as

Stony Run, Dead Run, Powder Mill Branch, Red Run, Western Run, Slaughterhouse Run and Horsehead Branch. These various streams have to be crossed and that of course means bridges. In fact Baltimore has been called "a city of bridges," for there are no less than 224 of them of which 100 are railroad bridges. Either the bridges are so well hidden or Baltimoreans have become so accustomed to them that few people are aware of this very Venetian aspect of their city.

In the early days the valleys of Gwynns Falls, Jones Falls and Herring Run presented charming sylvan scenes. Water furnished power for a succession of mills. A highway followed each stream and, from time to time, crossed it on quaint stone bridges. Then industry and the encroachment of the city blotted out the natural beauty of the valleys. In recent years Gwynns Falls Valley and Herring Run Valley have been recaptured and beautified with parkways.

Jones Falls, once the most impressive of the three, is alas! too far gone for redemption. The damp air rising from this stream made its banks an ideal site for cotton mills where moisture is needed during manufacture. While most of the textile industry has moved south the Mt. Vernon-Woodberry Mills and William E. Hooper and Sons still operate in Jones Falls Valley as reminders of the historic association. Numerous other factories have sprung up along its banks. From its entry into the city limits near Mt. Washington all the way to Mt. Royal Avenue, Jones Falls is little better than an unsightly open sewer. It has often been described as Baltimore's Cloaca Maxima. Sad to relate it is most conspicuous at Pennsylvania Station where travelers passing through get a superb view of it and judge Baltimore's sanitation accordingly. Once past the station the stream is mercifully swallowed up in an underground passage and is seen no more until its polluted waters appear just before emptying into the inner harbor.

Bisecting the city and serving as backbone and trunk line of its nervous system is Charles Street, running north and south. This was originally named Forest Street. Of almost equal structural importance is Baltimore Street, once known as Market Street. Like two outstretched arms it extends east and west from Charles Street. Beginning at Charles, streets are designated as either "East" and "West"; beginning at Baltimore, they are designated as either "North" or "South." Of all the streets in the city Charles is the best known and admittedly the most characteristic of the community. It represents a cross section of virtually the entire life and activity of the city.

South Charles Street passes through the wholesale produce market which supplies the city with food. Its lower extremity reaches almost to the harbor at Port Covington, one of the great terminals with its network of railway lines and elevators which are the sinews of the port's foreign trade. Between the market and the terminal is an unprepossessing neighborhood of row houses which are traditional in Baltimore. Modest though they are, they no doubt have the virtue of being owned by the people who live in them, for that is the general local custom.

South Charles Street has its place in the life of the city. But when mention is made of Charles Street it is North Charles Street that instinctively comes to mind. Where Charles Street crosses Baltimore it is anchored securely by the B. & O. Building, the Baltimore Savings Bank, the old home of the *Sunpapers* and a leading department store which bears the appropriate name of The Hub.

The six blocks of North Charles between Baltimore and Centre have been described as the local equivalent of London's Bond Street or Paris's Rue de la Paix. In this brief space are to be found banks and trust companies, restaurants, O'Neill's Department Store as well as The Hub, airline and travel bureaus, gift shops, florists, a de luxe grocery, book shops, jewelry stores and silversmiths, interior decorators, dress shops, sport shops, art shops, men's tailors, lawyers, doctors and dentists and furniture stores. In fact there are few human wants that this section of North Charles Street cannot supply from having a tooth filled or getting a will made to buying a trousseau or engaging passage around the world on a liner or airplane.

The majority of the business concerns are members of the Charles Street Association, a proud organization that undertakes to set standards for a neighborhood which is inclined to look down its nose at less distinguished thoroughfares. In such select company it is embarrassing to single out individuals for special comment. Yet certainly a word ought to be said about Cook, the florist. For this was the shop founded by John Cook whose name is famous among rose growers. He was born Johann Koch of Germany and he came of a long line of florists. After arriving in this country in 1853 he settled in Baltimore where he successively tended the elaborate flower garden of J. Howard McHenry at "Sudbrook" and that of William Frick at "Uplands," before opening his own establishment in 1870. To John Cook goes the glory of having originated that well-known and popular hybrid tea rose—Radiance.

Baltimore from earliest time has been famed for its skilled silversmiths and North Charles Street has long been the center of the local retail trade. As John Cook had many generations of florists behind him, so many Baltimore silversmiths were descended from craftsmen in the old countries. By way of illustration a story is told of the late Frank M. Schofield, a silversmith, whose place of business is across the street from Cook. One day there came to his shop Mrs. Charles H. Tilghman of "Gross Coate," the Tilghman stronghold on the Eastern Shore. She brought with her one of a pair of silver candelabra which had been inherited by her husband, Dr. Tilghman. The other had gone to another branch of his family. Mrs. Tilghman wanted to have the piece duplicated. Mr. Schofield examined its markings carefully, then willingly agreed to do the job. He pointed out that it would be a special pleasure since the original candelabra had been wrought in London by his great great grandfather John Schofield who plied his trade there between the years of 1740 and 1772.

A few more blocks up the street, at the corner of Charles and Franklin, is another establishment distinguished in the same line. It is the house of Kirk or, to be exact, Samuel Kirk & Son, Inc. Samuel Kirk, too, came of long lines of silversmiths and goldsmiths. Born a Quaker of Doylestown, Pennsylvania, he migrated to Baltimore and opened a shop on Baltimore Street in 1815. Kirk's, which does a wholesale as well as a retail business, is the oldest house of silversmiths in the United States. In the firm today are lineal descendants of Samuel Kirk. Kirk's claims the distinction of having introduced repoussé silver into this country. In its long history it also has turned out many famous pieces. Among them are a pair of silver goblets which were ordered by General Lafayette in 1824 and presented to a Baltimorean who had entertained him. One of Kirk's most ambitious undertakings was a silver service made for the U.S. Cruiser *Maryland*. It included a mammoth punch bowl and many other handsome pieces, each of which was etched with a picture having to do with the history of Maryland. All ships of the name Maryland having been decommissioned by the Navy, the silver service recently was returned to Baltimore and is now in the custody of the Maryland Historical Society.

Directly opposite Schofield's on Pleasant Street is the Women's Industrial Exchange. It is the relic of an age in which a gentlewoman's place was in the home; and, if she was so unlucky as not to find a husband, her only recourse was to throw herself on the mercy of a brother, take in "paying guests" or do fancy work, cooking and preserving. Many Southern cities had these exchanges where women's handiwork was assembled and presented for sale. There still, fortunately, are women in Baltimore who like to make pin money in this manner and Baltimore's exchange does a thriving business. The Exchange also conducts a restaurant where delicious food with a distinctly homelike flavor is served, and which tempts women on shopping trips to stop in for lunch and a shocking caloric orgy.

This section of Charles Street offers a choice of several churches. There is old St. Paul's Episcopal Church at Charles and Saratoga. A few blocks north on Cathedral Street, just off Charles, is the Catholic Cathedral. The residence of the Archbishop faces on Charles and in its garden are the crocuses whose appearance is annually heralded by the local press as the first sign of spring. Hard by, at Charles and Franklin, is First Unitarian.

During the Christmas season it is the custom of the Charles Street Association to decorate the lampposts in this section with red and green Christmas ornaments; and in spring, on the occasion of the Flower Mart, to deck them out with flower boxes. The Flower Mart comes off on a day in early May, at the foot of the Washington Monument where the two parked squares meet—Washington Place extending north and south and Mt. Vernon Place east and west. On this occasion the squares are roped off, traffic is diverted, and the square is made gay with booths, colored umbrellas and banners. Gardeners dispose of their seedlings, other garden wares are on sale, an open-air restaurant serves lunch, there are pony rides, balloons and other amusements and special refreshments for the children. The display is put on by the Women's Civic League and enthusiastically supported by the community.

The Charles Street neighborhood for several blocks south and north of the monument is a favorite location for social clubs. West and east of Charles on the narrow thoroughfare known as Hamilton Street are situated respectively the men's Hamilton Street Club and the women's Hamilton Street Club. The men's club is housed in one of the quaint early 19th-century dwellings which give Hamilton Street an unusual picturesqueness and the women's club is a remodeled stable of the same period. Both clubs are products of the 1920's.

The Hamilton Street Club (male) owes its beginning to some serious-minded young men in search of more intellectual stimulus than was to be found in the existing social clubs. They soon discovered, however, that their discussions lagged because everybody thought alike. It was decided therefore to take in a few members with diverse points of views. This turned out to be a case of the camel getting his head under the tent. Soon the outsiders had taken over while only the stoutest of the original group had the heart to stay on.

The men's Hamilton Street Club is primarily social. But, judged by the roster of its very limited membership, it seems to look out for men who have achieved distinction in their respective fields. It has included at one time or another lawyers, doctors, journalists, writers, architects, musicians, judges, many members of the Johns Hopkins faculty and a few businessmen. For many years one of the leading spirits of the club was the late William W. (Willie) Woollcott, brother of New York's Alexander Woollcott, but a wit and bon vivant in his own right. Willie had an aversion to a coat and seldom was in a crowd more than a few minutes before he was stripped to his shirt sleeves. An oil portrait of him, characteristically coatless, is the only one of a member permitted on the walls of the club.

A special claim to fame was his authorship of the song "I Am a One Hundred Percent American" which gained wide popularity among the unregenerate in the days of the Uplift, Prohibition and the revival of the Ku-Klux Klan. As originally composed the

song had five verses, but the number added by volunteers is almost unlimited. A verse written around the time of the Scopes
trial treated of the "anti-Darwin intellectual" who warned that
any man who said a nice young boy or gal "is a descendant of
the ape, shall never from Hell's fire escape." Another verse, in
which the singer identified himself as "just folks," asserted that
"in art I pull no high-brow stuff, I know what I like and that's
enough." Another dealt with the believer in osteopathy who held
that other kinds of therapy "may do for them damned foreign
ginks, who won't take medicine without it stinks." The fifth and
last verse, dedicated to the followers of Mary Baker Eddy, concluded that "disease is now laid on the shelf, and a dead man only
kids hisself."

A popular feature of the men's Hamilton Street Club has been
the monthly dinners to which many prominent figures have been
invited as guests. A speaker unprepared for the club's customary
reception would get a rude shock. Members claim the right to
interrupt, question, and sometimes contradict. In the early days
of World War II Lord Lothian, British Ambassador to this country, was guest of the club. A spokesman pointed out to him that
the club was unique in that it had no officers and no rules, that anybody could say what he pleased and talk as long as he pleased
but nobody was required to listen. When he got up to face the
assembly Lord Lothian prefaced his speech with the remark that
he was interested to know about so unique a club in this country.
He went on to say that he happened to be the member of just such
a club which had long had its home in London. He concluded,
"It's called the House of Lords."

The women's Hamilton Street Club was established about the
same time as was the men's. Like the men's club it seems to show
a preference for persons who are a bit outside the common mold.
Its membership runs to college graduates, professional women and
civic leaders. Much more elaborate, conventional and socially
exclusive is the women's Mt. Vernon Club, housed in one of the
handsome original Greek revival dwellings facing on Mt. Vernon
Place. Just across the way is Boumi Temple, Order of the Mystic
Shrine, luxuriating in the palace which was once the home of
Dr. and Mrs. Henry Barton Jacobs. At Charles and Madison
Streets is the University Club in a red brick building with brown

trimmings suggestive of the somber dignity of the members themselves.

Of all Baltimore's social clubs the most famous is the Maryland Club, housed in a massive gray stone structure at Charles and Eager Streets that is typical of the ponderous imagination of the architects of the 1880's. The club now lacks only a few years of being a century old. It was chartered by the Legislature in 1858, its declared purpose being "to promote regulated social relations among its members and the extension of hospitable courtesies to strangers." Its first president was Jerome Napoleon Bonaparte, son of Napoleon I's younger brother Prince Jerome who married Baltimore's Betsy Patterson. He was the first of many distinguished men to fill that office. In fact the presidency of the Maryland Club is just about the highest social honor to which a male Baltimorean can aspire.

The club was still in its infancy when it was caught up in the turmoil of the Civil War. Its sympathies were strongly with the South, a characteristic the Federal garrison soon recognized. Tradition has it that when General Ben Butler slipped into the town at night and occupied Federal Hill he trained one of his guns on the Maryland Club, letting it be known that at the first sign of trouble he would put a shot into it. The club then was in a house at the northeast corner of Cathedral and Franklin Streets. As a crowning indignity General Lew Wallace, the commanding officer in Baltimore, gave orders in 1864 that the club premises be used for the housing of those of Maryland's freed Negroes who had nowhere else to go. General Wallace was less well known as a soldier than as the author of the popular novel *Ben Hur*.

Today the Maryland Club is the last surviving stronghold of the conservative element which once ran the nation. Ever since President Hoover stepped out of office in March, 1933, its members have looked with increasing horror at the goings on in Washington. Yet the club itself gave Baltimoreans a shock one day in May of 1945, when people walking down Charles Street recognized a red flag as being the Hammer and Sickle of the Soviets waving from one of its windows. Confidence was restored when it became known that the flags were being flown in honor of "our gallant allies" on the occasion of VE-Day and the person in charge of the ceremonial had had no orders to snub the Russians.

However, later in the day the flag was quietly withdrawn. Perhaps the Maryland Club may lay claim to having been among the first to suspect that all was not well in that quarter.

Membership in the Maryland Club is a much sought privilege. There is an impressive waiting list almost as large as the membership of the club. The club always has enjoyed an enviable reputation for its food and makes a speciality of Maryland dishes. The ambition of most male Baltimoreans is to arrange their lives in such fashion that they can withdraw from the world and find a haven in the Maryland Club. It is a goal which only exceptional men achieve and then generally in the twilight of life. A very limited and fortunate few reach their objective sooner.

This recalls the story of a visit to the city some years ago of a man who, by the sweat of his brow, had risen in the steel industry from a puddler to chairman of the board. He was invited to Baltimore to attend the classic Preakness at Pimlico. After the race he was escorted to the Maryland Club and there turned over for entertainment to three of its most accomplished members, to wit, Mr. John Walter Smith (Monk) Foster, Mr. Lawrence Bailliere and the late Mr. Howell Parr. They fairly overwhelmed him with their charm.

As the evening wore on and acquaintances grew warmer, the steel magnate turned to Mr. Foster and Mr. Bailliere and inquired, "What do you gentlemen do for a living?" It was a surprising question to put to these two who had achieved early in life the goal vainly sought by so many Baltimoreans. One of them replied: "We don't do anything for a living. We just live." After a pause the steelman put the same question to Mr. Parr. "Why," replied Mr. Parr promptly, "I'm in business with these boys."

A block north of the Maryland Club is the Sheraton-Belvedere, the city's most ornamental hotel. From there on, Charles Street for a mile or more is a reflection of past grandeur, a drab example of the transition of a fashionable residential district to one of night clubs, rooming houses and miscellaneous commercial enterprises. There is nothing worthy of mention until Wyman Park is reached. This marks the southern approach to the Johns Hopkins University, at Homewood, which has carried Baltimore's fame to all corners of the world.

Fronting on Wyman Park is the Baltimore Museum of Art,

the very lively center of the artistic life of the city. Here, on Saturdays and Sundays in particular, the public flocks to see the fine permanent collection of paintings, sculpture, colonial interiors, prints and objects d'art or the special exhibitions that follow each other in rapid succession. The museum building, the University Baptist Church across the way and the Scottish Rite Temple, a few blocks to the north, are all the work of the New York architect, John Russell Pope, and afford an interesting contrast in the various expressions of his chaste style.

The Homewood area affords also sites for many of the city's largest and best-appointed apartment houses. Here also is the Protestant Episcopal Pro-Cathedral and beside it the residence of the Bishop of Maryland. A block to the east is the southern entrance to Guilford, Baltimore's most fashionable suburb. To the general public Guilford is best known for the Sherwood Gardens, a large open square adjoining the home of John R. Sherwood. Mr. Sherwood has planted the square with azaleas and other shrubs and with thousands of tulip bulbs. When they are in bloom in the spring people come by the hundreds from all over town to see them. This is Baltimore's most popular flower show.

From the point where University Parkway crosses Charles Street the city assumes a semirural character. Guilford was originally the country home of A. S. Abell, founder of the *Sun,* and the neighboring territory also was occupied by large estates. When, around the turn of the century, the real estate developers stepped in, they used rare insight in preserving the giant oaks and tulip poplars which were the crowning glory of the neighborhood. The houses here are built well apart and surrounded by spacious lawns, shrubs and shade trees. There is so much cover that wildlife is attracted to it. Within ten minutes by automobile from the very center of the city it is not at all unusual to encounter squirrels, rabbits, an occasional opossum and owls. Every once in a while a deer wanders into town. Sometimes the wild do not stop in the suburbs but are lured by green plots and open squares to the business district. There is authentic evidence of the call of a bobwhite having been heard in Preston Gardens within a stone's throw of the City Hall.

Half a century ago Charles Street ended abruptly below Wyman Park. Then somewhat timidly it undertook to add a few cubits to its stature and this addition was called "Charles Street Extended." Farther out it assumed the rather tautological name of Charles Street Avenue. There may be other cities in which a thoroughfare is designated at one and the same time as both a "street" and an "avenue." If so they do not at the moment come to mind.

Reminders of Baltimore's large Catholic population are Loyola College for men and Notre Dame College and School for women just beyond the cross street which bears the picturesque name of Cold Spring Lane. A few blocks farther north is the site for the new Catholic Cathedral which is to replace the old basilica near the center of town. Finally, as the city limits are reached, the golf course and clubhouse of the Elkridge Club are seen to the west of the Avenue. The club began as a hunt club in the 1870's. But many years ago the growth of the city ruined what had once been fine hunting country. Foxhunters, hounds and foxes moved farther afield and the club was taken over by the golfers.

So much for the city's skeleton. Now to pass on to its flesh and blood.

Chapter 3

THE PORT

MENTION the Port to the average Baltimorean and he will think you are talking about the little body of stagnant water lying at the intersection of Light and Pratt Streets. When reference is made to the business of the Baltimore port the picture it represents to him is one of the Norfolk boat, the *S.S. Bay Belle* and the *S.S. Tolchester* that take parties of jitterbugs down the Bay on moonlight excursions, and perhaps a nice white banana boat just in from Central America. For the inner basin is about all the average Baltimorean ever sees of his port.

Occasionally uptown one runs into officers of foreign merchant marines in their inconspicuous uniforms. More rarely the sound of a foreign tongue on the streets reveals a fresh arrival from abroad. But, except when they are rioting, merchant sailors are not easily distinguished from landsmen. In Baltimore sailors do their rioting within a short distance of the docks and in the small hours of the night. Brief references to it in the police court news next day escape the eyes of most people. So for the most part Baltimore ignores its port. Yet, the port was and still is the chief reason for the city's existence.

It is possible the average Baltimorean may recall vaguely having read somewhere that his is one of the five major ports of the Atlantic seaboard. He may have heard that Baltimore is second only to New York in gross tonnage of goods handled. If so, it made little impression.

There are, however, in the city no fewer than 40,000 persons who are very much alive to the port. For they are the 40,000 who owe their living directly to its activities. All of them are employed around it in some manner, from general managers of shipping companies and masters of vessels to stevedores and roustabouts. Add to these 40,000 their wives and children, and persons who run saloons, hotels and shops patronized by seamen, and at a conservative estimate the Baltimoreans dependent on the port may be placed in the neighborhood of 100,000 persons. That is more than one-tenth of the whole population of the city.

Experts who make up statistics figure that every ship which comes into the harbor spends from $15,000 to $25,000 on stores, fuel, repairs, docking charges and the like. All the various activities bring to the city business to the value of $200,000,000 a year. So, in spite of the indifference of the average Baltimorean to the port, he would be in a bad way without it.

When Baltimore Town was chartered in 1729 one of its chief purposes was to serve as a port of entry. Yet the beginning was slow. Not until 1739 is a record found of a boat taking on cargo. The boat was the *Parad and Gally* and the cargo a hogshead of tobacco. It is possible there were other cargoes before that which failed to be recorded. But, if trade had been brisk, surely some trace would have been left behind. The inference therefore is that it wasn't.

There was a good reason. Other ports of entry nearby at Whetstone Point, where Fort McHenry now stands, at Fell's Point and at Elkridge Landing, were more convenient both to the ships and to planters. So there was little reason for loading at Baltimore Town, almost hidden behind a marsh on the obscure northwest branch of the river. Yet, interestingly enough, this very obscurity was symbolical of the port's later greatness.

For the less convenient the port was to ocean-going vessels the farther inland it was and the closer to the rapidly expanding frontier. Skeptics might, for example, look at the 150 miles of bay that lie between Baltimore and the open sea and shake their heads. But shipping freight by water is relatively inexpensive as compared with shipping freight by rail. Viewed in that light the distance from the Virginia Capes to Baltimore, or from the coast to Baltimore by way of Delaware Bay through the Chesapeake and Delaware Canal represents a cheap transportation line. Baltimore is much closer than New York, Philadelphia and Boston to the Middle West with its great industries and rich farming regions. Because it is nearer it enjoys a lower freight rate. This asset is known as "the Freight Differential." It is Baltimore's joy and pride. It is spoken of with awe and reverence. The Freight Differential is to Baltimore what the Statue of Liberty is to New York, Independence Hall to Philadelphia or the steeple of Old North Church to Boston. The chief job of the Association of Commerce is to mount guard over it and warn of approaching foes;

for the city is in constant fear of being done out of it by its sly and crafty neighbors.

Forever looming up menacingly is the proposed St. Lawrence Waterway. Were it to be constructed Baltimore would cease to be the farthest port inland and the great present advantage of its differential probably would be lost. There is no surer way to lose popularity in Baltimore than to suggest that there is any merit in the waterway. Baltimoreans always refer to it as a nefarious scheme to pour public money into a ditch that would be frozen up half the year.

Like all other ports in colonial Maryland, Baltimore was designed primarily for the shipment of tobacco. But as time went on the business of the port became greatly diversified. Especially significant was a voyage made to Barbadoes around the year 1752 by the brig *Philip and James*, owned by Nicholas Rogers and one of two ocean-going vessels then boasted by Baltimore Town. It set sail with a mixed cargo of tobacco, corn, barrels of flour and bread, iron, staves and headings, peas, beans and hams. The voyage was typical of the kind of trade that was to develop between Baltimore and the West Indies. After two centuries that trade is still lucrative. Baltimore profits by being the nearest of the large Eastern ports to the Indies by a day's sailing.

Nevertheless as late as 1761 Baltimore's tobacco shipments still were valued at 140,000 British pounds compared with the value of 80,000 pounds for all the other exports, including wheat, corn, flour, lumber, pig iron, skins and furs. It was about that time that John Stevenson, the doctor turned promoter, made the successful experiment with his grain shipment to Ireland. So it turned out that, within the next forty years, grain and flour became more and more important in the port's trade. In 1774 the Patapsco Flour Mill, an ambitious enterprise for that day, was completed at Ellicott City, about ten miles to the west of Baltimore. By 1804, stimulated by the demand for foreign shipments, no less than fifty flour mills sprang up within a radius of eighteen miles of the town. Baltimore was beginning to be known as "the granary of the West Indies." Whether or not it was merely sales talk, Baltimore claimed that its product was "strong flour" which would stand up better than other flours on long tropical voyages.

Today John Stevenson's experiment is represented by three

mammoth grain elevators at the port's railway terminals with a total storage capacity of 12,000,000 bushels. One of them has the largest capacity of any grain elevator in any seaport in the United States. The three elevators combined are geared to deliver a total of 4,250,000 bushels of grain aboard ship in ten hours' time. In recent years, Baltimore contributed largely to the grain shipments involved in lend-lease and the Marshall Plan.

Baltimore first achieved real distinction as a port during the American Revolution. Until then Annapolis had held the limelight and the bulk of trade. In 1773 the port took a big step forward when Fell's Point, which lies nearer the mouth of the Patapsco was annexed to the town. Fell's Point provided deep water and a number of shipyards had already been established there. At Fell's Point was built the *Virginia,* the first frigate of the Continental Navy. The British who came into the Bay blockaded Annapolis but left Baltimore alone. A hostile fleet anchored only once more at the mouth of the Patapsco and then for a brief period. Baltimore took advantage of this oversight to send out a swarm of privateers to prey on enemy commerce. Considering that the great seafaring colony of Massachusetts dispatched in all 700 privateers, Baltimore's contribution of 248 is the more remarkable. The little town on the Patapsco was coming up in the world.

Immensely valuable to Baltimore has been its trade with the Orient. A pioneer was John O'Donnell, master of the merchantman *Pallas,* which sailed into the Baltimore harbor in August, 1785. The *Pallas* brought a cargo of tea, china, silks, satins and nankeens from Canton. It was the first of many cargoes to come from China. Captain O'Donnell liked the town, bought himself 1809 acres on the waterfront east of Fell's Point, built an oriental house on it and called the place Canton. And Canton it is to this day. Baltimoreans put the accent on the first syllable. Putting it on the second when speaking of Baltimore's Canton invites the scorn of the natives.

After the close of the Revolutionary War Baltimore continued its distinction in ship construction by building the frigate *Constellation,* a sister ship of the *Constitution* ("Old Ironsides"), and also the sloops-of-war *Maryland* and *Chesapeake* (not to be confused with the famous frigate of the same name which was built at Portsmouth, Va.) It was becoming more famous for its original contribution to marine construction through the evolution of the Baltimore clipper.

How the Baltimore clipper came into being is obscure. Some authorities say she was patterned after the French luggers that Americans got to know during the Revolution. A more romantic school traces her origin to two native Chesapeake Bay craft, the canoe and the bugeye, which on a small scale had the rakish lines that typified the clipper. Prior to the clippers ocean-going vessels tended to be broad of beam and rather tublike. To employ a modern term the clipper was "streamlined" to cut through the water much as a present-day automobile is streamlined to reduce air resistance. She was schooner-rigged and her two masts were set back at a rakish angle. Her bow and sternpost were raked too.

The clipper's great advantage was that she was designed so she could sail closer to the wind than other ships. She was so fast that nothing afloat could catch her. Speed demanded delicacy. In consequence the clipper did not stand up so well in the stormy weather of the North Atlantic or that encountered rounding the Horn. But she was ideal for the West Indian trade and for sailing in other tropical areas.

The clipper played a conspicuous part in the carrying trade that fell to the American merchant marine during the Napoleonic wars. A few years later clippers serving as privateers in the War of 1812 carried the conflict right to Britain's doorstep in the English Channel and the Irish Sea and earned for their home port the proud reputation of being "a nest of pirates."

The term "clipper ship" often is heard but generally it is used incorrectly. The original clipper was a schooner, and not a very large one at that. It was not until 1832 that the first true clipper ship was built in Baltimore. She was the *Ann McKim*, famous throughout the seven seas. Isaac McKim, a wealthy merchant, commissioned Kennard and Williamson, Fell's Point shipbuilders, to construct the vessel, for the China trade. Expense was no consideration. Mr. McKim's idea was a vessel built on the graceful lines of the clipper but of much greater size.

The *Ann McKim* when completed displaced 493 tons, was 143 feet long and 31 feet broad. Her frame was of live oak. She was copper-fastened throughout and her bottom was sheathed with imported red copper. Her interior was beautifully finished in Spanish mahogany. For her protection on the high seas she carrier a battery of 12 brass guns. She was square-rigged and, when all her sails were set, she was a swift and stately vessel, recognized and admired wherever she went. She sailed for years in the China trade and eventually ended her days in the Orient.

Another famous clipper ship of later years was the *Mary Whitridge*, of 877 tons. She was built in 1855 by Thomas Whitridge & Co., and astonished the shipping world by making the run from Cape Charles to the Rock Light, Liverpool, in the record time of 13 days, 7 hours. She, too, was long in the trade with China and the West Coast of the United States.

Supplementing Baltimore's commerce with the West Indies was her valuable Rio trade. Vessels left Baltimore for Brazil laden with flour and returned with coffee. In this manner a handsome profit was made going and coming. In 1851 Baltimore had the distinction of importing more coffee than any other port in the United States.

Still other Baltimore ships rounded Cape Horn to trade on the west coast of South America and of the United States. From Peru and Chile they brought back gold and silver. Even more valuable in the long run than the precious metals was an ill-smelling cargo that first appeared in the Baltimore port in 1844. This was guano from Peru, a natural fertilizer. Farmers in Southern Maryland, Virginia and the Carolinas found it an excellent stimulant to their exhausted soils. More than half the guano imported into the United States entered through the port of Baltimore.

As time went on the fertilizer industry was augmented by a product made of bones and other animal refuse. This eventually was replaced by the chemical fertilizer of today. With its great chemical plants in Curtis Bay, Baltimore continues to hold an important place in the industry.

Around the second decade of the 19th century Baltimore began to do an important business in human cargoes. These were not Negro slaves but immigrants from Europe, chiefly from Germany. When the Baltimore and Ohio Railroad reached the Ohio River it simultaneously stretched eastward across the Atlantic with a fleet of its own ships. This fleet later was replaced by a working agreement with the North German Lloyd which established regular passenger service between Bremen and Baltimore. Thousands of German immigrants, upon their arrival, settled in Baltimore. Many thousands more moved inland to people the Middle West. The North German Lloyd continued to land passengers at the B. & O. terminal at Locust Point until the outbreak of World War I in 1914.

Again in the 1920's an effort was made to revive trans-Atlantic passenger service through the establishment of the Baltimore Steamship Line with weekly sailings to Europe. The ships were small and trim and, for a time, it was quite the thing for Baltimoreans to set out for Europe from their own port. Some members of the crews came from old Baltimore families which added a homely touch. Sailing time was quite a social occasion. But the enterprise was financially uncertain from the start and the line failed to weather the great depression of the 1930's.

Sugar is yet another valuable item of import. From 1812 to 1855 between $30,000 and $40,000 worth of sugar was landed at the port every year. Then two refineries were built and a few years later annual imports grew to more than 8,500,000 pounds. Today the great plant of the American Sugar Refining Company rises like a fortress at the entrance to the inner harbor. Tobacco, too, continues to figure prominently in Baltimore trade. Today some 20 per cent of the Maryland crop goes to countries in Europe and all of it is shipped through Baltimore.

In the early days the Bay and its tributaries were the chief means of communication. Every planter had his boat and used it in visiting his neighbors. As Baltimore grew it became the center of trade and of the social intercourse which used the Bay as a highway. The sailboat gave place to the Bay steamboat. The first of these was the *Chesapeake* which began to operate in 1813. These trim white boats were a conspicuous feature of Baltimore and the Bay for more than a hundred years.

Around 4:30 o'clock every afternoon they would set out from the inner harbor. They carried both passengers and freight. There was quite a lot of rivalry among them, and as they reached open water, they often put on a race as they headed down the Bay. Those destined for the Eastern Shore turned east as they came opposite the Choptank and Tred Avon Rivers. One continued south to West Point, Virginia, where it connected with a boat train to Richmond. Another made for the Rappahannock and Fredericksburg. Still another rounded Point Lookout and started up the Potomac for Washington. It put in at plantation wharves in Southern Maryland and on the Virginia shore to discharge and take on passengers and freight. It used to be said that Baltimore was forty minutes from Washington by train and forty hours by boat.

There was also the *Emma Giles* that plied daily between Baltimore and Annapolis and was better known to many generations of midshipmen as the *Emmágilēs*. There were also the Tolchester and Love Point ferries. Gradually, however, automobiles and modern highways pushed their way into the picture. In comparison with these swifter means of transportation the Bay ceased to be an avenue of communication. Instead it became an obstacle. Trade that had gone to Baltimore from the Eastern Shore went instead to Wilmington and Philadelphia. In fact the Eastern Shore counties of Delaware, Maryland and Virginia began to think of themselves as an entity. They called themselves "Delmarva" and, when irritated with their state governments, threatened secession.

Southern Maryland meanwhile turned in the direction of Washington. The depression dealt the final blow. In 1932 the Baltimore and Virginia Steamboat Company went out of business. It was the last to operate the Bay boats. With it departed a picturesque and altogether charming institution. The new Bay Bridge, from Sandy Point to Kent Island and thence to the Eastern Shore, is expected to recapture the lost area. But it cannot recapture the romance of a trip down the Bay on a typical Bay steamboat. Vanished are memories of the *Talbot*, the *Dorchester*, the *Calvert*, the *Annapolis* and the *Anne Arundel*. Lost to the Baltimore vocabulary are such poetically named rivers as the *Sassafras*, the *Yeocomico* and the *Piankatank*.

Baltimore also was active in the coastal trade. A familiar sight on the Pratt Street docks were the black hulls and smokestacks, buff masts and white superstructure of the freight and passenger ships of the Merchants & Miners. They lacked the excursion atmosphere of the Bay steamboats. They looked definitely as though they had been built with an eye to seaworthiness. And they had to be. For they sailed to Norfolk and from there north along the Atlantic coast to Boston and Providence and south to Savannah and Jacksonville.

Customers were lured aboard by fastidious and conscienceless folders which enlarged on the delicious meals served aboard and spoke of appetites whetted by the tang of the salt sea air. The folders never alluded to the blow that could be expected on venturing outside the Virginia capes and the consequent rolling of the ship. Many a Baltimorean who could not afford a trip to Europe learned all about seasickness the inexpensive way on an M. & M. voyage.

The Merchants & Miners, too, succumbed to the motor-truck and other competition. The company went out of business after its ships had been taken over by the U. S. Government in World War II and many of them had been sunk by enemy submarines. It was the M. & M.'s *Dorchester* that carried the "Four Chaplains" to their death. Today, save for one Norfolk passenger boat and a few freighters, the business of the port is strictly with foreign countries.

If the average Baltimorean were to take the time to inspect his port today he would discover that it has 40 miles of berthing space including 290 piers. It is essentially a railway port. Its three great terminals are complete with grain elevators, facilities for loading coal, tracks to take care of thousands of freight cars, houses for storage, and other conveniences. They are located at Locust Point, Canton and Port Covington and are owned respectively by the Baltimore & Ohio, the Pennsylvania and the Western Maryland.

Other features of the port's equipment are coal piers that can load 9,700 tons of coal in 10 hours, tugboats, floating derricks, cranes, open-deck barges, car floats, tank barges for servicing ships with oil and water, and a fireboat on 24-hour duty. The port even has its own garbage disposal system and a taxi service to carry members of the crews to and from their ships.

The Baltimore port is equipped to handle 200 ships of various sizes at one time. It has 14 repair yards ready to handle anything from a rowboat to a freighter. In fact the port is self-sufficient and virtually a community in itself. It is estimated that some $200,000,000 have been invested in the port facilities and that replacement would cost three times that amount.

Intimately connected with the port are some 100 large industrial plants situated on the shore front. Most of them depend on the port for their business, including the delivery of raw materials and the shipment of manufactured goods. Among them is the Sparrows Point plant of the Bethlehem Steel Company which employs some 20,000 workers. Another conspicuous feature of the port area are the oil tanks at Canton and Fairfield of Standard, Continental and Mexican Petroleum and the Esso Standard refinery. As Baltimore in the past achieved distinction as the chief port for the importation of coffee and guano, so today it boasts being the largest port of entry in the United States for latex, or liquid rubber. The Baltimore & Ohio Railroad has a pier especially constructed for receiving and storing this product.

The Bethlehem Steel Company has sustained nobly Baltimore's reputation for shipbuilding. At Sparrows Point it has a yard where it turns out tankers. At Fairfield, across the harbor, during World War II it maintained another yard for the construction of cargo boats. While Mr. Kaiser was monopolizing the headlines, Bethlehem-Fairfield was quietly but steadily laying the keel for a new vessel as soon as its predecessor slid down the ways. At Bethlehem-Fairfield was launched the first Liberty ship—the *Patrick Henry*. Before the war ended Bethlehem-Fairfield had built 384 Liberty ships, 94 Victory ships, and 30 LST's. During the years 1942-1945 Baltimore shipyards completed a total of 608 ships in addition to repairing thousands of others.

There are two approaches to Baltimore from the open sea. Nature provided one by way of the Virginia capes. The other is by Delaware Bay, making use of the Chesapeake and Delaware Canal. This cut is about 15 miles long and connects Chesapeake Bay with the Delaware River. Plans for it were first projected in 1799, but work was not begun until 1829. For years it was too shallow to take vessels of deep draught. However, during the 1920's, the Federal Government took a hand and the canal was deepened and widened. Today one in every five deep-draught vessels entering and departing from the Baltimore port uses the C. & D. Canal. It saves a day's sailing for ships coming from or destined to north Atlantic points.

Baltimore port is distinguished for heavy bulk cargo. Its ten leading imports include iron ore and manganese, green coffee, crude rubber, liquid latex, crude petroleum, chrome, scrap iron and steel, bananas and fuel oil. Its ten largest exports are coal, grains, iron and steel products, fertilizer materials, machinery and parts, bricks and tiles, coal tar products, cement, autos and trucks, glass and glass products.

These cargoes weigh a lot but their cash value is small in comparison with their bulk. Critics maintain that Baltimore has gone far enough with its bulk cargo and should begin to encourage general cargo. The chief blame is leveled at the railroads which own the three great terminals and virtually control the port. The critics say better provision should be made for goods that come to the dock by trucks. The railroads, on the other hand, contend that they have made a large investment in the port and don't see why they are under obligation to do special favors for competitors.

The port made Baltimore. But in this new age commerce begins to move by air. So a city must have not only a seaport but an airport. Baltimore recognized this need. And, for all its dilatory ways, it has got one that is as up-to-date as an airport can be. It is the new Friendship International Airport on the southwestern outskirts of the city. It represents an investment of $12,000,000. The astonishing fact is that most of this came from the people of Baltimore and of Maryland, and very little from the Federal Government, a detail of which Baltimoreans are proud. There is grave concern over whether the new airport will pay its way. However that may be, Baltimore could hardly have held its place among the great cities without one. The name Friendship, by the way, was not picked at random. It was the name of a church whose site lay on part of the land condemned for the airport.

Chapter 4

THE FOUR MERCHANTS

AROUND the turn of the 19th century four men were born who were destined to become merchant princes and, through the generous use of their money, to leave a lasting imprint upon the city of Baltimore. They were George Peabody, Johns Hopkins, Enoch Pratt and William T. Walters. Because of the public institutions with which they are associated no other names are better known in the city today.

George Peabody and Johns Hopkins were approximately the same age, both having been born in 1795. Enoch Pratt entered the world in 1805, while William Walters did not make his appearance until 1820. Of the four, Johns Hopkins alone was a native Marylander; Peabody and Pratt hailed from Massachusetts, and Walters from the neighboring state of Pennsylvania. Baltimore, as is its way, graciously received the young men into its bosom and, for its magnanimity, reaped a handsome reward. Within one generation the city found itself the object of a veritable avalanche of philanthropy such as it had never seen before, nor has it seen since.

Each of these gentlemen burned with a desire to serve his fellow men. Each had a different idea as to how to go about it. When they were through Baltimore was richer by a university, a modern hospital, a superb scholar's library and conservatory of music, a free public library and an art gallery that for quality compares favorably with any in this country.

George Peabody was born of poor parents at Danvers, Massachusetts. His formal schooling was brief. At the age of eleven he was apprenticed to a storekeeper who dispensed groceries, drugs and the miscellaneous assortment of goods generally carried by country merchants. At sixteen he left Danvers to join his elder brother who had a draper's shop in Newburyport. Shortly after the shop was destroyed by fire and George lost his job. So he journeyed south to try his fortune with an uncle who had set up as a merchant in Georgetown, D. C.

At the age of nineteen years Peabody formed a partnership in the wholesale dry-goods business with one Elisha Riggs, who put up the capital; and in 1815 the house moved to Baltimore. It occupied the large building at Liberty and Baltimore Streets where the Continental Congress met in the winter of 1775-1776 and which still bore the name of "Old Congress Hall." Here, on his own evidence, Peabody made his first $5,000.

The firm prospered and opened branches in Philadelphia and New York. When Riggs retired in 1830 and Peabody became the senior partner, it had grown into one of the largest mercantile houses in the country. Peabody made his home in Baltimore for twenty years. He afterward said that, although he was a New Englander and sectional feeling even then was running high, he "never experienced from the citizens of Baltimore anything but kindness, hospitality and confidence."

In 1836 Peabody said good-by to his adopted home and went to live in England. He set up in business in London just in time to back the credit of the State of Maryland and other American interests during the financial panic of 1837. He never married. There are several stories of a shattered romance, all varying in detail. In any event he did not take a wife. But if he had no son to carry on the name he accomplished the same end through his benefactions. The name of Peabody, attached to libraries, tenements, museums and schools, is a familiar one in London as well as in many places in this country, from Vermont and Massachusetts in the north to Tennessee in the South. Baltimoreans are surprised, and a trifle resentful, at having Peabody associated with other places when they have imagined he was their exclusive possession. No doubt other beneficiaries feel the same way when they run into the Peabody tradition in Baltimore.

By 1850 Peabody had become a very wealthy man indeed and was beginning to distribute his fortune. Hard-luck stories did not move him. He believed that in such cases gifts of money did more harm than good. Thousands of appeals were addressed to him but few ever met his eye. He let his sister read them and use her judgment as to which should be approved. He made an exception once in the case of "a decayed English gentleman" who asked the loan of a few thousand pounds to establish a claim to an estate. The appeal ran to thirty foolscap pages. Peabody must have read it for he replied: "That you should have written such a letter would surprise your friends; that I should have read it would indeed surprise mine." There is no evidence, however, that Peabody advanced the cash. Even deserving charities often were turned down when they asked for money. Peabody liked to pick his own beneficiaries and to give when he was in the mood.

One of his most princely gifts was the group of tenements for laborers in London. This was a sort of pioneer slum clearance project. The grant of $3,000,000 was equaled only by the one he made for education in the South. In gratitude Queen Victoria offered him a baronetcy and the Grand Cross of the Order of the Bath. He politely declined them both but did accept a miniature portrait of the sovereign that was specially painted for him.

Peabody once remarked that he never ceased to feel and lament the want of an early education, and this no doubt was the motivation for his providing educational opportunities for others. As early as 1857, in a letter, he announced his intention of establishing an institute in Baltimore. It was, he said, "to teach political and religious charity, toleration and beneficence and prove itself to be in all contingencies and conditions, the true friend of our union, of the salutary institutions of free government and of liberty regulated by law."

The handsome white marble building, which faces on Mt. Vernon Place, was completed in 1861. But it was then too late for the Institute to foster the toleration that might have preserved the Union without the arbitrament of a bloody conflict. Because of the war the dedication had to be postponed until 1866 when Peabody, then seventy-one years old, returned to the city of his youth to take part in the ceremonies. It was a scene to warm the cockles of a philanthropist's heart and spur him on to do more good and distribute even more generously. The school children were given a day's holiday and, with their bright shining faces, lined up to bid the good man welcome. All the dignitaries of the community were on hand to express their gratitude and sing his praises.

Responding to an address by Governor Swann, Mr. Peabody said that his position with respect to the war had been misunderstood. It seems the charge had been made against him that his support of the Union was lukewarm. Never, he explained, during the war or after it had he allowed passion to interefere with the warm friendship he had formed with many people in the South. He laid the blame for the conflict on the extremists on both sides. But, he concluded, once the issue had been joined he saw no hope for the country except in the victory of Northern arms. Then, in the presence of the vast throng of people, young and old, which had assembled in Mt. Vernon Place, he declared:

> To you, therefore, citizens of Baltimore and of Maryland, I make my appeal; probably the last I shall ever make to you. May not this Institute be a common ground where all may meet, burying former differences and animosities, forgetting past separations and estrangements, weaving the bonds of new attachments to the city, to the State and to the nation? May not Baltimore, her name already honored in history as the birthplace of religious toleration in America now crown her past fame by becoming the day-star of political tolerance and charity?

Through succeeding years the plea has been heeded in a manner which would have gratified the founder. Supporters of the causes of the North and the South have sat together on the board of the Peabody in perfect amity and understanding. For more than eighty years the Institute has enjoyed a placid existence, astonishingly free from dissension and contributing largely to the cultural needs of the community. Graduate students of the Hopkins and other scholars have made good use of its excellent collection of books.

The Peabody Conservatory has been the center of the city's musical life. During the course of its existence hundreds of its students have gone out to all parts of the country as teachers and instrumentalists. In recent years the director of the Conservatory has "doubled" as conductor of the city's symphony orchestra and members of the faculty have played in it. The Peabody concerts, which take place on Friday afternoons during the winter, have long been a local institution and have brought many famous artists to the city. Peabody's gift to Baltimore represented an estimated value of $1,500,000. It was his third largest bequest. In all, Peabody gave away nearly 8½ million dollars, a princely sum in his day.

Johns Hopkins was the second son in a family of eleven children. His father, Samuel Hopkins, was a prosperous tobacco farmer in Anne Arundel County, which lies to the south of Baltimore. His mother, Hannah Janney, came from Virginia. The Hopkins were Quakers, and they owned a number of slaves who tilled the farm of 500 acres.

Being Quakers, the Hopkins had serious doubts about the institution of slavery. In the end Quaker conscience proved stronger than practical considerations. In the year 1807 they freed all their able-bodied slaves, retaining only the aged and the young. This meant that Samuel Hopkins and his two eldest sons had to go out into the fields and do the labor of the farm themselves. It meant also the end of formal education for the boys. Fortunately during the years he attended a local school Johns Hopkins acquired a taste for reading that never left him. His favorite subjects are said to have been history and English literature.

In 1812, when Johns Hopkins was seventeen years old, it was decided he should go to Baltimore to seek his fortune. There he joined his uncle Gerard Hopkins who had a wholesale grocery business. He had been with his uncle two years when he ran into the first serious test of his ability. In 1814 Uncle Gerard set out for Ohio to attend a Quaker convention, leaving young Johns in charge of the business. While he was away the British descended on Baltimore. Though the times were critical the youth, displaying sound judgment, rode out the storm. Not only did he keep the business going but he also expanded it.

At this time another crisis of a very personal nature occurred in the life of Johns Hopkins. While living in the home of Gerard he fell in love with his uncle's daughter, Elizabeth. When Gerard learned of the romance he refused to approve a match between first cousins. Elizabeth, being a dutiful daughter, would not go against the wishes of her father. So the romance ended there. Neither of the principals ever married. Johns Hopkins quit his uncle's house though the two remained on good terms. Eventually his mother and his two sisters came to make their home with him.

Johns Hopkins soon thereafter left Uncle Gerard's employment and, with his brothers, started a wholesale provision house under the firm name of Hopkins Brothers. They did a prosperous business in North Carolina and the Valley of Virginia. The Hopkins brothers had their own fleet of Conestoga wagons, veritable schooners on wheels drawn by four horses. These went out of Baltimore with manufactured goods and returned with provender from the frontier. Johns Hopkins was not averse to taking whisky from the country people in payment for his goods, and this he sold for a time under the brand name of "Hopkins Best." By so doing he incurred the displeasure of the Society of Friends and was turned out of meeting for a time. But he continued to sell the whisky. In later life he is said to have expressed regret at making money that way.

The austerity of the Quaker sect, however, did not extend to Johns Hopkins' table. He entertained lavishly and his formal dinners invariably included champagne and other fine wines. In fact it was rumored that he put through business deals by feeding his prospects sumptuously and getting them in a responsive frame of mind before making a proposition.

It was as a banker rather than as a wholesale grocer that Johns Hopkins achieved his greatest distinction in the business world. He had the reputation for being a shrewd judge of men and for distinguishing a good risk from a bad one. After twenty-five years he retired from the firm of Hopkins Brothers and, in the absence of Peabody, became the leading financier in the city. When the Baltimore & Ohio Railroad ran into difficulties Hopkins backed it with his credit. He was its largest stockholder and always showed a paternal interest in its affairs—a circumstance which later proved embarrassing to his other wards, the university and the hospital. During several serious financial crises the signature of Johns Hopkins on a piece of paper was all that was needed to restore confidence.

Among the people Johns Hopkins consulted on the subject of founding a university was Peabody who encouraged the idea. Peabody once remarked that the only person he had ever met who was more anxious to make money and more determined to succeed than himself was Johns Hopkins. The Hopkins fortune was estimated at $8,000,000. Of that sum $1,000,000 was distributed among the members of the Hopkins family and miscellaneous Baltimore charities. The rest went to the university, including the medical school, and to the hospital. Originally Johns Hopkins had intended to found an orphan asylum for Negro children but that project was abandoned. In the years since their establishment, the Johns Hopkins University and the Johns Hopkins Hospital have done more to make Baltimore known to the rest of the world than any other local institutions.

Many stories have been handed down to illustrate the frugality of these merchant princes. Peabody, it was said, would wait in a downpour of rain for a horsecar rather than pay the hire of a hackney coach. He seldom wore jewelry, and for years after he made his fortune managed to get along without a valet. He never kept house and it was generally believed that during the last ten years of his life his personal expenses did not exceed $3,000 a year. On the other hand, like Johns Hopkins, he entertained lavishly. One of the features of his residence in London was the large dinner at which he played host regularly every Fourth of July.

Enoch Pratt, however, was the chief butt of jokes over penny-pinching. He was careless, too, of his personal appearance. He is even said to have been mistaken for a tramp by another one of the fraternity who, seeing Pratt walking down toward his own house, called out to him: "There's no use going in there, Brother. You'll not get a damned crust." Baltimore ladies who met him in market whispered it about that he could be seen sampling the largest oysters before ordering the smallest ones. The most persistent legend was that, when Pratt was an old man, he would stop his carriage and get out to pick up a stray horseshoe nail in the street, the horseshoe business having been the original source of his fortune.

Like Peabody, Pratt was born in Massachusetts. He was the son of Isaac Pratt, a farmer of North Middleborough, the family being of old Puritan stock. Isaac Pratt turned from farming to running a sawmill and general store, and then to the wholesale hardware business. Nailrods were his speciality. In the early decades of the 19th century New England farmers used their spare time heating these rods and hammering them into nails. Enoch Pratt must have done this often in his youth.

Enoch was educated at a local academy. At the age of fifteen years he journeyed to Boston and there engaged as clerk in a wholesale hardware store, holding the job for seven years. The only detail recorded of this period of his life is that he was an active member of the Congregational Church to which he regularly subscribed $5 a year.

In 1831, at the age of twenty-two years, Pratt moved to Baltimore. In the national census of the year before it had risen to the rank of the second largest city in the United States. Pratt organized a company for the sale of nails, and of horseshoes and mule shoes. These goods were made in the towns and hamlets of New England, shipped in wagons to Boston, Hartford and New Haven, and from those cities by rail and boat to Baltimore.

This was the time of the great rift in the Congregational Church in New England which ended by the dissenting group establishing the Unitarian Church as a separate denomination. It so happened that a group of New Englanders living in Baltimore had established a Unitarian congregation and to it Pratt gravitated. The church became the center of his social life. It was there he met Maria Louisa Hyde, the young woman who became his wife. For years he was treasurer of the church and, after he amassed his fortune, frequently made up the deficits. He contributed material for the parish house, which still stands, and also for an organ which continues in use today.

In 1850, when Pratt was forty-one years old, he had accumulated $250,000. Two years before that he built a handsome four-story house at the corner of Park Avenue and Monument Street, which is now the home of the Maryland Historical Society, and he and his wife moved in. There were no children. Unrequited love and fruitless marriage worked to the advantage of Baltimore in that prolific era of benefactions. In 1855, now being comfortably off, Pratt set out alone for Europe and made an extensive tour of England, Scotland, France, Germany and Italy. He is known to have been impressed by the Advocate's Library in Edinburgh, a circumstance that may have turned his thoughts in that direction.

A year later Pratt returned to Baltimore to find the town seething over the issues of states' rights and slavery. There was no question about Pratt's stand. From the first he was a staunch Union man and advocate of freedom and education for the Negro. In the early days of the war this position was a dangerous one. His relief was natural when Baltimore awoke one morning to find General Butler and his troops occupying Federal Hill and guns pointing menacingly at the city. To his friends Pratt exclaimed: "Glory Hallelujah, Gentlemen. We are safe!"

The war greatly expanded Pratt's horseshoe and mule-shoe business. By 1865 he was handling a large consignment of stock from New England, and he controlled the major portion of Maryland's output as well. With the money he made in this line he bought a majority interest in a steamboat company providing night and day service on Chesapeake Bay. He served as president of the company for a time before selling out for two and a half times what he paid for his stock.

At the close of the Civil War Pratt joined the company of Johns Hopkins as one of the city's leading financiers. He was president of a bank and a director in numerous companies. Among his extracurricular activities he served as treasurer of Mr. Peabody's new institute. His interest in the Negro was evidenced among other things by membership in the American Colonization Society and his activity in establishing a reformatory for Negro boys. For this purpose he gave his farm, Cheltenham, in Prince George's County. Unfortunately this institution has not lived up to the expectations of its benefactor. In recent years Cheltenham has been a public scandal.

Meanwhile, getting on in years and being without children, Pratt was turning his thoughts to what he should do with his money. The idea of a university did not appeal to him. A university, in his opinion, served only a limited number of the wealthier members of the community. One afternoon when he was out driving with his pastor, the Rev. Dr. Charles R. Weld, he inquired abruptly what Dr. Weld considered Baltimore's greatest need at the moment. Dr. Weld hesitated to express an opinion. "Then," said Pratt, "I'll tell you—a free circulating public library, open to all citizens regardless of property or color."

Pratt was not a bookish man himself. His personal library consisted only of a few bookcases and there is no other evidence of his ever having been an omnivorous reader. Yet he had great faith in books as an educational factor. At that day Baltimore had no books to circulate among the general public. The few public libraries that existed were limited in membership and designed primarily to serve the well to do. The public library on the village green was still strictly a New England conception.

Pratt himself said that he turned the idea of a public library over in his mind for fifteen years. But he kept his plans secret. In fact the excavation for his central library building had been started before he let the public in on his scheme. Then his Yankee shrewdness came out. He couldn't resist the temptation to drive a bargain. So, in a letter to the Mayor and City Council, he offered the city $225,000 for a central public library building, plus $833,333.33, or a total of $1,058,333.33, provided the city would grant the library an annuity of $50,000 a year forever for its support and maintenance. The City Fathers accepted this condition.

Like Pratt, the people of Baltimore do not enjoy a reputation for being bookish. Their prejudice against buying books is notorious. Among the nation's large cities Baltimore ranks low in book sales. On the other hand, Baltimoreans are not averse to borrowing books. So Pratt's munificent offer met with immediate public response. A central library and four branches were completed. On January 5, 1886, the central library opened its doors with 28,000 books on the shelves. In the library's first year 26,000 cards were issued and 400,000 books were circulated. As Pratt hoped it would be, the library caters to all classes of society, regardless of race, creed or color. Its popularity has kept pace with the growth of the town.

The original central library no doubt deserved a reputation for its architectural beauty and general graciousness according to the taste of the late 1880's. But with changing architectural fashion it grew more and more forbidding as the years passed. The magnificent new building erected in the 1920's was by that time greatly needed to attract patronage. A unique feature is a series of twelve large show windows, whose displays are changed each month. Since they were built these displays have been the especial responsibility of Miss Kate Coplan of the library staff who has a genius for window dressing. In Baltimore customers are attracted to the public library to borrow books exactly as they are tempted to come and buy in the department stores a few blocks away. Current figures show that the collection of books has grown to around 1,000,000, cards taken out to nearly 200,000, and the number of books circulated during a single year to over 3,000,000. In addition to the central library building there are branches, and circulation also is assisted by a bookmobile that plies certain sections of the city on regular schedule.

In the early years of the library's career, Pratt himself served as president of the board. He took great delight in visiting the library at all hours to see how the public was enjoying it. An enthusiastic visitor was Andrew Carnegie who gave Pratt credit for being the pioneer in the planning of libraries in our country. Carnegie once said: "Many free libraries have been established in our country, but none that I know of with such wisdom as the Pratt." That was high praise from a man whose name is indelibly associated with public libraries in many parts of the nation.

Pratt lived to the ripe age of eighty eight years. A short time before his death he packed $1,500,000 in gilt-edged securities in a carpetbag. This precious burden he entrusted to two employes who boarded the night train for Boston. There the securities were conveyed to a bank for distribution to Pratt's six nephews and nieces in Massachusetts. This was Pratt's tidy New England way of avoiding the expense and red tape of the settlement of an estate.

The fourth and youngest of the merchant princes does not quite fit into the pattern with the other three. In the first place William T. Walters was not born a poor boy. His father was a country merchant in such comfortable circumstances that he could send his son to study civil and mining engineering in Philadelphia. Returning home young Walters found employment for a time in an iron furnace. But he did not long pursue his profession. In 1841 a canal was opened along the Susquehanna River, and he saw in it an opportunity to open trade between Baltimore and Pennsylvania. So he went to Baltimore and entered the produce commission business trading chiefly with his native state. This led to his interest in the Baltimore & Susquehanna Railroad which ran north from the city through York and Harrisburg and linked Baltimore with the canal. Walters became a controlling director of the road—the first indication of his genius in the field of railroading.

In 1847 Walters formed a partnership with one Charles Harvey in a company dealing in foreign and domestic liquors, and continued in the business until 1883. Unlike Johns Hopkins he never seems to have had any qualms of conscience about it. Meanwhile his commission business had shifted from Pennsylvania to Virginia and the Carolinas. Walters discovered the need for a fast freight line to carry perishable vegetables and fruits from the South to the Northern markets in Philadelphia, New York and Boston. He therefore conceived the notion of buying up a number of small bankrupt lines and consolidating them.

With a group of friends in Baltimore, Walters accomplished much before the outbreak of the Civil War to bring about the mergers through which the Atlantic Coast Line Railroad eventually was created. Through his business interests he developed a wide acquaintance throughout the South. In spite of his Pennsylvania origin he became an ardent sympathizer with the Confederacy. Such ardor, however, was not appreciated by the Federal troops occupying Baltimore. Walters found it advisable to leave town for the duration and go abroad.

From 1861 to 1865 he lived in Paris. This fortuitous circumstance worked to the great advantage of Baltimore. He once told a friend that with the first $5 he earned he bought a picture. In Paris, his infatuation with the fine arts reasserted itself. He soon was making the acquaintance of contemporary French artists and buying their works. Among the canvases that found their way into his collection were those of Corot, Millet, Millais, Delacroix, Detaille, Fortuny, Gerome, and Alma-Tadema. He also was among the first to appreciate and champion the sculptures of Antoine Louis Barye. About the same time he seized the opportunity to buy an important collection of Eastern ceramics.

Walters collected works of art chiefly for his own gratification, though he must have assumed that some day his collection would pass into the hands of the public. Yet from the very first he was generous about sharing the pleasure of his collection with others.

Long before he built his gallery he opened his residence on Mt. Vernon Place several days a week to persons who wished to view his art treasures.

William Walters had a son Henry who inherited his father's love of art. The two made frequent trips abroad together visiting the galleries and art exhibitions. Henry Walters, too, proved to be a competent railroad man and a successful financier. Following his father's death in 1894 he doubled the fortune that had been left him. He was reputed to be the wealthiest man south of the Mason and Dixon Line. He also greatly enlarged the collection begun by his father and built a handsome museum to house it.

It has been estimated that from the death of his father in 1894 up to 1931 Henry Walters spent $1,000,000 a year on art works. His purchases were not confined to painting and sculpture. They included also illuminated manuscripts, incunabula, textiles, ceramics, the work of goldsmiths and silversmiths, and what one authority describes as "probably the most important group of ivories, enamels and liturgical objects of the Byzantine and early Christian period ever brought together by one individual." This same authority states that the collection embraces virtually every known field of art, from the dawn of civilization to the present day.

Henry Walters died in 1931. Under his will the collection was bequeathed to the city. The bequest included not only the museum but it contained also a fund of $2,000,000 to maintain it.

For many years an air of mystery hung over the Walters residence at 8 W. Mt. Vernon Place because of a light that burned over the front entrance continually day and night year after year. Popular belief had it that William Walters' daughter offended by marrying a man her father did not approve, and that he had ordered her from his home. Later, according to this story, repenting his hasty action, he directed that the light be kept burning as an indication that she would be welcome if she ever returned.

The unfortunate part about this romantic tale is that it was not true. William Walters' daughter, Jennie, married Warren Delano, a charming gentleman of whom Mr. Walters highly approved and the marriage was altogether a happy one. The light has since been explained. Mr. Walters was frequently out of the city. Returning home one night he found a messenger boy at the door stumbling about in the dark. So he ordered that the light be kept on so that visitors could see what they were doing. To save the trouble of turning the light off and on he had it going all the time. As for the lighting bill, that was unimportant to a man of his financial resources.

In such manner has Baltimore profited by the presence of four merchant princes who found the city to their liking and showed their gratitude by endowing it with the essentials of a civilized society. Remove the names and works of Peabody, Johns Hopkins, Pratt and Walters and Baltimore would no longer be Baltimore. It would be just another town.

Chapter 5

SAGA OF THE IRON HORSE

THE FRENCH LINE, with its trans-Atlantic fleet, boasts that it is the "longest gangplank in the world," since once you are on one of its liners you are in France. The Pennsylvania Railroad might make a like boast that its platform is the longest in the world. For, once you are on it, you begin to experience every sensation of being in New York City. Typical of the metropolis are the throngs of people who push and shove to get through the gate, the express trains with interminable cars in which every seat appears to be already occupied, and train crews whose accent indicates a Pennsylvania or Jersey background.

The Pennsy's electrified trains speed through the country at from 70 to 80 miles an hour. On the run between Baltimore and New York, or Baltimore and Washington, there is a train each way every hour. The railroad is reliable and efficient. It gets you where you want to go. It does its job in a thoroughly impersonal way. As a railroad it is in a class by itself. But it isn't Baltimore.

If you are looking for local color you will find it on the B. & O., which had its origin in Baltimore. You will find it on the Western Maryland and the Maryland & Pennsylvania, which all Baltimoreans speak of with profound affection as "the Ma and Pa." You found it on the "Annapolis Short Line" and the "W.B. & A." (Washington, Baltimore & Annapolis) before rigor mortis set in.

The Baltimore and Ohio has played a unique role in the history of the city. Between the first Federal census in 1790 and the fourth in 1820 Baltimore, as we have seen, experienced a fivefold expansion. A writer in 1825 remarked that, "Among all the cities of America, or of the Old World, in modern or ancient times, there is no record of any one which has sprung up so quickly to so high a degree of importance as Baltimore." New inhabitants were being added at the rate of 4,000 a year.

Yet in spite of outward signs of prosperity and progress, the city stood in the shadow of economic disaster. In 1825 the Erie Canal was completed with the result that an unbroken waterway was established from the distant shores of Lake Superior all the way to New York City. Thus valuable trade that had gone south was diverted to New York, and New York leaped ahead at the expense of Philadelphia and Baltimore. Still another cause of misfortune for Baltimore was the appearance of steamboats on the Mississippi River. Prior to their coming it was customary for traders in the Middle West to ship their products by flatboat to New Orleans. A return journey upstream would have been far too laborious. So, after they had sold their cargo, they disposed also of their flatboats. With the cash they received in return they took passage on a sailing vessel through the Gulf and up the coast to Baltimore. There they bought manufactured goods which they took home with them overland in the great Conestoga wagons, veritable schooners on wheels which served as transportation to and from the frontiers. But steamboats made the return trip on the Mississippi possible. After their appearance Baltimore was left out.

Alarmed at these happenings some of the more timid merchants moved away to more promising fields. The majority, however, stayed on and, with admirable courage, applied themselves to the task of finding a solution to this vital problem. The best promise of a substitute for the North-South trade on the Susquehanna lay in tapping directly the resources of the rich and rapidly growing new territory of the Middle West.

At this point a Baltimorean named Evan Thomas made a trip to England. There he saw a steam railroad in operation between Stockton and Darlington and was greatly impressed by it. More important still, his observations greatly impressed his brother, Philip Thomas, a bank president and one of the leading merchants of the city. Philip Thomas in turn consulted George Brown, a keen businessman and son of Alexander Brown, founder of the banking house of Alexander Brown & Sons.

The upshot of these discussions was a meeting on February 12, 1827, at the home of Mr. Brown. To it were invited twenty-five influential merchants. Its announced purpose was "to take into consideration the best means of restoring to the city of Baltimore that portion of western trade which has lately been diverted from it by the introduction of steam navigation and by other causes." The venerable William Patterson, father of Madam Bonaparte, held the chair.

Evidently Philip Thomas and George Brown had handled the

preliminaries well. For before the evening was over a committee had been appointed, with Philip Thomas as chairman, to investigate and report on the practicability of a railroad from Baltimore to the Ohio River. In exactly a week the committee was ready with a report which proposed a double-track railroad and obtaining a charter for the same from the Legislature. The report was immediately adopted and a charter was drawn up by John V. L. McMahon, a competent lawyer. It was submitted to the Legislature which acted on it favorably on February 28, 1827. This was the first charter ever granted to an American railroad.

One month later books were opened in Baltimore, Frederick and Hagerstown for sale of the stock which was promptly oversubscribed. On April 24, 1827, the road was formally incorporated. Thus the elapsed time between the organization meeting on February 12th and formal incorporation was a bare seventy-one days. Yet Baltimoreans have a reputation for acting slowly and only after exhaustive deliberation, if they act at all!

The next great event in the history of the B. & O. was the laying of the first stone. A railroad was such a novelty that no one yet had thought of the more appropriate ceremony of driving the first spike. From time immemorial public buildings had been started on their way by the laying of a cornerstone. So why not a first stone for a railroad, even though in this case it would also be the last? Besides, Masonry was in full flower in Baltimore in those days. It alone knew how to conduct such ceremonies properly.

The date chosen for the great event was July 4, 1828. Everybody in Baltimore had a part in it and great crowds flocked in from the neighboring counties to witness the spectacle. Contemporary estimates placed the total attendance at between 50,000 and 60,000 persons. As usual in Baltimore the chief feature of the day was a monster parade. It started on Bond Street in East Baltimore and proceeded by way of Baltimore Street to the estate known as Mount Clare, two-and-a-half miles to the west of the town. It had been the home during his lifetime of Charles Carroll the Barrister, so designated to distinguish him from his cousin Charles Carroll of Carrollton. The distance covered by the marchers must have been at least four miles—a heartbreaking jaunt for a hot July day.

The procession was resplendent with great floats, blaring bands, military and civilian organizations. Heading the first division was a troop of horse. There followed the Grand Lodge of Masons, who were to lay the stone. After them came the President and Directors of the railroad, veterans of the American Revolution, the orator of the day, the Speaker of the United States House of Representatives and other honored guests.

In the second division were the trade associations and guilds, each with its own float. Among them were the Agricultural Society, the Farmers and Planters Association, gardeners, plowmakers, millers, bakers, victualers, brewers and distillers, tailors, blacksmiths, whitesmiths, weavers, bleachers, dyers and manufacturers of wool and cotton goods. Reminiscent of the days of Commodore Joshua Barney and his "Federalist" in a parade many years before was a ship on wheels named *The Union*, exhibited by ship captains, mates and seamen.

The leading figure in the proceedings was Charles Carroll of Carrollton, Baltimore's first citizen, and last surviving signer of the Declaration of Independence, who was to turn the first spade of earth. For all his ninety years the old gentleman was standing the physical strain of the celebration surprisingly well.

On a rise of ground in the center of a field at Mount Clare a pavilion had been erected. To this the dignitaries repaired. The exercises opened with a prayer which was followed by the reading of the Declaration of Independence. By way of an interlude a band burst into the lively strains of the Carrollton March, specially composed for the occasion. After that the Hon. John B. Morris delivered the oration that was then deemed essential to all public exercises.

When Mr. Morris had completed his speech and, amid applause, taken his seat, a deputation of blacksmiths advanced bearing a pick, spade, stone hammer and trowel. They were followed by a group of stonecutters surrounding a wagon on which rested the stone. All eyes were turned on the venerable Mr. Carroll as he took a spade from the blacksmiths and made a bold gesture of turning the earth. After that the stone was put in place by the masons, and there it remained for many years. With the changing of grades at Mount Clare the stone eventually was covered up and almost forgotten. In very recent times, however, it was dug up, polished off, remounted and given a place of honor near the original site.

If the leading merchants of the town lent their wholehearted support to the founding of the railroad, not so a generous segment of the citizenry. These gentry exercised the immemorial right of Baltimoreans to protest an innovation; since they were voters their obstructionist attitude had the support of the City Council. That august body first subscribed $500,000 toward the project, a generous sum. Then, fearful it had gone too far, it stipulated that the money should not be paid unless the Baltimore terminus of the railroad was located precisely at 60 feet above tidewater—no more and no less. How the Council arrived at 60 feet is not clear. Obviously it meant that the road could not be extended all the way to the waterfront to connect with ships in the harbor. The infant railroad was too helpless to do anything but agree. The spot chosen was in West Baltimore at the intersection of Pratt and Amity Streets.

Since the chief purpose of the railroad was to bring products from the hinterlands to the port the great question was how it was to reach the docks. Pratt Street, among others, was proposed as the route. No sooner did the citizens get wind of this than they raised more objections. The climax of the opposition was reached with a memorial addressed to the United States Congress expressing fear that every pump, hydrant, lamppost, awning post, tree and feeding trough on the street would have to be removed. The railroad, it was said, would scare the horses, parents would hesitate to send children to school across it, and no lady would ever go shopping if it involved crossing a railroad track.

In spite of the protests the railroad took the Pratt Street route to the docks, but for years no steam locomotive was permitted on the street. Instead horses hauled the coaches. As a matter of fact, at the outset nobody believed the new railroad would actually use steam locomotive power throughout its length. Even in England the steam locomotive was not yet being used over long distances. It was supposed, also, that the sharp curves on the American line could not be negotiated by a locomotive. No, the cars were to be drawn by horses and the space between the rails kept in condition with that end in view. The wheels of the cars were mounted on rails merely to make the going easier for the horses.

Thus the early experiments were concerned with animals. The record of the first years shows how twenty-seven persons were drawn in one car by a single horse at nine to ten miles an hour. It was demonstrated that two dogs could haul a car containing six persons. An experiment was made also with fitting a sail to a car. On one such trip a car equipped with a sail was reported to have attained a speed of twenty miles an hour. But, of course, there had to be wind: and, equally important, it had to be blowing in the direction you wanted to go. So the sail idea was abandoned.

The new railroad suddenly became the craze of the moment. Everybody wanted to enjoy the thrill of riding on it. By January, 1830, the line was ready for business from Mount Clare to the Carrollton Viaduct over Gwynns Falls, a few miles away. Excursions for the public were announced on a train of four cars with a capacity of 120 passengers. This was the first time in the United States that a railroad served as a common carrier.

Two men who were to make outstanding contributions to railroading appeared in Baltimore at this time. One was Ross Winans who hailed from New Jersey. He came to sell horses to the road, but, being of an inventive mind, he stayed on to experiment with equipment. It was he who invented the friction wheel which became standard with railroads. The other arrival was Peter Cooper of New York. Cooper had invested in land on the waterfront in the district known as Canton, to the east of the city, and was primarily interested in bringing the railroad closer to his property. He, too, was an inventor and he set to work to see what he could do to build a steam locomotive that could take the sharp curves of the American line. Winans helped him.

By the summer of 1830 Cooper's engine was ready for a demonstration. He christened it the *Tom Thumb*. The railroad now had been extended to Ellicott's Mills, some thirteen miles to the west of Baltimore. On Saturday, August 28th, President Thomas and the directors of the road were invited to take a trip to the end of the line in a car drawn by the *Tom Thumb*. There were twenty-six passengers in all. The *Tom Thumb* performed nobly, completing the thirteen miles in the elapsed time of one hour and fifteen minutes. The highest speed reached was eighteen miles an hour.

The return journey was uneventful until the Relay was reached, several miles outside the city. Here the party found a car drawn by a spanking gray horse. Car and horse belonged to Stockton and Stokes, the great stage proprietors of the day who recognized the challenge of the *Tom Thumb* to their business and the necessity of meeting it without delay. They proposed a race between the locomotive and the gray and the invitation was accepted. While the *Tom Thumb* was getting up steam the gray forged ahead. But, once the pressure was on, the *Tom Thumb* commenced to cut down the lead and finally passed the horse. At this critical juncture a part of the machinery which drove the blower on the engine slipped off; the pressure was released and the engine began to wheeze and pant. Mr. Cooper, who was acting as his own engine-man and fireman, tried to make hurried repairs, but to no avail. To his mortification and the delight of the stage proprietors the race was over and the horse had won!

In spite of this dramatic episode officials of the B. & O. were convinced that the locomotive was feasible. To speed progress they announced a competition for the design of a practical loco-motive adapted to a curved road. Among those who read the an-nouncement was Phineas Davis, a watchmaker of York, Penn-sylvania, and he at once set to work building a locomotive after his own ideas. When it was finished he christened it the *York*, and set to work on the tedious business of hauling it by way of the York Road from his home to Baltimore, some fifty miles to the south. Davis's *York* proved an immediate success and was the first locomotive to be put into regular service on the B. & O.

The next few years saw feverish activity as the line was pushed westward and constant experiment led to rapid improvement in locomotives, cars and other equipment. The Mount Clare shops hummed under the combined inspiration of Winans, Davis, Cooper and others. The railway car, for example, began as a rough market cart. From that it was transformed into a nine-passenger carriage. To Winans went the credit for building the first eight-wheeled coach.

Meanwhile the engineers were working miracles cutting a right of way through virgin territory, building bridges and calculating grades that eventually would carry the line through the Blue Ridge and Allegheny Mountains. Outstanding among the achieve-ments was a curving stone viaduct 77 feet long over the Patapsco River, just to the south of the city. The floor of the viaduct rested upon eight elliptical arches, each of them 60 feet wide and rising 65 feet above the level of the stream. This majestic structure was designed by Benjamin H. Latrobe, a gifted Baltimorean, son of the architect of the United States Capitol in Washington and of the Catholic Cathedral in Baltimore.

The Thomas Viaduct, named for the B. & O.'s first president, has been called one of the finest bits of railroad architecture in the entire nation. Because of its ambitious design it was dubbed "Latrobe's Folly." But Latrobe built better than he or his contemporaries knew. The viaduct still stands and is one of the oldest stone-arch viaducts in continued use in the world. Constructed to carry six-ton locomotives and cars commensurate with them, it today bears without perceptible strain great monsters weighing 300 tons, hauling trains beside which those of the 1830's would be pygmies.

On December 1, 1831, the railroad was completed to Frederick, Maryland, and, for a season, was the longest stretch of railroad in the world. August 25, 1835, was another red-letter day in the road's history when the first train was run from Baltimore to Washington. Evidence of the vast progress that had been made since the founding seven short years before is that this time 1,000 passengers rode on the excursion train that inaugurated the line and pulled up in the new Washington depot at the foot of the hill back of the capitol. The event was not without its tragic episode. On the return trip the locomotive jumped the track. Phineas Davis, who was riding in the cab on this great day, was thrown beneath the wheels and killed.

It was not a cheap business projecting a railroad line through a wilderness and over lofty mountain ranges. But there was no doubt that, through the courage and ingenuity of its leading merchants, Baltimore had found an answer to the Erie Canal, had taken a new lease on its economic life and that the future of the city was guaranteed for years to come.

The 1850's was the period in which great railway stations were being erected throughout the world. The management of the B. & O. was determined not to be left behind. Baltimore must have a station commensurate in grandeur and in modern facilities with such impressive monuments as Euston, Charing Cross, and Paddington Stations in London.

There was nothing niggardly about the B. & O.'s plans. In 1852 a sum of $500,000 was alloted to the purchase of three city blocks in the southwest section of the town. There Camden Station came into being. At the time of its completion it was the largest station in the United States and one of the largest in the world. One smiles on looking at Camden Station today and what our ancestors regarded as magnificent. By present-day standards it is a structure of exceedingly modest proportions. Without major alterations Camden Station has been in constant use for almost a century. Among the celebrated passengers who have passed through it in their time are Abraham Lincoln, Henry Ward Beecher, George Bancroft, Charles A. Dana, Commodore Matthew Calbraith Perry, and Robert E. Lee, to mention only a few.

Perhaps the B. & O. had gone too far and too fast. For just about this time the company was confronted with a financial crisis. One trouble was that, because of the stock holdings of the State and the municipality the management was riddled with politics. Two stockholders then particularly interested and influential were Johns Hopkins and John W. Garrett. The latter was the son of Robert Garrett, one of the town's leading bankers. The Garrett firm, under the name of Robert Garrett & Sons, after more than a century is still actively engaged in the investment banking business.

Hopkins and Garrett joined forces to put an end to the political control of the road. Hopkins, the largest individual stockholder, proposed Garrett as president, and the resolution was duly passed. The new executive was thirty-eight years old, a man of massive frame and of equally massive intellect and will power. The election took place on November 17, 1858. Mr. Garrett's first act was to effect economies that enabled his first report to show net earnings. In his second year the board was released from political control.

The B. & O. now was to be harassed by something far more formidable even than politics. It found itself a key to strategy in time of war. On the outbreak of hostilities between North and South in 1861 the "Main Stem" between Baltimore and Cumberland, Maryland, was vital to the movement of Union troops and supplies. It passed through Harper's Ferry where it was exposed to the Confederate Army in the Valley of Virginia under the astute leadership of Stonewall Jackson.

Jackson was not the man to overlook so valuable a prize. During the early days of the conflict the Confederates for six months were in control of 100 miles of the road. Even when they were not in permanent control they subjected the line to destructive raids. Rails and ties were ripped up. Fires were made of the ties and over them the rails were heated red hot and then twisted around the nearest tree. Bridges, in that period constructed chiefly of wood, were burned. So were rolling stock, stations, shops and other property. Jackson even hitched teams to some of the locomotives and hauled them down the valley pike for use on Virginia railroad lines. Nevertheless under the driving power of the vigorous young president the damage was repaired almost as fast as it was made. The Mount Clare Shops during the war worked night and day turning out railway equipment. The extent of the damage done during hostilities is revealed by the indemnity of $3,000,000 which the B. & O. received from the Federal Government at the close of the war.

In spite of many personal ties with the South, Mr. Garrett was a staunch Union man. He was on intimate terms with Edward M. Stanton, Secretary of War, and valuable military information that was picked up along his line was promptly relayed to the Government in Washington. One of President Garrett's greatest achievements was the movement of 20,000 Federal troops from the Potomac to Chattanooga in 1863, one of the first great military rail-transport movements in history.

The B. & O. also made history in 1863 when President Lincoln traveled to Gettysburg for the dedication of the battlefield cemetery. The official party left Washington at noon on November 18, traveling over the B. & O. At 1:20 P.M. the presidential special rolled into Camden Station. There the Marine Band played while horses were being hitched to the President's car to haul it up Howard street a mile or so to the Bolton Station of the Northern Central Railroad. On this occasion Union sympathizers were out in force. They thronged the sidewalks and the President appeared on the rear platform of the car to acknowledge the applause.

The dedication ceremony took place on the 19th and with it the famous address. At 7 P.M. the President entrained for the return journey. It was 11 P.M. when his special again reached Bolton Station. The town had gone to bed and the streets were deserted, so the President stayed in his car while it was being hauled back to

Camden Station. This was Lincoln's last visit to Baltimore until 1865 when the funeral train bore his body into the city on its way to its final resting place in Illinois.

The days that immediately followed the Civil War saw the building of great railway empires whose creators were as ruthless as those of political empires. John Garrett was not one to refuse a fight and he was determined that the B. & O. was not going to yield by default to its younger adversaries. The Pennsylvania, founded in 1847, had by now become a dangerous rival. Each company bedeviled the other with petty annoyances. The Pennsylvania depended on the B. & O. for service between Baltimore and Washington, the B. & O. on the Northern Central (a subsidiary of the Pennsylvania) for service to Harrisburg. These services were given grudgingly. There were rows also with the Philadelphia, Wilmington & Baltimore which B. & O. patrons used when bound from Washington to New York. The P. W. & B. eventually was absorbed by the Pennsylvania. The upshot was that, to achieve independence, the Pennsylvania paralleled the B. & O. to Washington while the B. & O. paralleled the P. W. & B. to Philadelphia and then negotiated with other roads to carry its trains to Jersey City.

Mr. Garrett took the offensive also on his western front. He defied the Pennsy by boldly moving into Pittsburgh. He gained a foothold on Lake Erie and also entered Chicago. His ambition did not end with the land; he claimed the sea also as part of his dominion. At Locust Point, on the northwest branch of the Patapsco River, he built great docks, warehouses and grain elevators. Immediately after the Civil War he also bought several ships from the Government and for two years had them running on a regular schedule across the Atlantic.

It was a popular saying in Baltimore that the B. & O. had three periods of history: Before Garrett, Garrett and After Garrett. No other president left so permanent an imprint. The Garrett incumbency saw the B. & O. at its peak. After his death it yielded place to the Pennsylvania and thereafter played second fiddle to that extensive and powerful system.

An outstanding event of the later history of the road was the digging of a tunnel under Howard street from 50 to 65 feet beneath the surface. Its purpose was to connect Camden Station with an uptown station on Mt. Royal Avenue. The tunnel was opened to the first passenger train on May 1, 1895. On September 1, 1896, Mt. Royal Station received its first passengers. As Camden Station at the time of its construction in 1857 was considered the last word in railway stations, so, too, was Mt. Royal. The station was not distinguished for its size but for its design and setting. Its most distinguishing feature is a lofty Romanesque clock tower. The tracks are cleverly concealed behind the station, which is set down in an open space embellished with shade trees, flower beds and lawns, giving the area the character of a public park. Like Camden Station, Mt. Royal continues in regular use today. A detail that never fails to attract attention are the rocking chairs in the waiting room. In late years they have been reduced to two or three, thus constituting little more than a gesture. There is also a gracious open fireplace in the main waiting room. This sometimes is used on special occasions, such as the Christmas holiday season.

Among the various presidents of the railroad the one next in importance to Garrett was Daniel Willard. His administration began in 1910 and ended with his retirement in 1941, the longest tenure in the history of the road. Unlike most of his predecessors who had been financiers or lawyers Mr. Willard was a practical railroad man. A native Vermont farm boy, he attended an agricultural college with the idea of becoming a scientific farmer. But serious trouble with his eyes forced him to withdraw. He then started railroading as a laborer, and became successively a fireman, engineer and brakeman. He used to say he never asked for a promotion and saw no reason why anybody should have to do so. He underestimated his industry, intelligence and executive ability which was quickly recognized and carried him to the pinnacle of his profession. Mr. Willard lost none of his Yankee crispness and energy through life in Baltimore.

By the time he became president of the B. & O. the age of railroad expansion had passed. His contribution lay in rebuilding and modernizing the road. He also had a powerful hand in humanizing it. He realized that the B. & O. could never match the Pennsylvania in volume of travel; he therefore aimed to give a personal touch to the service provided the select few who traveled over it. Mr. Willard was an avid newspaper reader, and he also kept his ear to the ground. If he read in the public print or heard any criticism of his road he was very likely to search out the author of it and send one of his officers around to inquire if the critic had any constructive suggestions to offer for the improvement of the service.

Mr. Willard's administration, like that of John W. Garrett, saw the nation's participation in another war. Fortunately in this instance the B. & O. was not the target for enemy raids. But, like Garrett, Mr. Willard found many opportunities to be of use to the President of the United States and the Secretary of War, in mobilizing the nation's railroads for the war effort. He served as a member of the Council of National Defense and Chairman of the War Industries Board.

Mr. Willard did not confine himself purely to railroad affairs. He was an active leader in the community. In keeping with the old B. & O.-Hopkins tradition, he was invited to membership on the Board of Trustees of the Johns Hopkins. Very soon he was elevated to the presidency of that august body. To his railroad colleagues and the Baltimore public at large he was known affectionately as "Uncle Dan." His name must be added to those of the long line of gifted New Englanders who have contributed handsomely to Baltimore's well being.

Allusion has been made to the Western Maryland as also being typical of the Baltimore scene. Origin of the road is owed not to Baltimoreans but the residents of Carroll County which lies to the west of the city. A charter was obtained in 1852 for the building of a railroad whose purpose was to recapture the trade centering around Hagerstown that was being diverted to Philadelphia.

Twenty years before, the Northern Central had built a branch from the Relay House at Lake Roland through the Green Spring Valley to Owings Mills. The Western Maryland purchased this as its entrance into Baltimore with the understanding that, whenever it obtained its own right of way into the city, it would sell the branch back to the Northern Central. Through the 1860's and 1870's the Western Maryland continued to extend its line westward through Westminister, Union Bridge, Thurmont and Hagerstown. It was not until 1874 that the road got its own right of way into the city and made a contract with the Pennsylvania to use its tunnel and Union Station on the way to its own station on Hillen Street. Hillen Station, which still stands, was built in 1876 and ranks next to the B. & O.'s Camden Station in age.

In 1881 the Western Maryland had the distinction of being the only means by which the ordinary public could reach the Pimlico Race Track, then in the dead of the country and otherwise accessible only to those who could afford horse-drawn vehicles. The Western Maryland tapped it with a spur from Arlington. The Western Maryland is primarily a freight line with its coal pier, grain elevator and other facilities at its Port Covington terminal. Passenger service has been reduced to two trains each way per day in and out of Baltimore. Conductors and coaches share a stately dignity in defiance of the modern craze for streamlining. They remind one of an aristocratic limousine and chauffeur, vintage of 1910.

Most picturesque of all Baltimore's railroading is the Maryland and Pennsylvania or, more familiarly, the "Ma and Pa." Its right of way is said to be the most winding and roundabout in fixed rail transportation. It starts at a little station under the east end of North Avenue bridge, follows the Jones Falls valley for a brief space and then turns off to parallel its lesser tributary, Stony Run. The route cuts through the city's fashionable northern suburbs, skirting Roland Park and the Elkridge Club. It passes through Towson, the seat of Baltimore County. With the aid of wooden trestles it traverses Baltimore County, crosses the line into Harford and eventually arrives at its terminus in York, Pennsyvania.

By the Northern Central Railroad (subsidiary of the efficient Pennsy, of course) the distance from Baltimore to York is 56 miles; by the highway it is 50 miles. By the "Ma and Pa" it is 80½ miles! Because it carried milk to town from the dairy herds of Baltimore and Harford Counties the road was once known as "The Milky Way." But it has long since lost that business to trucks and its chief revenue comes from bulk freight. There are two passenger trains and one freight train each way on week days.

That is hardly what would be called heavy traffic. Yet there was enough going in each direction over the single-track line in May, 1920, to cause a serious head-on collision between a passenger train and a freight. The accident occurred just southwest of the Charles Street Avenue crossing and beside the Elkridge golf course. The engineer of the passenger train was killed instantly. The fireman on the freight had his foot caught between his engine and the tender.

It so happened that at the time Dr. J. M. T. Finney, one of the nation's leading surgeons, was playing golf over the club course and was summoned to the scene of the wreck. Unable to free the fireman, he got a saw from the club toolhouse, mounted the cabin and, in a cloud of steam that was pouring from the engine, amputated the man's foot. The fireman was released but died of shock on reaching the hospital.

The "Ma and Pa" is known far and wide to the connoisseurs of quaint railway lines. People come long distances just to ride on it. It is a favorite way of taking an all-day outing. It was not uncommon a few years ago for the engineer on the arrival of the train in Baltimore to stand by his engine and inquire of passengers as they passed, "Did you have a nice trip?" For a long time Engine No. 6, relic of a bygone era, hauled the passenger train to the delight of the sentimental. But in 1947, steam locomotives gave way to diesels.

Old No. 6 was in action on September 14, 1947, when Lucius Beebe was the chief figure in a literary excursion launching his book *Mixed Train Daily*, in which the "Ma and Pa" was among the roads featured. The train that day was dubbed "the Champagne Special." Beebe and his 37 guests came dressed in the fashion of the Gay Nineties and made the trip to Delta, Pennsylvania and return. An annual feature is the picnic of the Paint and Powder Club, the local amateur organization which produces musical shows. Members of this, too, attend in costume. On such occasions the train usually is equipped with an open flatcar from which the passengers may the better see the country.

To passengers who pass through Baltimore the most memorable feature of the railroads are the two long tunnels. These are on the Pennsylvania line on either side of the station. In the days of steam locomotives the smoke was terrific. In spite of heroic efforts on the part of the train crews to close all windows, the coaches were saturated with it. Most people therefore associated Baltimore with a slow and painful death by asphyxiation. The substitution of electricity for coal has changed all of that. Even so the impression of the city as obtained from the railway rights of way is anything but pleasant.

Chapter 6

BALTIMORE MILITANT

BALTIMORE was little more than a hamlet at the outbreak of the French and Indian War in 1756. That war was in part financed by a tax on bachelors, from 5 to 20 shillings each according to the size of his income. Baltimore levied on thirteen bachelors and this seems to have been its sole contribution to the conflict.

The war did, however, give Baltimore its first experience with displaced persons. These were French Acadians expelled by the British from Nova Scotia. A group of them found their way to Baltimore Town. Being Catholics they received a cordial welcome from their co-religionists. A priest from the chapel at Doughoregan Manor, the country estate of the Carroll family, came to town to say mass for them in a private dwelling. They found lodging on South Charles Street and that neighborhood for years after bore the name of Frenchtown.

Immediately prior to the Revolutionary War Baltimore had become a place of considerable importance. Including the adjoining settlement of Fell's Point, which had recently been annexed, it counted a population of 6,755. It was strategically placed on the main route linking the colonies of the eastern seaboard. When in 1774 the people of Boston protested the Port Bill, the Baltimoreans promptly showed their sympathy by holding mass meetings. They also formed a committee of correspondence. In fact the claim has been made that a resolution passed at a meeting in Baltimore on May 31, 1774, presided over by Captain Charles Ridgely, was the first to propose a congress to the other colonies. Further evidence of Baltimore's enthusiasm was the dispatch of a shipload of food to the suffering patriots of Boston.

Because of its location on the main highway of travel the town played host to a succession of Revolutionary celebrities. Among the first to arrive in 1775 were members of the Virginia delegation on the way to the meeting of the Continental Congress in Philadelphia. They put up at the Fountain Inn, at that time the leading hostelry. Included in the delegation was Colonel George Washington whose military reputation already was sufficiently marked to warrant a turning out of the militia and the firing of a salute. Before departing, Colonel Washington also reviewed four companies of troops that were drawn up on the common.

In a letter to a member of the Convention at Annapolis Captain Mordecai Gist states that as early as December, 1774, he recruited in Baltimore a company of militia "composed of gentlemen, men of honor, family and fortune." The statement is significant since it is from this body that Baltimore's infantry regiment in the National Guard today claims direct descent. A company answering Gist's description formed part of the Maryland Line which fought through the Revolution. It constituted a corps d'élite and was distinguished by its bright scarlet uniforms and smart appearance which earned for its members the then popular term "Macaronis."

The Baltimoreans proved as gallant in battle as on parade. The Maryland Line had the exacting task of acting as rearguard in the Battle of Long Island and the bluest blood of Maryland was shed in holding back the British, thus protecting Washington's retreating army. This action won special praise for the Marylanders from the Commander in Chief.

On July 29, 1776, Baltimore Town had its own personal celebration of the Declaration of Independence. The great document was read with ceremony before a throng of citizens in front of the Courthouse. To add further color to the scene the local militia was drawn up at attention and a cannon was fired. In the evening the town was illuminated and an effigy of King George III was carted through the streets before being committed to the flames.

An important local revolutionary body was the Committee of Observation. Today, it would be known as a counterintelligence group. Its chairman was Samuel Purviance, Jr., member of a prominent family. The committee's task was to search out subversive elements and bring them to book. Theoretically it disapproved threats and violence, though its claims were questioned by some of the Tories singled out for investigation and ordered to appear before it.

The committee once went so far as to dispatch one Captain Samuel Smith (of whom more will be heard) to Annapolis to take into custody the last royal governor, Robert Eden. It so happened that, in spite of his official position and English affiliations, Eden was popular with the Annapolitans. Besides, Annapolitans did not like the idea of upstart Baltimoreans interfering in their affairs. So they advised Chairman Purviance and his committee to mind their own business. Soon thereafter Governor Eden discreetly took his departure. The more radical elements of the committee later organized as the Whig Club, which continued its campaign of vigilance against the Tories. Most of the latter found it expedient to leave town.

In the autumn of 1777 Count Casimir Pulaski, a Polish patriot who had embraced the American cause and been commissioned a brigadier in the Continental Army, arrived in Baltimore to recruit an independent corps of 68 horse and 200 foot. Pulaski paid a flying visit to Bethlehem, Pennsylvania, a Moravian settlement, and the nuns there presented him with a handsomely embroidered silk banner. This was carried by his corps until Pulaski's heroic death at the siege of Savannah in 1779. It later found its way to Baltimore and for more than a hundred years has been in the possession of the Maryland Historical Society. Pulaski's name has been immortalized in that of a street. Pulaski Day is regularly celebrated by Baltimore's Polish colony and a bas-relief in his honor has recently been erected in Patterson Park.

In the spring of 1781 the dashing young Marquis de Lafayette rode into town at the head of his troops on the way south and stopped for the night. The good women of the town organized a ball in his honor. A pretty story is told of the Marquis looking disconsolate in spite of all the beauty and gaiety around him. Being asked the reason he replied that he could not help thinking about his poor ill-clad soldiers. A hint was all that was needed. The townspeople at once came through with flour and Mrs. David Poe headed a committee of ladies that set to work making 500 "garments" for Lafayette's troops.

This is the first mention of "garment-making" by Baltimore women. A garment is not necessarily a loose-fitting nightshirt, as the name implies. It may be almost anything that Baltimore ladies see fit to cut out and sew together. "Garments" have since been made by them for combatants in the nation's wars as well as in peacetime for the victims of fire, flood, starvation and disease, for lepers in the South Seas, for repentant sinners at home and converted heathen abroad.

In September of the same year (1781) General Washington again visited the town and put up for the night at the Fountain Inn. The French fleet, under command of the Comte de Grasse, had recently arrived in Chesapeake Bay. In honor of this auspicious turn in events the town again was illuminated and a banquet held at Lindsay's Coffee House. A flowery address was presented to the General by a group of citizens and the General delivered an equally flowery response. One wonders if the American custom of ghost writing did not originate with these tedious ceremonial affairs.

Still another distinguished visitor in Revolutionary days was the Comte de Rochambeau who arrived with his suite on his way to the Virginia battle front. After the surrender of Yorktown Rochambeau returned at the head of his troops and encamped on a hill on the outskirts of the town. The hill is now the site of the Catholic Cathedral. In the Archbishop's garden still stands an ancient elm which shaded the Count and his men in 1782 as today it shades pedestrians at the busy intersection of North Charles and Mulberry Streets.

During the Revolution Baltimore shipyards, as we already have seen, played a conspicuous part in ship construction. The town also gave to the infant United States Navy a colorful figure in the person of Joshua Barney. Barney's reputation probably does not suffer from the fact that he was primarily his own biographer and chief witness to many of his daring exploits.

At the outbreak of the Revolution he volunteered his services to the Navy and took part in a number of expeditions and engagements. He claimed to have used in recruiting the first United States flag received in Baltimore from Philadelphia. A ship he commanded in the West Indies, which flew the Stars and Stripes, was said to have been the first to receive a salute from the governor of a foreign power. Barney's most distinguished achievement in the war was as commander of the *Hyder Ally,* 16 guns, which engaged and defeated the British sloop *General Monk,* 18 guns, off Cape May.

Barney married a daughter of Associate Justice Samuel Chase. An ardent Federalist like his father-in-law, who was impeached by the Republican administration of Thomas Jefferson, Barney devised an ingenuous method of celebrating Maryland's ratification of the Federal Constitution in 1788. He built the model of a full-rigged ship 15 feet in length. This was mounted on wheels and drawn in a parade which featured the local observance. After that the model was parked for a time on the eminence to the south of the inner harbor which ever since that day has borne the name of Federal Hill.

As a final romantic gesture Barney launched his ship and, single-handed, sailed it down Chesapeake Bay, past Point Lookout and up the Potomac to Mt. Vernon, where he presented it to General Washington in the name of the merchants and shipmasters of Baltimore. Washington's letter of thanks, while couched in polite and graceful language, does not quite hide the General's astonishment at the gift and his perplexity as to what to do with it.

A Baltimorean as distinguished for his services on land as Barney was for his services at sea was Colonel John Eager Howard. Howard entered the continental service as a captain, having raised a military company in Baltimore and Harford Counties. He was with the Maryland Line in numerous battles, was promoted and commanded a regiment at Germantown. History says of him that he "delighted to meet the foe in the close encounter of crossed bayonets." The high point of his military career was reached in the Battle of Cowpens. There, according to tradition, he personally received the swords of seven British officers. An engraver immortalized the scene, depicting Colonel Howard clutching in his arms the seven swords and looking rather like a perplexed juggler who has fumbled his act.

In gratitude and affection his fellow citizens honored Howard by electing him three times Governor of Maryland and twice to the United States Senate. He on his part generously gave many acres of his land for the site of the Catholic Cathedral, for the laying out of streets to the north and west of the town and for various civic improvements. His name lives today in Howard Street, one of the city's noblest thoroughfares in the shopping district. There also are a John Street and an Eager Street. If one were to try to choose Baltimore's first citizen throughout all its history John Eager Howard would come close to filling the bill.

For several months during the war Baltimore was the seat of

national government. Driven from Philadelphia by the British the Continental Congress took refuge in Baltimore. It held its sessions in a large building owned by one Jacob Fite situated at what is now Baltimore and Liberty Streets. For years after the building, long since gone, was known as Congress Hall. The Congress convened on December 20, 1776, and remained until February 27, 1777, usually the bleakest and dreariest season in Baltimore. That winter seems to have been no exception. Some of the members were none too pleased with their surroundings and accommodations. Among the loudest complainers was John Adams who, in his diary, referred bitterly to the bleakness and the mud. This cannot be laid entirely to the propensity of the Adams family to find fault. Local history records that, about the same time, the roads in Baltimore were in such wretched condition that a mounted drummer boy passing through the town with troops fell into a mud puddle and he and his horse were almost lost to view.

There were Federalists in Baltimore in 1812, but the rank and file of its people were Republicans, disciples of Jefferson and Madison and therefore keen for the war with England. As in the Revolutionary War, Baltimore was the home port of many of the privateers which preyed on British commerce. Thomas Boyle, though New England born, sailed the *Chasseur* out of Baltimore and boldly attacked British merchant vessels in their home waters. He wrote an impudent note to the Admiralty claiming all British bays, inlets and rivers as his domain. Baltimore's Joshua Barney, returning from service in the French navy with the rank of Commodore, cruised in the *Rossie* as a privateerman and captured and destroyed property to the estimated value of $1,500,000. No wonder the English charged Baltimore with being a "nest of pirates" and singled it out for special punishment.

Baltimore volunteers figured conspicuously also in the American attack on Canada. William H. Winder deserted a lucrative law practice to take the field. He was captured and imprisoned. Nathan Towson, another native son, commanded a battery of artillery that performed with distinction in the Battles of Chippewa and Lundy's Lane and in other major engagements.

Baltimore now was a prosperous city of some 46,000 population, exceeded in size only by New York and Philadelphia. If captured it could afford to pay a handsome ransom. By comparison the young capital city of Washington was insignificant. That is why General John Armstrong, the Secretary of War, assumed that the invading force under General Robert Ross and Admiral Sir George Cockburn was aimed at Baltimore, not Washington.

But when Washington was attacked Baltimore's General Winder was the hapless commander of the defending troops and Stansbury's brigade of Baltimoreans was in the advance guard that met the shock of the enemy attack at Bladensburg. Of that unhappy engagement and the demoralization of the American army, the flight of the Government and the sacking of the capital, the less said the better. William Pinkney, who at the time was Attorney General of the United States, fought gallantly in the forefront of the battle until he was wounded. Still another Baltimorean to give a good account of himself was the redoubtable Barney. He commanded a flotilla of gunboats that fled up the Patuxent River pursued by the British fleet. When the flotilla could go no farther Barney blew up his boats and marched his sailors and his guns to join Winder's army at Bladensburg.

Barney's flotilla men, veterans of many a naval engagement, were the only Americans to put up any sort of a fight. The Commodore himself was wounded by a ball that lodged in his thigh. He was captured by the British who knew him by reputation and treated him with great courtesy.

When the British a few weeks later launched an amphibious attack on Baltimore with the same troops that captured Washington, the city had made preparation to meet it. Star-shaped Fort McHenry, on Whetstone Point guarding the approach to the inner harbor, represented the very last word in the military engineer's art. It was manned by militia, volunteers and regulars under Lieutenant Colonel George Armistead, of the regular establishment. Details of citizens, working in shifts, had constructed a strong line of fortifications on Loudenslager's Hill (now Patterson Park) covering the eastern approach to the city which a landing force co-operating with a fleet would be most likely to take.

Baltimore also had two stout defenders in the persons of John Eager Howard and Samuel Smith, both veterans of the Revolutionary War. Some of the fainthearted merchants, seeing more than fifty British sails off the mouth of the Patapsco and knowing that aboard them were regiments of Wellington's regulars, very naturally regarded defense of the town as hopeless. They proposed buying the enemy off. The debacle in Washington was still fresh in everybody's mind.

But Colonel Howard would have none of it. He who "delighted to meet the foe in close encounter with crossed bayonets" rose nobly to the occasion. "I have," he declared, "as much property at stake as most persons and I have four sons in the field; but sooner would I see my sons weltering in their blood and my property reduced to ashes, than so far disgrace the country."

The immediate problem was what to do about Winder. Though he had been, so to speak, knocked out of the box at Bladensburg, he was still officially in command and he arrived in Baltimore to assume his duties. But the Baltimoreans at that moment wanted no more of Winder, native son and sincere patriot though he was. It was old John Howard as much as anybody else who used his influence to sidetrack Winder and give the supreme command to Sam Smith, now a general of militia.

The courage of the Baltimoreans was well rewarded. The British landed on September 12, 1814. While the main body of the defenders, some 10,000 strong, manned the fortifications on the hill, the City Brigade under General John Stricker sallied forth to meet the foe, commanded by General Ross, advancing up the North Point peninsula after landing from the fleet. The stand of the American advance guard was brief. After a brisk fight with the enemy lasting less than an hour the inferior defending force retired on the main body in the fortifications. But in the initial skirmish General Ross was killed by sharpshooters. The deed was popularly attributed to two teen-age youths, Daniel Wells and Henry McComas, who themselves later fell in action. The death of General Ross decidedly discouraged the invaders.

Next day the British fleet bombarded Fort McHenry almost continuously from morning until after midnight. Though more than 1,000 bombs were rained on it, the fort held out. From the British fleet, where he was being kept a prisoner, Francis Scott Key saw the Stars and Stripes still flying and knew the fort had not surrendered. Inspired by the sight he dashed off a few lines on the back of an envelope. Next day, upon his release by the British and his return to Baltimore, he showed the verses to his brother-in-law, Judge Joseph H. Nicholson, who urged Key to publish them. In such manner was born the National Anthem.

After the death of Ross and the successful defense of Fort McHenry the invaders concluded not to try an attack on the fortifications on the hill. So the main body saw no action. The 10,000 defenders, who had taken no active part in the operations, survived to produce offspring. It was a great battle for the making of distinguished ancestors.

The 5th Regiment, under command of Colonel Joseph Sterett, was present both at Bladensburg and in the sharp little battle waged by the City Brigade on the North Point Road. The 5th claimed descent from Mordecai Gist's company in the Maryland Line in the Revolution. The 5th, too, was composed of sons of the leading families of the city. Both at Bladensburg and at North Point it held its ground until other units gave way; then it had no other choice than to retreat or be surrounded and captured.

On May 23, 1846, Monument Square was the scene of a mass meeting to stir up public enthusiasm over a war with Mexico. Among the distinguished guests was General Sam Houston of Texas. The oratory had the desired effect, for two weeks later a company bearing the name "Baltimore's Own" was mustered into the Federal service and brigaded with troops from the District of Columbia. The organization was commanded by Lieutenant Colonel W. H. Watson, a native son, who died gloriously in the Battle of Monterey.

A tragic role awaited Baltimore in the Civil War. Both the Confederacy and the Union had their ardent sympathizers and clashes between the two factions were frequent. When South Carolina seceded Southern sympathizers raised the state flag. When a Southern sympathizer appeared on the street wearing in his hat a cockade of Southern colors he would be greeted by the opposing faction with hisses and groans. Fist fights followed. Colonel George P. Kane, marshal of the newly organized police force, was a zealous man and did his best to intervene and preserve order but without great success.

A particularly mischievous incident was the report of a plot to assassinate Abraham Lincoln, the President-elect, on his way through Baltimore to his inauguration in Washington. Investigation has revealed that the report was a figment of the imagination of a detective, but at the time it was taken seriously. Lincoln made one of the few blunders of his career when he was induced to change his schedule and slip through Baltimore secretly in the dead of night. An innocent crowd assembled at the depot next day to catch a glimpse of him. When Mrs. Lincoln and the children appeared without the President and the truth was learned the Baltimore public was indignant that it should have been suspected, and at the same time ridiculed Lincoln for what it imagined was cowardice. Consequently, when Fort Sumter was fired on and the President called for 75,000 volunteers, Baltimore was already seething with resentment.

This was the situation when, in response to the call, volunteer troops from the North began to pass through Baltimore. One detachment, whose arrival was reported in advance, got through safely under the protection of Marshal Kane's men. There was no such prior notice when, on April 19, 1861, the 6th Massachusetts Infantry, comprising 1,200 men, arrived at the President Street Station of the Philadelphia, Wilmington and Baltimore Railroad. President Street Station was to the east of Jones Falls. Since a city ordinance forbade steam locomotives on the streets, it was customary for passengers bound for the south to remain in the coaches which were drawn by horses along Pratt Street to Camden Station of the Baltimore & Ohio Railroad. There the cars again were coupled to a locomotive and the journey was continued on to Washington. Marshal Kane learned at the last minute of the arrival of the Massachusetts troops. He mistakenly assumed if there was any trouble it would be at Camden Station and there he took station with his men.

Meanwhile a mob of several thousand persons gathered on Pratt Street, halfway between the two stations. A number of carloads of soldiers got through safely. Then the mob, growing bolder, put obstructions on the track so that the troops had to abandon the cars and walk. The commanding officer made the mistake of ordering the double quick which gave the appearance of running away, so the mob attacked with sticks and stones while the soldiers retaliated by firing into the mob.

The hero of the day was Baltimore's nervy little mayor, George William Brown. Mayor Brown was in his office when news came of the arrival of the troops. He at once went to Camden Station and joined Marshal Kane and the police. It was there that he heard of the rioting on Pratt Street. Umbrella in hand the Mayor hurried to the scene. He introduced himself to the commanding officer and urged him to countermand the double-quick order. Then, still holding tight to his umbrella, he marched at the head of the troops. People in the mob recognized him and, for a time, were cowed. But it was only a few minutes before the battle was renewed. In this tragic encounter thirteen Baltimore citizens were killed and four wounded, while the losses of the 6th Massachusetts Infantry were four killed and an undetermined number wounded.

News of the bloody incident was flashed to the North where it instantly created bitter resentment and a public outcry for revenge. Fearful of similar outbreaks Mayor Brown hurried to Washington and begged President Lincoln to send no more troops through Baltimore. To make sure none would get through the authorities in Baltimore had the railroad bridges to the north destroyed. For the time being the Washington Government acquiesced, but only until it felt strong enough to deal with the situation. On the night of May 13th a strong body of troops under command of Brigadier General Benjamin F. Butler slipped into town, seized Federal Hill and trained a battery of guns on the city. From then on, until the close of the war, Baltimore was treated as a captured enemy city. The writ of habeas corpus was suspended and prominent citizens suspected of Southern sympathies were clapped into the dungeons at Fort McHenry. In spite of his sincere effort to protect the Massachusetts troops on April 19th Marshal Kane was included among those taken into custody. Mayor Brown also was put under arrest.

It must be confessed that the forces of occupation had their hands full dealing with the Southern faction. Young men of prominent families were stealing away daily and going south to join the Confederate Army in Virginia. Their families, friends and sweethearts carried on the war in Baltimore. There were subtle ways of showing loyalty to the Confederacy. They are revealed by Federal orders forbidding the display or sale of secession badges, flags, pictures, songs, photographs, music and neckties. There was even a ruling that infants were not to be exhibited in socks in the red and white colors of the South.

In the forefront of these agitators was a group of attractive young women known as the Monument Street Girls. Prominent among them were the daughters of Colonel Wilson Miles Cary, Jenny and Hetty. The Carys were a Virginia family. Mrs. Cary conducted a fashionable girls school. Hetty had a reputation for beauty while Jenny was the musical member of the family. They took delight in annoying the Federal authorities by wearing rosettes of red and white in their hair and white aprons trimmed in red.

About this time a Maryland-born teacher of English in a small college in Louisiana was inspired by the attack of the Baltimoreans on the Massachusetts troops on April 19th. Getting up in the middle of the night he put pen to paper and set down the verses as they came to him. The poet was James Ryder Randall; the inspired verses were "Maryland, My Maryland." Shortly thereafter the poem appeared in a local Louisiana newspaper and soon was republished throughout the South. It appeared in print also in Baltimore.

Among the various activities of the Monument Street Girls was the organizing of a glee club which held its meetings alternately in the homes of the members. It came the Cary girls' turn to arrange a program. Hetty suggested Randall's poem. The question was what music to set it to. Hetty recited the verses and Jenny exclaimed "Lauriger Horatius," the name of a popular college song. Experiment showed that the words fitted the music. When the glee club met Jenny sang the song in her deep contralto voice. It was an immediate hit. The story has it that the windows were open and persons outside, moved by the stirring music, took up the refrain. Then the proposal was made to get the song published. Rebecca Nicholson, whose father was a commodore in the United States Navy and loyal to the Union cause, volunteered to get it done. By an interesting coincidence she was a granddaughter of the Judge Nicholson who was instrumental in the publication of "The Star-Spangled Banner."

The music and verses were submitted to the local musical publishing house of Muller and Beacham, whose place of business was on Charles Street near Baltimore. Eventually the words were adapted to the more stately measures of the German air "Tannenbaum, O Tannenbaum" from which "Lauriger Horatius" derived.

The work of adaptation was done by Charles Ellerbrock, a German-born teacher of music, whose heart was with the Southern cause.

The city's historic 5th Regiment did not serve as such in the Civil War. But a large number of its members journeyed south to fight in the Army of Northern Virginia. Many of them joined the 1st Maryland Regiment which also was known by the old Revolutionary name of "The Maryland Line." Most of these men were sons of the old-established families of the city and state. The roster included such names as Howard, Symington, Post, McKim, Gilmor and Steuart. The younger men entered the service as privates; but, being well educated, most of them soon were commissioned.

Another Maryland Regiment, composed of Union sympathizers with a generous sprinkling of Baltimore Germans served with distinction in the northern Army of the Potomac. At Front Royal, Virginia, the opposing Marylanders met in battle. The Southern group boasted that they drove the Maryland Yankees from the field. News of the engagement soon reached Baltimore where the battle was renewed by the opposing forces on the city streets.

Three times the Confederates invaded Maryland. Each time the report was spread that they were on their way to Baltimore. Such reports were received with mixed feelings by the populace. But only once did they prove to be true. That was in the summer of 1864 when veteran Confederate combat troops to the number of 5,000, under command of General Jubal A. Early, marched up the Valley of Virginia to Harper's Ferry, sweeping all before it, and continued on to Frederick, Maryland.

Some elements of Confederate cavalry, leaving the main body, actually reached the outskirts of Baltimore. They contented themselves with burning the country home of Governor Bradford, a Union man, whose estate was on the present Charles Street Avenue, just across the city line, and now the site of the Elkridge Club.

April of 1865 was eventful. On the 3rd all work stopped while Northern sympathizers celebrated the fall of Richmond by illuminating their homes and places of business. On the 11th Admiral Farragut arrived in the city and was treated by the Northern contingent in a manner fitting a hero. On the 14th the city was stunned by news of the assassination of Abraham Lincoln. The tragedy was all the more personal since John Wilkes Booth had spent much of his boyhood in Baltimore and the Booth family had many ties there. On this occasion there was no clash between the opposing factions. Baltimoreans had long since come to know Lincoln better than they had on his first unhappy trip through the city. Many buildings were draped in black and the grief of the entire community was genuine.

The town had a chance to pay its respects to the departed president when, on April 21st, the funeral trains arrived in the city. A procession was formed and the coffin was borne from Camden Station to the rotunda of the Exchange where for two hours it lay in state. In that brief time it is said that 10,000 persons viewed the remains.

The 5th Regiment was among the National Guard outfits that volunteered for Federal service in the Spanish-American War. But, like most of the others, it got no farther than the southern states. Spoiled canned food and typhoid fever were the worst foes it met, though they were bad enough. The regiment had long borne the popular title of "the Dandy Fifth" as a token of the blue bloods to be found on its roster, and reminiscent of Mordecai Gist's "Macaronis" of Revolutionary fame. The turn of the century found the regiment in a fine new armory at the foot of Bolton street.

The 5th next entered the Federal Service in 1916 when war threatened with Mexico. It served on the border for six months. Then it returned home but scarcely had time to unpack before it was again called to get ready for service with the American Expeditionary Force in France in World War I. The 5th formed part of the 115th Infantry Regiment in the 29th, or Blue and Gray Division, composed of National Guard units from Maryland. Virginia and the District of Columbia. It conducted itself with distinction in the Meuse-Argonne campaign which preceded the collapse of Germany.

Meanwhile a new National Guard organization appeared on the scene to challenge the social prestige of the "Dandy Fifth." Even at so late a date some people were still naive enough to imagine that a military organization could be socially exclusive. The new unit, a battery of light field artillery, first bore the name of Battery A. Its original officers came from the oldest families. The ranks were filled with the graduates of Yale, Princeton, Harvard and the Hopkins.

Battery A was incorporated in the 29th Division as the 110th Field Artillery. Long before it went to France its personnel was recognized as being composed almost entirely of officer material. Virtually all the original members were commissioned, some staying with the regiment and others being transferred to new outfits. The 110th Field Artillery never reached the front. It was still in training when the war ended.

Still another Baltimore unit that saw active service in World War I was the 117th Trench Mortar Battery. This began as a coast artillery company. When the famous Rainbow Division was being built out of units from every state, a picked group from the coast artillery company was organized into a trench mortar battery as Maryland's contribution. This battery conducted itself with particular gallantry in the Battle of Champagne which saw the turning back of the last German offensive. The remainder of the coast artillery company also saw service in France as heavy artillery.

Baltimore, too, shared ownership in the 79th Division of the National Army which was in part recruited in Maryland and trained at Camp Meade, a few miles to the south of the city.

As usual in time of war Baltimore's women rose nobly to their responsibility, showing stout hearts when sons, brothers and lovers went off to the front. They busied themselves knitting socks, sweaters and hoods, making bandages for the Red Cross and maintaining their famous tradition for turning out "garments." More important still they sustained their reputation for hospitality and making themselves charming. The houses of the city were thrown open to the soldiers at Meade and many romances stemmed from the war.

Baltimore, like other cities, celebrated the "false armistice" that preceded the real one by several days. The war left one other mark on the city. There was a street to the south of Baltimore Street that bore the name of German. In the heat of the war the name was altered to Redwood in honor of George Buchanan Redwood, a young officer who won the Distinguished Service Cross and was among the first Baltimoreans to die on the field of battle in France.

Baltimore's last military venture was quite in keeping with its enviable tradition. With commendable wisdom our military authorities have realized in the destructive wars of today the catastrophic risk involved in recruiting any unit from one geographical area. In consequence Baltimoreans in World War II were found widely distributed through the Army, the Navy, the Coast Guard and the Merchant Marine in all the theaters of operations.

However the city continued to hold a special place in its heart for the peacetime Baltimore units of the 29th Division, which is to say the 175th Infantry, the 110th and 224th Field Artillery Battalions and the 104th Medical Battalion. As in World War I many Baltimoreans were transferred long before the 29th Division went abroad. Nevertheless quite a sprinkling of the original officers remained with the outfit.

So it was that Baltimore watched with particular interest the training of the 29th Division at Camp Meade and its eventual departure for England where it continued to train for another year. The still local character of the units based on Baltimore was evidenced by such typical Baltimore names on the roster of officers as Whiteford, Purnell, McKenrick, McIntosh, Slingluff, Cadwalader, Cooper, Beehler, Boykin and King, to mention only a few.

These Maryland units of the Division, be it remembered, still carried the picturesque quartered arms of the Calverts and Crosslands as their regimental colors. And wherever the Maryland flag was unfurled it was admired and complimented, and questions were asked about its history.

At last news of the assault and landing on the Normandy Beaches was flashed to the world. Then it was revealed that, selected to spearhead the attack along with the famous 1st Division of the Regular Army was the 29th Division. So it came about that the 175th Infantry, that boasts as its progenitor Mordecai Gist's Macaronis, and the "Dandy Fifth" whose men fought under Grant and Lee in 1865, under Pershing in 1918 now held the post of honor under Eisenhower in 1945. Surely there could be no finer climax for Baltimore's long and worthy record of participation in the nation's wars.

During the Civil War, as has been mentioned, the 5th Regiment did not appear on either side as a unit. But a large number of its men organized as the 1st Maryland Regiment of the Army of Northern Virginia. The U.S. Congress recently recognized this service and granted the 175th, as a lineal descendant, the right to carry streamers for participation in a number of Civil War battles. Furthermore along with the Stars and Stripes and the Maryland State Flag the regiment now carries also the battle flag of the Confederacy. Baltimore's unique tradition as a border state, torn in two directions by its loyalties, persists.

Chapter 7

"THE MONUMENTAL CITY"

THE YEAR 1815 was outstanding in the annals of Baltimore for monuments. As early as 1809 a group of prominent citizens had applied to the Maryland Legislature for permission to raise $100,-000 by lottery to erect a monument to George Washington. The request was granted but the war with England intervened and for the time being Baltimore had as much as it could do to defend itself against the invader. So the Washington monument project had to be postponed.

However, with the signing of the Treaty of Ghent in December, 1815, and the nation once more at peace, plans for the monument were resumed. The original intention was to erect the monument on the site of the old courthouse which had recently been torn down. This area, which now lies on Calvert Street between Lexington and Fayette, had been converted into a square surrounded by some of the handsomest dwellings in the city. But when the owners of these houses saw Robert Mills' design for a lofty column they lost their enthusiasm. They were afraid it might topple over on them. Even if it were to stand up they thought it would attract lightning. So they exercised the true Baltimorean's inalienable right of veto to any novel proposal. Being persons of consequence their will prevailed. Besides, by this time another and less formidable monument was being contemplated and the dwellers on the square had their eye on that.

It looked as though the proposed Washington monument would have nowhere to go when Colonel John Eager Howard came to the rescue. As he had done with the Catholic Cathedral, the University of Maryland, the market and several other community enterprises he graciously offered a piece of his property. This was on a commanding hill to the north of the town with plenty of open space around it. If a monument were to fall it wasn't likely to land on anybody. This elevation was then known as Howard's Woods. So it came about that on July 4, 1815, Baltimore staged another mammoth ceremonial. A crowd estimated at between 20,000 and 30,000 persons assembled in the woods. Levin Winder, Governor of Maryland, was there. So was Edward Johnson, Mayor of Baltimore. So were the managers who had handled all the plans, members of the local chapter of the Society of the Cincinnati, and distinguished officers of the Army and the Navy. Lined up in military formation was the 3rd Brigade of Maryland militia commanded by Samuel Sterett, now a brigadier general. Less than a year before, as a colonel, he had led the 5th Regiment at Bladensburg and North Point.

A volunteer band, under the direction of "Professor" Bunzie, enlivened the occasion with patriotic airs. The church was represented by the Right Reverend James Kemp, Protestant Episcopal Bishop of Maryland, and the Rev. James Inglis of the Presbyterian Church. Since the purpose of the assembly was the laying of a cornerstone, the Most Worshipful Master and lesser dignitaries of the Masonic Order were on hand with trowel and mortar. Conspicuously displayed nearby was a large oil portrait of the Father of His Country executed by Rembrandt Peale. Finally, to give the public an idea of what was to come, a drawing of the monument by Robert Mills, the architect, also was conspicuously exhibited.

Under the skilled direction of the Masons the stone was securely cemented into place. Simultaneously Professor Bunzie raised his baton and the volunteer band struck up "Yankee Doodle" while a salute of 100 guns was fired by the artillery. This was followed by three volleys from the infantry. The ceremony was continued in the evening with a grand display of rockets at Fort McHenry and a similiar one in front of Colonel Howard's mansion in the park. It was altogther an auspicious event. Even Baltimore's uncertain weather co-operated. For, say the chroniclers, "Divine Providence seemed to smile upon the occasion, the air was delightfully cool and the firmament serene." Thus was commenced the first monument in the United States to do honor to the great statesman and patriot who a few brief years before had expired at Mt. Vernon.

Between the Enabling Act of 1807 and the laying of the cornerstone on July 4, 1815, Baltimore passed through the most critical moment in its whole history. It had been assaulted both by land and by sea by the British. It had gallantly defended itself and repelled the invader. These stirring events took place on September 12 and 13, 1814. Active in organizing the public for the defense of the city was the Committee of Vigilance and Safety. It continued in existence after the crisis had passed to finish up the odds and ends of its business. On March 1, 1815, the Committee met and resolved unanimously to erect a monument to perpetuate the memory of those who fell fighting in defense of the city in the preceding September. It was this monument that the timid householders in the old courthouse square seized upon in preference to the lofty and ominous memorial to George Washington. Since they were influential citizens in an age when influence meant something they had their way.

On September 12, 1815, the Baltimore populace, having got its breath after the ceremonies of July 4th on Howard's Hill, again girded itself for another impressive civic rite. All business was suspended for the day. In keeping with the fact that the monument was to be in honor of the gallant dead the occasion assumed the nature of a public funeral. A procession formed on East Baltimore Street. Professor Bunzie and his volunteer musicians once more were on hand to render appropriate music. On this day he was assisted by "Professor" Neninger. The procession was built around a funeral car drawn by six white horses and escorted by a detachment of the Independent Blues, the city's crack cavalry outfit. In place of the customary corpse, the hearse bore a plan of the proposed monument which had been prepared by Maximilian Godefroy, the city's leading architect. It was he who drew the plans for the Exchange and for the Unitarian Church.

Present also were the militiamen who had taken part in the battle and their leaders. Among the latter were Major General Sam Smith, the Generalissimo; Brigadier General John Stricker, who commanded the City Brigade at North Point, and Lieutenant Colonel George Armistead, of the regular army, who kept the flag flying at Fort McHenry. Again Bishop Kemp was present to offer a prayer while Dr. Inglis, the Presbyterian divine, this time made the chief address. During the progress of the procession the bells of Christ Protestant Episcopal Church, muffled for the occasion, were rung, and minute guns were fired. The cornerstone was put in place under the direction of General Smith, General Stricker and Colonel Armistead and the ceremonies closed with an artillery salute.

Commencement of the erection of these two ambitious monuments within a few months of each other directed the attention of the nation toward Baltimore. From that day forward it came to be known as "The Monumental City" quite as widely as by the less flattering title of "Mobtown."

It was not until late in 1829 that the Washington monument was completed. On November 25th of that year the last piece of the statue was raised to the summit. This ticklish job was accomplished with aid of a pair of shears attached to the cap of the column and a capstan and pulleys. Fortunately the idea of embellishing the column was abandoned. So it stands in its Doric simplicity, a shaft of beautiful proportions. It is made of marble from the quarries at Hampton, in Baltimore County, donated by the owner, General Charles Ridgely. The statue of Washington on the top is the work of an Italian sculptor, Henrico Cancici. It is in three pieces and was cut out of fine white marble from quarries on the York Road, also in Baltimore County, and presented by Mrs. F. T. D. Taylor of the same county. The sculptor has depicted Washington in the act of surrendering his commission. The posture is particularly appropriate in a Maryland monument since the incident took place in the senate chamber of the State House at Annapolis. The statue is sixteen feet in height which gives it majesty when viewed from the ground.

Colonel Howard died in 1827, two years before the completion of the monument, and immediately after his death his heirs made plans for developing the land in the vicinity. Open squares with grass plots and trees were laid out respectively to the north and south and to the east and west. Building lots facing these squares were offered for sale. The squares running north and south were named Washington Place and those running east and west Mt. Vernon Place. By 1850 the city had grown out to the monument and the area was well built up. The spacious Georgian mansion on the north side of Mt. Vernon Place which now houses the Mt. Vernon Club was built by William Tiffany in 1842. The Thomas and Walters houses, which still stand on the south side of the square, were built around 1848. The architects for the former were Niernsee and Neilson. The modern generation knows the Thomas house as the residence of the Francis M. Jencks family which has occupied it for over half a century.

In the course of their long history Washington Place and Mt. Vernon Place have been subjected to numerous changes in accordance with prevailing whims and fashions. At one time the trees were permitted to grow to considerable height and the grass plots were inclosed with fences. Somewhat later the fences were removed, the trees cut down and the grass plots alone were left. This severe treatment no doubt was adopted the better to display the Barye bronzes and other statuary presented to the city by William T. Walters.

Antoine Louis Barye, the Frenchman, was one of the leading sculptors of his day. He made a speciality of animals. Mr. Walters was among the first to appreciate his genius and invest heavily in his productions. In consequence Baltimore boasts one of the best Barye collections in this country. The gifts to the city include a noble lion, the original of which is in the Tuileries Gardens in Paris, and four symbolic groups representing War, Peace, Force and Order. The originals of these, wrought in stone, stand in a court of the Louvre. Mr. Walters also gave the city a bronze statue by Paul Dubois entitled "Military Courage"; it commands the western approach to Mt. Vernon Place. The original is in Nantes Cathedral.

In fact today the squares around the monument have assumed the proportions of an out-of-doors sculpture exhibit. To the works already mentioned must be added the statues of George Peabody, Chief Justice Roger Brooke Taney and Severn Teackle Wallis, and the equestrian statues of John Eager Howard and Lafayette. Wallis was a man of letters, a leader at the bar and a political reformer in the 1880's. Today those accomplishments are overshadowed by the fact that it is from him the Duchess of Windsor derives the given name of Wallis. Erection of the statue to Lafayette was accompanied by much controversy. The site on which General Joffre, on a visit to Baltimore after World War I, turned a spade of earth was abandoned, and the hard-riding horsemen of Green Spring Valley were highly critical of the bridle and Lafayette's seat.

Completing the sculpture display are Henri Crenier's "Boy and the Turtle" in the fountain on West Mt. Vernon Place and Edward Berge's "Sea Urchin" in the fountain on South Washington Place. Crenier's work formed part of a temporary exhibit that was arranged in the square in 1924. It looked so much at home there that the Municipal Art Society bought it as a permanent fixture.

The "Sea Urchin" was presented to the city as a memorial to Mr. Berge, a local sculptor. For many years it exercised a strange fascination for vandals. Several times it was removed and discovered in strange places. On a number of mornings it appeared before the public draped in odd garments. Fortunately the joke, if such it can be called, seems to have worn itself out. More recently the "Sea Urchin" has assumed the nature of guardian of the city's wishing well. It has become the custom to make wishes and then toss coins into the fountain. The wishes at least benefit the human Baltimore urchins who fish out the coins.

To return to the memorial honoring the city's defenders, it took the name of Battle Monument and its site became known as Monument Square. It was financed by popular subscription, most of the money being raised by survivors of the battle. Although the cornerstone was laid in 1815 the monument was not completed until 1825. It consists of an Egyptian pyramidal base surmounted by a pedestal with eagles at the four corners. From the pedestal rises a column and on top of the column is a female figure ten feet high. The lady symbolizes the city of Baltimore. She wears a mural crown and holds a laurel wreath in one hand while the other hand rests on the rudder of a ship. At her feet are an eagle and a bomb. On the column are bas-reliefs of the engagements at North Point and Fort McHenry. The over-all height of the monument is fifty two feet.

Godefroy went all out in the matter of symbols. There are lachrymal urns, fillets, cannons with balls issuing from their mouths, fasces and other details, each with some special significance. But generations of grime have neutralized the whole so that Baltimoreans of today scarcely notice the details. As early as

1827 the outline of the monument was adopted as the city seal. It also is superimposed on the black and gold colors of Lord Baltimore to form the flag of the municipality.

Ever since 1815, September 12th has been known as Old Defenders' Day and celebrated as a public holiday. For many years it was the annual custom for the veterans of the battle to form in procession and march to the monument wearing cockades in their hats and crepe on their arms. This was continued up to the death of the last surviving veteran. His name was James Morford, and when he was too old to walk he was driven around the monument. In recent years the official ceremony has been reduced to the Mayor of the city laying a wreath on the monument while traffic passes by paying little heed to what is going on.

Unlike Mt. Vernon Place, Monument Square has lost completely its original character. All the handsome dwellings which once flanked it have long since gone. So too have Barnum's Hotel and Guy's Hotel which succeeded some of the early dwellings. The monument now is dwarfed by the Court House, the Post Office, the Baltimore branch of the Federal Reserve Bank and several skyscrapers. The square itself is obscured by parked cars and lanes of bustling traffic. Battle Monument has always enjoyed its share of public veneration. Even during the bank riot, when Reverdy Johnson's house on the square was burned and a bonfire was made of his library, the rioters respected the injunction to look out for the monument. Even today when attention is called to it as a traffic hazard and proposals are made to move it to some less congested spot there are still champions to rise up and protest such a desecration.

Almost a quarter of a century before the dedications of the Washington Monument and the Battle Monument there was erected still another one worthy of justifying Baltimore's name as the Monumental City. It still stands though few Baltimoreans know it and even fewer appreciate its significance. It is a slender obelisk of brick covered with concrete, 44 feet 6¾ inches high from the ground to the peak of the capstone, and it stands at the northeast corner of the intersection of North Avenue and Harford Road. It is the first monument erected to the memory of Christopher Columbus in the United States. A more doubtful claim has been made that it is the first monument erected in memory of Columbus anywhere in the world. There is an interesting story as to how it got where it is.

Some years prior to the Revolutionary War there appeared in Baltimore a gentleman from Normandy, France, glorying in the name of Charles Francois Adrian de Paulmier, the Chevalier d'Anmour. He returned to France, espoused the American cause and soon was back in this country as a secret agent. In 1779 he was appointed Consul General to this country from France. At the close of hostilities, having become attached to life in the United States, he acquired land outside Baltimore and called his estate Belmont, or Villa Belmont.

D'Anmour had an intense admiration for Christopher Columbus. On the occasion of the 300th anniversary of the discovery someone remarked in his presence that it was strange no monument had ever been raised to Columbus in this country. D'Anmour was impressed and immediately pledged himself to correct the omission. On August 3, 1792, the date of the departure of Columbus from Laos in Spain, the cornerstone was laid. The monument is said to have been completed by August 22nd. On October 12, 1792, the date of the landing on San Salvador, it was officially dedicated.

Though the monument has been on the present site for more than a century and a half it is still in remarkably good condition. Its authenticity is attested by contemporary newspaper accounts and the research of historians of the Johns Hopkins University. Nonetheless a local legend has grown up to the effect that the monument is not actually a memorial to Christopher Columbus, the discoverer, but to a horse of that name. In consequence the Italian colony for years would have none of it. Baltimore Italians erected their own monument to Columbus on the shore of the lake in Druid Hill Park; it was dedicated on Columbus Day, October 12, 1892, the 500th anniversary of the landing, and ever since has been the scene of local Columbian celebrations. The original Columbus monument, a whole century older, stood in dignified solitude, until Columbus Day, 1950. Then Mayor D'Alesandro, himself of Italian blood, had the courage to recognize it by giving it a wreath.

Quite the most picturesque landmark of the city is a lofty tapering brick tower which rises to a height of 234 feet and stands out against the skyline on East Fayette Street. It so resembles a medieval fortification that one would not be surprised to see a warrior in armor appear above its castellated summit. This is the Shot Tower.

The tower is the remaining one of three built in Baltimore soon after the War of 1812. Up to that time the better grades of shot had been imported; the war revealed the need for domestic production. The surviving tower was erected in 1828. Old Charles Carroll of Carrollton was called on to lay the cornerstone for it as he had been called to lay the first stone of the Baltimore & Ohio Railroad in the same year. It is estimated that more than 1,000,000 bricks went into its construction. The shot was made by passing molten lead through colanders and letting it fall from stations high up in the tower into buckets of water at the base. The passage through the air rounded the lead into shot.

In 1878 the interior of the tower was burned out, and a few years later the tower method of making shot was outmoded by modern machinery and the tower was closed. Several times there have been threats to pull it down and salvage the bricks but each time interested citizens have come to the rescue and saved it.

Baltimore raised the first monument to Christopher Columbus in the nation. It raised the first monument to George Washington in the nation. But that is not all. So far as is known Baltimore also has the distinction of being the only city in the nation that has raised a monument to the memory of Adam.

Both the idea and the memorial are credited to John P. Brady, a retired contractor. Mr. Brady erected the monument in 1909. It is a concrete shaft 3½ feet high surmounted by a sundial, and it stands on a plot of ground in Gardenville, near Bowley's Lane, on the Philadelphia Road. On the shaft is the inscription: "This the First Shaft in America is Dedicated to the Memory of Adam, the First Man." Around the base of the sundial is the inscription: "*Sic Transit Gloria Mundi.*"

Once when Mr. Brady was asked his reasons for erecting the monument he said: "There is no serious reason why there should not have been thousands of memorials to Adam. It has made me feel sad to see every public committee or board leave its name on the public buildings of the city. If it is so easy to get one's name graven in stone I thought it was high time Adam had something to show for having been here. Adam had a pretty hard time of it. He was something of a hero, after all."

According to Mr. Brady's calculations the birth of Adam took place on October 28, 4004 B.C. Consequently every year, on October 28, it was his custom to assemble a group of friends and conduct them to the memorial to pay their respects to the departed First Man. Mr. Brady died in 1925. In recent years the memorial has belonged to Mr. and Mrs. Conrad M. Breitschwerdt, who have lived up fully to their responsibility as guardians and protectors, keeping the concrete freshly painted and planting evergreens around the shaft. Stimulated by the success of his memorial to Adam, Mr. Brady a year before his death raised a monument to the Constitution of the United States. For, said he, the Constitution had passed away because of amendments, constructions and interpretations. The monument bore the simple inscription, "In Memory of the Constitution of the United States. Gone, But not Forgotten."

There now is also in Baltimore a memorial to Eve. This was erected the year of the death of Mr. Brady, and was the work of the Rev. Dr. Benjamin B. Lovett, an Episcopal clergyman. Dr. Lovett felt that if Adam was a hero then surely Eve was a heroine and that the First Woman had quite as hard a time of it as the First Man. The Eve Monument stands on property that was the site of Dr. Lovett's summer home on Idaho Avenue, off the Belair Road. It too has taken the form of a sundial mounted on a shaft of stone and concrete. The inscription on it reads: "Erected in Memory of Eve, the First of Her Good and Noble Kind. B.B.L. Fecit 1925."

Others of the nation's wars have served as inspiration for various monuments. There is a shaft with a female figure on top of it in memory of the Maryland Line in the American Revolution, which stands at the intersection of Cathedral Street and Mt. Royal Avenue. Though most Baltimoreans know a monument is there practically nobody can describe it. It seems to occupy a blind spot. The Mexican War is commemorated in a single monument to Colonel Watson, who was killed while leading the lone regiment of Baltimore volunteers.

The Civil War is a popular subject. Since Baltimore was a border city, both sides have been memorialized, though the South comes off the winner on the basis of the deadweight of stone and bronze employed. There is a Confederate Soldiers and Sailors Monument on Mt. Royal Avenue in which a dying soldier is supported by a winged female figure symbolizing Glory while on the base is the inscription: *"Gloria Victis."* This is balanced by a monument erected in honor of the North in which a male figure, turning from the plow and anvil to buckle on a sword, is being pushed forward somewhat reluctantly by two females representing respectively Victory and Bellona. Still another monument, at the corner of Charles Street and University Parkway, glorifies the women of the Confederacy.

The most recent addition to this Civil War gallery is the double equestrian statue of Robert E. Lee and Stonewall Jackson in Wyman Park. It was dedicated on May 1, 1948. The sum of $100,000 was bequeathed for the purpose by J. Henry Ferguson, a Baltimore banker. In his will Mr. Ferguson stated that: "They were my boyhood heroes and maturer judgment has only strengthened my admiration for them. They were great generals and Christian soldiers. They waged war like gentlemen and I feel that their example should be held up to the youth of Maryland."

Mr. Ferguson entrusted the details of the monument to the Municipal Art Society, though he proposed that it should depict the two generals as they appear in the famous engraving of their last meeting on the eve of the Battle of Chancellorsville. A competition was won by a woman, Laura Gardin Fraser, who has been very successful in catching the spirit of that momentous occasion. Appropriately enough the cadet corps of the Virginia Military Institute formed a guard of honor at the dedication while the chief address was delivered by Dr. Douglas Southall Freeman, the biographer of Lee. The military procession, the music, the attendance of notables and the oration were reminiscent of the dedication of monuments in earlier days.

Francis Scott Key, author of the Star Spangled Banner, is a local hero who has been immortalized by the sculptors in two monuments of questionable merit. The Federal Government erected a memorial at Fort McHenry which takes the form of a heroic statue of Orpheus undergoing strange contortions of his body as he strikes a lyre. The second monument is a local enterprise. A bronze Francis Scott Key, in a stone rowboat rowed by a bronze sailor, addresses his song to a bronze Columbia who holds aloft a gilded banner. Although it may not rate high as a work of art, it is an unending delight to little boys who keep an eye out for the cop while they join Key and the sailor in the boat.

General Sam Smith and Lieutenant Colonel George Armistead, who saw to the laying of the cornerstone of Battle Monument in 1815, are themselves now immortalized in bronze. So, also, are such miscellaneous assortment as Cecilius Calvert, William Wallace, the Scotchman (the statue was given the city by a namesake, William Wallace Spence), Martin Luther, Edgar Allan Poe, Johns Hopkins and Sidney Lanier.

Of late years one seldom hears Baltimore referred to as the Monumental City. But the name Monumental lives on in some thirty five assorted commercial establishments, ranging from a 5-and-10-cent store to a distillery.

Chapter 8

BELLES and BEAUTIES

LIKE MOST CITIES Baltimore boasts of the charm and beauty of its women. But, in addition, Baltimore can produce some impressive substantiating evidence in the persons of a number of its daughters who have achieved fame extending far beyond the local scene.

From the earliest times Baltimore women exhibited a keen interest in fashions. Since it was a seaport hardly a ship put in from Europe whose hold was not stocked with silks, satins, millinery and other choice materials to delight the feminine heart. As the local merchants made fortunes their wives found opportunity to gratify a taste for clothes. Contemporary advertisements in the newspapers regularly heralded the arrival of this finery and there are many references also to the "mantuamaker," as the dressmaker of the day was called. Early 19th-century portraits and miniatures show that Baltimore's ladies of fashion of that period could hold their own with those of other cities in this country and abroad.

Baltimore's reputation as a center of fashion continued until recent times when the dress shop replaced the dressmaker. Around the turn of the present century the establishments of Maggie O'Connor, Fuechsl and Mrs. Hall for dresses, and Mesdames Stuart and Schoen for hats attracted clients from a distance as well as from the city. Many Southern women made a practice of coming to Baltimore for their clothes and so did Washingtonians. It was not unusual at one time to see a White House automobile parked on North Charles Street while the womenfolk of a President of the United States shopped or went through the ordeal of fittings.

In spite of its universities and colleges Baltimore is distinguished as much for its social as for its intellectual life. And social life demands smart clothes. Baltimore women find opportunities to show them at the Cotillon, the Assembly, the Supper Club, and the dinners, dances and other social occasions sponsored by the country clubs. Smart clothes are seen in the boxes at the opera, in the boxes at Pimlico, at luncheons which precede the point-to-point races during the spring season, at debutante receptions and wedding receptions.

Smart clothes are by no means confined to the socially elect. Easter parades on North Charles Street and in several other sections of the city illustrate what Baltimore women in the aggregate can do. On Pennsylvania Avenue, the colored devotees of fashion put on a show that rivals that of their white neighbors. Any weekday of the year a walk on Lexington Street, North Charles Street and Howard Street, where Baltimore women congregate from all over town to shop, is enough to convince that it is exceptional to see a woman who is indifferent to her appearance. All may not succeed; but it is obvious that the great majority have worked hard to get a smart effect.

In the antebellum South the popularity of Sir Walter Scott's romantic novels has been credited with inspiring a revival of the age of chivalry. In the country districts "knights" rode in tournaments and it was the privilege of the victor to choose one of the young ladies present and crown her "Queen of Love and Beauty." No town of any size was without its reigning belle. Her daily stroll down the main street was like a royal progress. The local poets wrote verses about her. Duels were fought over her. She was an important part of the local tradition. Baltimore was enough of a Southern town to share in this cult.

Of the various periods in Baltimore history distinguished for its belles the foremost was the early 1800's. It was the age made famous by Betsy Patterson, the Caton sisters, the Pascault girls and their contemporaries. Betsy Patterson of course achieved world-wide fame through her marriage with Prince Jerome Bonaparte, younger brother of the Emperor Napoleon I of France. She was the daughter of William Patterson, a poor boy from the north of Ireland who came to this country to make his fortune and was one of the numerous merchants of the town to prosper along with Baltimore's sudden postwar expansion. Mr. Patterson's wealth was said to be second only to that of Charles

Carroll of Carrollton, and at a time when Carroll was reputed to be the richest man in the United States.

Betsy Patterson therefore was born to all the advantages usually enjoyed by the daughter of a man of wealth. She had a quick mind and received a sound education. Most important to her career, she learned French from nuns of that nationality at a convent school in Baltimore. In 1803 she arrived at the age of eighteen years and mature womanhood. As was customary among young women of fashion, she had her portrait painted and the artist chosen for the task was the celebrated Gilbert Stuart. He shows her in full, three-quarter face and profile. The hazel eyes and dark curly hair, the perfect lips, the soft clear skin, the proud nose and graceful shoulders as the artist painted them are proof that her reputation for beauty was not exaggerated. There is the word of the subject herself that Stuart was the only painter who made her live. Long after time had altered her it is said she was accustomed to stand in rapt admiration before this testimony of her youthful loveliness.

At this time momentous events were taking place in Europe. Napoleon Bonaparte had recently revealed his military genius by his brilliant campaign in Italy. As First Consul he had become the most powerful figure in France. His numerous brothers and sisters were swept into power with him. Youngest in the family was Jerome. Fifteen years junior to Napoleon he was rather more in the position of a son than a brother, and Napoleon spoiled him badly. In his youth Jerome might have been considered handsome. His dark eyes, swarthy skin and curly black hair betrayed his Corsican background. From the start he was fastidious and delighted in dressing himself in gaudy uniforms.

General Leclerc, who married Jerome's older sister Pauline, was sent by Napoleon as head of an expedition to Haiti, and Jerome was ordered to follow him there. The adventure ended in disaster, most of the French army dying of yellow fever. Jerome came down with it but recovered. He soon grew tired of the monotony of life in the West Indies and trumped up an excuse to make a trip to the United States.

Late in the summer of 1803 he landed in Norfolk, Virginia, with his retinue and set off for the national capital. Washington then was a struggling new settlement of a few houses. There he ran into Commodore Joshua Barney, whose previous service in the French navy served as a bond between them. The Commodore invited the young man to go with him to Baltimore and be introduced to the sights and people of the bustling community on the Patapsco. Pichon, French chargé in Washington, doubted that Barney was a suitable companion for Jerome and said so. Jerome told Pichon to mind his own business and set out with Barney for Baltimore.

In England it is the boast of many an ancient manor house that Queen Elizabeth once slept there. In Baltimore there are few ancient families which do not boast that it was at a ball given by their ancestors that the first meeting of Betsy Patterson and Jerome Bonaparte took place. Then as now Baltimore had its fall racing season. In those days the track was at Govans, northeast of the town. One story has it that it was there Jerome's eye first fell upon the Baltimore beauty. Another tells of the prophetic incident at a ball when a gold chain worn by Betsy became entangled in Jerome's uniform.

Betsy herself used to say the meeting was at a fashionable dinner given by Louis Pascault, the Marquis de Poléon, in honor of his lovely daughter Henriette. Mr. Pascault was a merchant and, with his family, had been resident in Baltimore some twenty years. According to Betsy's story she was standing with Henriette Pascault when two handsome young men approached. "I will marry that one," said Henriette, pointing to one of the young men. "Then I will marry the other," replied Betsy. She remarked in later years, "Strangely enough we both did as we said." One young man was Jerome. The other was Captain Reubel, a member of Jerome's retinue and the son of one of the Directors of France.

The infatuation was immediate. Jerome showed marked attention to Miss Patterson who gave every appearance of looking upon his suit with favor. The romance caused concern in several quarters. The French officials in this country were beside themselves, knowing that Napoleon would not approve a serious love affair. No less opposed was William Patterson, Betsy's father. He even sent his daughter on a trip to Virginia to give her passion time to cool.

Betsy returned no less determined to have her way. Jerome was as obstinate as she. When Mr. Patterson saw he could not stop the match he did what he could to regularize it. Bishop John Carroll, a personal friend and the highest Catholic dignitary in the United States, graciously consented to perform the ceremony which took place in the house of the bride's father. To give the marriage still further appearance of official sanction the Mayor of Baltimore and the French consul also were present.

The solemnity of the occasion did not suppress Betsy's customary audacity. One shocked guest remarked that the bride's wedding dress was so scanty he could have put the whole thing in his pocketbook. Proclaimed man and wife the young couple set out on a honeymoon and round of gaiety that was to continue for more than a year. A few weeks after the marriage they were in Washington. Describing Betsy's appearance at a fashionable ball there Mrs. Samuel Harrison Smith, formerly Miss Bayard of Philadelphia, and wife of the editor of the *National Intelligencer* wrote:

Of Madame——— I think it is no harm to speak the truth. She has made a great noise here and mobs of boys have crowded round her splendid equipage to see what I hope will not often be seen in this country, an almost naked woman. An elegant and select party was given her by Mrs. Robert Smith, [another Baltimorean and wife of the Secretary of the Navy]. Her appearance was such that it threw all the company in confusion, and no one dared look at her but by stealth; the window shutters being open a crowd assembled round the windows to get a look at this beautiful little creature, for everyone allows that she is extremely beautiful.

Her dress was the thinnest sarsnet and white crepe without the least stiffening in it, made without a single plait in the skirt, the width at the bottom being made of gores; there was scarcely any waist and her arms uncovered and the rest of her form visible. She was engaged the next evening at Madame P's. Mrs. R. Smith and several other ladies sent her word that if she wished to meet them there she must promise to have more clothes on. I was pleased with this becoming spirit in our ladies.

When Napoleon learned what Jerome had done he was outraged. Not only had his brother violated the French law by contracting a marriage without his family's consent but he had seriously interfered with the plans Napoleon was making for him. The First Consul then was about to declare himself Emperor. To strengthen his position he proposed to raise his brothers to the rank of kings. Jerome he proposed to ally by marriage to some old and legitimate royal family. Napoleon therefore appealed to Pope Pius VII to annul the marriage, but this the Pope refused to do. Napoleon then had a scurrilous notice printed in a Paris newspaper to the effect that while Jerome might have a mistress in America he could not have a wife. He also ordered Jerome to return home at once on pain of being charged with desertion. Like the spoiled child he was Jerome ignored the order.

It was not until March, 1805, that Jerome and his wife actually got away in the *Erin,* one of Mr. Patterson's own ships, bound for Lisbon. Arriving there they were met by an agent of Napoleon who had orders not to let Betsy land. To his inquiry as to what he might do for "Miss Patterson" she is said to have replied, "Tell your master that *Madame Bonaparte* is ambitious and demands her rights as a member of the imperial family."

Betsy seems to have assumed that her charm would work even on Napoleon. He on his part was determined not to give it a chance. He firmly forbade Madame Bonaparte to enter France. Jerome at last left her, protesting his eternal devotion and promising to rejoin her shortly. In spite of his promises he never saw her again except for one brief accidental glimpse many years later. Napoleon compensated him for giving up his wife by making him a handsome allowance, directing that he be addressed as "Imperial Highness," investing him with the grand cordon of the Legion of Honor, and raising him to the rank of rear admiral. To cap it all Jerome was elevated to the throne of the newly created Kingdom of Westphalia and presented with a royal wife, Catherine, the dowdy daughter of the King of Wurtemberg.

Denied entry into France Madame Bonaparte took refuge in London where she gave birth to a son whom she named Jerome Napoleon. Jerome, the elder, wrote her occasional letters still declaring his devotion. But if she had really ever trusted him, which is doubtful, Betsy lost all faith in him now. A few years later, through the influence of Mr. Patterson, the Maryland Legislature granted her a divorce. Madame Bonaparte was not too proud, however, to accept from Napoleon an outright gift of $20,000 and a $12,000 annuity.

For many years Madame Bonaparte spent much of her time in Europe. Her ambition now was transferred to her son. When young Bo, as he was called, reached his teens she arranged for him to meet the Bonaparte family. She hoped for recognition from them and also that he would make a brilliant marriage. By now the elder Jerome had a son by his second wife and refused to grant Bo any recognition that would interfere with rights of this younger half-brother.

Nor was Madame Bonaparte any more successful in arranging a marriage for Bo in Europe. Eventually he married a Miss Susan May Williams of Baltimore. She was not royalty; not even the spurious Bonaparte kind. So when she was informed of the engagement Madame Bonaparte was indignant. She wrote: "As the woman has money I shall not forbid a marriage which I never would have advised. . . .I hope too that, as seems likely, he has not been cheated in the settlements."

Though Baltimore has made Betsy Patterson one of its immortals she, on her part, never pretended to any affection for the city or its people. At the time of Napoleon's death she made a point of praising his genius despite the fact that "he hurled me back on what I hated most on earth, my Baltimore obscurity." She was to suffer that obscurity for a long time. In 1840, at the age of fifty six years, she returned from Europe for good and all to take up residence in the city she so much disliked. No doubt she bored many an audience discoursing at length on the romantic days of her youth. In later years she remarked: "My ruling passions have been love, ambition, avarice. Love has fled, ambition has brought disappointment, but avarice remains."

This was more than a neat epigram. In his will, which may still be seen in the Baltimore Courthouse, William Patterson stated that his daughter Betsy had caused him much expense and trouble in her youth. In consequence he limited his bequest to her to a few city lots and houses. These and the sums she received from Napoleon were her only capital. But she was a shrewd business

woman and, as she grew older, she became more and more of a
miser. She is last remembered as a shrunken old lady, all traces
of beauty gone, carrying a dilapidated umbrella and living in one
room in a boarding house on Cathedral Street. In 1879, at the age
of ninety four years, she died. Even in death she continued to
observe an aloofness from her fellow Baltimoreans that distinguished her in life. Her body rests in Greenmount Cemetery in
a lot all by itself.

"Bo" died several years before her. He had two sons whom he
named Jerome and Charles Joseph. Jerome, the elder of the two,
went off to serve in the French army and Baltimore saw little
more of him or his descendants. The last of these died in New
York City a decade or so ago. Charles J., on the other hand, made
Baltimore his home and became one of its most distinguished
citizens. He was a staunch Republican and served in Theodore
Roosevelt's Cabinet first as Attorney General and then as Secretary of the Navy. He was instrumental, too, in bringing about
civil service reform. Old Baltimoreans still recall the smart Bonaparte carriage, with coachman and footman in livery on the box,
which was a familiar sight at the turn of the last century. Charles
J. had no children. In consequence nothing is now left of the
American Bonaparte line.

The three Caton girls—Mary, Eliza and Louisa—were the
daughters of Richard Caton and Mary Carroll, daughter of
Charles Carroll of Carrollton. Richard Caton was an Englishman
whose chief distinction in life was as a sire of comely daughters.
The Caton girls had quite a reputation for beauty. Also appealing
were their prospects of inheriting fortunes from grandpapa. Betsy
Patterson's brother Robert married Mary, the eldest of the three
Caton sisters and generally regarded as the most beautiful. A few
years later plans were made for a trip to England on which the
Robert Pattersons were to be accompanied by Louisa and Eliza
Caton.

Before sailing they got from the British Minister in Washington
a letter of introduction to none other than the great Duke of
Wellington, then at the height of his power. The warrior was
quite swept away by the charm of the Baltimore beauties. He
made the necessary arrangements for them to be presented at the

Court of George IV. He also introduced them into the most exclusive English society. Tradition has it that, on seeing Mary Caton Patterson, King George IV exclaimed: "Is it possible the world can produce so beautiful a woman!" The fame of the Catons spread far and wide and they soon became known as "The three American Graces." As "the Three Graces" they are still remembered by posterity.

The first of the Catons to marry in England was Louisa, the youngest. She won the heart and hand of Wellington's aide-de-camp, Colonel Sir Felton Bathhurst Hervey. Sir Felton died shortly thereafter and Louisa's second husband was Francis Goldophin D'Arcy Osborne, eldest son of the Duke of Leeds. Francis Osborne eventually succeeded to the title and Baltimore's Louisa Caton became the Duchess of Leeds. Eliza Caton, the second sister, made a somewhat less distinguished marriage. However she too joined the English nobility as the wife of Baron Stafford.

In 1822 Robert Patterson died and his widow by way of assuaging her grief went abroad to join her sisters. Once more she exercised her fascination on the Duke of Wellington. Through him she met his elder brother Richard, the Marquess of Wellesley, who was credited with having the brains of the family. While his younger brother was fighting battles Richard was serving as Governor General of India. In 1822, when he met Mary Caton Patterson, Wellesley was a widower of sixty five years. He had been appointed Lord Lieutenant of Ireland, but he was said to be deeply in debt. The widow Patterson's beauty, charm and fortune made an irresistible appeal. The Marquess proposed and was accepted. The marriage was duly solemnized in Dublin Castle and there the Wellesleys set up a court that many said was even more glamorous than the English court of George IV.

Thus by a strange series of events the prosperous little city of Baltimore in the young State of Maryland produced a sister-in-law for each of the great protagonists on the world stage in the opening years of the 19th century—Napoleon Bonaparte and the Duke of Wellington. Equally remarkable, the two women in question were themselves sisters-in-law through the earlier marriage of Robert Patterson, Betsy's brother, to Mary Caton.

While this highly gratifying alliance between English nobility and American wealth and beauty was being arranged Madame Bonaparte was living in Paris. When she heard about it she turned green with envy. To young James Gallatin she exclaimed: "Had I but waited, with my beauty and my wit, I would have married an English duke instead of which I married a Corsican black-guard." The three Caton sisters lived to a ripe old age. None of them had children, so Baltimore's influence on the upper reaches of English society died with them. A fourth Caton sister, Emily who was her grandfather Carroll's favorite, made a less distin-guished match. She married John L. McTavish, British consul to Baltimore, and unlike her sisters did leave descendants.

Next among Baltimore beauties to create a sensation was Hetty Cary, daughter of Wilson Miles Cary. She played her part against the somber background of the Civil War. An account already has been given of her launching "Maryland, My Maryland" with the help of her sister Jenny. A story is told of a company of Union soldiers marching past the Cary home on Hamilton Terrace and of Hetty waving a Confederate flag from an upstairs window. One soldier called the incident to the attention of his captain. But the captain had seen the face behind the flag. Chivalry, after all, was not a monopoly of the South. "Never mind," replied the captain, "she is so pretty she can do as she damn well pleases."

Perhaps that explains why the Cary girls found it so easy to move backward and forward through the lines, traveling from Baltimore to Virginia and back. In the early days of the conflict, it will be recalled, they visited General Beauregard's head-quarters near the field of Bull Run. In those days it was customary for literary men in the South to dip their pens in perfume and rhapsodize over feminine beauty. Perhaps the Carys' visit was the inspiration for a piece that appeared shortly thereafter in the New Orleans *Crescent*. It read:

Look well at her, for you have never seen, and will probably never see again, so beautiful a woman! Observe her magnificent form, her rounded arms, her neck and shoulders perfect as if from the sculptor's chisel, her auburn hair, the poise of her well-shaped head. Saw you such color on a woman's cheek? And she is not less intelligent than beautiful. . . . She is dressed in pure white.

It is worth a king's ransom, a lifetime of trouble, to look at one
such woman. No wonder Beauregard pronounced her the most
beautiful in that city of lovely women—Baltimore.

During the war Richmond saw much of Hetty Cary. There,
as in Baltimore, she was the leader of a set of young people who,
through their gaiety, tried to brush aside morbid reflections on the
imminence of death. Brief furloughs in the Confederate capital
between battles were brightened by music and dancing and love
making. When the Confederacy was in its last death agonies
Hetty Cary, who had attracted so many men, made her choice.
It fell upon Major General John Pegram, a handsome and gallant
young officer. There could not have been a more fitting mate for
the reigning beauty.

The wedding at St. Paul's Church was the most fashionable
and romantic of the time. After a brief honeymoon General
Pegram returned to his command with General Lee in front of
Petersburg. He had hardly resumed his duties when he was
killed in battle and his body was brought back to Richmond.
In St. Paul's Church the funeral service was read over him by the
same clergyman who had performed the wedding ceremony a
few weeks before. The chief mourner, shrouded in black, was the
young widow who so short a time before had been a beautiful
bride. Hetty Cary Pegram returned to Baltimore and, years later,
became the wife of a Hopkins professor. The rest of her life
passed as quietly as the days of her youth had been tempestuous.

A revival of the traditional cult of beauty took place as recently
as 1939, with the death of Alfred Jenkins Shriver. Mr. Shriver
was a bachelor, a scholar and a bon vivant. For years he served
as a president of the University Club and there staged dinners
for his intimate friends, regaling them on terrapin, oysters, crabs
and other delicacies washed down with choice wines from his
private cellar.

Mr. Shriver attended the Johns Hopkins in the golden age of
Gilman. At the age of twenty he won an essay prize in an inter-
collegiate contest against a field of over 2,500 competitors. Phi
Beta Kappa and a law degree followed. After that he practiced
law and wrote lawbooks. Yet these academic pursuits did not

blind him to the wealth of feminine beauty that abounded in Baltimore in the days of his youth in the early nineties. So when his will was opened after his death it was found to contain an unusual bequest.

To his alma mater, the Johns Hopkins University, Mr. Shriver left a gift of $800,000 for the construction of a lecture hall. But a condition was attached to it. To qualify for the bequest the University must agree to display in the hall the portraits of ten Baltimore women distinguished for their beauty in Mr. Shriver's youth. The portraits were to be painted by the best available artist. Each of the women was to be portrayed as she looked "at the height of her beauty." The ten women he named were: Edith Johns, Louise Morris, Harriet Wade, Anne Foster, Lota Robinson, May Handy, Marie Stirling, Ida Wade, Frances Lurman and Mary Washington Keyser.

Edith Johns first married Jesse Tyson, a man twice her age and richly endowed. After his death she took as her second husband a dashing young officer of the United States army, Major Bruce Cotten. Major Cotten forsook his military career and thereafter devoted his time and talents to the cultivation of domestic felicity. The Cottens were for years leaders of Baltimore society. They were famous for their Sunday night suppers at Cylburn, Mrs. Cotten's country estate. Mrs. Cotten kept her face and figure to the day of her death.

Louise (or Lulu) Morris shared honors with Harry Lehr in scandalizing society by wading through the fountain on Mt. Vernon Place. She married as her second husband a Clews of New York and spent more than thirty years in Paris, so Baltimore saw little of her. Ida and Harriet Wade were Virginia girls who took Baltimore husbands. Ida became Mrs. James T. Dennis. Harriet was first married to William Wallace Spence. As a widow she became the wife of Charles Morris Howard, a leader at the bar and a member of one of Baltimore's oldest families.

Anne Foster was a native of Hartford, Connecticut and came to Baltimore as the wife of N. Winslow Williams, a prominent attorney. Hers was a delicate beauty that reminded one of a French china ornament. It was a beauty that even in her old age never lost its freshness and vivacity. Marie Stirling, a daughter of Rear Admiral Yates Stirling, married J. Lee Tailer of New York, and thereafter was lost to Baltimore.

Mary Washington Keyser is the daughter of H. Irvine Keyser, a member of one of Baltimore's most prominent families in the period following the Civil War. Her mother was Mary Washington of Virginia. Mary Washington Keyser, the daughter, has the statuesque beauty that Sargent liked to paint. She is distinguished, too, for her coloring, her perfect features and her imperial carriage. Her first husband was John Stewart, one of the "Valley" Stewarts. After his death she married DeCourcy W. Thom, an accomplished lawyer. Of the Shriver beauties she alone survives.

The right of Lota Robinson to be included among the ten has been questioned. She was distinguished rather for her brilliance and vivacity, and was a favorite not only in Baltimore society but also in that of New York and Newport. She was the only one of the ten who never married, though it was said she could have had among others Frank A. Munsey, the New York publisher. May Handy was born in Baltimore but her early life was spent in Richmond, Virginia, where for years she reigned as a queen, worshiped alike by white and Negro, rich and poor. She had many suitors in Richmond but eventually married James Brown Potter of New York. Mr. Potter needed consolation since his first wife shocked New York society by running away with Kyrle Bellew, the handsome English actor who was a matinee idol of the nineties.

Frances Lurman, better known as Fannie, was the last of the ten beauties to marry. For a long time it looked as though she would follow the example of Lota Robinson and continue a maiden through life. She made her debut in Newport and she was a belle also in Philadelphia as well as in Baltimore. To the surprise of Baltimore society, Miss Lurman while in a hospital bed married Dorsey Williams. This was the culmination of a romance that began sixty years before.

While no one quarreled with Mr. Shriver's choices there was criticism of several startling omissions. Notable for their absence were the names of Josephine Fairfax and Elizabeth S. Clarke. Josephine Fairfax was the sister of Lord Fairfax and became the wife of Tunstall Smith. Elizabeth Clarke, a Virginia beauty, was first married to Douglas H. Gordon, of Baltimore. After many years of widowhood she was wedded to J. Wilmer Biddle of Philadelphia. Following Mr. Biddle's death she became for a brief period the wife of Alexander Gordon, a cousin of her first husband. Mrs. Gordon's beauty is a rare combination of classic features, golden hair, deep blue eyes and a flawless complexion.

There has, of course, been much speculation as to how the terms of the will are to be carried out. From the standpoint of the university one factor may simplify the matter: there is no stipulation as to the size the portrait of each of the ten women is to be!

After the turn of the century, save for its unexpected eruption in the Shriver will, the cult of beauty died out in Baltimore as it did pretty much everywhere else. Had the tradition been continued a number of Baltimore women could have met the exacting qualifications of the reigning beauties. Among them is Mrs. Redmond C. Stewart, Sr., the former Katharine Small, of York, whose beauty has a freshness suggesting days in the hunting field and other vigorous exercise in the out of doors. There is also Ellen Keyser, wife of James Bruce, the former United States Ambassador to Argentina. Families like the Carters and the Dulanys have had their good looks passed on from one generation to another.

There are the three Watts sisters—Dorsey, Gladys and Elsie. When they were in their teens the Watts household was a popular rendezvous for Johns Hopkins undergraduates. Every evening saw the beaux arriving en masse. The congestion was such that time had to be rationed, each young man being allowed a limited number of minutes of conversation with one of the three sisters. Dorsey, the eldest, married Robert W. Forsyth and went to live in California. Gladys, now Mrs. H. Irvine Keyser, and Elsie, who is Mrs. Vogel H. Helmholz, have remained in Baltimore and continue to invoke admiration wherever they appear. Gladys Keyser is singled out every year as one of the best-dressed women in the city.

Another beauty of this same generation is Mrs. William Wallace Lanahan, the former Eleanor Williams. When, at a Democratic National Convention, the late Governor Albert C. Ritchie's name was presented as a candidate for President of the United States, Eleanor Lanahan was picked to appear on the platform, wave a Maryland flag and start a landslide for him. That the land-slide did not materialize was not due to lack of beauty on the part of the Maryland flag or of its fair waver. There is Anne Steele, now Mrs. Harold Smith, and there is Mrs. George C. Carey, Jr., a daughter of Baltimore by adoption. She was Margaret Blow Elliott, of Wilmington, North Carolina, whose blonde beauty suggests Helen of Troy and Byron's famous line: "Is this the face that launched a thousand ships." A regal beauty is that of Mrs. Alexander E. Duncan, the former Anne Ranson. The list is, of course, quite incomplete. It is offered merely to indicate that Baltimore still has a right to the claim of being called a city of lovely women.

This brings us to very recent times and to another incident in which the charm of a Baltimore woman shook an empire to its foundations. January 20, 1936, upon the death of his father, King George V, Edward, Prince of Wales, ascended the throne of Great Britain and Ireland as King Edward VIII. From the time he reached manhood the Prince was recognized as being the most eligible bachelor in Christendom. His accession to the throne merely served to enhance a reputation that made him the object of devotion, either secret or freely admitted, of virtually every impressionable woman. No matinee idol or star of the screen was the victim of more crushes than he. All the world made conjectures as to what lucky girl from the limited number of eligibles he would choose as his wife.

Yet the handsome young prince showed no inclination to settle down and marry. He appeared equally indifferent after he had ascended the throne. Such was the situation when suddenly gossip spread that the King was showing marked attention to one woman—an American and a divorcee.

The person in question was identified as Mrs. Ernest Simpson, the former Wallis Warfield of Baltimore.

Immediately all eyes turned on Baltimore and the question asked was, "Who was Wallis Warfield?" Though it had been many years since she made her home in the city many people still remembered Wallis. To the surprise of the older generation even a passing acquaintance with her now became a matter of boast. It had not always been so.

There was no difficulty in identifying her, for the Warfields are an old and prominent Maryland family. Her father was Teackle Wallis Warfield; her mother Bessie Montague of Virginia. Wallis was born in 1896 in a cottage near Monterey Inn, a fashionable summer resort at Blue Ridge Summit, Pennsylvania, then greatly patronized by Baltimoreans. Soon after the birth of his daughter Teackle Wallis Warfield died. The child was christened Bessie Wallis; but, when she grew up, she dropped the Bessie and called herself Wallis.

Mrs. Warfield, a young widow, was faced with the problem of supporting herself and her child on very limited means. She took a modest house on Biddle Street, one of an identical row such as then was typical of the city's building. After Wallis became famous the house was for a time opened to the public for a small admission fee and visitors were invited to gape at a tub in which the Duchess of Windsor was supposed once to have bathed.

It was the events of this period that led to the report that Wallis was the daughter of a boarding-house keeper. The story seems to have been based upon the fact that relatives from Virginia lived with Mrs. Warfield while attending school in Baltimore. Some old Baltimoreans recall that she ran a tearoom and others that she made money by doing fancy needlework. However, the problem of living was solved when, in 1908, Mrs. Warfield became the wife of John Freeman Rasin, son of the Democratic boss of Baltimore and a man of comfortable means. During her childhood Wallis spent much time with her grandmother, Mrs. Henry Mactier Warfield, who lived nearby on Preston Street. It was there rather than at her mother's that she entertained her friends.

Like the children of most Baltimore families of social prominence Wallis attended private schools. She first was a pupil at the Arundell School, an elementary institution a few blocks from her home. Later she transferred to Oldfields, a fashionable boarding school for girls in Baltimore County. There, according to some accounts, she learned to ride. In fact in the first glow of discovery her various newspaper biographers attributed to her marked ability also in tennis and golf as well as horsemanship. If she had such gifts they have been forgotten by her intimate friends. They recall no special talent for outdoor sports. They do remember that she was an excellent dancer and a genius in matters of dress.

Above all, her friends remember her as being first-rate company, a good listener and capable of rapierlike thrusts in repartee. She was credited with a keen sense of humor and being quick to laugh at other people's jokes. Her distinction in matters of dress was not altogether due to her own talent. Even when money was short her mother saw to it that Wallis had the best in clothes. She was a regular customer of Maggie O'Connor.

Wallis Warfield laid no claim to ravishing beauty. But she was superlatively smart. Her dark hair, white skin, violet eyes and trim figure compensated for undistinguished features. She soon realized that, in the Baltimore of her day, if a girl of good family but without money wanted to get anywhere socially she had to live by her wits. She was very much the Becky Sharp of the local scene. From her mother she inherited those indefinable qualities that attract men and which in Virginia have always been regarded as the natural attributes of the Montague women. While she was still at the Arundell School she demonstrated her ability to attract boys.

In the winter of 1914 Wallis was eighteen years old, through school and ready to be presented to society. On December 7, 1914, in accordance with local custom she made her debut at the Bachelors Cotillon. The Warfield uncles made this possible. Uncle Sol (S. Davies Warfield) then was president of the Seaboard Air Line Railway. Wallis's partners were her cousin, Henry M. Warfield, Jr., and Major General George Barnett, commander of the Marine Corps, her uncle by marriage.

For the occasion Wallis appeared in "an exquisite gown of white satin combined with chiffon and pearl trimmings." She carried American beauty roses. Among the other debutantes was Mary Kirk, of the silversmith family, an intimate of Wallis' who was to figure later in the London episode. A society editor of one of the local newspapers commented next day that "never has a more charming bevy of buds been presented." After the ball, which always closes at the respectable hour of 1:30 A.M., Wallis, Mary Kirk and their own smart little circle repaired to the Baltimore Country Club and danced until dawn.

The debutante year is over all too soon. The next year finds the earlier group on the shelf making room for the new. Wallis escaped this humiliation by spending much time in Washington with her aunts, Mrs. Barnett and Mrs. Buchanan Merryman, who

introduced her to society in that city. She also began to appear at
the "hops" at the Naval Academy in Annapolis. In 1916, two
years after her debut, her engagement was announced to Lieutenant Earle Winfield Spencer of the United States Navy.

The wedding, which took place November 8th, in Christ
Protestant Episcopal Church, was a fashionable event with a full
quota of bridesmaids and groomsmen. Wallis wore a family wedding veil and a gown made for her by Maggie O'Connor. She was
given in marriage by her Uncle Sol. Following the wedding the
Spencers set out on their honeymoon and a tour of duty that carried them away from Baltimore. The city of her childhood and
her youth was to see little more of her. Fate decreed that she was
to play her role on a larger stage. Another reason for breaking relations with her native city was that, in 1921, after the death of Mr.
Rasin, Wallis's mother married a third time and moved to
Washington.

In 1927 Wallis and Earle Spencer were divorced. That same
year she joined an old friend in New York, the former Dorothea
Parsons, whose husband was Ernest Simpson, a shipping man.
Soon thereafter the Simpsons parted company. Wallis sailed for
England. Simpson followed her there, proposed marriage and was
accepted. They were married in Chelsea in the summer of 1928.

Wallis's charm, her cleverness at turning out fried chicken á la
Maryland, sweet potatoes topped with marshmallows and other
popular Baltimore dishes are credited with having given the
Simpsons a place in ultrasmart London society. Such briefly was
her career up to the years 1930-1936 when she became the friend
of the Prince of Wales. How they first met and Wallis' unusual
appeal have been fully described in the Duke of Windsor's memoirs. His account indicates that what charmed him was just the
same naturalness and good company that Wallis' Baltimore friends
recalled most vividly.

It was on December 1, 1936, that the Bishop of Bradford
brought the "Simpson affair" into the open by declaring that the
King "needs God's grace as much as any of his subjects." Wallis
then was on the point of obtaining a preliminary decree of divorce
from Ernest Simpson. While Prime Minister Stanley Baldwin
made frantic trips to Fort Belvedere, King Edward's country
place, in the hope of bringing him to reason, and while the Arch-

bishop of Canterbury threw his weight into the battle to uphold the British constitution, the Baltimore public rooted for the home town girl. They joined in the then popular refrain:

Give three cheers, and three cheers more,
For the lovely lady from Baltimore.

The Baltimore *Sunpapers,* ever alert to give their readers the most reliable information, free from bias and sensationalism, put in a long distance call to London on December 4th. Through the call contact was made with an Englishman of high position reputedly in possession of the facts. It announced to its readers: "Despite the prevailing impression—supported by events of the last few weeks—that the king is really in love with Mrs. Simpson, he is, as a matter of fact, it was said, beginning to grow just a little tired of her, and it is but a question of time before this affair goes the way of the others."

Never in their long history of furnishing news to the Baltimore public had the *Sunpapers* been so far wrong. For six days later, on December 10th, the King delivered his memorable broadcast in which he announced that, because he could not have it and wed "the woman I love," he was abdicating the throne!

With the rest of the world, and with a special pride of personal possession, Baltimoreans followed the development of the romance until its culmination in the wedding of June 3, 1937, at the Chateau de Conde, in Monts, France. Those interested in running down all the details of the affair did not overlook the eventual disposition of Wallis's discarded husband. Ernest Simpson found consolation in a marriage with the divorced wife of one Jacques Raffray. And Mrs. Jacques Raffray was none other than the other Baltimore belle, Mary Kirk. How small the world is—where Baltimore women are concerned!

Four years later, in the autumn of 1941, Baltimore at last had an opportunity to extend a formal welcome to "the little lady" who once more had put the old town on the map. The occasion was the visit of the Duke and Duchess of Windsor to the latter's uncle, General Henry M. Warfield. Uncle Sol had died a number of years before.

General Warfield was every inch a Maryland gentleman, dignified, courteous and modest as became a descendant of Pagan de Warfield, the English knight whom the Maryland Warfields claim as progenitor of their line. Throughout all the notoriety that attended the royal romance he displayed an admirable reserve. Fellow commuters on the Northern Central's "Parkton Local" could hardly believe that the quiet white-haired and mustached gentleman with the military bearing, his face partially hidden behind his newspaper, was the uncle of the Mrs. Simpson all the world was talking about.

The General and Mrs. Warfield, the former Rebecca Carroll Denison, lived quietly with their only child Anita and their son-in-law, Zachary Lewis, on the General's country place, Salona Farms, in the picturesque Dulany Valley, north of Baltimore. Though the Warfields enjoyed all the bodily comforts to which the old county families are accustomed, their house and its equipment had not been designed for the entertainment of royalty.

Mrs. Warfield, for example, was baffled when she was told that the Duke could sleep only between linen sheets and that these must be changed every day. The Warfields, however, enjoyed a large circle of devoted friends who generously came forward with offers of their goods and their services. The countryside supplemented the Warfield supply with more than enough linen sheets to meet the royal requirements. Friends and relations volunteered informal entertainment. Besides this purely private aspect of the visit, Mayor Howard W. Jackson let the Warfields know that Baltimore city wanted to add an official welcome to the homecoming.

The fateful day arrived. The Windsors, returning from the Duke's E. P. Ranch in Canada, entered Maryland by way of the Northern Central Railroad. The express with the Duke's private car attached, halted at Timonium, a flag stop in Baltimore County a few miles north of the city line. There General Warfield and Anita Lewis were waiting to greet them. It was the first meeting of Wallis and her Uncle Henry in eight years and they embraced affectionately. The Duke appeared without a hat. Fair-haired, slender and below average height he presented a decidedly boyish appearance. The three pedigreed Cairns that accompanied the royal party were whisked off to the Baltimore County Humane Society while the others set off by automobile for Salona Farms.

It was a relief to everybody to discover that the Duke was natural and unassuming. He smoked a pipe much of the time and was especially interested in General Warfield's turkeys that strutted about the lawn in front of the house. There were nice little bits of etiquette to be observed, as for example waiting for the Duke to enter the house first. But the Warfields adjusted to it quickly.

October 13th was the day of the public welcome. Shortly after lunch the Duke and Duchess and General and Mrs. Warfield left Salona Farms by automobile. Following in other cars were the Lewises and various members of the Warfield family and of the Windsor entourage. At the city line cars were met by a motorcycle escort which rushed them direct to the City Hall. There the Duke and Duchess were received by the officialdom of city and state.

While these ceremonies were taking place at the City Hall, all work in the city was suspended. In the downtown area women left off shopping and crowds began to pour out onto the sidewalks along the route of the return trip which had been announced in the press. On Charles Street, from Lexington to Mt. Vernon Place, thousands of people were jammed together battling for vantage points. Those who could get no nearer than three or four rows from the curb stood on tiptoe and craned their necks to see.

There was a muffled roar from the crowd as the motorcycle cops cleared the way and an open car appeared in which were the Duke and Duchess and Mayor Jackson. In England the Duchess might be snubbed and denied a right to the title of Royal Highness. But from her own people she received a wholehearted and tumultuous welcome. Cheers went up as the car dashed up Charles Street and the Duke and Duchess, perched on the folded top, bowed acknowledgment. The Duke from his childhood up had been through this sort of thing hundreds of times. For the Duchess it was a new and thrilling experience.

The royal progress continued all the way to University Parkway where it turned toward Roland Park and the Baltimore Country Club. There a reception was held to which several hundred of Baltimore's public figures and socially elect had been invited. Those who had wives brought them along. Assisting Mayor Jackson as chairman of the reception committee and master of ceremonies was Frederick R. Huber. This was "old stuff" for the Mayor and Freddie. It reminded them of several years before when together they rolled out the crimson carpet for Marie of Rumania.

Though the Duke wore a dark blue double-breasted lounge suit and word had gone out that dress was to be informal the more elegant Baltimoreans were not to be denied the opportunity to put on their best bibs and tuckers. According to official count one top hat, six morning coats and a like number of pairs of striped trousers were displayed. In the receiving line besides the Duke and Duchess were Mayor Jackson and his daughter-in-law Mrs. Carle Jackson, the former Rosa Ponselle, of the Metropolitan Opera. So, too, were Governor O'Conor and Mrs. O'Conor and Mr. and Mrs. Wallace Lanahan. To give a domestic touch to the proceedings Rosa Ponselle Jackson sang "Home Sweet Home."

The Duchess was exceedingly gracious. She greeted Mrs. Spalding Lowe Jenkins with "It was sweet of you to come." And when Mrs. Sanchez Boone, her former schoolteacher, appeared, the Duchess recognized her immediately and stepped out of the receiving line to embrace her. The Duke appeared equally pleased at the warmth of his wife's reception by her fellow Baltimoreans. In a letter of thanks to the Mayor he said that he had been "more than touched by the dignity and simplicity of the reception and by the cordial friendliness of the crowds."

So ended the official festivities. The Windsors returned to Baltimore once more to visit but never again in an official capacity. In the autumn of 1941 the Baltimore public had said its say. From then on Wallis Warfield was given a place beside Betsy Patterson, the Caton Sisters, Hetty Cary and Alfred Shriver's Ten in the charmed circle of Baltimore's beauties and belles. History offers few other examples, if any, of a man who has given up an empire for the love of a woman. Baltimoreans will not believe it was purely an accident that when King Edward VIII made his fateful decision the woman in question was one of their own fair daughters.

Chapter 9

"NOT BY BREAD ALONE"

In John Moale's sketch of Baltimore Town made in 1752—the oldest drawing of the town extant—the most conspicuous feature is a church. It sits on a hill overlooking the inner harbor. There is a church on the same spot today.

In subsequent sketches of Baltimore, churches continued to be conspicuous features. In modern Baltimore churches of whatever denomination are as much a part of every neighborhood as the drugstore, the market and the filling station. There are synagogues as well. It is impossible to find reliable figures on church membership but it is safe to say that the number of Baltimoreans associated with Christian and Jewish congregations is well above average. A study made some years ago indicated that half the city's population is connected with some religious sect. Of the Christian population about half is Catholic and the other half divided among innumerable Protestant denominations.

In Baltimore the Sabbath Day is kept relatively holy. It is still fashionable and customary to go to church, though tennis, golf and other similar diversions have made inroads. Only in recent years has the strict religious observance of Sunday been relieved by the movies and professional football and baseball games. These, however, are reserved until after church hours and the dispensation was won only after bitter battles with such strict religious constructionists as the Lord's Day Alliance. Baltimore's conservatism with respect to an open Sunday is no doubt due to the fact that of the Protestant denominations the Methodist is by far the largest.

If Baltimore may lay claim to having an exceptional religious atmosphere it comes by it naturally, for in its long history it has sat in at the birth of several important religious institutions. Within little more than a square mile in the center of the town are to be found the scenes of great moments in the annals of these various churches.

Since Baltimore was founded in colonial days, it is natural that the oldest parish in the city should be that of the Established

Church of England, later to become the Protestant Episcopal Church in the United States. The Revolution of 1688 in England, which resulted in the abdication of the Catholic King, James II, was followed in the summer of 1689 by the Protestant Revolution in Maryland. From then on the government of the colony was controlled by the Protestants.

In 1730, the year following the granting of a charter to Baltimore Town, the Maryland Assembly acted to erect a parish church in the new community. This parish took the name of St. Paul's, claiming as its parent a St. Paul's parish set up previously in Patapsco Hundred, to the east of the town. Lot No. 19 on the original town plan was set aside as the site of the church. It was on an eminence perhaps a mile to the north of the harbor and situated at what is now the intersection of Charles and Saratoga Streets. Lot No. 19 extended east to the present St. Paul Street and south to Lexington Street. A brick church was begun on the site in 1731 and completed in 1739, and it is this church which is shown in the Moale sketch of 1752.

In the year 1779 the vestry of St. Paul's resolved to build a new church. The cornerstone was laid in 1780. As had become the custom among all good church people in Baltimore, including even the straight-laced Presbyterians, funds for the construction were raised through a lottery. The new edifice was completed in 1784, all of the old church with the exception of the bell tower being torn down. At this period the remainder of the church property was used as a graveyard. This second building served the congregation for thirty years. Then in the spring of 1814 the cornerstone for a third church was laid. This church was finished in 1817 and continued in use for thirty-seven years until it was destroyed by fire in 1854. The congregation set to work at once to replace it and on January 10, 1856, the fourth church was completed and dedicated.

This plain Norman edifice in the form of a basilica and constructed of red brick is in regular use today. It is known affectionately as Old St. Paul's. Where the first church was a landmark that could be seen by mariners far down the Patapsco River, the present church nestles in comparative obscurity in the shadow of a modern skyscraper and several other tall buildings. The graveyard disappeared long years ago when the bodies were moved to a new location well to the west of town. Save for the land occupied by the church itself, Lot No. 19 is given over to shops, office buildings and parking lots. Thus for over two centuries there has been a St. Paul's Church exactly where there is one today.

A newcomer to downtown Baltimore might well rub his eyes when he looks north on Liberty Street toward Saratoga. For before him lies a green terraced lawn behind a retaining wall some six feet above the level of the street. Beyond the lawn he will see a quaint red brick Georgian dwelling with a white doorway, above the doorway a Palladian window with white trimming, and dormers breaking out of the roof. The house is set off by a tree or two, lilac bushes and other shrubs. One might imagine it had been set up there as a model for a suburban home by some construction firm. Certainly it looks out of place in the company of parking lots, retail businesses and the noise and turmoil of the center of the city. But the old dwelling stands there as it has stood for over 150 years, observing quietly and sedately the march of progress. This is the rectory of St. Paul's parish. It was built in 1791 and it still houses the rector of St. Paul's Church and his family.

Twice the "Old Parsonage" was threatened by fire. In the summer of 1873 a conflagration raged virtually across the street. The Great Fire of February, 1904, missed it by only a few blocks. Yet the most serious threat to it came in the lush days following World War I and preceding the financial collapse of 1928. An ambitious construction corporation hit upon the property as an ideal site for a modern office building. The promoters approached the vestry of St. Paul's with a proposition to buy it. The Rev. Dr. Arthur B. Kinsolving was then rector of the church and residing in the parsonage with his extensive and charming family.

The vestrymen explained to the promoters that, aside from its intrinsic worth, the congregation of St. Paul's placed a sentimental value on the old house. They felt quite sure that, regardless of how generous the offer might be, members of the church would not consent to the destruction of the rectory. But, replied the promoters, they had no intention of destroying the rectory. They proposed to preserve every brick of it and use it as a penthouse on top of the skyscraper. They even offered to install a private elevator so that Dr. Kinsolving could take his model-T Ford right up to a garage on the roof. The vestrymen declined this generous offer. And so—for a further period of years—the rectory was saved. It continues to be one of the most unusual and charming landmarks of downtown Baltimore.

Though Maryland was a Catholic colony Baltimore Town began as a strictly Protestant settlement. Soon after its founding German settlers appeared on the scene and introduced the Lutheran and German Reformed Churches. Members of the German Reformed persuasion established a congregation around the year 1750 and for eight years the Lutherans worshiped with them. Members of the Presbyterian faith erected a small log meeting house on a lot on Fayette Street in 1763, and three years later built a new church at Fayette and North Streets.

The first Catholics to settle in Baltimore were immigrants from Ireland and the French Acadians. Private dwellings were used for the celebration of the mass until 1770. By that time the Catholics had become so numerous it was decided to build a church. A lot on the northwest corner of the present Saratoga and Charles Streets was obtained opposite St. Paul's. Here was erected a plain brick church which was given the name of St. Peter's. The Revolution caused delay in construction and the church was not completed until 1783.

One of the first priests to serve in the parish of St. Peter's was the Rev. John Carroll, a cousin of Charles Carroll of Carrollton. Father Carroll was an accomplished scholar who had received an excellent education in Europe. As was the case with a distinguished successor of his, Protestants flocked to St. Peter's to hear him preach. During the Revolution Father Carroll accompanied Benjamin Franklin, Samuel Chase and Charles Carroll of Carrollton on a mission to Canada—to try to persuade the French Canadians to support the American cause, but without success.

Prior to the Revolution the few Catholics in the American colonies came under the spiritual jurisdiction of the bishop of the London district of the Catholic Church. The independence of the colonies and the establishment of the Federal Union called for a reorganization, and the Catholic clergy in Maryland and Pennsylvania appealed to the Holy See to choose a superior. The Pope gave a favorable response in 1786 by appointing Father Carroll Vicar General of the Roman Catholic Church in America. Four years later Father Carroll became the first Catholic bishop in the United States. His consecration took place in the chapel of Lulworth Castle, in Dorsetshire, England, on August 15, 1790. All of the thirteen original states were included in his diocese.

The following year Bishop Carroll founded Georgetown College in the District of Columbia. Simultaneously St. Mary's Seminary for the training of young men for the priesthood was established in Baltimore by the Sulpicians. Particularly striking were the cordial relations existing between John Carroll and the Protestant clergy of the town. In 1786 he joined forces with the Rev. William West, of St. Paul's Episcopal Church, and the Rev. Patrick Allison, the Presbyterian minister, to establish an academy for the study of the learned professions. Unfortunately this bold experiment in interdenominational education was short-lived.

In 1795 Dr. Carroll, now elevated to the rank of bishop, was found again in company with Dr. Allison and the Rev. Joseph G. Bend, successor to William West at St. Paul's, improving the intellectual atmosphere of the community by establishing the Library Company of Baltimore and purchasing a collection of books for circulation among the subscribers. Many of the books are now in the Maryland Historical Society.

In his zeal to promote education Bishop Carroll did not even flinch from contamination with the Masonic order. In 1800 he joined with Mr. Bend and the Rev. John Crawford, a leading Mason, in organizing a society which bore the imposing title of "The Maryland Society For Promoting Useful Knowledge."

Bishop Carroll's rare gift for spiritual leadership among his fellow Catholics and his distinguished contribution to the community did not escape the keen eye of the Holy See. In 1808 Baltimore was elevated to the rank of a metropolitan church and Dr. Carroll was invested with the dignity of Archbishop, the first of that rank in this country. Thus Baltimore enjoys the distinction of being the birthplace of the Roman Catholic hierarchy in the United States. The Baltimore diocese continues to take precedence over those later established.

On July 7, 1806, a solemn procession made its way up the hill to the north of the town in the direction of Belvidere, the country estate of Governor John Eager Howard, Revolutionary hero and statesman. The central figure was Bishop Carroll and he was going to lay the cornerstone for a Roman Catholic cathedral on property on North Charles Street deeded to the church by the Governor. The procession must have passed under the welcome shade of the elm tree where General Rochambeau's army had camped during the Revolution. Arrived at the spot where the foundations of the new edifice already were in place, Bishop Carroll performed the ceremony of laying the stone.

The Cathedral, usually described as Greco-Roman in style, was designed by Benjamin Latrobe who also designed the Capitol in Washington. The War of 1812 interrupted construction and the building was not under roof until 1818. It is an impressive structure of Patapsco limestone with a gilded dome and a portico supported by massive Ionic columns. Two bulbous towers after the Russian manner have since been added. In spite of its somewhat conglomerate nature the cathedral presents a dignified and pleasing appearance. Archbishop Carroll did not live to see the consecration of the building which took place in 1821. He died six years before at the venerable age of eighty years, lamented by a community whose affection and respect he had earned.

Meanwhile, literally within a stone's throw of the cathedral, another religious group of a very different nature had established itself. At the turn of the 19th century the Congregational Church in New England was seething over the issue of Unitarianism. This might reasonably have been considered a matter of little concern in Baltimore. But here again the persistent influence of New England on the town asserted itself. The New Englanders resident in Baltimore brought to this religious issue the same boldness and imagination that distinguished their business dealings.

On February 10, 1817, a number of gentlemen, the great majority of whom were of New England origin, met at the home of one Henry Payson at 21 Hanover Street. There, after due deliberation, they formed a society known as the First Independent, or Unitarian Church of Baltimore. The conservative element in the Congregational Church at the time brought the charge that many ministers of liberal persuasion were abandoning the doctrine of the Trinity as stated in the Athanasian and Nicean creeds and embodied in all Protestant orthodox creeds. The liberal ministers did not deny the charge but defended their action on the ground that they were merely developing the principles of religious freedom on which Congregationalism was founded. Such was the disturbed atmosphere in which a small body of New Englanders, far removed from the center of the conflict, met and acted in Baltimore.

The next concern was the erection of a church. With enviable good judgment the congregation engaged the services of Maximilian Godefroy, a highly talented architect. Godefroy's design, interestingly enough, followed that of Latrobe's cathedral in its general lines though on a much more modest scale. That is to say, it also had a dome and a portico supported by columns. A charming feature was the group of carved figures in the pediment. It still is, for Godefroy's church, like Latrobe's cathedral, thus far has escaped the ravages of time and the hand of the despoiler.

The cornerstone of the Unitarian Church was laid on June 5, 1817, and the building was ready for its first service on November 1, 1818. Shortly thereafter the Rev. Jared Sparks of Cambridge, Massachusetts, was called to the pastorate, but his association with Baltimore has been largely forgotten. He is best known to posterity as a president of Harvard and the biographer of George Washington.

The ordination of the new pastor was set for May 5, 1819. Invited to preach the ordination sermon was Dr. William Ellery Channing, an eloquent leader of the Unitarian movement. His discourse was devoted to a formal statement of the tenets of his liberal brethren, their mode of interpreting the Scriptures, their views concerning God and Christ, their idea of the nature of His mission and mediation.

As is so often the course in theological controversy Unitarianism first consisted of a group within the Congregational Church. Then came the definitive break and the establishment of a wholly new and independent denomination. Dr. Channing's Baltimore sermon is taken by Unitarian historians as the first tangible evidence of the parting of the ways. Some six years later, in 1825, the American Unitarian Association was formed. This is the date usually accepted as marking the formal separation from the Congregational Church and the beginning of organized Unitarianism in the United States. Dr. Channing's sermon is used as justification for inscribing over the front door of the church edifice in Baltimore "The Birthplace of Unitarianism in the United States."

The year 1729, in which Baltimore Town was founded, saw religious meetings in Oxford University, England, organized by a group of undergraduates led by John and Charles Wesley. These earnest young men adopted a system of religious discipline so strict they were given the name of "Methodists." The Wesleys and their friends went out of Oxford as ordained ministers of the Church of England to spread the new discipline. Among other places Methodism took firm hold in Staffordshire, England, where, in the summer of 1745, one Francis Asbury was born. His mother was passionately religious. She divined that her son would some day become a prophet and planned his education with that end in view. While he was still in the cradle she read the Bible aloud to him, and so successful was the indoctrination that it was said that, at the age of six years, the child Asbury could read the Book to himself.

As he grew up Asbury reveled in the prospect of the career his mother had chosen for him. He shunned all fun and frivolity. Naturally he was fair game for his contemporaries who made his life miserable. Yet he found joy in his martyrdom. At sixteen years of age he had gained so much self-confidence that he preached before meetings of his mother's friends. He took orders as a priest of the Church of England but at the same time came under the spell of the Wesleys, embraced Methodism and volunteered as a missionary to the American colonies.

In the autumn of 1771 Asbury arrived in Philadelphia. He had then reached the age of twenty-six years, and was the eighth Wesleyan preacher to come to this country. A society of Methodists already existed in New York and there were societies also in Philadelphia and in Maryland. Asbury struck out through New Jersey, preaching on the way. He is said to have picked towns where public executions were to take place. He found it impressive and convincing to his hearers to tilt against sin while the mortal remains of a malefactor dangled from a gallows beside him.

In 1772 Asbury received from John Wesley a letter appointing him general assistant in America. This virtually made his power absolute. He set out on horseback to tour Pennsylvania, New Jersey, Delaware and Maryland. Asbury was preceded in Maryland by Robert Strawbridge, another Methodist prophet, who established the first society in Frederick County and also journeyed through the colony preaching. Still another Methodist exhorter in Maryland was one John King. King is credited with having delivered the first Methodist sermon in Baltimore from a blacksmith's block. He repeated the performance on militia day, always a festive and jovial occasion. But,in this instance, his audience was in no mood for a lecture on sobriety. Some of those in the crowd attacked and knocked him down. Nevertheless King made an impression on the godly for he was invited to preach at St. Paul's. But he screamed so loudly and raised such a general commotion that he was not asked to preach there again. Thereafter Methodist preaching was conducted in private houses until chapels were built.

Such was the state of Methodism in Maryland when Asbury eventually reached the colony on his tour. He at once quarreled with Strawbridge who refused to do battle and retired to a farm outside Baltimore to spend his declining years. Asbury entered Baltimore on January 3, 1773, and preached in several private homes. He had a rare gift for making converts and the ranks of the Methodists swelled. Soon it was found necessary to rent a sail loft for use by the congregation. This temporary place of worship was succeeded in 1774 by chapels in Strawberry Alley and in Lovely Lane. A census of the Methodists in the colonies at this time showed a total of 1,160, nearly half of whom were in Maryland. This was testimony to the force of Asbury's preaching and personality. Even more so it was evidence of the very poor quality of clergy Lord Baltimore had appointed to livings in the Established Church.

Asbury's mission was directed chiefly toward the poor and persons of moderate means. But he also made friends among the wealthy planters and members of the professional classes and included some of them among his converts. A particularly advantageous conversion was that of Harry Dorsey Gough, one of the most influential planters in Maryland. He was reputed to have a fortune of $300,000 and his estate, Perry Hall, on the road to Bel Air, was one of the showplaces in Baltimore County. Mrs. Gough was an elder sister of Governor Charles Carnan Ridgely of Hampton, who was more influential in the colony than his brother-in-law. Through these connections Methodism became fashionable in Maryland.

Mrs. Gough no doubt was influenced by her aunt, Rebecca Dorsey Ridgely, wife of Charles Ridgely, the builder of Hampton and uncle of the Governor, for Rebecca had come under the spell of Asbury and embraced Methodism. When Charles Ridgely completed his handsome Georgian mansion house he celebrated the occasion with an elaborate banquet. Mrs. Ridgely meanwhile would have no part in the feasting and merrymaking and retired with a group of women to a room upstairs to hold a prayer meeting while the revelry was going on below.

One of the guests at the banquet suddenly gave a cry of alarm, announcing that he had been paralyzed. One leg, he said, was numb and useless. Had Asbury appeared at the moment he would have found an easy convert, for the poor fellow was sure his end was not far off. Fellow guests showed their sympathy and the banquet was on the point of breaking up when the cause of the seizure was discovered. Next to the gentleman's chair was a wine cooler packed with ice. In his exuberance he had put his leg into it. A little rubbing, the "paralysis" disappeared, the leg was as good as new and the revelry was resumed.

The conflict between the mother country and the American colonies was now coming to a head. John Wesley, being resident in England, counseled loyalty to the crown. As the crisis reached a climax he ordered his Methodist ministers home. But Asbury, with a political astuteness that was characteristic of him, disregarded Wesley's order and stayed on. His attitude during the Revolution has been described as one of "sympathetic neutrality." Because of the known attitude of Wesley, Methodist preachers were looked upon as spies and Tories, and this did not make the situation easy for Asbury.

In the early years of the war Asbury journeyed to Virginia where he took part in revivals at which miracles were performed and converts made in gratifying numbers. In 1776 he returned to Baltimore, preached there and then went on a mission to Annapolis. The next year, however, he was told he could not remain in Maryland unless he took the oath of allegiance. Since taking oaths was contrary to his conscience he left Maryland and found refuge in Delaware. But he made good use of his time there by converting 1,800 persons.

Asbury did not spare his body and, in consequence, he was sick most of the time. But, in spite of aches and pains he plodded along, preaching several times a day. He also made it a practice, while riding circuit, to pray ten minutes out of every hour. For many years it was his habit to pray for every Methodist missionary in the colonies by name.

The Revolution over and the colonies having won their independence, Wesley again became solicitous for his followers in the new country. For the first time he took it upon himself to consecrate a bishop in the person of Thomas Coke and assigned him as superintendent of the Methodist societies in America. Bishop Coke arrived in New York on November 3, 1784.

At 10 A.M. on Christmas Eve of the same year a conference was convened in Baltimore with Dr. Coke as presiding officer and Asbury as the dominating force. Pursuant to Wesley's instructions the conference decided to establish an episcopal church. On Christmas Day Asbury was ordained a deacon by Coke and on December 26th he was elevated to the rank of elder. On December 27th he was consecrated bishop. This solemn ceremony was performed in the Lovely Lane Meeting House, the site of which today is occupied by the Merchants Club. Thus as the Reverend John Carroll was consecrated the first Roman Catholic bishop in America, so Francis Asbury was the first Methodist bishop to be consecrated in the United States. Furthermore at this same historic conference the Methodist Episcopal Church in the United States was born.

Among the distinguished clerical guests present at the consecration of Bishop Asbury was the Rev. Philip William Otterbein, a minister of the German Reformed Church. He was there by special invitation of Asbury. Otterbein was a Prussian by birth and in his youth began his studies for the ministry. He was soon distinguished by his evangelical zeal and a strictness of discipline that rivaled that of the Wesleyans. His methods found little favor with his superiors. They were relieved to see him depart as a missionary to the New World where he arrived in 1752, pursuing his ministry among the German Reformed congregations in Pennsylvania and Maryland. In the course of their activities Asbury and Otterbein met and were mutually attracted to each other. Asbury was said to have been instrumental in bringing Otterbein to Baltimore where the latter established an independent reformed church on Methodistic lines. It was called the Evangelical Reformed Church.

At this church Otterbein continued as pastor for twenty-nine years. To the end of his life he was a member of the German Reformed Church. Nevertheless he encouraged the organization of an independent group which became a separate church under the name of the United Brethren in Christ. At a conference in 1800 Otterbein was chosen bishop of the new denomination. So Otterbein became the third of the three pioneer bishops whose careers were intimately associated with Baltimore. His church building was erected in 1786. This quaint brick structure with a tower still stands in South Baltimore. It has the distinction of being the oldest church building in the city. Tucked away on Conway Street a few doors east of Sharp its history and its location are known to few Baltimoreans. The Church of the United Brethren in Christ recently has merged with the Evangelical Church to form the thirteenth Protestant denomination in number of members in the United States. It has sometimes been described as the German branch of the Methodist Church, so close have been its practices to those of the Wesleyans.

Following the founding of the Methodist Church in the United States and his consecration as bishop, Asbury took full charge. He introduced the circuit rider system; and in spite of ill health and advancing years toured the country from Maine to Georgia and also visited the western frontiers. It is estimated that this indefatigable man covered 5,000 miles in a year. In the spring of 1816 he was on tour when he fell ill in Virginia. There he died on March 31. Two months later his body was conveyed to Baltimore where it lay in state in Light Street Methodist Church while outside the streets were thronged with mourning Methodists.

The funeral was held on May 10th. The chief feature was a public procession in which 20,000 persons marching eight abreast made their way slowly to the Eutaw Street Church. There the body of America's first Methodist bishop was laid to rest in a vault. And there it remained until June, 1854, when it was disinterred and transferred to Mt. Olivet Cemetery, in southwest Baltimore, where it rests today.

While all this religious history was being made the greatest of Baltimore churchmen was not yet born. That event took place quietly in a modest dwelling on Gay Street in the year 1834. It was the home of an Irish family that had recently immigrated to

Baltimore. The child was James Gibbons. Shortly thereafter the family returned to Ireland, but it was back in this country a few years later. The incident of James Gibbons' birth in Baltimore's Gay Street is significant, for he was first and foremost an American. Of his many achievements probably the greatest was his defining of the dual loyalty to the church and to the nation which served as guide to thousands of his fellow Catholics.

Young Jimmy Gibbons was below average height and sparsely built, and he had an alert, intelligent face. He studied for the priesthood at St. Mary's Seminary in Baltimore and was ordained at the age of twenty-seven years. At that moment the nation was plunged into a bloody civil war and the unhappy city of Baltimore became a house divided. The young priest's pleasing personality and sincerity soon impressed themselves on his superiors. In 1865 he was appointed secretary to the Archbishop of Baltimore. Three years later, at the surprisingly early age of thirty-four years, he was consecrated a bishop in the Baltimore Cathedral and dispatched to North Carolina as Vicar Apostolic.

There were relatively few Catholics in North Carolina in those days, but Bishop Gibbons did not confine himself to the members of his own church. His humanity and simplicity made him at home in all classes of society and among people of a variety of faiths. The young bishop deemed it his duty to preach the Gospel wherever he might find hearers. In this period of his career he preached in Protestant churches, in courthouses, public halls and even in Masonic lodge rooms.

From North Carolina Bishop Gibbons was transferred to Richmond, Virginia, and installed in St. Peter's Cathedral. The success his preaching had achieved in North Carolina followed him to Virginia where he attracted to his services almost as many Protestants as Catholics. On one occasion, when he was preaching in the town hall at Culpeper, Virginia, the local judge adjourned court so that all might hear him. Inspired by his cordial reception at the hands of Protestants he wrote the book entitled *The Faith of Our Fathers*. It was directed primarily at them and sold in the neighborhood of 1,000,000 copies.

As Archbishop Bayley of Baltimore was in failing health, Bishop Gibbons in 1877 was named his coadjutor. On the death of the archbishop a few months later Bishop Gibbons succeeded him in office. From then on his activities centered around Baltimore which became his permanent home. Since the days of John Carroll no Catholic Archbishop had been so well known to the community. Typical of the attitude of the Archbishop to those outside the faith and their response to him is an incident described by a visitor to the city. He and the Archbishop were walking together and passed a church where the congregation was letting out. Archbishop Gibbons at once was the object of cordial greetings from all sides. The visitor was impressed. "You seem to be well acquainted here," he said. "Oh, yes," replied the Archbishop cheerfully. "These are our Episcopal friends."

When, in 1886, Baltimore learned that its beloved archbishop was to be made a cardinal, public enthusiasm broke all bounds. His selection was regarded as a mark of honor for the whole community. Protestants joined with Catholics in paying their respects to a fellow citizen whose signal attributes had won the highest recognition of the Holy See. Other activities were suspended while the city gave itself over to the reception and entertainment of virtually the whole American hierachy which assembled in Baltimore for the installation.

An immense crowd was on hand to witness the colorful procession through the streets to the cathedral. This was headed by a crucifer, after whom marched the students from St. Charles College, of which the Cardinal-elect was an alumnus, and seminarians from St. Mary's.

There followed the regular and secular clergy, monsignori, bishops, abbots, Capuchin fathers, Benedictines, Lazarists, Dominicans, Jesuits and Franciscans. Then came Archbishop Kenrick of St. Louis, and after him the Papal Delegate and Count Muccioli in the uniform of the Noble Guard. Last of all walked the cardinal-elect. The procession wended its way into the cathedral and there, in front of the high altar, in the presence of that distinguished religious company and with impressive ceremony, James Gibbons was elevated to the exalted station of a prince of the Church.

Following the ceremony at the cathedral a dinner was held at St. Mary's Seminary at which the new cardinal presided, clad in his scarlet robes. The celebration was continued throughout the city until far into the night with illuminations and the burning of red fires which lit up buildings decorated with the Stars and Stripes and banners of the Papacy.

For the next thirty-five years Baltimore saw much of Cardinal Gibbons. He was honored everywhere as its first citizen. He made several visits to Rome and his return invariably was the excuse for a public demonstration in which the Mayor of the city, the Governor of Maryland and other dignitaries took part. Crowds met him at the station and accompanied him to his residence on Charles Street, east of the cathedral. Once he had entered the house the people waited for him to appear at the bay window overlooking the street and acknowledge their applause.

In spite of the fuss that was made over him Cardinal Gibbons remained a simple, modest man. He delighted in walking and almost any fine afternoon found him striding up Charles Street. The only evidence of his rank was the edge of the scarlet zuchetta, or skullcap, which could be seen under the edge of his soft black felt hat.

No public meeting was complete without the Cardinal. He shared the platform indiscriminately with Methodists, Jews and Quakers. In 1893 he took part in a so-called Parliament of Religions held in Chicago, appearing on the program as the first speaker. Following immediately after him was one Ameer Ali, a Mohammedan of Calcutta. Once at a mass meeting at Brown Memorial Presbyterian Church a visiting Protestant minister charged Cardinal Gibbons with obstructing reforms in the Belgian Congo whose rule under Leopold II was at the time a world-wide scandal. In an instant a Presbyterian minister and a Methodist minister were on their feet vigorously defending the Cardinal.

The Cardinal's humility and good fellowship were displayed on another occasion when he was taking part in a public function in the company of the clergy of various Protestant denominations. Present also was Bishop Paret, of the Protestant Episcopal Diocese of Maryland. As the procession was forming Bishop Paret turned to the Cardinal and said: "Your Eminence, it is the custom in our church for the inferior to precede the superior. So, if it meets with your approval, I will go first." To this the Cardinal quickly replied, "My dear Brother, we will go together." And so they marched, side by side.

In the hundred years since its organization by Bishop John

Carroll in 1789 the Catholic Church in the United States had experienced a tremendous growth. There were an estimated 40,000 Catholics in 1789; there were 9,000,000 in 1889. Many of them were immigrants to whom this country was new and strange. They were perplexed as to what their attitude should be. In the solution of their problem Cardinal Gibbons was tremendously helpful. He saw the great danger of maintaining and encouraging racial groups in this country. His attitude was expressed in a sermon to a congregation in Milwaukee composed largely of foreign-born persons. "Next to love of God," he exhorted them, "should be love of country. Let us glory in the title of American citizen. It matters not whether this is the land of our birth or adoption. It is the land of our destiny." Little wonder he enjoyed the warm friendship of Grover Cleveland, Theodore Roosevelt and other Presidents.

Cardinal Gibbons joined with Cardinal Manning of England, in defending organized labor at a time when such support created powerful enemies. He helped smooth the way for arbitration when Great Britain and the United States exchanged hot words over Venezuela and he used his influence to put an end to the Louisiana lottery which had become notorious. That last action caused the Rev. Dr. Lyman Abbott, the distinguished Congregationalist, to exclaim in a sermon: "Thank God for Cardinal Gibbons! Long may he wear his red cloak and red cap, and if there should be an election now, and you and I could vote, I would vote to make him Pope."

The Cardinal lived to the ripe age of eighty-seven years. Death came to him quietly in 1921. After a funeral befitting his high ecclesiastical station he was laid to rest in the crypt of the Baltimore Cathedral, beside Archbishop Carroll and his other predecessors in the Archdiocese of Baltimore. No more acceptable compliment was ever paid the city than that of Cardinal Gibbons when, returning from his last visit to Pope Leo XIII and acknowledging the welcome of his fellow citizens he remarked: "No country is so dear to me as America; no place like Baltimore!"

Maryland prides itself on its Act of Religious Toleration which was passed in 1649. The statute is revered as one of the first statements of the principle of the right of the individual to worship God in his own way. Critics have questioned the true significance

of it and Marylanders have not always lived up to its noble purpose. How far Baltimoreans have responded to its influence it
would be hard to say. Yet surely there is exceptional breadth about
a city that has maintained an Episcopal church on the same spot
for 200 years, preserves the ashes of the first Catholic bishop,
and the first Methodist bishop in the United States, witnessed
the labor pains that attended the birth of the United Brethren
Church and the Unitarian Church and contains the landmarks
of this conglomerate church history within the compass of a
square mile of the City Hall.

Chapter 10

"MOBTOWN"

FOR MORE than a century Baltimore was known throughout the nation under the unsavory name of "Mobtown." The title owed its origin to the speed and frequency with which the citizenry found excuse to riot. The Baltimore tough of the 19th century knew no peer. But there also were times when the best citizens took a conspicuous part in these public disorders. In the early days political feeling ran high and politics often was at the bottom of the trouble. However, when the populace was in the mood for going on a rampage almost any reason would do.

The first instance of mob action sufficiently important to become a matter of public record occurred soon after the outbreak of the American Revolution. It involved a clash between the principle of freedom of the press and the call of patriotism. In the summer of 1773, there arrived in Baltimore Town one William Goddard, a Rhode Islander, and his sister Mary. Goddard established the town's first newspaper under the name of the *Maryland Journal and Baltimore Advertiser*. The first number appeared on August 20th and in it editor Goddard announced that "the paper shall be free and of no party." He did a good job of reporting and kept his readers informed of such events as the Boston Tea Party and the Battle of Lexington. Goddard was a versatile man and did not confine himself to journalism. He found the time also to organize a postal system, employing post riders to carry the mail between the larger towns of the colonies.

As the Revolutionary War got going in dead earnest Goddard began to show a critical attitude toward the American cause. When, in 1777, Lord Howe made his peace overtures, the editor used his privilege of free speech to print a letter in the *Journal* giving it high praise. The letter was signed "Tom Tell-truth."

About the same time the patriots of Baltimore organized themselves into the Whig Club. Members swore a solemn oath "to detect all traitors and discover all traitorous conspiracies against the State." When the Tom Tell-truth letter appeared in the columns of the *Journal* the master minds of the Whig Club decided that Goddard met the specifications of the type of public enemy they were after. A committee therefore waited upon him and ordered him to present himself before the club.

This Goddard refused to do. In consequence a crowd of angry men armed with sticks and swords descended upon his house. They were led by Commander James Nicholson, of the Navy, and Colonel Nathaniel Ramsay. Included in the crowd were David Poe, David Stewart and George Turnbull, all members of Baltimore's most prominent families. Commander Nicholson entered the printing room where Goddard stood surrounded by his workmen and seized the editor. This was the signal for a free-for-all.

Goddard was overpowered and dragged down the stairs. A cart was brought up and there were threats of giving him a coat of tar and feathers. Mary Goddard, who had been a witness to all this, begged Captain Galbraith of the town guard to rescue her brother from the mob, but he refused to interfere. Goddard then was ordered to leave town. He lost no time making his way to Annapolis and putting his case before the State authorities. In response Governor Thomas Johnson censured the Whig Club for its riotous and unseemly behavior and sent Goddard back to Baltimore under the protection of the State.

There is no further record of trouble with Goddard until the summer of 1779. He then printed a series of queries which were interpreted by the public as reflecting on the character of George Washington. Again a band of patriots descended on him. This time they were led by Colonel Samuel Smith, then a young man. During his long life Sam Smith was to figure conspicuously in the dramatic events of Baltimore. The party, numbering about thirty, was composed of Continental Army recruits, mulattos, Negroes, pipers and drummers. This motley committee demanded that Goddard appear before their main body at the Coffee House.

Goddard seized a sword and prepared to defend himself. But before matters went further a truce was arranged under which Goddard promised to meet their demand next day. He was as good as his word. He not only showed up but he brought his sword with him. A cart was produced and the proposal was made to haul Goddard through the town with a halter around his neck. Goddard again appealed to the magistrates who as usual sided with the crowd. So he confessed that the queries were the work of Colonel Charles Lee. The mob then forced Goddard to sign an apology begging Washington's pardon. This he retracted two days later. In spite of his waywardness Goddard continued to edit his paper until 1793 when he sold out to a partner and returned to his native Rhode Island.

So far as the record shows Baltimore was free from rioting and mob action until March of 1794. In that month Congress declared a 30-day embargo on foreign commerce, at the time a hot political issue. At its conclusion one Captain Ramsdell lowered his ship's flag to half-mast by way of indicating his displeasure. Seeing this, one Captain David Stodder and other persons of the opposite political persuasion seized Ramsdell and a young man named Senton and tarred and feathered them. These grave disorders occurred on the waterfront at Fell's Point. Apprised of what had happened Judge Samuel Chase, a staunch Federalist and a very fiery gentleman, issued a warrant for the arrest of Stodder and other ringleaders of the mob.

On their way to court the prisoners were followed by a crowd marching to the music of fife and drum. Arrived before Judge Chase spokesmen of the mob informed him that, if the prisoners were sent to jail, the mob would tear the jail down and demolish the judge's house for good measure. In reply the judge gave the prisoners a choice of posting bail or going to jail. Though several men of prominence offered security the prisoners refused to accept it.

"Then you must go to jail," declared Judge Chase. Whereupon he ordered the sheriff to seize Captain Stodder. The sheriff refused, replying that it was more than he could do single-handed. The judge suggested that, in that case, he summon a *posse comitatus*. But the sheriff insisted that he could get no one to serve on it. "Summon me, Sir," the judge proposed.

At this point the prominent gentlemen again intervened begging the judge to yield to the mob and warning him that his life was in danger. But Chase stood his ground.

"God forbid," he declared, "that my countrymen should ever be guilty of so daring an outrage; but, Sir, with the blessing of God, I will do my duty. They may destroy my property, they may pull down my house from over my head. Yea, they may make a widow of my wife and my children fatherless. The life of one man is of little consequence compared to the prostration of the laws of the land. With the blessing of God, I will do my duty, be the consequences what they may."

Even a Baltimore mob was not a match for such eloquence. Judge Chase did relent to the extent of giving the prisoners until next day to think it over. And, by the next day, they changed their minds, gave security and the incident was closed. This was the same Judge Chase who later was elevated to the Supreme Court of the United States. His trial before the United States Senate in an unsuccessful effort to impeach him has gone down in history as a *cause célèbre*.

The next threat of mob action occurred fourteen years later. It was a by-product of the trade dispute with England which culminated in the War of 1812. On September 30, 1808, Baltimoreans opened their newspapers and saw before them in bold type an address directed "To the People of Maryland." It stated that the brig *Sophia* had arrived in Baltimore harbor with 720 gallons of Holland gin in her hold. On the way across the Atlantic the *Sophia* had been overhauled by a British man o'war, forced to put into an English port and, in accordance with a British order in council, made to pay a tax on her cargo before being allowed to proceed on her voyage.

Immediately on publication of the address a town meeting was called and a protest raised against the payment of this "infamous tribute." By public acclaim a decision was reached to burn the gin. The owner, knowing the temper and ferocity of Baltimore mobs, concluded that discretion was the better part of valor, and agreed to the destruction of his property. The day set for the execution was October 4th. A monster parade was organized. In the van were 1,200 horsemen, preceded by a trumpeter. Following in line were 400 sailors and, after the sailors, ordinary civilians to the estimated number of 1,000. A conspicuous feature of the procession was a full-rigged barge on wheels from whose rigging were suspended patriotic slogans.

The procession moved out to Hampstead Hill on the east of the town where Patterson Park now lies. Here already was assembled a throng of some 15,000 people. The 1,200 horsemen formed a circle and in the center of the circle was erected a gallows. On the gallows was stacked the 720 gallons of gin. A band struck up "Yankee Doodle," a torch was applied, flames leaped high in the air and, to the accompaniment of the cheers of the crowd, the gin was consumed by the flames. The Boston Tea Party has been signalized as one of the outstanding events in American history. But, alas! the Baltimore Gin Party not only has been ignored by the nation but is unknown even to most Baltimoreans.

It was the outrageous behavior of the mob in the summer of 1812 that was most responsible for Baltimore's notoriety as "Mobtown." As in the Goddard incident in the Revolution a fiery editor was again responsible. A few days before, Congress had declared war on Great Britain, a step to which the Federalists were bitterly opposed. Baltimore was a Republican stronghold and most of the people were in favor of the war. Nevertheless Alexander C. Hanson, a Federalist editor and publisher of the *Federal Republican*, a Baltimore newspaper, printed a strong editorial lamenting the war.

June 22nd a mob armed with axes, hooks and other implements descended upon Hanson's printing office, pulled down the building and destroyed the press. The mayor of the town and a judge of the local court were on the scene but took no action to halt the destruction. Hanson left town. But on July 26th he was back again accompanied by a group of Federalist friends. Prominent among them was Richard Henry Lee, "Light Horse Harry" of Revolutionary fame and father of Robert Edward Lee, then a child of five years. Hanson and his friends took over a house on Charles Street and strengthened it against attack. Then, on July 27th, they issued a paper containing another inflammatory article against the war.

Nothing happened during the day. But as darkness fell around 8 P.M. a carriage was seen to drive up to the door and deliver some muskets. A group of boys collected across the street and began to stone the house; Hanson's group inside retaliated by firing muskets from the windows. Meanwhile the crowd was growing larger and more menacing every minute. At last a charge was made on the house, window sashes were smashed and an attempt was made to batter down the front door. This was met by more gunfire from the house and one of the attackers was killed.

Now at last the authorities took steps to quell the riot. The militia arrived on the scene and opened negotiations with the inmates of the house. Hanson and his friends agreed to surrender on a guarantee of being escorted to the city jail. Pursuant to this arrangement at 7 A.M. on July 28th, Colonel Lee and twenty-one other persons filed out of the house, and gave themselves up. Upon their departure the mob broke into the house, destroyed all the furniture and wrecked the interior. Meanwhile the prisoners reached the jail in safety, the mob dispersed and quiet prevailed throughout the town. The authorities were so confident the trouble was over that they dismissed the militia.

But it was the calm before the storm. No sooner had night come than a crowd began to gather in front of the jail. Finding that the militia had left, it stormed the building, overpowered the jailer and, with clubs and other weapons, set out to massacre the unarmed and defenseless prisoners. One was killed immediately; eleven others were brutally beaten and tortured. Eight, presumed to be dead, were thrown out in front of the jail. They were saved only by lying still. Its appetite for blood sated the mob departed from the scene leaving its victims in agony behind. "Light Horse" Harry Lee never recovered from the terrible beating he received. Following this unhappy incident, the bloodiest and most brutal in Baltimore's history, members of the mob were brought to trial. But all of them were acquitted.

This outburst at least created an immunity against mob action for a long period. It took more than twenty years for the cycle to come around again. But when it did the mob fever broke out with all its accustomed virulence.

The year 1835 was distinguished for the Bank riot. In the spring of 1834 the Bank of Maryland closed its doors; one of a number of financial institutions which failed, resulting in loss to the public of several millions of dollars. For seventeen months creditors of the bank waited for a settlement; but none was forthcoming. At last their patience was exhausted. Among the directors of the bank was Reverdy Johnson, a prominent lawyer and leader in the community who lived in a handsome house on fashionable Monument Square. On August 6, 1835, a small crowd moved on Mr. Johnson's house and showed its displeasure by smashing his windows. This seemed to satisfy its desire for redress and it dispersed.

Fearing a renewal of the disorder Mayor Jesse Hunt himself

undertook to guard the Johnson house. He was assisted by bail-
iffs, watchmen and a number of citizens. During the evening of
Friday, August 7th, a hostile crowd appeared and, regardless of
the presence of the Mayor and guard, proceeded to smash a few
more windows. Mayor Hunt addressed the crowd and at last persuaded it to leave.

More trouble was expected next evening so the Mayor this time
summoned thirty armed horsemen to his support and formed a
cordon across the entrance to the square. About 7 P.M. a large
crowd congregated in Baltimore Street and marched north on
Calvert running into the Mayor and his guard. Brickbats were
hurled but the guard stood fast. The crowd, thwarted in its attempt to break through, suddenly changed its plan and marched
off to the Charles Street home of John Glenn, another director.
The Glenn house was without a guard but the door had been
barricaded. The mob first smashed the windows then broke down
the front door, burst into the house, threw the furniture out into
the street and proceeded methodically on its job of demolition.
It did not stop until the whole of the front wall had been torn
down. This time special guards and police arrived on the scene,
but though they fired into the mob they could not make it disperse.

Next day, which was Sunday, the mob returned to the Reverdy
Johnson house. It broke in, sacked the house, hurled Mr. Johnson's valuable law library out into the street and made a bonfire of
it. As in the case of the Glenn house the greater part of the front
wall was torn down. By now all semblance of law and order had
vanished and the mob took full control of the town. It next attacked and pillaged the house of John B. Morris, still another director, and that of Mayor Hunt. It then wreaked its vengeance on
the residences of Evan T. Ellicott, a Captain Bentzinger and a
Captain Willy whose only fault had been to protest the action of
the mob. Baltimore fully merited the name of Mobtown that
Sunday night while the populace pursued its grim work of destruction by the light of the bonfires and amid the shouts of the
throng, the discharge of small arms, bloody fist fights and the
crashing down of walls.

Unless Baltimore was to be leveled to the ground by its own
people it was evident that something drastic had to be done. In
this critical hour, as in 1814 when the British assaulted the city,

the better element turned for leadership to General Sam Smith. He had saved the city from the invader; could he save it from the blind rage of its own people? The General was now an old man of eighty-three years, yet he rose boldly to the occasion. A mass meeting was held at the Exchange building. Mayor Hunt resigned. General Smith took over and called for volunteers to march with him to Howard's Park, which was on a hill to the north of the town where the newly completed monument to George Washington stood. A great crowd immediately responded to the General's appeal. He gave them instructions to get arms and assemble at the City Hall. When it was marshaled his force numbered 3,000, more than enough to overawe the mob. Before General Smith took over an appeal for help had gone out to Annapolis and Washington and Federal troops were already on their way. But they were not needed. By the time they arrived the mob had disbanded, the town was quiet and there was nothing for the troops to do.

There was one change in the normal pattern of rioting in Baltimore. In this instance the best legal talent was represented among the victims of the mob. Probably on that account the full force of the law was brought to bear on the miscreants. The ringleaders were singled out, brought to trial, fined and imprisoned. Those citizens whose houses had been wrecked and property destroyed filed suits for damage against the State of Maryland for its failure to protect them. They won their cases and the State paid them a total of $100,000.

A striking example of Baltimore's virtually psychopathic urge to mob violence is found in the Nunnery Riot of August 18, 1839. On that day a woman wearing the habit of a nun was seen running through the streets of East Baltimore. She begged protection from passersby declaring that she had escaped from imprisonment in the Carmelite Convent nearby on Aisquith Street. In short order her dramatic story and her entreaties drew a large crowd around her. Somebody suggested a march on the convent.

The Bank Riot had occurred only four years before and the memory of its excesses was still vivid. Sheppard C. Leakin had succeeded General Sam Smith as Mayor of the city and he was summoned to the scene. He begged the crowd, which had become very excited by this time, to keep the peace. While the Mayor was pleading with it a hurry call was sent out for the City Guard. To this was added 200 special policemen as well as many volunteers. So the convent soon had an impressive number of protectors who stood guard over it throughout the night. Meantime the woman who had been the cause of all the excitement was questioned by the authorities and examined by the medical faculty of Washington University nearby which found her to be insane. The authorities and the doctors at last succeeded in convincing the public of the facts and proving that there was really no need to tear down the convent.

The 1850's in Baltimore were distinguished for another outburst of rioting. These disorders were entirely political, in large part inspired by the Know-Nothing Party, a national political organization violently opposed to the foreign-born immigrants. Throughout Baltimore the Know-Nothings were organized into political clubs bearing such suggestive names as the "Plug-Uglies," "Rough Skins," "Rip-Raps," "Blood Tubs," "Black Snakes," and "Tigers." Activities of these 19th-century gangsters were not confined to politics. The Baltimore police force was corrupted and crime went unpunished. Conditions grew so bad that respectable citizens did not dare go about alone in the street after dark for fear of being set upon by toughs. Election days resembled a battle. Muskets and pistols were used freely. In one instance a cannon was brought into action. In an election in 1856, eight persons were killed and more than 250 wounded.

At last decent people were stirred to action. The best citizens in the community organized themselves into the City Reform Association, a non-partisan group whose object was to clean up the mess. To show its strength the Association held a large and enthusiastic mass meeting in Monument Square on September 8, 1859. In a last gesture of defiance the old political clubs staged a rival mass meeting in the same place a few days before the November election. A favorite weapon of the Know-Nothings was a shoemaker's awl. This was used to jab voters of the opposing party and drive them away from the polls. So brazen were the Know-Nothings by this time that they brought to their meeting enormous models of the awls as well as banners and placards displaying clenched fists and bleeding heads. The crowd was addressed by Henry Winter Davis, the town's outstanding rabble-rouser. As he spoke, there stood below the platform a forge at which blacksmiths fashioned awls to be used at the coming election.

Like others which had preceded it the 1859 election was violent. But, in spite of the bullying tactics of the clubs, the reform bills were passed. Foremost among them was one directing the reorganization of the police. To free the force from the control of the political clubs in the city it was turned over to the Governor of Maryland. And there it remains to this day. In the election of 1860 not a shot was fired nor a knife drawn. An old inhabitant of "Mobtown" would not have recognized it as a true example of the democratic processes as they had recently been practiced in Baltimore.

The reformed police force did not have to wait long for a major test. Its trial came on April 19, 1861, in the bloody riot which attended the progress of the 6th Massachusetts Infantry across the town. In this instance the Mayor of the city and the Marshal of police performed their duty courageously and well at the risk of their lives. Yet, ironically enough, both the Mayor and the Marshal were relieved of their official duties and held under arrest by the Federal military authorities.

The summer of 1877 saw a revival of the mob spirit in connection with the Baltimore & Ohio Railroad strike of that year. During the protracted depression that followed the Civil War the railroad, like others throughout the country, lost money and felt it had to cut the wages of its employes. The brakemen and firemen retaliated by striking. Rioting first broke out in Cumberland where important shops of the road were located. The Governor of Maryland ordered the 5th Regiment of the State militia, stationed in Baltimore, to go to Cumberland and restore order. At the same time the 6th Maryland Regiment was to repair to its armory to act as a reserve.

The 5th set out for Camden Station to entrain. On arrival there the militiamen were set upon by a large crowd that reached the station ahead of them. The mob was finally dispersed but not until it had set fire to several engines, passenger cars and part of the station platform. Next day was Sunday, always a favorite day with Baltimore rioters, and the mob reassembled at the station. Though it numbered several thousand it was controlled by the police and some 200 of its members were arrested. On this occasion the regular police handled the situation so well there was no need to use the Marines, artillery and 500 special police which arrived on the scene.

The bitter election of 1895 was attended by another outburst of violence though on a minor scale. Once more the polls had got into the hands of a corrupt political machine, and once more the respectable element in the city was aroused from its customary political lethargy. The Reform League was organized to insure an honest count of the votes, and a call was sent out for volunteer watchers. Among those who responded was Howard A. Kelly, a young man just beginning his distinguished career as one of the great surgeons of the new Johns Hopkins Medical School and of the Johns Hopkins Hospital.

Dr. Kelly was assigned to the Marsh Market, an especially tough neighborhood. Tradition has it that he appeared for duty in a golf cap and knickers, in themselves enough to start a riot in that neighborhood. Though Dr. Kelly was small in stature he survived the day with only minor injuries. Another volunteer was Leigh Bonsal, a member of one of Baltimore's old families, a graduate of Harvard and a rising lawyer. Mr. Bonsal had been a football player and was stoutly built. A hostile crowd surrounded him, swept him off his feet and trampled him unmercifully before he could be rescued. But this was child's play compared to the brutality and carnage of the old days.

Baltimore's last demonstration of mob action took place on April 1, 1917, on the eve of the convening of the extraordinary session of Congress called by President Wilson to decide whether this country should declare war on Germany. As in the cases of Goddard and the Whig Club and of Hanson and the war party of 1812 the conflict on this occasion arose between groups favoring and opposing the declaration.

A group of Baltimoreans opposed to the war arranged a mass meeting of protest at the Academy of Music. It had as its chief speaker Dr. David Starr Jordan, then Chancellor of Leland Stanford University. Among the local sponsors were Mr. and Mrs. A. Morris Carey, prominent members of the Society of Friends, William F. Cochran, a man with a passion for supporting minority causes, the Rev. Richard W. Hogue, an Episcopal clergyman with

Socialistic views, and the Rev. Dr. Peter Ainslie, a Congregational Minister similarly inclined.

The meeting was attended also by a group of young men who were not at all in sympathy with its aims. Some of them were members of Battery A, a National Guard outfit recently formed by young men of social prominence. There were prowar sympathizers outside the theater as well. They included such well-known Baltimoreans as C. Harry Reeves, Carter G. Osburn, Jr., Louis McLane Merryman, Robert G. Lowndes, J. Allison Muir, William D. Tipton and Douglas Ober. Muir was to lose his life in the war while Tipton was destined for a distinguished career in the nation's stripling air force.

Disgusted with the trend of the speeches at the meeting Carter G. Osburn went outside and, raising a large United States flag, paraded up and down Howard Street until he had attracted a crowd of several thousand people. Someone suggested that they stampede the meeting and the proposal met with a favorable response. Dr. Jordan was in the middle of his speech when the invaders forced their way past a police guard at the door of the theater, entered the auditorium and marched to the stage.

This demonstration was enough to break up the meeting. Dr. Jordan left the theater by a rear door, a circumstance the local newspapers made much of. On the whole the rioters showed good nature. The only casualties were caused by the police who used their espantoons rather freely and bruised several heads. Next day Congress voted a declaration and that was the end of antiwar demonstrations in Baltimore.

The April 1, 1917 incident had an interesting sequel. Nine years later, in November, 1926, Carter Osburn, who had been a ringleader in the demonstration, addressed an open letter to Dr. Jordan. In it he offered a humble apology for his behavior and concluded "You were motivated by the principles of civilization, while I was motivated by the passions of barbarism."

If Mr. Osburn's theory is accepted then civilization has supplanted barbarism in Baltimore and kept control for more than thirty years.

During World War II the shipbuilding and the mass production of war materials brought thousands of laborers to the city. The arrival of so many strangers necessarily led to severe racial and social tension and it was feared that at any moment serious trouble might break out. Yet the crisis passed without a single instance of mob violence.

The most startling case of provocation was "That Poem." It was alleged to have been written by a warworker involuntarily imprisoned in the city for the duration. This is the way it appeared in the *Evening Sun* in October, 1945:

BELOVED BALTIMORE, MD.

Baltimore, oh Baltimore, you moth-eaten town
Your brick row houses should all be torn down.
Your winters are cold and your summers are hot,
The air is so foul with mildew and rot,
The land of bad colds and sore throat and flu,
Of still aching muscles and pneumonia, too.

You're a blot on the landscape, the nation's eyesore,
Your people are dull-witted and, gad, what a bore!
The home of white steps and bumpy thoroughfares,
With your rough riding street cars and 10-cent fares,
You live among filth and you don't mind the rats,
They thrive on that filth and the scarcity of cats!

You don't speak English, you speak Baltimorese,
And the stench off the bay is what you call breeze.
You make us pay double for all you can sell,
But after the war you can all go to hell.
And when you reach Hades and Satan greets you,
You'll feel right at home—he's from here, too.

Yes, Baltimore, oh Baltimore, it isn't all gravy
To be planted on your doorstep by the Army or Navy.
The WMC and the draft boards, too
Have frozen us here and we're stuck with you.
The worst of it is that you think you are swell,
You think you are perfect and that gripes like hell.

You're dead and rotten; you think you're alive,
You think you're a place; instead you're a dive.
You're not worth this paper, you're not worth this ink,
You can take it from us, Baltimore—YOU STINK! !

Nobody was brought to book for this outrageous libel. Not a stone was hurled or a head broken. For a few days the letter columns of the newspapers sizzled with communications from irate natives asking, "Why don't you go back home?" But that was all. On the contrary most of the community thought it funny. No doubt about it, Baltimore had lost its claim to the title of Mobtown.

Chapter 11

THE HOPKINS AT HOMEWOOD

ON AN ELEVATION on the west side of Charles Street just south of University Parkway stands a handsome Georgian mansion of red brick with a white-columned portico, green-shuttered windows and wings. It is shaded by a grove of beeches and lofty tulip poplars. Like St. Paul's parsonage in the downtown district it belongs to an earlier age. But unlike the parsonage it is not all alone. For farther from the street and partially screened by trees are to be seen numerous other buildings of red brick with white trimming and more white-columned porticoes. These buildings are on a decidedly larger scale but it is obvious that their architectural features were suggested by the mansion. The whole scene is hospitable and inviting. There is an atmosphere of warmth and quiet, associated more with domestic establishments than institutions.

This is the Johns Hopkins University. Rather it is the Homewood campus where are located the graduate and undergraduate departments, the school of engineering and various vocational and extension activities. The medical school is several miles across town on Broadway in proximity to the John Hopkins Hospital.

During the first half of the 19th century there was in the United States no educational institution that bore resemblance to a university according to the European definition of the term. Yale, it is true, gave a Ph. D degree as early as 1861; but faculties in the old-established colleges were too occupied with their undergraduates to devote time and attention to graduate students. The doctorate was not then considered prerequisite to appointment to a teaching position in a college. In 1873 not more than 25 doctorates were conferred in all the American universities and even as late as 1900 the number was still less than 400.

Young men who wished to prepare themselves for teaching by pursuing graduate work therefore went abroad. Their objective usually was either one of the numerous flourishing universities in Germany or the Sorbonne in Paris. This system had two obvious disadvantages: it took the student far away from home, and the lack of a true university in this country gave Europe an unfavorable impression of American scholarship. The question of what was to be done about it was being freely discussed in academic circles here.

Just about the same time Johns Hopkins was approaching the end of a successful career as the leading Baltimore merchant of his day. Being a bachelor he had no direct descendants to whom to pass on his fortune, and he faced the problem of how best to dispose of it. As early as 1867, Mr. Hopkins made his decision. He would leave his money to establish a hospital and a university. The university was to include a medical school to be closely associated with the hospital. In that year a board, whose members he himself had chosen, was incorporated for the purpose of establishing a university for "the promotion of education in the State of Maryland." Simultaneously another act of incorporation was passed for the establishment of a hospital. With two exceptions the boards of the university and of the hospital were composed of the same men.

It was not, however, until 1874, after the death of the founder when his will was probated, that the bequests became effective. There has always been much discussion over what Johns Hopkins had in mind when he spoke of a university. It usually is assumed that he was not aware of the agitation in the academic world for an institution on European lines. It is more reasonable to believe that he envisioned an undergraduate school of the arts and sciences and associated with it professional schools of medicine and law according to the customary American pattern. There are some who hold that, realizing his limitations in matters of education, he deliberately left the terms of his bequest vague.

In the advice he gave his trustees with respect to handling the corpus of the bequest, he made a provision which later was to cause embarrassment to the university. It resulted from the founder's endeavor to kill two birds with one stone. Johns Hopkins was greatly attached to the Baltimore & Ohio Railroad, being a large stockholder and a member of the board. With the help of John W. Garrett, having rid the company of political control, he didn't want it to revert to that control after his death. The primary foundation of the university as set forth in the will was 15,000 shares of common stock in the B. & O. The founder directed the trustees not to touch the principal for construction or current expenses, which proved to be sound advice. Less sound were his instructions to the trustees not to sell the B. & O. stock and to vote it so that the management would be free from politics. The advice served well enough when dividends from the stock amounted to $150,000 a year. But lack of diversification brought financial disaster to the university years later when the railroad went into receivership and the stock stopped paying.

Johns Hopkins showed his shrewd business sense in the selection of his trustees. There were fourteen of them on his original boards. Eight were kinsmen by blood and marriage. At least ten had had the advantage of college or university training. In religious affiliations they presented a composite picture. Seven of them like Hopkins himself, were Quakers; four were Episcopalians, one was a Presbyterian, and one a Swedenborgian. In establishing the foundation for the hospital, Hopkins stated specifically that he wished it to be free from sectarianism. This very soon became also the policy of the university.

The trustees were for the most part business or professional men of insight and intelligence. They took their responsibility very seriously. Among other things they volunteered to take a course of reading the better to fit them for their task. It comprised a comprehensive list of the latest books on education. Their next move was to send committees to visit other universities to see how they were being run. Their third, and perhaps most important move was to invite three of the nation's leading educators—all of them college presidents—to Baltimore for consultation. These advisers were Eliot of Harvard, White of Cornell, and Angell of Michigan. An important result of these consultations was that the trustees began to think of their university as a graduate school after the European model.

Finally the trustees asked their three counselors to recommend a man to head the new institution. Without joint discussion or previous arrangement they returned the same name. It was that of Daniel Coit Gilman, a person then unknown to Baltimore. Gilman was born in 1831 in Norwich, Connecticut, the son of a merchant of that town. He was sent to private schools and from them to Yale where he was graduated in 1852. There followed a year of graduate work at Harvard; and after that a year of diplomacy with the American legation in St. Petersburg. Geography was his special subject. He found time to do quite a bit of traveling in Europe and to attend lectures at the University of Berlin before returning in 1863 to Yale's Sheffield Scientific School as professor of physical and political geography. Thus by the age of thirty two years Gilman had received a far better-rounded education than the average young American and also had seen a good deal of western Europe, then the center of culture.

In 1872 Gilman was called to the newly established University of California as its first president. But the university was involved in politics and he was not happy there. Consequently when the Hopkins trustees began looking for a head and Gilman's name was mentioned by the leading American educators of the day, he was in a receptive mood. The trustees invited him to come to Baltimore and he agreed to meet them there. In the interview which followed Gilman was much impressed with their sincerity and common sense. It was then that he revealed his ambitious plans. The University he proposed was not to be a mere local institution. What he had in mind was one that would extend its influence far and wide to promote scholarship of the highest order. First and foremost in his thoughts was the faculty. It was his plan to pick his men from the top rank in their respective fields, pay them decently, give them enough graduate students to stimulate them and look to them to publish the results of their researches.

These ideas impressed the trustees, they offered Gilman the presidency and he accepted it. For the time being it was agreed that the negotiations were to be kept secret. Therefore to his waiting family in California Gilman wired the cryptic message: "Chesapeake Bay oysters have a fine flavor." The family caught his meaning. The meeting of Gilman and the trustees took place in December, 1874. The following year was devoted to developing plans for the university. In May, 1875, the trustees concluded to postpone for the time being the establishment of schools of law and medicine and to concentrate on a literary and scientific department for graduate students. It was definitely settled between the president and his board that this was to be a university not of buildings but of men. Dr. Gilman set himself to the task of picking his faculty at which he excelled.

The research professors chosen were five in number. In looking for the very best Gilman set no geographic limits. Foremost among them was Joseph Sylvester who came from England, recognized as one of the foremost British mathematicians. He was a graduate of St. John's College, Cambridge. Strange as it seems to us today Sylvester, in spite of his great academic accomplishments was long denied a formal degree from his university because he was Jew.

To head the chemistry department Gilman came upon a young man named Ira Remsen, a native of New York City. Another importation from abroad was Henry Newell Martin, a biologist and an Irishman. Martin was a graduate of the University of London and of Cambridge. More important than that, he had served as assistant to the great English scientist, Thomas Huxley.

From the South came Basil L. Gildersleeve to head the department of the classics. Gildersleeve was born in Charleston, South Carolina, but his father was a New Englander. The younger Gildersleeve was graduated from Princeton in 1848 and from there went abroad to do advanced work in the classics at the German universities of Berlin, Bonn and Gottingen. From Gottingen he got his Ph. D degree and returned home just in time to enter the military service with Lee's Army of Northern Virginia. He was professor 'of Greek at the University of Virginia when he accepted Gilman's call to the Hopkins.

Last of the group of research professors was Henry A. Rowland, a physics prodigy whose genius Gilman discovered when he took him on a trip to Europe. One of Rowland's early reports on his researches was turned down by the leading American publisher of scientific matter on the ground that Rowland was "too young to publish such." Rowland had to send the paper to England where the scientific world was sufficiently informed to appreciate its worth.

With the exception of Sylvester, who was sixty two years old, this first faculty was astoundingly young. Rowland and Martin

were each twenty eight years old. Remsen was thirty. Gilman and
Gildersleeve were but forty five. Yet it was not long before they
were recognized as giants in their respective fields. There was no
false modesty about them. Gildersleeve unhesitatingly admitted
to his intimates that he was the first classical scholar in the United
States. Of Rowland it is told that, in his later years, he was called
to give evidence as an expert witness in a lawsuit. Asked who was
the greatest physicist in the United States he replied calmly, "I
am." When a friend later expressed surprise at such a self-laud-
atory statement Rowland replied that he had no alternative. For
he explained, "I was under oath to tell the truth."

On February 22, 1876, Dr. Gilman was formally inaugurated
as president of the University. It is from that formal occasion
that the Hopkins counts its age. Word of the intellectual renaissance that was taking place in Baltimore went out through the
entire academic world and bright young men from all parts of
the country turned their eyes in that direction. As an added inducement the University offered twenty scholarships of the then
princely sum of $500 each to graduate students. Among the first
to take advantage of the offer were Walter Hines Page, later to
become a distinguished editor and diplomat, and Josiah Royce,
the philosopher. There also was a recent graduate of Princeton
who had gone from there to the law school at the University of
Virginia. He now entered the new university to work for a Ph. D.
He signed himself Thomas W. Wilson. Forty years later he was
to become better known to the world as Woodrow Wilson.

One of the first decisions to be made by the trustees was the
choice of a site for the university. Well to the northeast of the
city John Hopkins had a beautiful and extensive country estate
of over 300 acres of rolling terrain. There was little doubt that he
intended his university to be placed there. But in 1876 Clifton
was far beyond the city limits and altogether inaccessible. There
were no easy means of transportation from the center of the
town, no gas or other modern conveniences. Therefore in the
face of strong popular objection President Gilman and the trustees decided to locate the university on North Howard Street
in the heart of the city.

Indeed by this time many good citizens were looking with a

decidedly jaundiced eye on this whole university business. It was surprising how many people imagined they knew exactly what Johns Hopkins would have wanted done. Now that he was dead they came forward voluntarily to protest the manner in which the trustees were disregarding the wishes of the founder. They called attention to the section of the charter of incorporation which read "to promote education in Maryland." How, they asked, was education in Maryland to be promoted by a school for graduate students from all parts of the country? Obviously what came more closely to the founder's idea would be agricultural and trade schools for deserving Maryland youths. It was bad enough to propose a graduate school. But it was adding insult to injury to place it in the center of the city instead of on the estate which Johns Hopkins had reserved for it. John W. Garrett was so heartily in favor of Clifton that, when the majority of the trustees voted against that site, he resigned from the board.

No whit discouraged by popular disapproval Dr. Gilman and his trustees went right ahead with their plans. A major advantage of the downtown site was that it was within a few minutes' easy walk of the library of the Peabody Institute. This contained a scholarly reference collection of 60,000 volumes such as it would take the university years to assemble. For his graduate students the inside of the Peabody library with its dingy stacks looked more inviting to Gilman than the woodlands, rolling hills and great open spaces around Clifton. This was many, many years before the most important factor in laying out a university was picking a site for the stadium. So it was that the infant university began to take shape on the west side of North Howard Street where it joins Centre. Next-door neighbors were the City College, Baltimore's glorified high school, and the Academy of Music, which was as new as the university. Contemporary accounts described the Academy as being the most modern and beautiful theater in the nation.

In contrast the university's buildings were unimpressive. One of the most important ones, Hopkins Hall, was actually formed by two dwellings thrown together under a single roof and with the dividing wall knocked out. There was, of course, no such thing as a campus, or even a quadrangle. In fact the university was so insignificant and so much a part of the neighborhood that it escaped public notice. Strangers who asked for "the University" were regularly directed blocks away to the medical school and law school of the University of Maryland. Kirby Flower Smith, who later held the chair of Latin, recalled that when he first inquired for the Johns Hopkins he was informed that it was "near the Academy of Music." He went on to say that he walked past it several times without recognizing it. And this was the university that already was beginning to acquire an international reputation!

The neighborhood of Howard and Centre Streets when the university was in session presented the throbbing, feverish enthusiasm of the early days of the Renaissance. Learned societies were organized at a great rate in which faculty members and graduate students met to read and discuss papers. Among them were The Philological Association, the Scientific Association, the Historical and Political Science Club, the Metaphysical Club, the Naturalists' Field Club and the Archeological Society. Popular belief to the contrary, Baltimoreans in those days were not all fox hunters and bons vivants. The town boasted a number of intellectuals, especially among the lawyers and the clergy. These local gentlemen, though not members of the university, were invited to take part in its symposiums. After papers had been read at the various societies they were published. The Johns Hopkins University Press was established to perform this task and was the first press in this country to bear the name of a university. It was this stimulus that led to Baltimore becoming a center for the publication of scholarly works, whether the text called for characters in Sanskrit, complicated mathematical formulae or a print showing a section of the human liver in color.

Although the Hopkins was primarily designed for advanced students it was never without an undergraduate school. In fact Gilman felt that such a school was needed as a feeder for the department of graduate studies. The undergraduates in those days numbered not more than 200 and most of them came from Baltimore and the vicinity. The Hopkins had no dormitories. Graduate and undergraduate students who came from far away found lodging in boarding houses near the university. Two of them, with the conn... ...ce of the sexton, rigged up a room in the mid-section of a church steeple and lived there in great ease and comfort.

In those quaint days money went a long way, so that students thirsty for knowledge could live high in Baltimore on modest incomes. Excellent table board was to be had at the homes of Southern gentlewomen impoverished by the Civil War. Furnished rooms were offered at $6 a month. The equivalent of today's "snack bar" offered sandwiches at a nickel apiece and milk at 3 cents a glass. At nearby Lexington Market bananas, right off the banana boats, brought only 8 cents a dozen.

Most famous among the establishments of the day was the home of Mrs. DuBois Egerton at 132 West Madison Street. This had the reputation for being the leading salon of the South. Mrs. Egerton prided herself on providing her guests with all the deli-cacies for which Baltimore was then famous. At various times one found at Mrs. Egerton's members of the Hopkins faculty and distinguished visiting lecturers. Among those who graced her board were G. Stanley Hall, the pioneer psychologist, James Russell Lowell, William James and Sidney Lanier, the poet, and his family. Tradition has it that Oliver Wendell Holmes was once a guest there and that it was Mrs. Egerton's table he had in mind when he coined his famous phrase about Baltimore being the gas-tronomic center of the universe.

On McCulloh Street, to the northwest of the university in a distinctly Scotch Presbyterian neighborhood, was another popu-lar boarding house where Woodrow Wilson lived while working on his doctorate. Here he returned with his family in later years when he came to lecture at the university. These lectures from the start were an important feature of the university and also of the community, since they generally were open to the public. They have continued to be an important feature to the present day.

One of the most famous took place on the opening of the first session of the university. The day was September 12, 1876, and the lecturer was Thomas Huxley. It was a bold choice for Gilman to make. For Huxley was a disciple of Charles Darwin and the American public was still reeling from its impact with the *Origin of Species* which seemed to them a negation of all they had been taught in the Bible to believe. Baltimoreans may have nodded assent when, in his inaugural address six months before, Gilman laid down the expostulate that, "Religion has nothing to fear from science, and science need not be afraid of religion." But they had not expected the theory to be put so quickly to a practical test.

A Baltimore newspaper seized upon the arrival of Huxley to proclaim that there was "no more frightful heresy" than the theory of evolution. But despite their qualms, the Baltimoreans filled every seat in the Academy of Music for Huxley's lecture. When it was over the severest criticism leveled at the meeting was that it had not been opened with prayer.

Because the student body was small there were frequent opportunities for informal social meetings between students and faculty impossible in larger institutions. It was a regular custom for professors to invite their students in to family dinner. Morris, of the Latin Department, made a practice of calling in his young men periodically and regaling them with oysters, beer, cigars and classical allusions. It was not long before a Johns Hopkins University Club was organized with rooms behind the fashionable grocery store of Jordan Stabler. Inviting food was brought in from Gordon's restaurant across the way. Gordon's, through its strategic location on Madison Street, was for years a popular institutions among undergraduates. Here they would gather at night for beer and pretzels or a light repast. A city ordinance then required that, after midnight, restaurants should be closed to all except registered guests. So at Gordon's, when the clock struck twelve, a hotel register was passed around the tables for signatures. The Hopkins undergraduates delighted in setting down the names of all the dignitaries in town. Cardinal Gibbons would have been astonished—and no doubt amused—had he known how often, according to the register, he was a guest at Gordon's.

All things considered it would have been difficult to find in any academic community a happier and more enthusiastic band of scholars than the one which assembled around North Howard Street in the early days of the university. Yet already sinister forces were at work to upset the serenity of the place. In his first inaugural President Gilman touched briefly on a delicate issue. It was that of admitting women to the university. Even at that early date the feminist movement was beginning to give trouble. The good doctor remarked that he hoped for the establishment of a women's college in the city. For, said he, he did not wish to expose women to the "rougher influences found in colleges and universities where young men resort." That should have settled the matter surely. But it did not. "Rough influences" or not, would-be students began to knock at the door. The university was still in swaddling clothes when a Miss Nunn sought admission to regular courses in biology. Her request involved no complications; it was promptly denied.

Soon thereafter another application was made which, because of a personal consideration, gave the trustees considerably more food for thought. The applicant this time was Miss M. Carey Thomas, a recent graduate of Cornell. The personal consideration was that she happened to be the daughter of Dr. James Carey Thomas, a member of the Board of Trustees. How could the trustees gracefully refuse the daughter of one of their colleagues? Miss Thomas's ambition was a master's degree in Greek which involved work under the great Gildersleeve.

In their dilemma the trustees attempted a compromise. They ruled that Miss Thomas might be guided in her studies by members of the faculty and take examinations. But she was refused permission to attend Dr. Gildersleeve's seminars. There is a story to the effect that she was told she might sit behind a screen and listen to the learned discussions on the other side. Whatever the offer Miss Thomas declined it. She said it would merely make her a special student of Dr. Gildersleeve. The rebuff, however, did not discourage her. She contrived to take some courses at the Hopkins and completed her graduate work in Europe, helped organize Bryn Mawr College, eventually became its president. She also headed the woman suffrage movement, thus making herself even more objectionable to reactionary gentlemen who continued to believe firmly that woman's place is in the home.

It devolved upon a devoted friend of Miss Thomas and companion in mischief to bring the trustees to heel. The lady was

Miss Mary Garrett, daughter of John W. Garrett, president of the Baltimore & Ohio Railroad and former Hopkins trustee. At the very moment the university lost its income from the B. & O. the Hopkins medical school was just getting started and in pressing need of funds. The ladies were quick to take advantage of the university's financial embarrassment to further their own ends. A committee of feminists headed by Mrs. Nancy Morris Davis offered the university a gift of $100,000, but on one condition. It must agree to admit women to the medical school. The financial predicament of the trustees was so acute that they had to pocket their pride, act counter to their better judgment and accept the gift on these terms.

The $100,000 was not enough. Miss Garrett, however, offered $360,000 more on the same condition. Again the trustees had to eat humble pie. But their defeat was not complete. Even though they had to accept women in the medical school they still reserved the right to exclude them from undergraduate premedical courses. They also managed to keep them out of all graduate departments until 1907. Before they were admitted, however, the head of the department had to give his consent. In retrospect it is hard to determine which party was more culpable in bringing this desirable reform about—the women who would descend to blackmail or the men who permitted themselves to be bribed.

The "female undergraduate problem" solved itself in a most satisfactory manner. In spite of the opinion of learned educators to the contrary, women persisted in their claim that they had minds and were capable of profiting by higher education. In Baltimore this persistence resulted in the founding of the Woman's College of Baltimore under the auspices of the Baltimore Conference of the Methodist Episcopal Church. The new institution received its charter in 1885 and opened its doors to students in 1888. In the year 1910 it changed its name to Goucher College in honor of its benefactor and second president, the Rev. Dr. John F. Goucher.

Goucher recently has moved from its restricted quarters in town to the purer atmosphere of Hampton, in Baltimore County. From the very beginning its aim has been to make available to women the very highest standards of scholarship. So young women have not needed to go to the Hopkins for their undergraduate training, and run the risk of the rude contacts with men which alarmed Gilman. Goucher can give them all they need. Relations with the Hopkins, though most cordial, are strictly social and—let it be hoped—when Hopkins men are on their best behavior.

The decision to build the university in downtown Baltimore proved not to be too farsighted. Very soon small businesses and other undesirable neighbors began to encroach upon the property. The advent of the streetcar added greatly to the noise of the downtown district while at the same time it enabled more people to move into the suburbs. It began to dawn upon Dr. Gilman that the present location was untenable and there would have to be a shift to a place where there was more tranquility and less congestion.

In the summer of 1894 the president of the university was on an outing in Chesapeake Bay as guest of Mr. William Keyser on the latter's yacht. Mr. Keyser was the wealthiest of the university's trustees. His father, Samuel S. Keyser, was a Pennsylvanian of Dutch ancestry who came to Baltimore in the early 1800's and prospered. William, too, had amassed a handsome fortune with his copper works and various other industrial enterprises. The sunshine, the cooling breeze, the blue waters of the bay and the comfortable deck of the yacht all combined to create a seductive atmosphere. Dr. Gilman was convinced that this was a propitious time to set to work solving the university's most pressing problem. First he remarked quietly that the Howard Street site was too small, too noisy and too dirty and that a move to the country was necessary. Then, after a pause, he turned to his host looked him in the eye and declared: "Mr. Keyser, I think you are the only man who can do this!"

Dr. Gilman wielded an uncanny power over his trustees that many another college president must have envied. The record does not show that Mr. Keyser made the slightest protest. He fell in with Gilman's proposal. In 1895 Clifton was sold to the city for a public park and ceased to be a consideration, and in 1898 a solution offered itself so appropriately that it is hard to believe it was not actually inspired by Mr. Keyser.

Living on an estate of 60 acres in the northern outskirts of

Baltimore was William Wyman, Mr. Keyser's first cousin. Another 60 acres adjoining was owned by William Wyman's brother Samuel who made his home in New York. Both the Wymans were widowers and Samuel was childless. It was presumed that at his death he would leave his Baltimore property to William. One day William Wyman remarked to Mr. Keyser that he was anxious to protect his estate against the city which was rapidly advancing in his direction. In order to do this he had thought of giving part of his property to the city as a public park and the rest to the Johns Hopkins University and Hospital. Mr. Keyser immediately saw in this proposal the possibility of a solution to his problem. He realized also that for its purpose the university would need Samuel's 60 acres as well as the 60 acres of his brother. He therefore encouraged William Wyman in his idea and urged him to take up the matter with his brother.

But the proposal failed to appeal to brother Samuel. In fact Samuel cared so little for it that he changed his will and left his property to a sister instead of to brother William. Then he died. By this time William Keyser was convinced that the Wyman properties were the perfect site for the university. From the trustees of Samuel Wyman's estate he wheedled an option on the 60 acres. He himself made a gift to the university of $200,000 and persuaded other friends to donate tracts of land to round out the property. William Wyman was induced also to make a gift of his property at once, retaining only the right to occupy the house on it during his life and that of his only daughter.

The matter had been so deftly handled that on the University's Commemoration Day on February 22, 1902, Mr. Keyser was in a position to announce that 180 acres had been given without condition to the university for its new site. Other friends of the university were so inspired by this display of generosity that in short order they pledged a gift of $1,000,000. Thus the university was assured a new home. The deal went through barely in time. In 1903 Mr. Wyman died. In 1904 Mr. Keyser died and that same year occurred the Great Fire.

The new site of the university was once the property of Charles Carroll of Carrollton. The estate bore the name of Homewood, the origin of which is obscure. In 1800 Carroll deeded land to his only son Charles for the site of a dwelling on the occasion of his marriage to Harriet Chew of Philadelphia. On it young Charles commenced the charming brick structure that now looks down on Charles Street from the university grounds. The interior was finished with mahogany doors, white woodwork, handsomely carved mantels and other elaborate ornamentation. The Carrolls moved into the uncompleted house in the summer of 1802. Thereafter, in keeping with local custom, young Carroll assumed the name Charles Carroll of Homewood to distinguish him from his father, Charles Carroll of Carrollton, as well as from Charles Carroll the Barrister whose country seat was Mount Clare.

Sad to relate, the palatial house failed to bring happiness to Charles Carroll and his bride. Soon thereafter they were divorced. In 1839 the property, including the house, was purchased by Samuel Wyman the elder, and from him passed to his sons. The graceful lines of the mansion can be traced in Gilman Hall, the Johns Hopkins University Club and other structures. Another charming red brick building with an ornate cupola dates from the same period. It actually was the Homewood stable. To undergraduates of today it is popularly known as "The Barn." Since most of them are city boys they could not well be expected to distinguish between a stable and a barn.

In 1901, having arrived at the age of seventy years, Dr. Gilman retired from the presidency, honored on all sides as one of the greatest educators of his day. Dr. Charles W. Eliot of Harvard, one of Gilman's three original sponsors, was on hand to contribute to the encomiums showered upon him. Before the assembled company Eliot testified that the Harvard Graduate School had been a feeble thing until the example of Johns Hopkins forced the faculty to put their energy into the development of instruction for graduate students. "And," he added, "what was true of Harvard was true of every other university in the land which aspired to create an advanced school of arts and sciences."

Gilman was succeeded in office by his right-hand man, Dr. Remsen, who reluctantly abandoned his beloved chemical laboratory to take up the uncongenial task of administration. Remsen stuck at it doggedly for ten years, then turned in his resignation in 1912. He was followed by Dr. Frank Johnson Goodnow, a professor of law at Columbia University. Goodnow came to the Hopkins by way of China where he acted for a time as adviser to China's first president, Huan Shi-Kai. It was during the administrations of Remsen and Goodnow that the university moved to Homewood. The major construction of academic buildings and a dormitory was accomplished under Goodnow.

Universities are notoriously in need of money and the Hopkins has been no exception. Since the founding there have been some nine special campaigns for funds. It has been estimated that the gifts received from friends during its life have been more than ten times the value of the original gift of Johns Hopkins.

In all the university has had six presidents. Dr. Goodnow resigned in 1929 and was succeeded by Dr. Joseph A. Ames, professor of physics and the university's dean. Dr. Ames was affectionately known as "Joe" by faculty, graduate students, undergraduates and townsmen. He was sixty five years old when he took office and his was generally regarded as an interim appointment. But during the five years of his incumbency he displayed surprising zeal and was every inch a college president. He brought both dignity and homespun wisdom to the task. As a physicist he contributed largely to the theory of aeronautics and the development of the airplane in this country.

On a less exalted plane an astounding and original contribution to academic thinking in this country was his expressed belief that it is "most improper for an institution of learning itself to charge admission fees for athletic contests." Equally astounding is the fact that, shortly after the retirement of Dr. Ames, the Hopkins actually put the principle into practice. Thus simply it solved the problem of commercialism in athletics. It has had to pay no lip service to a "sanity code." There are no athletic scholarships and the football coach does not rank above the president of the university. Some day when our universities and colleges grow up and gain true sanity in place of a "sanity code," Joe Ames of the Hopkins will be revered as a pioneer in the return to amateur standards.

On his seventieth birthday Dr. Ames stepped down to make way for Dr. Isaiah Bowman. Like Gilman, Dr. Bowman was a geographer with a Yale and Harvard background. He is remembered chiefly for his leadership of the Hopkins' effort in World War II. Under him the university's physicists played an important part in the development of the atomic bomb and guided missiles. Dr. Bowman himself was useful as a specialist with the United States delegation both at Dumbarton Oaks and San Francisco in the creation of the United Nations. He, too, resigned on reaching the age of seventy years, and died shortly thereafter. He was succeeded by Dr. Detlev Bronk, a physicist of the University of Pennsylvania.

The Hopkins has always had an undergraduate department but it has been relatively small. It has been overshadowed by the graduate school and lost in the great city about it. Hopkins undergraduates have been too few in number to riot and defy the police. Besides, many of them live at home. In consequence the Hopkins has been decidedly lacking in the drama associated with other campuses. College life for the undergraduate has been limited to membership in a fraternity, activities at the "Y" and occasional dances. The only undergraduate activity that gives the Hopkins distinction among other of the nation's universities and colleges is the lacrosse team.

In consequence Baltimore's young men who are in search of glamor go in throngs to Princeton. In smaller numbers they are found at Yale, Harvard, Dartmouth, Cornell and Williams and in universities to the South.

At one of the early commemoration days shortly after the founding of the university the orator was Severn Teackle Wallis, a lawyer distinguished for his eloquence. He asked his audience to imagine a Spanish galleon crammed with ingots of silver sailing into the Baltimore harbor and unloading its precious cargo for free and equal distribution among all the citizens. The tangible and enduring worth of a great university would, he concluded, exceed such largess a thousandfold. In the more than seventy years of its existence the Hopkins has proved to be an asset of incalculable value to the community. It has educated many of Baltimore's sons and some of its daughters. It has made and is making scientific studies of local soils and of the marine life of Chesapeake Bay. It has provided professional advice on traffic problems and tested materials used in the building of State and city roads. It has done its share toward developing weapons in time of war.

As Gilman intended, the Hopkins has contributed magnificent-ly to American scholarship. During the 75 years of its existence, 116 of its alumni have served as presidents of various universities and colleges. Over 3,000 of its sons have devoted their lives to university and college training. That is exclusive of the graduates of its medical school. Of the ten institutions in the United States having the largest number of alumni among the scientists of great distinction figures recently showed Harvard leading with 507 and the Hopkins second with 291. The accepted criterion of distinction in the field of science is membership in the National Academy of Sciences. A few years ago of its 447 members, 46, or over 10 per cent, were either alumni of the Hopkins or members of its faculty.

Though Baltimoreans may be clumsy in expressing their emo-tions they have a profound appreciation of the galleon that the plodding Johns Hopkins filled with treasure and headed for the port.

Chapter 12

SOCK AND BUSKIN

On the north side of Fayette Street between Howard and Eutaw stands a drab three-story red brick building with brown trimming that would escape the notice of passersby were it not for the billboards at each side of the main entrance and a canopy extending over the sidewalk. A mansard roof with dormer windows makes a pretense at being a fourth floor, but the sham is immediately revealed when it is looked at from either side. Like an elderly spinister in the presence of a teenager the ancient structure seems to be reproving the frivolous behavior of a flashy new motion-picture house across the way.

This is Ford's Theater. In spite of its forbidding aspect it is probably as intimately associated with the history of the American stage as any other surviving structure in this country. It is the refuge of the last vestige of the professional legitimate stage in Baltimore whose record goes back to colonial days. The legends of the great actors, who throughout some two centuries have performed for Baltimore audiences, are an important part of local tradition.

In the spring of 1752 a theatrical company set sail from England under the management of one Lewis Hallam. It was popularly known as the American Company. Arrived in this country it repaired to Williamsburg, Virginia, and established a theater which is reputed to have been the first opened in America by a company of regular players. Almost simultaneously a theater was erected in Annapolis and two members of Hallam's troupe—Messrs. Wynell and Herbert—appeared as the chief actors. There is even a suggestion that the plays may have been performed in Annapolis while the American Company was still waiting for the theater in Williamsburg to be made ready. Annapolis then was a flourishing metropolis and the center of a fashionable society while Baltimore was still a frontier outpost.

However Hallam seems to have been willing to put on a play wherever there was a prospect of finding an audience. How soon

[174]

he considered Baltimore worth his while is not quite certain. A market house at Gay and Baltimore Streets may have been used as a theater some time between the years 1751-1763. But it is not until around 1773 that Hallam's name appears in association with one Douglas in the staging of plays in a warehouse at Baltimore and Frederick Streets. The producers must have been well received for they next built a small theater at Lombard and Albemarle Streets, and continued to produce plays there until the outbreak of the Revolution. During hostilities plays were forbidden and Hallam retired to the West Indies for the duration.

Meanwhile in 1781 the town's first brick theater was built on East Baltimore Street, and on January 15, 1782, it was formally opened with Shakespeare's *King Richard III.* Judging by the number of times it was presented this play must have been a prime favorite with Baltimore audiences. Perhaps the offer of a kingdom for a horse appealed to the local fox hunters.

In 1785 Hallam returned from exile and first resumed his productions in Philadelphia. Being coldly received there he came to Baltimore accompanied by a fellow actor, John Henry. In Baltimore a warmer welcome awaited them. Yet they were not sure of their ground. Henry's position was all the more ambiguous because he had rheumatism, walked with great difficulty, and in consequence acquired a coach in which to travel between his home and the theater. In those days ownership of a coach by an actor was considered presumptuous. To forestall public criticism Henry had a pair of crutches, crossed,emblazoned on the door of his coach and under them the inscription "This, or These."

Even today Baltimoreans are prejudiced against anything smacking of affectation. But they do make allowances for members of the theatrical profession. A popular saying is that when a man is seen on the street in Baltimore carrying a cane he is either lame or an actor.

The year 1794 was epochal in the theatrical history of Baltimore. Two years before a member of Hallam's Old American Company named Wignell broke away from it and entered partnership in the show business with one Reinagle, described as a Philadelphian and a professor of music. Together they built a theater on Holliday Street. Under the name of The New Theater it was opened to the public on September 25, 1795, with a variety of fare which included a comedy, dances, overtures and a comic opera. Playbills enjoined the ladies and gentlemen who bought their tickets at the box office to bring the exact change. The suggestion also was made that servants be sent to the theater before a quarter to five o'clock in the evening to hold seats for their masters. They were then to withdraw as soon as the company was seated and *on no account were they to remain to see the show.* One can imagine the reluctance of the servants to leave just as the curtain was going up after they had spent an hour or more waiting for their masters.

Following the death of Wignell in 1803 and of Reinagle in 1809 management of the theater was assumed by William Warren, who married Wignell's widow, and William B. Wood. During this period the playhouse was distinguished by the performances of John Howard Payne, a native New Yorker, the popular idol of the day. He was a playwright and a composer as well as being an actor, and the author of an opera entitled *Clari, or the Maid of Milan* which was produced in Covent Garden, London, in 1823. The production was significant in that the opera included the song "Home, Sweet Home." Payne's words were adapted to an Italian air. The song made an immediate hit which has been sustained well over a hundred years.

It was customary in those days to designate a performance as a benefit in which all the proceeds went to the actor. His popularity could be gauged by the box-office receipts. At one such benefit for Payne the total reached $1,160, some of the patrons signing checks for as much as $50.

Baltimore was visited periodically by epidemics of yellow fever. The disease then was believed to be transmitted through the breathing of foul air by large assemblages in closed buildings. Therefore an ordinance was passed forbidding theatrical performances from June 1st to October 1st.

So successful was the venture on Holliday Street that the management decided to tear down the first building and erect a new one on the same site. The promoters were undaunted by the fact that at the moment the nation was engaged in a war with England and the enemy was unpleasantly close to Baltimore.

What was described in contemporary accounts as "a fine brick edifice" took the place of the old wooden one. Long before this the wooden theater had ceased to be called "New" and acquired the name of the "Old Holliday." The brick theater started its career as the "Baltimore," but it too eventually inherited the name of "Holliday Street." As it reached a venerable age it also came to be known affectionately as "Old Drury."

The second theater on the Holliday Street site was officially opened on May 10, 1813. Especially for the occasion handsome new scenery was purchased in Philadelphia. It was shipped overland to the head of Chesapeake Bay and thence was to go by boat to Baltimore. At this very moment a British fleet under the command of Admiral Cockburn was on a marauding expedition in the upper Chesapeake and the scenery reached Havre de Grace just as the British did. The warehouse in which it was stored was fired by the invaders so the opening night at the Holliday Street had to get on as best it could without the new scenery. However, fate ordained that the theater was to have a sweet revenge on the British. For, in the following year, the British were again active in the Bay. This time they attacked Baltimore both by land and by sea and were repulsed. The stout defense of Fort McHenry inspired Francis Scott Key's "Star Spangled Banner."

The Battle of Baltimore took place in September, 1814. A few weeks later, on October 19, 1814, Key's verses set to the tune of the drinking song, "Anacreon in Heaven" were sung from the stage of the Holliday Street Theater by an actor named Hardinge. The song was an immediate success and for many nights thereafter, according to the custom of the time, the audience called for it to be repeated. The management of the theater was quick to capitalize on its popular appeal. Soon thereafter the singing of the "Star Spangled Banner" was accompanied by a scene representing Fort McHenry under bombardment and illuminated by the fire from the enemy's bomb ships. This was the golden age of "illuminations" and "transparencies" and the effect was no doubt very fine. Thus the Holliday Street Theater, Baltimore's Old Drury, had the honor of launching the song which a century later was to be adopted as the National Anthem.

The next important event in the annals of the Holliday Street

Theater was on April 24, 1821, when Edmund Kean, the great English tragedian, made his first appearance in Baltimore. He must have been warned in advance of the taste of the natives for he opened his engagement with the town's old favorite, *King Richard III*. This was followed by other Shakespearean plays. Kean drew the largest audience that had been seen in Baltimore up to that time. Six months later there appeared at the Holliday Street Theater still another English actor who came to this country with a considerable reputation. He was Junius Brutus Booth. Though still a young man Booth already was beginning to rival Kean. He liked Baltimore and Maryland and decided to make his home there. He found himself a city house on Exeter Street, then went out to Harford County and purchased a farm several miles outside Bel Air. On it he built a house which he called Tudor Hall and there he repaired frequently to relax from his professional labors.

Junius Brutus Booth had eccentricities which, as time went on, were hardly distinguishable from insanity. The presence of death in any form completely unnerved him. His grief over the death of a son and daughter is understandable. Less reasonable was his calling a clergyman to his hotel room to conduct a funeral service over the remains of two spring chickens. When he lived at Tudor Hall Booth had a pony which he rode back and forth on his journeys between his farm and Baltimore. When it died Booth was inconsolable. He ordered Mrs. Booth to put on a white gown and sit on the corpse while he stood watch with a shotgun. Neighbors heard about what was going on and closed in on him. They managed to pinion his arms and take the shotgun away from him. Once overpowered Booth made no further resistance and invited his captors to join him in a drink.

Outstanding among Booth's performances was his portrayal of *King Richard III*. Baltimoreans had seen the part played many, many times and in many ways. But Booth had a special surprise for them. Once he became so absorbed in the part that he imagined he actually was King Richard on Bosworth Field. Brandishing a sword he drove his antagonist off the stage and down through the audience.

Rivaling the Baltimoreans' fondness for *King Richard III* was their delight in equestrian acts. Horses demanded more room

than was customarily to be had in the conventional theater. Therefore to accommodate this particular form of amusement a
theater and a circus combined were erected on Front Street in
1829. It operated under the name of the "New Theater and Circus" or the "Front Street Theater." This spacious building boasted
three tiers of boxes and a pit. It could seat 4,000 persons. Fire
destroyed it in 1838 but it was promptly rebuilt.

The most famous performance there, however, had nothing
to do with horses. It was the appearance of Jenny Lind, "the
Swedish Nightingale," on December 8, 1850. This was her first
visit to Baltimore. Two hours before the concert was to begin
the doors were opened and the crowd streamed in. Front Street
was so blocked with carriages, omnibuses and pedestrians that it
was extremely difficult to reach even the entrance to the theater.

By 8 P.M. every nook and cranny of the great building was
filled. Some people were reported to have paid as much as $100
for a choice seat. When the concert began there was only enough
room left on the stage for the Nightingale and the orchestra
which accompanied her. Miss Lind gave four concerts in Baltimore, the receipts from which reached a total of $60,000. She
boasted a glamor which held our ancestors enthralled. With all
due respect to her genius it is not altogether impossible that her
brilliant success was influenced by the fact that her tour was arranged by the great showman, P. T. Barnum.

The Holliday Street and the Front Street Theaters figured in
another famous episode in the 1840's. This involved the bitter
rivalry between the English actor, William Macready, and the
American Edwin Forrest. In 1843 Macready arrived in this country where the native-born Forrest already had achieved a reputation as a tragedian. Annoyed by Macready's invasion of his
territory Forrest, to prove his superiority duplicated the visitor's
repertoire, matching him play for play. The rivalry grew even
more bitter when Forrest carried the offensive to England. There
he was driven from the stage by Macready's followers.

In 1848 both actors were back in the United States touring the
same towns. On December 11th of that year Macready began
an engagement at the Front Street Theater as Macbeth while, on
the same night, Forrest undertook the identical role at the Holliday Street Theater. In Baltimore the incident had no serious

consequence. From Baltimore the actors carried their rivalry to New York. There the ardent admirers of the two men met in a bloody riot in front of the Astor Place Theater where Macready was to perform. When at last the police had dispersed the mob and restored order it was found that twenty two persons had been killed and thirty six wounded. Jealous as it was in those days of its reputation as Mobtown it is surprising Baltimore should have let New York outdo it.

Two other establishments which figured prominently in the early history of the stage in Baltimore were the Old Baltimore Museum, which stood at the northwest corner of Calvert and Baltimore Streets, and the Howard Athenaeum and Gallery of Arts on the northwest corner of Baltimore and Charles Streets. The museum served to house Rembrandt Peale's collection of portraits, stuffed birds and animals and other curiosities when, in 1830, he moved it from its original home on Holliday Street. Rembrandt was emulating his father, Charles Willson Peale, who established a similiar museum in Philadelphia. The exhibit was not a financial success so eventually the two upper floors of the building were remodeled as a theater. Most of the leading actors performed there. In 1850 the management was assumed by John E. Owens, an English comedian, who made Baltimore his home and became prominent in civic affairs as well as in the theater. He also at one time managed the Athenaeum and Gallery of Arts. This house was distinguished chiefly for the claim that on its stage John Wilkes Booth made his debut as Richmond in *King Richard III.*

In the spring of 1829 was born in Baltimore a man destined to leave his imprint on the theater not only in his native city but throughout the eastern seaboard. He was John T. Ford. At the age of twenty years Ford felt the call of the stage and journeyed to Richmond, Virginia, where he joined a minstrel troupe. His genius for administration soon was revealed and he became manager of the company.

In the late 1840's ill fortune at last fell upon the Holliday Street Theater and for a number of years it was dark. Ford had by this time made money with his troupe and was looking for a good investment. So in 1856 he joined with two partners in the purchase of "Old Drury." The next year he assumed sole management and soon had the place back on its feet. A performance of note in 1859 was that of *She Stoops to Conquer* in which a young man named Stuart Robson played the part of Tony Lumpkin. Robson became famous in that role and played it again and again for the next forty years until his death in 1903. There are today many people whose introduction to the theater was seeing Robson as an old man still playing the part of the youthful Tony. Ford is credited also with giving Edwin Booth his start by engaging him to play for four weeks in *King Richard III* and *Hamlet*.

In 1870 Ford bought the theater outright for $100,000. It was burned in 1873, he rebuilt it and opened it again the next year. But by this time his interests were centered elsewhere so he sold the property back to the people from whom he had bought it. But the career of "Old Drury" was far from over. For a time it was run successfully by John W. Albaugh, an actor-manager and another luminary of the local theatrical world. At last the theater grew shabby, the neighborhood became run down, and the Holliday Street Theater yielded place to newer and more modern houses. At the turn of the century it was the home of melodrama. The last indignity it had to suffer was when it was converted into a motion-picture theater. Finally in 1917 it was razed to make way for the City Hall Plaza. Thus the active career of the Holliday Street Theater—if the succession of playhouses on the same site may be called one theater—extended over a period of more than a hundred years.

Encouraged by his success in Baltimore, Ford in 1862 bought a theater in Washington and extended his activities there. The first building was burned and he at once replaced it. The playhouse bore his name. It was in Ford's Theater, in the spring of 1865, that President Lincoln met his death at the hands of John Wilkes Booth. Baltimore was deeply involved in the tragic event, since the owner of the theater was a Baltimorean and the assassin had spent many years of his life there. Booth's handsome face and his gifts as an actor had won him many friends who were horrified at his crime.

It so happened that the Booth family owned a lot in Greenmount Cemetery, Baltimore's most fashionable burying ground. After the death of John Wilkes, when public excitement over the assassination had to some extent died down, Edwin Booth approached officials of the cemetery and claimed the right to bury his unfortunate brother there. Since the lot was the property of the Booth family, the officials could not refuse. So very quietly the body of John Wilkes was buried in the family lot in an un-marked grave. Even to this day the exact location of the grave is known only to officials of the cemetery.

Five years later Ford settled upon plans for the erection of a new theater in Baltimore. In order to disassociate it from the very recent tragedy at Ford's Theater in Washington he gave it the name of Ford's Grand Opera House. So it was known for most of its long career though very rarely was grand opera actually staged there. Only in late years has it reverted to the name of Ford's Theater. The first public performance took place there before an enthusiastic audience on October 2, 1871. The play was *As You Like It* and the star the English actor James W. Wallack. Wallack led a procession of famous actors across the stage at Ford's—from Jefferson, Robson and Adelaide Neilson to Tallulah Bankhead, Beatrice Lillie and the Lunts. There are few stars either of the English or American theater who have not played to audiences there.

To Ford's in their day came E. A. Sothern and Julia Marlowe in Shakespearean repertoire. There appeared the famous beauty Lily Langtry, "the Jersey Lily," whose name Victorian gossip linked with Edward, that Prince of Wales who reigned briefly as Edward VII. There Mrs. Leslie Carter shocked our grand-parents with her lush portrayal of Du Barry. In the procession were John Drew and all the Barrymores, Robert Mantell and Forbes-Robertson in Shakespearean repertoire, and Richard Mansfield who also played Shakespeare but was better known for his gruesome portrayal of *Dr. Jekyll and Mr. Hyde*.

The stage at Ford's saw also a succession of great magicians whose annual visits were as keenly anticipated by the small fry of the town as were those of Buffalo Bill and Barnum and Bailey's Circus. They included Hermann, Kellar, Thurston and Houdini. Then there were the equally popular blackface ministrels—That-cher, Primose and West; Primrose and Dockstader, and finally Lew Dockstader alone in a clever, but impudent, blackface im-personation of Theodore Roosevelt. Ford's also claims the distinction of having been the scene of the original performance in this country of Gilbert and Sullivan's *Pinafore*.

Soon after the theater was opened in 1871 contemporary writers grew rapturous in their praises of its many advantages. "The whole structure," said one of them, "has a solid and at the same time elegant appearance. The building is richly and tastefully furnished and is provided with all the elegant conveniences of the most finished theaters in the country." Those who know the quaint structure today will smile at that glowing description.

The senior Ford, as time went on, was assisted in the management of his Opera House by his four sons, Charles E., John T., Jr., George T. and Harry M. He maintained a handsome house on Gilmor Street where he frequently entertained distinguished visitors to the city. When Charles Dickens arrived in Baltimore on his American tour, among the persons to whom he handed a letter of introduction was Mr. Ford. Mr. Ford also was a public-spirited man who served in the City Council and sometimes acted as mayor.

Shortly after Mr. Ford opened his "Opera House" a group of local capitalists formed a company for the purpose of erecting a so-called "Academy of Music." This building, occupying a lot on the west side of Howard Street opposite Centre, was officially opened on January 5, 1875. At the time its sponsors claimed that it was one of the finest theaters in America. It boasted central steam heating, and its auditorium was lit by electricity with a magnificent chandelier suspended from the ceiling. The official opening was signalized by an oration delivered by Severn Teackle Wallis, a leader of the Baltimore Bar, followed by a Grand Inaugural Ball. For such occasions a floor could be laid which converted the theater into a handsome ballroom.

At the Academy, fresh from the World's Fair in Chicago, the Great Sandow performed feats of strength in the season of 1893. The famous strong man headed "The Sandow Trocadero Vaudeville Company." Sandow's manager was a keen young man with an ambition to go places. His name was Flo Ziegfeld.

Here, too, in 1894 another young man who was greatly interested in physical culture hired the Academy for a lecture on that subject. The lecture was to be illustrated by a comely young woman in tights. The lecturer was Bernarr McFadden. Those were strait-laced days in Baltimore and young McFadden was not sure how the local police would take this daring proposal. So, to make sure, he hired a local lawyer to sound out the chief. After thinking the matter over carefully the chief concluded that, since the tights were black, there was nothing immoral about them.

In 1895 the Lyric, built to heroic proportions, rose majestically on Mt. Royal Avenue. Unfortunately the money gave out before the front facade was completed. It continued without embellishment from then on. Here, truly, was the home of grand opera, boasting a stage on which even the heftiest Brunhilde and her attendant Valkyries did not look out of proportion. Here, too, a symphony orchestra with close to a hundred players could sit without crowding, and whole troupes of ballet dancers could be perfectly at home.

The Lyric has always been famous for its acoustics. Its formal opening was signalized by a concert of the Boston Symphony Orchestra with Nellie Melba as soloist. After Madame Melba had sung, thirty-two-year-old Henry Randall, architect of the building, was brought to her dressing room to be presented to her. The singer congratulated young Randall on the acoustics remarking that in her opionion the only other hall in the world that did her voice full justice was the Gewandhaus in Leipzig. To this young Randall replied with a smile that it was the proportions of the Gewandhaus he had followed closely in designing the Lyric.

For years the Lyric has served the community. It will be noted elsewhere that, with level floor laid, it has for years been the scene of the Bachelors Cotillon and the presentation to society of the season's debutantes. Here, too, the Metropolitan Opera gives three performances a year. Whatever the occasion, the lobby of the Lyric is graced by its personable manager Freddy Huber who, next to George Washington on top of the monument, is the most widely known figure in Baltimore. In its long career, like most authentic Baltimore institutions, the Lyric has had its financial crises and many times has had to be "saved." Nevertheless it has managed to keep rolling along.

Shortly after the turn of the century James L. Kernan, seized with a sudden inspiration to do something gigantic, thrilled Baltimore with what was advertised as his "Triple Million Dollar

Enterprise." It consisted of the erection of two theaters at How-ard and Franklin Streets with a hotel in between. These were merely the major attractions. Appended to them were a rath-skellar under one of the theaters, an art gallery, a Turkish bath, a pool-and-billiard parlor and a saloon with what was described as the longest bar in the city. This last feature embraced a slab of marble some sixty feet long. The two theaters were known respectively as The Auditorium and The Maryland. The Audi-torium was designed primarily for musical shows and The Mary-land became the home of the best vaudeville, being on Keith's circuit. During the intermissions patrons of The Maryland were privileged to view the collection of pictures in the art gallery free of charge.

Kernan already had done well with another enterprise in a less fashionable part of the town overlooking Jones Falls. This was his Monumental Theater. Because of its location it was popu-larly known as "The Bridge." It catered to stag audiences with burlesque. It was the testing ground for comedians, many of whom later gained national fame. Among these was the great team of Weber and Fields.

So it was that around 1900 Baltimoreans every week were given a wide choice of theatrical fare. The best plays and musical shows, with the current stars, were to be found at Ford's and the Academy of Music. There were musical shows as well at the Auditorium, vaudeville at the Maryland, melodrama at Holliday and Blaney's and burlesque at the Monumental, the Odeon and several other houses. The Lyceum, a charming little playhouse in the heart of the fashionable residential district on North Charles, was the home of Stock. Baltimore audiences could afford to be blasé and they were. The city got a reputation for being the hardest in the country to please. Until recent years Baltimore frequently was picked as a tryout for shows before they were presented on Broadway. Among the show people there was a belief that if a show went with a Baltimore audience it would go anywhere.

Yet even while the legitimate theater appeared to be at the height of its powers the forces of destruction already were in being. Patrons were being lured to motion-picture houses by films put out by Biograph, Pathé Freres and other pioneer concerns featuring such favorites as Mary Pickford and Charlie Chaplin. Among the first of the screen's lovers was Francis X. Bushman, a Baltimorean. With the money he made in pictures he bought a handsome estate in Baltimore County just off the fashionable Green Spring Valley and lived like a country squire until the public found a new favorite.

As the motion-picture industry expanded the legitimate theaters closed their doors. Some were torn down, others were remodeled for the showing of films. Fate caught up with the Academy of Music in 1926. It had lasted about fifty years. The Maryland, early home of vaudeville, within the year has been torn down to make room for a parking lot.

John T. Ford's namesake alone goes on. Fortunately it was on the leeward side of the flames during the great fire of 1904. After more than eighty years it continues to serve the purpose for which it was originally intended. The three tiers of boxes which flanked each side of the stage have given place to flat surfaces decorated with white curlicues like the writing on a birthday cake. The old dressing rooms also have been rebuilt and refurnished. Otherwise the interior and exterior remain much as many generations have known them. Were the ghosts of Joe Jefferson, Stuart Robson, Edwin Booth and other great figures of the past to return to Baltimore today they would surely recognize it.

Though the professional stage in Baltimore is a mere shadow of its former self the tradition has been kept much alive by the amateurs. There are a number of active little theaters and even more theatrical groups in the colleges, high schools and churches. Donald Kirkley, playwright and theatrical critic of the *Sun*, recently estimated that there are more people in Baltimore acting in or helping to produce plays than the total number of people in the whole professional theater from coast to coast. In the very first performance produced in Baltimore of which a program survives there is mention that several parts are being taken "by gentlemen for their amusement." Such, after some two centuries, is the prevailing custom among the gentlemen and ladies of Baltimore today.

Two amateur groups have had such long careers that they are regarded as established institutions of the city. They are the Paint and Powder Club and the Vagabonds. The former was

organized in 1894 by a group of young men "of social prominence." Its primary function has been to produce comic operas
after the manner of such college organizations as Harvard's Hasty
Pudding, Princeton's Triangle Club and the University of Pennsylvania's Mask and Wig. Both male and female parts originally
were played by the men. Such groups usually are organized to
exercise the talents of some particular individual. In the instance
of the Paint and Powder Club the inspiration came from A. Baldwin Sloane. An original comic opera written and composed by
him was the club's first offering. Particular distinction was added
to this first production by the appearance of Harry Lehr as one of
the ladies in the pony ballet. He was soon thereafter to win national fame as a social figure in Newport.

The Vagabonds were Baltimore's response to the little-theater
movement which had its beginning in England and swept this
country in the early years of the second decade of the present
century. In June, 1916, a Shakespeare Tercentenary Pageant was
produced in Baltimore and Constance D'Arcy MacRaye, a pro-
ponent of the little theater came to town to direct it. She is credited
with providing the original inspiration for the local group. A
spare room on the ground floor of the St. James Apartments,
designated as 3 West Centre Street, was rented and there the first
performance was presented on November 16. The announced
object of the Vagabonds was "to present one-act plays of literary
as well as of entertainment value."

The enterprise was viewed skeptically and unsympathetically
by the local press. The dramatic cirtics, as a rule, regarded the
Vagabonds as amateurs beneath professional consideration. Nevertheless the Vagabonds kept manfully on. While still in swaddling
clothes they survived World War I though many of their players
were called into the service. During World War II they kept
alive by presenting plays for the amusement of the military.

The Vagabonds now lay claim to being America's oldest little
theater still in operation. They have been going for thirty four
years. During that period there have been several moves; the last
one to the old basement bar of John L. Kernan's "Triple Million
Dollar Enterprise." Because a conventional stage was impracticable they have undertaken an experiment with a theater-in-
the-round.

The Vagabonds have occasionally encouraged local playwrights by holding playwriting competitions and producing the winning play. But, for the most part, they are content to repeat Broadway successes. They claim the credit for having introduced fifteen noted playwrights to Baltimore for the first time—from Eugene O'Neill to Pirandello. Some twenty two others—including Masefeld and Cork—have had their works produced in Baltimore by the Vagabonds alone.

During the thirty four years of their existence the Vagabonds have produced well over 300 plays. Their audiences total from 10,000 to 15,000 persons annually. They seldom hesitate to attempt the production of a play because of practical difficulties. For their thirtieth anniversary they selected the jubilee play *Victoria Regina*. It was produced by a veteran charter member of the organization, Helen A. F. (Mrs. Nick) Penniman.

In fact Mrs. Penniman's unflagging interest in theatricals long antedates the Vagabonds. She was a member of the "New Wednesday Club" which succeeded the "Family Circle" which sprang from the "Old Wednesday Club" which flourished about the time of the Civil War or shortly thereafter. There are still some ancient Baltimoreans who trace the lineage of the Vagabonds back to the dark ages of the "Old Wednesday Club." They say it was Mrs. Penniman reviving the "New Wednesday Club" and not the little theater movement that actually got the Vagabonds started. At any rate there is no question she has kept them going.

Chapter 13

INDIAN QUEEN AND PROGENY

ON THE EVENING of February 21, 1948, Mr. A. J. Fink, manager of the Southern Hotel entertained a distinguished company of some 250 persons at a "Fountain Inn Dinner." The occasion heralded the publication of a small book entitled *The Fountain Inn Diary*, the work of the Baltimore historian Matthew Page Andrews. The book had been prepared at Mr. Fink's instigation and in it Mr. Andrews showed how the Southern Hotel could claim direct descent from the ancient Fountain Inn which stood on the same site. Mr. Fink spared neither pains nor expense to give his dinner the magnificence that characterized the public banquets of the parent house.

The Fountain Inn was opened in 1773, but it was not the earliest of Baltimore hostelries. In John Moale's famous sketch of Baltimore Town as it looked in 1752 two inns are to be seen. Older also than the Fountain Inn was the Indian Queen which stood at the southwest corner of Baltimore and Hanover Streets. The date of its establishment is uncertain but it is believed to have been quite early in the history of the town. Daniel Grant, who had managed an inn in Philadelphia, conducted the Indian Queen before moving on to take charge of the new Fountain Inn. The first issue of Baltimore's pioneer newspaper, the *Maryland Journal and Baltimore Advertiser*, announced that Mr. Grant had "opened an inn and tavern at the Sign of the Fountain." It added that the inn could provide everything "for the accommodation of Gentlemen, their servants, and horses in the best manner." The inn, like many an old one in London, was built around an open court shaded with trees on which a series of balconies looked out.

To Fountain Inn came George Washington in May, 1775, as a member of the Virginia delegation on the way to attend the meeting of the second Continental Congress in Philadelphia. Evidently Washington was pleased with his treatment for this was the first of a number of visits. He was a guest again on his way to Yorktown in 1781 and on the occasion of his trip to Annapolis in 1783 to surrender his commission to the Congress which was then sitting there. On this last visit he was tendered a formal dinner at the inn. Martha Washington also stopped there from time to time when going to join the General in camp. She was with him also when, after the close of the war, he reappeared in Baltimore as a private citizen and was honored by another dinner followed by a ball.

During the days of the Revolution the Fountain Inn was definitely the most popular hostelry in town. Here the Whig Society, which kept a close watch on Tories, and the Council of Safety held some of their meetings. Here, after his victories in the South, Nathaniel Greene was received as a guest and honored with a public dinner. When Congress met in Baltimore John Adams might have put up at the Fountain Inn had he not been so concerned over the expense. As it was he took lodgings in a house nearby, the while complaining of the high cost of everything.

Another memorable evening at the Inn was February 2, 1814. This was the occasion of a public dinner in honor of young Commodore Oliver Hazard Perry whose victory over the British fleet in the naval battle on Lake Erie was still only a few months old. President Madison drove all the way over from Washington to be present. In that moment of exaltation the President little dreamed that, before the year was out, the enemy would be in his capital and he and his Cabinet would be fugitives. Daniel Grant had long since passed from the scene. The inn was now managed by John H. Barney, brother of the colorful Commodore. Either John shared his brother's gift for the dramatic or else the Commodore had an active hand in the evening's arrangements, for they were sensational. The banquet hall was elaborately decorated with United States flags. From the ceiling was suspended an American eagle of impressive size, and in its beak was a scroll bearing in large letters the slogan, "A nation's gratitude, the hero's best reward."

Another conspicuous feature of the setting was an elevated platform built to represent the quarter-deck of a ship, on the stern of which appeared the name "Niagara" in large letters. It was on the *Niagara* that Perry won his battle after transferring from the shattered *Lawrence*. Seated in the center of this impressive platform were Commodore Perry and President Madison. Taking up an entire end of the hall was a transparency depicting the battle of

September 10, 1813. The evening was an inspiring one that certainly tested the capacity of those present. According to the account handed down to posterity, in addition to nineteen formal toasts prepared in advance, there were no fewer than twenty-five volunteer ones.

Commodore Stephen Decatur was similarly honored at the Inn. So too was General Winfield Scott who just then was getting fairly launched on his long and distinguished military career. When Lafayette returned to Baltimore as an elderly man in 1824 he found a handsome suite of rooms prepared and waiting for him at the Inn. This was forty-three years after his first visit to Baltimore. Yet at the public banquet given in his honor he did not forget to propose a toast to Mrs. David Poe and the other ladies of the town who in 1781 so promptly met the appeal to clothe his ragged troops. Could there have been, as today, some useful person in his party to remind the general of these pleasant little episodes?

The first city directory, published in 1796, listed no fewer than ninety-eight taverns and inns. However, many of these were no more than lodgings for sailors near the waterfront. Other popular locations for the hostelries were at points where the highways entered the town. Thus, for example, Howard Street was the terminus for traffic coming from the western frontier. Near the intersection of Howard and Saratoga Streets the great Conestoga wagons, drawn by teams of four or six horses, pulled up for the night. While the teams were unhitched and tied to the wagon poles, the wagoners went off to eat and drink at such establishments as "The Golden Horse," "The White Swan," "The Golden Lamb," "The Black Bear" or "The Maypole." These were among the favorite resorts west of Jones Falls also for the horse dealers and the cattlemen. Farmers coming to town by the Harford Road stopped east of the Falls in Old Town at "The Bull's Head" or "The Rising Sun."

In the second decade of the 19th century, with the arrival of large numbers of immigrants from the continent of Europe, the prototype of the English Inn, with its quaint sign, gave way to the less picturesque and more elaborate "hotel." As time passed the old inns were torn down. Yet one or two buildings survived on Howard Street almost to the close of the last century. Only a few years ago the dramatic collapse of a house at Paca and Pratt Streets revealed it to have been "The Three Tuns," probably the last survivor of these ancient hostelries.

In an effort to keep up with the prevailing fashion the Inn in the 1820's changed its name to The Fountain Hotel. Because of its location within a few blocks of the basin where the Bay boats came in, it continued to enjoy popularity with the planters of the Eastern Shore and Southern Maryland; also with travelers arriving by water from Norfolk, Virginia, and other points in the South. The building was a year short of a century old when, in 1871, it was torn down at last to make way for a new and up-to-date establishment. This was the Carrollton, named for the country estate of Charles Carroll. It covered more land than the Fountain Inn since it extended from German Street (now Redwood) all the way to Baltimore, an entire block. The new hotel was a mammoth building rising seven stories. To assist the guests to reach these dizzy heights the hotel was equipped with that most modern invention—the elevator. The Carrollton flourished until it was destroyed by the Great Fire of 1904.

Eleven years later, under the leadership of Mr. Fink, capital was assembled and the Southern Hotel was named and incorporated as an establishment to be erected on the site previously occupied by the Fountain Inn and the Carrollton Hotel. The new hotel opened its doors on March 6, 1918. The Carrollton and the Southern in their turn maintained the tradition of their predecessor in attracting celebrities. The old register of the Carrollton bears the names among others of Sarah Bernhardt, General George B. McClellan, Henry Ward Beecher, Lillian Russell and Thomas Nelson Page. The Southern in its time has acted as host to Theodore Roosevelt, Cardinal Gibbons, Helen Keller, Franklin D. Roosevelt, William Howard Taft, Will Rogers, Warren G. Harding, Herbert Hoover, General John J. Pershing, Gilbert K. Chesterton, Sir Philip Gibbs, Victor Herbert, Marshal Foch, Georges Clemenceau, General Jan Smuts, William Jennings Bryan, Calvin Coolidge, Dean Inge, James H. Doolittle (when he was just a lieutenant and not a general), Major General Douglas MacArthur, Dr. Chaim Weizman, Knute Rockne, Charles A. Lindbergh and Rear Admiral Richard Evelyn Byrd.

The Southern continues its usefulness today. Its proximity to the basin still makes it convenient for visitors who arrive by the Norfolk boat. Since it is in the heart of the banking district its dining room is regularly patronized by the city's financiers. On any day from Monday to Friday one could select from the tables in its main dining room a board of directors of which any local corporation would be proud.

Hotels, like fair women, have their period of brilliant success. After that the dazzling quality of youth is replaced by mature dignity. Then old age overtakes them and they yield to gradual decay. When Daniel Grant left it to inaugurate the Fountain Inn the Indian Queen continued to carry on under other owners and managers until well beyond 1832. But it never again was a serious rival of the Inn. While the Fountain Inn was still enjoying a gratifying popularity a new competitor appeared on the scene. This was Barnum's City Hotel, destined to become one of the most famous hostelries in the country. Associated in the enterprise were David Barnum, W. Shipley and J. Philip, Jr. In 1825 they commenced the erection of the new structure on Monument Square at the southwest corner of Fayette and Calvert Streets. Mr. Barnum, a Pennsylvanian, had served an apprenticeship as manager of the Indian Queen.

The new structure must have caused consternation among the conservative Baltimoreans of wealth who hitherto had enjoyed something of a monopoly of the square with their charming Georgian dwellings. The new hotel reached a commanding height of seven stories. A columned portico, reached by steep flights of steps on either side, lent magnificence to the main entrance. Many of the windows on the upper floors were set off by wrought-iron balconies. The interior was equally elegant with heavy red velvet curtains, plush carpets and great glass mirrors in heavy gilt frames of baroque design extending from the floors to the lofty ceilings. Barnum's Hotel was, in fact, in keeping with Baltimore's importance at the time as the second largest city in the country. Its luxurious appointments symbolized the wealth then being amassed by its merchants and industrialists. When in other parts of the country mention of Baltimore was made people invariably thought of Barnum's Hotel. Travelers from the South who put up there were in a seventh heaven. Its fame spread also to all parts of the East and abroad as well.

The hotel was little more than a year old when it was honored with a visit from President John Quincy Adams who came to attend a dinner for the Order of the Cincinnati and for the officers and men wounded in the Battle of North Point. President Adams was the first of a long succession of distinguished guests. A year later Henry Clay appeared. In 1833 John Randolph of Roanoke was entertained as he passed through Baltimore on a journey just before his death. Scorning the railroad that had been inaugurated a few years before he traveled in his own coach. Too ill to walk he was carried into the hotel by his favorite body servant Juba.

Among others who put up at Barnum's were Charles Dickens, Washington Irving, Thackeray, Jenny Lind, Adeline Patti, Edward, Prince of Wales who later ascended to the throne as Edward VII, Edwin Booth, Joseph Jefferson and Sarah Bernhardt.

David Barnum was a gracious host and a liberal provider. All the delicacies of the market were found at his table. On special occasions terrapin, wild duck, venison, crabs and other local dishes were featured. Dinner, for which the charge was $1.50, was attended with much ceremony. A large bell was rung through the halls to summon the guests who seated themselves at a long table. Negro waiters, holding their loaded trays ready, stood behind the chairs of the guests waiting for a signal from the captain. When that was given each waiter stepped forward to serve and dinner was begun. As late as the 1920's, at a private dinner at the Belvedere Hotel, waiters performed a similar ritual. While the captain stood behind the chair of the host they took their places at equal intervals behind the guests with dishes poised. As the captain dropped his arms the waiters in unison began to serve. The guests found the ritual highly amusing. Could the captain of the waiters have been descended from a member of the Barnum staff? And was he in fact reviving an old custom practiced at the famous hotel?

Among the guests at Barnum's in the 1830's was one G. W. Featherstonehaugh, a Londoner and author of a book entitled *Travels in the Slave States of North America,* which he published in 1844 after his return to England. He presents a vivid description of dining off a pair of canvasback ducks with his host, Mr. Barnum. When the birds arrived on the table he remarked that there was no gravy and that, in consequence, he was not going to enjoy the ducks. But his countenance changed when Mr. Barnum put a knife into the breast of one of the ducks and the blood-red juice gushed out. He then records his complete enjoyment of this local delicacy eaten "with currant jelly and a soupçon of Chateau Margaux."

Charles Dickens, who was a guest in 1842, reversed his usual custom of making unpleasant comments on his experiences in this country. In his American Notes he said: "The most comfortable of all the hotels of which I had an experience in the United States, and they were not a few, is Barnum's, in that city (Baltimore); where the English traveler will find curtains to his bed for the first and probably the last time in America . . . and where he will be likely to have enough water for washing himself, which is not at all a common case."

It was probably at Barnum's that Dickens drank his famous julep with Washington Irving. In a letter to a friend written after Irving's death he thus described the incident: "We sat, one on either side of it, with great solemnity (it filled a respectable-sized round table) but the solemnity was of very short duration. It was quite an enchanted julep, and carried us among innumerable people and places that we both knew. The julep held out far into the night, and my memory never saw him afterwards otherwise than as bending over it, with his straw, with the attempted air of gravity (after some anecdote involving some wonderfully droll and delicate observation of character) and then, as his eyes caught mine, melting with that captivating laugh of his, which was the brightest and best I have ever heard."

The unusual atmosphere of Barnum's is attributed in great part to the servants. Most of them grew up with the hotel. Mr. Barnum supplied them with a book of instructions in which he admonished them on no account to stand around as though waiting for a tip. Nevertheless, in spite of any show of indifference they may have assumed, they did exceedingly well. Many of them were, of course, slaves. Before the Civil War one waiter made enough to pay for his own freedom and that of his wife and daughter. A chambermaid who died shortly after the war was reported to have left an estate of $20,000.

David Barnum died on May 10, 1844, at the age of seventy-four years. His funeral, held from the hotel, was attended by all the dignitaries in the city and received impressive notice in the local newspapers. He was succeeded by his son Zenus and his son-in-law, Andrew McLaughlin, who enlarged the building and continued to carry on the hostelry's enviable tradition. In 1855 Zenus withdrew, leaving McLaughlin as sole proprietor. After the Civil War the hotel passed from one owner to another. As time went on the painted ceilings, the velvet curtains and the baroque mirrors lost much of their freshness, but they still served to impress members of the oncoming generation with the past grandeur of the establishment. Barnum's did not close its doors until 1889. It then was razed to make way for the Equitable Building which stands on the spot today.

In its last years Barnum's began to meet with stiff competition from the Carrollton and still another more modern hotel—the Rennert. The latter was founded by Robert Rennert, a German-American. Mr. Rennert started business in 1871 in a building across the square from Barnum's and called his place the Rennert House. He had a genius for preparing and serving food and his establishment became one of the most popular eating places in Baltimore.

The United States Government, looking for a site for a new post office, took a liking to Mr. Rennert's property and bought it from him in 1881. Mr. Rennert then built his Hotel Rennert, at Saratoga and Liberty Streets. It was formally opened on October 5, 1885. Contemporary accounts described it as being "the highest type of American hostelry." It soon became as much of a local institution as the Fountain Inn and Barnum's had been before it. The Rennert had two main entrances facing on Saratoga Street. One opened directly onto the lobby and the clerk's desk. The other, which resembled the entrance to a private residence more than to a hotel, ushered the new arrival into a drawing room especially reserved for ladies. In such manner were the delicate females of the day spared the embarrassment of walking past ogling men seated in large leather chairs well within range of brass spittoons.

The Rennert made a specialty of Southern cooking. Terrapin, redhead duck, oysters in all styles, crabs and other seafoods were featured on its menu in season. The Rennert was the scene of practically all the public banquets. These ran through countless courses with an appropriate wine for each course. Midway in this enormous feast it was customary to serve a sherbet, presumably with the idea of coaxing the stomach to accept another installment of food. The hotel's raw oyster bar was especially popular with the public. It was presided over by two Negro barmen who shucked oysters as fast as a patron could eat them. Meanwhile they carried on an unrehearsed dialogue that rivaled the humor of "Amos and Andy" and "The Two Black Crows." It was their invariable custom to shuck thirteen oysters to the dozen, giving each customer the impression that he had been particularly favored and, in this pleasing manner, inviting a tip.

Eventually with the advent of more modern hotels the Rennert ceased to be the place of fashion it had been in its prime, though it never lost its appeal to visitors from the counties. It evolved into the unofficial headquarters of the city Democratic machine. Here the boss, Sonny Mahon, was to be seen in the lobby during the day issuing orders to his lieutenants and receiving the long line of people who came seeking favors.

Nine years younger than the Rennert was a modest establishment which rose in 1894 on Washington Place, within the shadow of the Washington Monument. This was the Stafford Hotel, the property of Dr. William A. Moale, member of Baltimore's most ancient family. The Stafford was small, quiet and exclusive. Theatrical stars favored it in preference to the larger and noisier hotels farther downtown.

The paneled bar of the Stafford was almost as exclusive as that of the Baltimore Club across the street. The report was widely circulated that not everybody could get a drink there. Before being so privileged you had to pass muster before the Stafford's discriminating bartender. The Stafford, now at the ripe age of over fifty-five years, is still very much alive. In fact in recent years it has passed through a process of rejuvenation. Its interior has been remodeled and redecorated and it continues to attract patrons who do not like crowds.

As the Rennert passed its prime need was seen for a larger and more up-to-date hotel. The demand was answered by the Belvedere Hotel which was opened to guests in December, 1903. This was indeed by far the most impressive hotel edifice Baltimore had yet seen. Erected on the southeast corner of Charles and Chase Streets it dominated what was at that time the fashionable residential district of the city. The hotel took its name from the country estate of John Eager Howard, on the site of which the hotel was built. Calvert, Cecil, Balmar and Oriole were among the suggestions for names made before Belvedere was chosen. Then a question arose as to the proper spelling. Should it be "Belvidere" or "Belvedere"? The *Century Dictionary* was consulted and gave Belvedere as the more approved of the two. Nevertheless the directors announced publicly that they would look up the name on the deed to the property, find out how Colonel Howard spelled it, and follow his style. In the end they adopted Belvedere. Oddly enough, "Belvidere" was the way Colonel Howard actually spelled it.

The Belvedere has been to Baltimore what the Bellevue-Stratford is to Philadelphia and the Touraine to Boston. In the course of its long history it has passed through numerous managements and various vicissitudes of fortune. On one occasion it was taken over by a bank. There have been times when its red plush carpets and rich draperies have looked drab indeed. A few years ago it was absorbed into the hotel system known as the U. S. Realty-Sheraton Corporation, which operates some twenty-three other hotels. It has been renovated, refurbished and rechristened the Sheraton-Belvedere. On the top floor, high above the city are a magnificent ballroom and a small theater. The ballroom often is the scene of the coming-out parties of the city's debutantes. Here, too, the Assembly has met occasionally. The Belvedere also is a popular place for dinner, and many a New Year has been noisily welcomed in its dining room and around its bar.

Two other hotels which in this modern age might be said to continue the tradition commenced by the Indian Queen and the Fountain Inn are the Emerson and the Lord Baltimore. The

Emerson was built in 1911 by Captain Isaac Emerson, who at the time was at the peak of his fortune created by the popular headache and morning-after remedy, "Bromo-Seltzer." The Emerson, at Baltimore and Calvert Streets, occupies a site next door to where Barnum's City Hotel once stood.

Isaac Emerson was a poor drug clerk in Annapolis when he hit on his miraculous formula while looking for a cure for his wife's migraine headaches. As its sale brought him wealth he moved to Baltimore and built an elaborate city house on Eutaw Place. Beside the house was an Italian garden resplendent with sculpture. On Sunday afternoons in the early 1900's the public, passing by on the way to Druid Hill Park, would pause in open-mouthed wonder at the garden's magnificence. The garden was protected by a side wall and, to discourage trespassers, broken glass was embedded in cement on top of the wall. The glass was unmistakable. It was the same dark blue of the bottles in which Bromo-Seltzer came.

The Captain was divorced from the first Mrs. Emerson. Following his second marriage he moved away from unfashionable Eutaw Place and the broken blue bottles and joined the select in the Green Spring Valley. There he took ownership to Brookland-wood. This was originally the country seat of Richard Caton, son-in-law of Charles Carroll of Carrollton and father of the "Three Graces." Here Captain Emerson ran a farm which supplied the hotel with poultry, fresh vegetables and milk. A conspicuous feature was a herd of purebred Guernsey dairy cattle. During the 1920's and 1930's Brooklandwood was a favorite objective for family automobile parties on week-end afternoons. The dairy did a thriving business in ice cream, chocolate milk and other dairy and farm products.

Following the death of Captain Emerson the hotel was sold to the Robert Meyer hotel group which had previously leased it. The Emerson has taken the place of the Rennert as headquarters of the Democratic party. Here the political leaders meet at lunch. The small fry meanwhile patronize Bickford's restaurant across the way or stand on the sidewalk outside keeping an eye on who goes in and out of the Emerson.

Last to join the group of modern hotels is the Lord Baltimore.

It was opened in 1928 and stands on the northeast corner of Baltimore and Hanover Streets, a site previously occupied by the Hotel Caswell whose manager, Harry Busick, was the prime mover in the building of the new hotel. Had the Lord Baltimore been built on the southeast corner instead of the northeast it would have been on ground hallowed by the Indian Queen and might have claimed descent from that ancient hostelry.

Like most other institutions the Baltimore hotels of today have become standardized. Local dishes are served occasionally; but, as a rule, a guest waking up in one of them would not know either from his food or his surroundings whether he was in Baltimore, Boston, St. Louis, Cleveland or Detroit. He can, however, count on a clean bed, food inspected by the health department and water that is almost undrinkable because it is so full of chemical purifiers. Sanitation and local color, alas, seldom go hand in hand.

Chapter 14

ENTER THE GERMANS

So FAR as the records show no Germans had a part in the founding of Baltimore. Yet no racial group, other than the English-speaking, exercised a more profound effect upon the city's growth and development. If the Germans were not in at the birth they were not far behind it. Tradition has it that Baltimore's first butcher was a German, Andrew Steiger by name. His house bore the date of 1741 and that portion of Jones Falls valley where his cattle grazed long was known as Steiger's Meadow. It is now the site of the new home of the *Sunpapers*. Baltimore Town was only twelve years old when Steiger put in an appearance.

Soon after, other Germans arrived. They came down the York Road from Pennsylvania or by way of the frontier of the Maryland colony which is now Frederick County. They came also direct from the old country, landing at Annapolis. These last were the precursors of thousands of immigrants who were to play a vital part in building the nation. Two Germans who deserve special mention arrived from York, Pennsylvania, in 1748. They were Leonard and Daniel Barnetz and they made a permanent place for themselves in local history by setting up the town's first brewery.

The most vital factor in the growth of Baltimore was the work of Germans who may never have seen the town at all or who did no more than pass through it on the way west. They were the Germans who farmed the frontier. Instead of following the example of the planters of Southern Maryland and the Eastern Shore by growing tobacco they turned their attention to wheat. Thanks to them, Baltimore became an important grain port on the East Coast and it still is one. In the course of the town's history many fortunes have been made through the export of grain.

In a report on the colony written in 1754 Governor Horatio Sharpe spoke disparagingly of the Germans in Baltimore. He described them as small merchants and prophesied that the town would never amount to much so long as it depended on them.

The pre-Revolutionary arrivals he was talking about were weavers, smiths, cobblers, bakers, clockmakers, saddlers, other craftsmen and more butchers like Mr. Steiger. They were humble folk, but they made good burghers. What Governor Sharpe failed to consider was that they produced just the sort of goods people come to town to buy. He overlooked also that most great merchants start as small ones.

The first printer in Baltimore also was a German. In 1765 one Nicholas Hasselbach got himself a press and opened a printing shop. But he died five years later and was overshadowed in history by William Goddard, the New Englander, who took over the plant from Hasselbach's widow and published Baltimore's first newspaper.

These pre-Revolutionary Germans were Protestants, either Lutheran or German Reformed. They tried to worship together but differences soon arose and the plan was abandoned. In 1755 the Lutherans founded Zion Church which became the center of all the social and religious activities of German Lutherans in Baltimore. In the course of its long history it attracted many distinguished pastors from Germany. Sermons were preached both in English and in German. They still are; for, after nearly two centuries, Zion Church still flourishes in a picturesque edifice in the very heart of Baltimore and in the shadow of the City Hall.

Zion Church, too, was a pioneer in the education of youth. As early as 1770 the congregation solemnly stated that "It is an incontestable fact that a good school education lays the foundation to our future happiness. It takes men of intelligence to realize the importance of such an undertaking (as organizing a school), men that are convinced that money spent for that purpose is very usefully spent indeed."

There was a naturalization law even in colonial days, but it was complicated and few of the early Germans took advantage of it. Since they were not English subjects it was not hard for them to shift their allegiance from England to America. The German clergy were virtually unanimous in supporting the cause of the colonists, and German laymen, too, played an important part in the Revolution. In Baltimore the names of Barnet Eichelberger and George Lundenberger are found on political committees.

One Captain George Keeports, a German, supplied arms, powder, tents, horses, clothing, shoes, flour and meat to Washington's army. Engelhard Yeiser provided meat for the militia. German craftsmen turned out powder cartouche boxes, bayonets, belts, gun slings and other military equipment.

A German of unusual distinction in Baltimore at this period was Dr. Charles Frederick Wiesenthal, a man of superior social position and culture, who was said to have been a physician to Frederick the Great. Not only was he a leader in his profession but he was also active in the Revolution. Prior to the outbreak of hostilities he was elected to the Committee of Observation of Baltimore County. He then was chosen to superintend the manufacture of saltpeter in Maryland, an essential ingredient of the powder used by the Revolutionists. In 1776 he became surgeon of the 1st Maryland Battalion in Smallwood's command. He also examined candidates for the medical service and served in an advisory capacity to the Continental Army on medical matters.

Dr. Wiesenthal was a recognized leader in all German affairs in the town. A founder of the Zion Church, he took a keen interest in the school connected with it. He served as first president of the German Society, a benevolent organization that had an enviable record in correcting the barbaric treatment meted out to German immigrants and in finding them jobs in their new home.

The first directory of the town, published in 1796, showed 10 per cent of the names listed as German. Among them were laborers, tanners, carpenters, cordwainers, bricklayers, wagoners, weavers, locksmiths and harnessmakers in addition to the other craftsmen previously mentioned. But now the white-collar class was putting in its appearance. Listed also among the German names were those of an innkeeper, a merchant, a musician, a notary public and a clergyman. Some years before this two Germans, Charles Gartz and John Leypold, built and started to operate a sugar refinery, thereby inaugurating another one of Baltimore's important industries. And one Henry Dulheuer established the town's first German newspaper of which there is authentic record.

This period witnessed the arrival of still another German who was to play an important part in the commercial and social life of the city. He was Frederick W. Brune, a native of Bremen, Germany, where his family was prominent in business. Largely as a result of his efforts and his family connections there grew up between Baltimore and Bremen a trade relationship that was highly profitable to both ports. The German farmers in Frederick County had promoted Baltimore as a grain port; now the German merchants in the city promoted it as a tobacco port. From it they shipped Maryland tobacco to Bremen from which it was distributed throughout Germany. Ships returned from Germany to Baltimore with manufactured goods and human cargoes of immigrants.

It has been estimated that in the three decades prior to the Civil War some 200,000 German immigrants were landed in Baltimore. Part set out to people the Middle West, but many remained to swell the population of Baltimore. Two other Germans contemporary with Frederick Brune and, like him, well above the average in birth and education, were Christian Mayer and Lewis Brantz. They prospered in the tobacco export trade and soon had Maryland tobacco going, not only to Germany, but also to Holland, Denmark, Italy and even to India. Lewis Brantz also was a skilled cartographer. He made the first scientific survey of Chesapeake Bay and embodied it in a map. His map was standard until very recent times when it was replaced by one of the U. S. Coastal Survey.

The language barrier was a formidable one. Save for a few notable exceptions, Germans were looked upon as foreigners. Add to that the fact that they preferred German customs to those of their adopted country and found their own company more congenial than that of other people. As a result they kept to themselves and developed their own social system apart from the rest of the community.

As the German population increased social distinctions grew up as between Germans. Particularly characteristic of this German social scheme was the elaborate organization of clubs, each catering to a different class. At the top of the pile was the Germania Club which was founded in 1840. It was the most exclusive of all and its membership was confined to the wealthy merchants. Prominent among them was Albert Schumacher, son of a City

Counselor of Bremen. He arrived in Baltimore in 1826 and joined an exporting firm that shipped goods from the local port to all parts of the world. Mr. Schumacher amassed a large fortune in these operations. He was president of the Germania Club and of the German Society and also was active in Zion Church and Zion School. He was highly regarded in the business world, serving on the board of the B. & O., of the Chamber of Commerce and the boards of various banks. He and his family seem to have taken no part in the social life of the city outside German circles.

Next to the Germania in social importance was the Concordia, founded in 1847. This club emphasized a literary and musical program that appealed to the intellectuals of the upper middle class. Its musical and dramatic divisions sponsored ambitious productions that gave it unusual distinction.

A cut below the Germania and the Concordia were the singing societies. The oldest of these was the Liederkranz which was organized in 1836 out of the choir of Zion Church. It claimed to be the oldest singing society in the United States and is believed to have presented the first Beethoven symphony performed in Baltimore. The Liederkranz made a specialty of oratorios and even ventured on the production of operas. Other singing societies stemming from choirs and catering to a lower social group were the Harmonie and the Arion. On the other hand, the Germania Mannechor, founded in 1856, was reserved primarily for the families of the wealthy merchants. These various singing societies met annually with similar societies in Philadelphia and other cities for a national sangerfest.

At the bottom of the social scale were the gymnastic clubs. These appealed to the rank and file of immigrants and were part of the Turner movement whose basic concept was a healthy mind in a healthy body. The Turners went in for tumbling and other acrobatics. A favorite stunt was the human pyramid. The tights and handlebar mustaches of the participants added an awful splendor to the completed human design. Photographs were taken and handed down as treasured heirlooms to succeeding generations.

The two most active Turnvereine in Baltimore were the Sozialdemocratische Turnverein, founded in 1849, and the Turnverein Vorwarts which made its appearance after the Civil War. The Turners also were closely allied with the liberal movement in Germany. The Sozialdemocratische was largely a child of the Forty-eighters who fled Germany after the failure of the assault on the autocratic government of the day. The Turners were for the most part free thinkers as well as liberals.

Among the Forty-eighters were also many intellectuals, including writers, journalists, professors, musicians and lawyers. Many regarded themselves as being in temporary exile awaiting a return to Germany. They arrived in this country just in time to take part in the bitter debates on slavery that preceded the Civil War. With rare exception they sided with the North. At the outbreak of hostilities the Baltimore Turners were so closely allied with the Union cause that their hall was attacked by Southern sympathizers. They volunteered in large numbers for service with the Northern armies. On the other hand, the wealthy German merchants favored the South where they had many close business ties.

Soon after the American Revolution German Catholics arrived in Baltimore in sufficient numbers to warrant a proposal to establish distinct German congregations. This Archbishop John Carroll stoutly opposed as did one of his most distinguished successors, Cardinal Gibbons. Nevertheless it was found expedient to introduce German Catholic churches for immigrants of the faith who could speak no other language. By the time of the Civil War the German Catholic population had grown to a point where there were four German Catholic churches.

Mention already has been made of Zion Church's early interest in education and the founding of a school in connection with it. As time went on the minister and congregation grew indifferent and the school and its few pupils were neglected. Such was the situation when Heinrich Scheib arrived as pastor in 1835. In addition to his gifts as a pastor Scheib had a genius for teaching, and he at once attacked the problem of the school. His first step was to dissociate its instruction from the church and make it purely secular education in spite of its being sponsored by the church and headed by the minister. Then, in the face of determined opposition from other people, he introduced instruction in English as well as in German. Baltimore parents recognized good education when they saw it and in those days the public school system had not been fully developed. It was not long therefore before pupils other than German were beating a path to Scheib's school to benefit from its excellent instruction.

A decade and a half later there arrived from Germany still another born educator in the person of Friedrich Knapp. He appeared first as tutor in the family of William A. Marburg, a wealthy tobacconist. A few years later, in 1853, he opened a school with sixty pupils. Herr Knapp stated his policy clearly and frankly. "Everyone," he said, "the State as well as the Church, the communities as well as the government, tries to control and influence schools and teachers. The Knapp school emphatically refuses any such influence."

This bold announcement evidently pleased the Baltimoreans for Knapp's school grew and prospered until it was the most important private school in the city. At the height of its success, during the Civil War, F. Knapp's German and English School had 700 pupils. As the public school system expanded the demand for private schools such as Knapp's declined. Yet it continued on into the eighties including in its enrollment students of various racial backgrounds. One of its most distinguished pupils in the twilight period was H. L. Mencken who began his formal schooling there.

As the Germans in Baltimore increased in numbers during the mass immigration period they grew also in political power. Eventually they were in a position to demand and get German-English schools under the public school system. By 1897 there were as many as seven such schools in the city. No other white racial group ever enjoyed such a privilege.

Through thrift and application small German businesses in the course of years grew into large ones. Baltimore's German merchants achieved national, and in some cases world-wide, prominence. For example, there were William Knabe and Charles M. Stieff, piano manufacturers, and Gustav Christian Dohme, of the famous drug firm of Sharp and Dohme. There was George William Gail who entered into partnership with Christian Ax to form one of the largest tobacco companies of the day in the United States. As Baltimore grew in importance as a tobacco market the German tobacconists increased in wealth and prestige.

Among the German names prominent in the industry were Schmeisser, Marburg, Gieske, Lauts, Felgner and Niemann.

A century after a German established the first brewery in Baltimore Town Germans continued to monopolize the brewing of beer which had become a leading industry. German names associated with it were Gunther, Weisner, Vonderhorst, Gottlieb, Bauernschmidt, Strause and Brehm.

When the English-speaking people made money they immediately proceeded to follow the customs of the British upper classes, spending it lavishly on country estates and good horseflesh. They aspired to making a place for themselves in society and went in for elaborate entertaining. During the last three decades of the 19th century there were many Germans in Baltimore of abundant fortune who could gratify any wish. Yet for the most part they continued to live comfortably but modestly in their own circle, and also to marry inside it. Among the few who broke away were the Brunes, the Middendorfs, the Marburgs, the Fischers, the von Kapffs, the von Fersens, the von Lingens, and the Lurmans. These allied themselves with the old Baltimore families, rode to hounds, danced at balls, had their daughters formally introduced to society at the Cotillon and otherwise adopted the mores of the English-speaking group.

In 1887, according to an unofficial estimate, there were 100,000 German-Americans in Baltimore out of a total population of 425,000 and a white population of 360,000. In other words, more than a fourth of the white population was of German extraction. The rise of the German Empire after the Franco-Prussian War in 1870 inspired these people with a new pride in their German origin and at the same time retarded their amalgamation with the rest of the city's native population. The situation gave rise to the German-American movement which was nationwide and reached its climax with the outbreak of World War I.

In Baltimore, as elsewhere throughout the country, the beginning of hostilities in 1914 found the German-Americans almost solidly behind the Kaiser and actively at work to stem the growing sympathy of Americans for the Allied cause. Some of the most prominent Baltimore Germans were suspected of being implicated in plots to sabotage the manufacture of munitions for the Allies. When the United States entered the war the authorities at once centered their attention on the German-Americans. In some places they were interned. However, thanks to the restraining influence of Federal Judge John C. Rose, who kept his head and sense of proportion, Baltimore's German-American population went unmolested. In spite of divided loyalties they gave no trouble and many of their sons served honorably in the armed forces of the United States.

Because of the qualities inherent in their nature the Germans have played a leading part in the musical and artistic life of the community. Mention has been made of the singing societies. By 1900 there were no fewer than fifteen of them and in 1903 the national sangerfest was held in the city. To the Germans goes the credit for having organized the first philharmonic orchestra in the city. They, too, were the inspiration of a Haydn society, dedicated to the performance of classic orchestral music.

Baltimoreans of German birth naturally gravitated to the Peabody Conservatory, center of musical life in the city. Otto Ortmann, a German, was long a director of it as well as professor of music at Goucher College. Franz C. Bornschein was a violinist and a composer, Frederick R. Huber was director of Municipal Music and Gustav Strube was a composer and orchestra conductor.

In the field of art there have been a number of painters of German blood. But sculpture has been the German's most conspicuous contribution to the Baltimore community. In fact no single group has done more to adorn the city's parks and public places than the Baltimore-German school of sculptors. Earliest among them was William Henry Rinehart, a Carroll County boy who had his first contact with marble while working in a quarry. He came to Baltimore as an apprentice to a firm of marble and stonecutters, and also entered the Maryland Institute as a student. While there he attracted the attention of William T. Walters, the art collector. Mr. Walters sent him abroad to complete his training, after which Rinehart returned to design the bronze doors of the national Capitol in Washington. In Baltimore his most familiar work is the seated statue of Chief Justice Taney in Mt. Vernon Place. Then there was Ephraim Keyser who, among other works, executed the DeKalb Monument which stands on the State House grounds at Annapolis as well as busts of Cardinal Gibbons, Sidney Lanier and Daniel Coit Gilman.

Most prolific of all has been Hans Schuler who was born in Lorraine when it was a German province and came to Baltimore at the age of six years. His work fairly dominates North Charles Street in the vicinity of the Johns Hopkins University. The monument to the founder is his. So, too, are the odd green bronze likeness of the poet Sidney Lanier, flattened against a stone on the university grounds several hundred yards to the north, and the statue of General Sam Smith in Wyman Park to the south.

Still another prolific member of this school was Edward Berge. He also was a student at the Maryland Institute before going to Paris to become a pupil of Rodin. Familiar to all Baltimoreans are his statue of Lieutenant Colonel William H. Watson, Baltimore's only memorial to the Mexican War, and his statue of Lieutenant Colonel George Armistead at Fort McHenry. He did the Indian study in Clifton Park called "On The Trail." Best known of all, however, is his "Sea Urchin" in the fountain in Washington Place. Were all the works of the German sculptors removed Baltimoreans would scarcely recognize their city.

Two wars waged against their homeland and the break in the flow of immigrants combined to put an end to the German-Americans. The third generation had forgotten its German and spoke English. It could not maintain loyalty to a country from which it was so far removed. When Hitler's true nature was revealed only a few extremists among the Baltimoreans of German descent embraced the Nazi cause.

Sergeant Paul J. Wiedorfer, the only Baltimorean to win the Congressional Medal of Honor in World War II, was German on both sides of his family. Yet, when he returned home to receive a public ovation, nobody thought of him as being German any more than a person named Jones would be thought of as Welsh. Today the Germans have been completely absorbed into the rest of the population. Their names survive. In the obituary columns in the newspapers every day at least a third of the names can be recognized as being of Teutonic origin. But as a race apart the Baltimore Germans have ceased to exist.

Chapter 15

JEWRY'S CONTRIBUTION

THE *Maryland Journal and Baltimore Advertiser* of December 9, 1773, carried a notice to the effect that Benjamin Levy "has just opened a store on Market Street, at the corner of Calvert Street, where he sells wholesale and retail, for ready money only, a large variety of articles including liquors, spices, drugs, foodstuffs and dry goods."

The notice is significant as being the first surviving reference to the presence of a Jew in Baltimore. Levy must have enjoyed a favorable reputation for, in 1776, he was one of a number of men who was authorized by the New American Congress to sign bills of credit for money. So far as the record shows he was the first of many Jewish merchants who were to leave their imprint on the community.

While occasional individuals like Benjamin Levy are mentioned there appears to have been no Jewish colony in Baltimore before the Revolution. Growth was slow. In 1825 it was estimated that there were not more than 150 Jews in the whole of Maryland and, in 1835, not more than 300.

The first Jew to make his mark was Solomon Etting. He came to Baltimore from York, Pennsylvania, in 1789, at the age of twenty five years and opened a hardware business. His widowed mother, Shinah Solomon Etting, and five of her other children had preceded him. Shortly thereafter the widow of Israel Cohen of Richmond, Virginia, a daughter and five sons arrived. The Ettings, the Cohens and the Solomons were superior people and immediately gained recognition in the community.

At that period a State law forbade a Jew to hold public office. From 1818 to 1825 at every meeting of the Legislature an effort was made to erase this disability. The so-called "Jew Bill" had the support of a number of the leading gentiles but nevertheless met with stout opposition year after year. It finally was passed in 1825. The same year Solomon Etting was elected president of First Branch of the City Council and Jacob I. Cohen to membership in it. Meanwhile Etting's hardware store had expanded into a general shipping and commercial business and Etting was a rich man as well as a prominent one. He was on a committee to protest to General Washington the terms of Jay's treaty with England. He was a director of the new Union Bank and of the Baltimore Water Company. And, soon after he ascended to the presidency of the upper chamber of the Council, he was elected to the first board of directors of the new Baltimore & Ohio Railroad.

The first synagogue was formed in 1826 and held its meetings in a room over a grocery store in East Baltimore. It received a charter in 1830 and took the name of the Baltimore Hebrew Congregation which in later years has been also known as the Madison Avenue Temple. Other important congregations which followed were Oheb Shalom in 1853, Har Sinai in 1842, Bikur Cholim in 1865 and Chizuk Amuno in 1871.

In time of war Baltimore's Jewish citizens were found taking their part in the country's defense. During the American Revolution one Nathaniel Levy served under Lafayette in the "First Baltimore Cavalry." Perhaps he was a son, or at least a kinsman, of Benjamin Levy, the pioneer merchant. When the United States almost went to war with France in 1798 Reuben Etting, son of Solomon, was elected captain of the Independent Blues and prepared for action which never came. Later he was appointed U. S. Marshal by Thomas Jefferson.

Among the defenders at Fort McHenry who kept the flag flying in September, 1814, were Philip Cohen, Mendes Cohen, Samuel Etting, Levi Collmus, Jacob Moses and Samuel Cohen. To get a little ahead of the story, Baltimore Jews also offered their services in the Mexican War; some saw active duty and one, Leon Dyer, rose to high rank. An all-Jewish company was formed with Levi Benjamin as first lieutenant but it did not become engaged. Dyer, as a youth, worked in his father's beef-packing plant, which was said to have been the first such plant in America. He was a man of powerful physique and commanding presence. He went as a volunteer to join the Texas forces in their struggle for independence; later when the United States entered the war he became Quartermaster General in the American forces. He at one time was acting Mayor of Baltimore and was elected president of the Baltimore Hebrew Congregation, a post his father held before him.

Most of the Baltimore Jews were of a German or Dutch extraction. Some came direct from Europe, while the rest arrived by way of other American cities or the West Indies. The great influx began around the year 1835. The vast majority of them were poor and tried to make a living by peddling goods. With a compassion characteristic of the race those who were well off set to work to look after their less fortunate brethren. The 1850's and 1860's saw the establishment of a "Society for Educating Poor and Orphan Hebrew Children," a "Hebrew Ladies Sewing Society" to make clothes for the poor, a "Hebrew Hospital and Asylum Association," a "Hebrew Free Burial Society," and a "Hebrew Orphan Asylum." Most of these organizations or their successors exist in Baltimore to this day.

The Baltimore Jewish Community has now grown to the neighborhood of 75,000 persons. Like many other racial groups, on their arrival in Baltimore they settled near the harbor and then, as they became better off, moved farther afield. Of the present 75,000 Jews in the city it is estimated that there are still 15,000 in East Baltimore near the harbor. The other 60,000 make their home in the western part of the city in the Park Heights Avenue and Forest Park neighborhoods.

Jews have played conspicuous parts in the medical and legal professions. The late Dr. Harry Friedenwald was one of the country's leading ophthalmologists, as is his son Jonas. Dr. Louis Hamburger and Dr. Charles Austrian have been outstanding in medicine. Judge Eli Frank and Judge Jacob Ulman served with distinction on the Supreme Bench of Baltimore City as does Judge Joseph Sherbow at the present time. Philip B. Perlman after having risen to the top of his profession in the city was appointed by President Truman as Solicitor General of the United States and has run up an astonishing record of victories for the Government in his pleadings before the United States Supreme Court. Jews are found on most civic committees, and several Jewish banking firms maintain the ancient tradition of the Jew's peculiar genius in finance.

Jewish scholars have made valuable contributions to learning as members of the faculty of Johns Hopkins. Mention already has been made of Sylvester, the mathematician, who came from England at Gilman's invitation. Others have been Jacob H. Hollander, political economist; Aaron Ember, Egyptologist; William Rosenau, religious studies; Dr. Cyrus Adler, Semitic languages; George Boas, philosophy; David S. Blondheim, Romance languages; and Dr. Florence E. Bamberger and Dr. David E. Weglein in education. Dr. Weglein also was for years superintendent of the Baltimore public schools.

But it is the Jewish merchants whose names are best known in the community and whose activities affect thousands of their fellow citizens. The Hochschilds, the Kohns, the Hutzlers, the Hamburgers, the Hesses, the Gutmans, the Katzs, the Hechts, the Schleisners, the Slesingers, and Bonwits in the retail trade, the Blausteins in oil, the Greifs and Sonneborns in wholesale clothing, Polan Katz in umbrellas—these are a few on whom Baltimoreans are dependent for clothes, household furnishings and other essentials of civilized living.

Aside from these very practical services the influence of the Jews on the Baltimore community is felt in their generous support of all cultural enterprises, especially in the fields of music and art. They subscribe in large numbers to the symphony concerts and other musical programs at the Lyric. They in large part make possible the annual season of the Metropolitan Opera Company.

Through their gifts of art treasures and money the Jews have added immensely to the scope of the Baltimore Museum of Art. One of the first large benefactors of this institution was the late Jacob Epstein, founder and directing head of the Baltimore Bargain House. Starting out in 1881, at the age of seventeen years, with $600 capital Mr. Epstein built up a wholesale mail-order business that ran to millions of dollars annually and brought him a handsome fortune. He became an art collector and, at his death, bequeathed his collection to the art museum then recently established by the municipality. This included painting and sculpture. The paintings were largely representative of the old masters —Van Dyck, Hals, Raphael, Titian, Goya and Reynolds. The sculpture collection contains pieces by Rodin and Barye, not to mention a bust of the Baltimore merchant Jacob Epstein by the English sculptor Jacob Epstein. No doubt in years to come one of the most valuable items in the collection will be a sly portrait of the benefactor by the contemporary English master, Sir William Orpen.

By far the most important of the museum's Jewish benefactions is the Cone Collection, gift of the two sisters Claribel and Etta Cone, daughters of Herman and Helen Guggenheim Cone. They were born in Tennessee, came to Baltimore as girls and spent most of their life there save for frequent trips to Europe.

Of the two, Claribel was the dynamic leader and Etta the quiet follower. Claribel was the first woman to receive a medical degree from the Johns Hopkins University. She dressed with a flourish and had an imperial carriage. She was regularly seen at Lyric concerts draped in Oriental shawls, laden down with exotic jewelry and her coiffure stabbed through by silver skewers. There was a story to the effect that once in the lobby of the Munich opera house Kaiser Wilhelm II offered her his arm, mistaking her for a duchess. Sister Etta, on the other hand, affected delicate laces. She, too, did the housekeeping.

The Cones were cousins of that other intriguing personality, Gertrude Stein. On the first of some twenty eight trips to Europe around 1900 they joined the Stein family group in Paris—Gertrude, Leo and Mr. and Mrs. Michael Stein. Just then a school of young French artists were breaking away from the classical tradition and attempting some daring things. Gertrude introduced the Cones to what was then known as modern art.

The two sisters became enthusiasts and bought up the works at a time when nobody else wanted them. They were particularly intimate with Matisse and ended by buying forty one of his paintings, quantities of his sketches and his more important sculptures. These paintings are said to reveal the artist's development more comprehensively than any other group in America. While the works of Matisse predominated their purchases included also Cézanne, Van Gogh, Renoir, Manet and Picasso.

The Cones brought their collections back to their apartment—actually three apartments in one—in the Marlborough, on Eutaw Place. Here in a series of small rooms with gray-green walls and dark mahogany trim were spread in delightful confusion priceless oriental rugs, Renaissance and Queen Anne tables and chairs, chests and armoires, and draperies of red damask and embroidered burgundy velvet. Dominating the scene were the paintings in gold frames, occupying every inch of wall space from living to bathroom.

Dr. Claribel died in 1929. She knew Baltimore for the conservative place it is, and questioned whether this collection of modern art would ever be appreciated by the community. So strong were her doubts that she left directions to Sister Etta that, unless "the spirit of appreciation of modern art" showed evidence of growth in Baltimore, her share of the collection was to go elsewhere.

It was fortunate that, prior to the death of Miss Etta Cone, in 1949, the director of the museum was Mrs. Adelyn Breeskin. The loudest criticism of Mrs. Breeskin and her staff has been that they are far too partial to the moderns. However far they may have erred from the conventional pattern their attitude was immensely helpful in keeping Miss Etta Cone's interest in Baltimore alive. So it came about that by the time Miss Etta had to make a decision as to the disposal of the collection she was convinced that Baltimore had given evidence of the growth in appreciation stipulated by Dr. Claribel. So the Baltimore Museum of Art got the collection. To make it more of a documentary educational group Miss Etta added to it examples of Matisse's predecessors, Delacroix and Corot. The collection, in addition to some 350 paintings and drawings and 50 pieces of sculpture, includes quantities of jewelry, tapestries, laces and furniture said to be worth $3,000,000. Miss Etta also left a bequest of $400,000 in cash to be used to build a wing to house the collection.

Time marches on. What was modern in the collecting days of the Cones has now become virtually classical. More recent artists have dared to venture into even stranger fields. Again thanks to a Jewish woman the Baltimore Museum of Art has been able to keep abreast of the movement. This new benefactor was Mrs. Saidie A. May. Mrs. May was born Saidie Adler, daughter of a wholesale Baltimore shoe dealer. She was herself an artist with a taste for all kinds of art and a special liking for the very latest departures. Through the years she contributed to the museum a vast treasure of classic and modern art. Her benefactions included also a 17th-century room and examples of stained glass from the 13th and 14th centuries. Most significant are the examples of the latest modern art. This collection picks up where the Cone collection leaves off. It begins with impressionism and embraces postimpressionism, cubism, expressionism, surrealism, primitivism, nonobjective art and constructivism. The Baltimore public can hardly be expected immediately to know what all of this means. The museum people assure that this, plus the Cone collection, "offers a comprehensive survey of the entire background and development of the 20th-century European painting."

Mrs. May also presented the museum with $300,000 in cash for the construction of a children's wing to be known as The Saidie A. May Young People's Art Center. Here the beginners are provided with the facilities for trying out their talent. Presumably they will be given the opportunity to find out what modern art is all about, which, unfortunately has not been vouchsafed to their somewhat perplexed parents.

Other Jewish benefactions are the Juilius Levy collection of oriental art combined with an endowment fund for the purchase of additions, and gifts to the museum's graphic arts department by Miss Blanche Adler, sister of Mrs. May.

Surprisingly enough the best-known Jew of Baltimore birth throughout the world at large is least known by the vast majority of people in her native city. She is the Zionist leader Henrietta Szold. Miss Szold was the daughter of Benjamin Szold, a native of Hungary, who came to Baltimore around the middle of the 19th century as rabbi of Oheb Shalom congregation. He served the congregation as rabbi for thirty four years and as rabbi emeritus for nine years more. He was a distinguished Hebrew scholar and the author of a number of religious books.

Henrietta was born December 21, 1860, on Eutaw Street, the eldest of eight daughters, and inherited the scholarly attributes of her father. Attending Western High School she was graduated at the head of her class with an average of 99.8 and delivered the address at the graduation exercises at Ford's Grand Opera House. She was the only Jewess in the class. Following graduation she taught in a private girls' school conducted by a Southern gentlewoman. She is said to have been shy and reticent as a girl, but judging by her letters, she appears to have overcome those weaknesses effectually.

The Szold household with its eight girls was intimate with the

Friedenwald household and its five boys. A special friendship developed between Henrietta Szold and Harry Friedenwald. In later life that gave rise to a collaboration between the two in Zionism. Dr. Friedenwald was the first president of the Zionist Federation. Some of the letters she wrote him reveal the passionate nature of her support of the causes to which she adhered and the violent distaste for certain other human foibles. In a letter written in 1887 from Old Point Comfort, Virginia, where she had gone on a vacation she noted that "the hotel was crowded with that despicable class of people—the Virginia aristocracy with the unjustifiable purse pride and shoddyism, or, if possible, even more ignorant pride of blood."

Miss Szold was quite as severe on her fellow Jews. Of them she wrote in 1888: "American Jews, American rabbis, are giving the world at present such a sad spectacle of their own utter worthlessness that I am beginning to understand the scorn the anti-semite harbors for our co-religionists." Again she wrote: "Why are we so hated, and why indeed are we so hateful?" "The pride of the rich Jew, the parvenu, is intolerable. His bearing toward the Russians, for instance, is inexcusable."

Reference to the Russians is significant. For in 1881 the Czar Alexander II of Russia was assassinated and this act was made the excuse for bloody pogroms throughout his empire. Russian Jews fled to this country and, for the first time, they made their appearance in Baltimore. Already they were imbued with the spirit of Zionism and it was from them that Henrietta Szold caught the first fire. Rabbi Szold felt great compassion for these refugees and took the leading part in helping them. Henrietta assisted him in this work. She journeyed over to East Baltimore at night to give instruction in English in what was the first night school for the education of immigrants.

In 1888 Miss Szold was active in organizing a group of Hebraists. In 1893 she helped form the Zionist Association in Baltimore which probably was the first Zionist Society in the United States. In 1903, following the death of her father, she left Baltimore for good and all, going to live in New York. A visit to Palestine, contrary to the expectation of her friends, strengthened rather than reduced her intense enthusiasm for the Zionist movement.

Miss Szold's greatest achievement was the part she played in the organization of Hadassah. It came out of a meeting in 1912 of a handful of Jewish women in the vestry room of a temple in New York. Its program was propagation of Zionism in America and the furtherence of health work among women and children in Palestine. Thereafter the organization of Hadassah became Miss Szold's paramount interest. In the 1920's she was sent to Palestine and from then on, save when she was commuting to New York, she spent her remaining years there. In 1927 she was elected one of the three members of the Palestine Executive Committee of the World Zionist Organization. She was the first woman to serve in that capacity. In 1945 she died at the age of eighty four years. From its humble beginning Hadassah now has more than 100,000 members. Its health work in Palestine has greatly expanded and its annual budget runs into the hundreds of thousands of dollars.

There is relatively little intermarriage among Jews and Gentiles in Baltimore though many instances could be cited in which such alliances have turned out happily. Nor is there widespread social intercourse between Gentiles and Jews. The Jews have their own social stratas, exclusive clubs, dancing classes and balls, their own private schools. They live in overwhelmingly Jewish neighborhoods although they are, at the moment, rapidly pushing the old hunting set out of the Green Spring Valley. The two groups meet for joint activity in charitable enterprises and in civic and business affairs. It would be futile to deny a tacit distinction between the two racial groups, yet between them there is mutual respect and a modicum of friction.

Chapter 16

THE MEDICAL FACULTY

WHEN Baltimore Town was laid out in 1729 two of the commissioners appointed to perform that important task were Dr. James Walker and Dr. George Buchanan. Thus from the very outset the doctors staked a claim which they have successfully maintained for more than two centuries.

As early as 1769 Dr. Henry Stevenson was inoculating against smallpox. He built an elegant house on the York Road and called it "Parnassus," but to his neighbors it was known as "Stevenson's Folly." Folly or not, he used it as a hospital and patients came from far and wide to seek immunity from a scourge which did not respect even so exalted a personage as George Washington.

Henry Stevenson was an Irishman who got his medical training in England. He and his elder brother John, also educated as a doctor, came to this country together. John, however, abandoned the profession to become a promotor to the great advancement of the town. Henry continued to practice until the outbreak of the American Revolution when his Tory sympathies forced him into exile and his property was confiscated. During the war he served in the British navy. When it was over he returned to his old house, resumed his practice and died in Baltimore at a ripe old age, much loved and lamented.

Possibly because of his own early experience with smallpox Washington sought to protect his stepson, Jacky Custis. The boy then was living at Annapolis in the home of the Rev. Jonathan Boucher, who was acting as his tutor, and came up to Baltimore for the inoculation. In Washington's correspondence is found a letter to Mr. Boucher, written in 1771, thanking him for his "attention to Jack in the Small Pox." So even at that early date the town had laid the foundation for its reputation as a medical center.

The Stevensons were by no means the only doctors. Scharf's

Chronicles lists some sixteen contemporary practitioners. Prominent among them was the German immigrant Dr. Charles Frederick Wiesenthal who, it will be recalled, performed valuable service with the Continental Army in the Revolution. Baltimore was being exploited by quacks who went through the country playing on the ignorance and superstition of the public by professing to cure all sorts of ailments through the use of Chinese stones and powders. The record shows that Dr. Wiesenthal, on December 15, 1788, called a meeting "on behalf of the faculty" to petition the Assembly for the better regulation of the practice of physic throughout the State. Unfortunately he died six months later and nothing came of the plan.

In the years immediately following the Revolution Baltimore grew by leaps and bounds and the medical profession kept pace with it. On numerous occasions when epidemics threatened doctors were appointed temporarily as health officers to handle the situation. In the summer of 1793 Philadelphia was having one of the worst of its yellow-fever visitations and Baltimore was fearful that it, too, would fall a victim to the malady. To meet the crisis a Committee of Health was officially appointed on September 12th, and continued to serve regularly. When Baltimore Town was incorporated as Baltimore City in 1797, the name of the body was changed from the "Committee of Health" to the "Commission of Health" and it has continued uninterruptedly to this day. Baltimore therefore claims the distinction of having the oldest health commission with an unbroken record in the United States.

In spite of past failures a group of physicans from Baltimore City and Baltimore County in 1799 petitioned the Assembly for the right to incorporate as a medical society. The Assembly responded favorably and on January 20th passed an act to establish a "Medical and Chirurgical Faculty." The Faculty has had a continuous existence and serves to bind together the local societies throughout the State. The act granted to the faculty the important power of creating a Medical Board of Examiners to examine candidates and grant licenses.

Dr. Henry Stevenson in his inoculations for smallpox employed the ancient method imported from the East in which a scab from a human being suffering with the disease was used and the subject was given an actual case of it. Sometimes these artificial cases proved as virulent as the natural ones. This crude method was replaced by that of Dr. Edward Jenner, a doctor of Gloucestershire, England, who substituted vaccination for inoculation. Jenner reported his first successful case in 1796. In 1801 William Taylor, a Baltimore merchant, received a supply of vaccine from his brother in London and distributed it among the medical practitioners in the town. Thus, in spite of primitive communications, within five years after the discovery of vaccination Baltimore doctors were protecting their patients with it.

Evidence of the increasing importance of Baltimore at the expense of Annapolis was the arrival of Dr. John B. Davidge from the latter town. Dr. Davidge had been educated for his profession at the University of Edinburgh, then famous as a medical institution. He was a skillful surgeon and also gifted as a lecturer and teacher. At the time of his taking up residence in Baltimore a proposal was made to start a medical college and a committee was appointed to make a study of it. Rather than wait for official action Dr. Davidge decided to start a school of his own. In 1802 he commenced lectures with a few students and prospered sufficiently to erect an anatomical hall at the southeast corner of Saratoga and Liberty Streets for the term of 1807.

To this hall Dr. Davidge brought for dissection the body of a man who had been hanged for murder. News of the presence of the corpse spread around the town and soon a crowd gathered in front of the building, while indignation grew against Dr. Davidge and his students. It resulted in an attack being made on the hall and its complete destruction at great personal loss to Dr. Davidge. Yet the disaster had a far-reaching effect, for it impressed the doctors with the necessity of getting the protection of the State. So it was that Dr. Davidge and two associates, Dr. John Shaw and Dr. James Cocke of Virginia, applied to the Legislature for the privilege of establishing a medical college in Baltimore.

January 20, 1808, the Legislature obliged by passing an act for the creation of a college to be known as "the College of Medicine of Maryland." The act stipulated that the privileges and honors of the college were to be available to all without enforcing any religious or civil test or urging attendance of the students upon any particular plan of religious worship or service. Shortly thereafter seven pupils matriculated in order to take advantage of the privileges and honors offered. There being no other place of assembly they were instructed in the homes of members of the faculty. Such was the beginning of the Medical School of the University of Maryland.

A few years later John Eager Howard, who was forever disposing of his real estate for public purposes, gave land for the site of the school. On May 7, 1812, he laid the cornerstone for the first building at Greene and Lombard Streets where the university remains to the present day. By the summer of 1813 the new quarters were ready and the faculty was boasting that "the apartments provided for the classes are more spacious and convenient than any other in America, and deemed inferior to none in Europe."

The new medical school prospered. By 1825 the enrollment had risen to 300 students. Then the Legislature passed an act taking the school out of the hands of the medical men; the public lost faith in the institution and the student body dropped to 18. But in 1839 the management was restored to the regents, and since then the school has prospered save for a break during the Civil War.

In the early 19th century there were several instances in which groups of doctors joined together around a hospital which provided clinical material and incorporated as a medical school. One such institution was Washington Medical College which was incorporated in 1833. It pursued its course with varying fortune for more than forty years, eventually merging with a similiar institution, the College of Physicians and Surgeons. The lasting distinction of Washington College was that its medical school was built around the hospital to which Edgar Allan Poe was taken in his last illness and in whose ward he died. The hospital was situated on the present Broadway and continues to flourish today as the Church Home and Hospital under the auspices of the Episcopal Church. The College of Physicians and Surgeons, with which Washington College was merged, was incorporated in 1872. It was eventually absorbed by the University of Maryland as was also the Baltimore Medical College, another independent school of like character. All that survives today of the College of Physicians and Surgeons is its name worked out in brick high up on the east facade of Mercy Hospital at Calvert and Saratoga Streets.

In the middle period of Baltimore's medical history, which is to say from 1800 to 1888, there is found among the practitioners an occasional giant whose fame survived him. One such was Dr. George Frick who wrote the first book on ophthalmology in the United States. Dr. William Gibson, who got his medical education in Edinburgh, was a surgeon of rare talent. It was he who extracted from the shoulder of General Winfield Scott the ball received in the Battle of Lundy's Lane in the War of 1812.

An even more famous doctor was Nathan Ryno Smith, a New Englander. He had inherited his professional gifts from his father, Nathan Smith who enjoyed the rare distinction of having founded three medical schools respectively at Dartmouth, Yale and the University of Vermont. Nathan Ryno, who was born in Cornish, New Hampshire, came to Baltimore in 1827 to occupy the chair of anatomy at the University of Maryland's school of medicine. His students called him "the Emperor of Surgeons." Nathan Ryno in turn had a son, Dr. Alan Penniman Smith who was a close personal friend of Johns Hopkins and is sometimes credited with having influenced the latter to assign part of his fortune to the establishment of the medical school and hospital bearing his name.

Still another famous medical family in Baltimore which made its start at the turn of the 19th century is the Chatards. First of the line was Pierre Chatard, a Frenchman, who fled with his family from an uprising of slaves in San Domingo and came to this country in 1797. He settled in Baltimore in 1800. A graduate of the University of Paris he had broad experience with tropical diseases through his sojourn in the West Indies and this made him a particularly valuable man during yellow fever epidemics. Pierre Chatard practiced in Baltimore for forty five years.

Pierre's son, Ferdinand Edmé Chatard, also became a doctor. He practiced as a physician and surgeon from 1829 to 1884. He and his father together are said to have brought no fewer than 9,609 Baltimore babies into the world. The family tradition next was sustained by Ferdinand Edmé Chatard, Jr., who practiced until his death in 1900. He was joined by his son J. Albert Chatard. The Chatard line is at present represented by J. Albert and his son, Ferdinand Edmé, the third bearer of that name and representative of the fifth generation of Chatards to practice in Baltimore. Thus this one family alone has rendered the local community more than 150 years of unbroken medical service.

Other names famous in the period are Colin Mackenzie, Charles O'Donovan, James McIntire, Samuel Chew, John Whitridge, Julian Chisholm and John Buckler. Many of the names that were distinguished in the medical profession are borne by their descendants. The Charles O' Donovan of today represents the fourth generation of his family in practice in Baltimore.

In this middle period Baltimore made history also in the sister science of dentistry. Credit goes to Horace H. Hayden, a New Englander, and to Chapin A. Harris, from up-state New York, for doing pioneer work in this field. Both were doctors of medicine as well as dentists. Dr. Hayden had a national reputation as a geologist, too. He moved to Baltimore and began practice in 1800. He was sufficiently schooled also in surgery to serve as an assistant surgeon at the Battle of North Point, during the British invasion of Baltimore in 1814. He taught small classes in dentistry at his home at night and also lectured on dental physiology and pathology at the University of Maryland.

Harris, who was thirty seven years younger than Hayden, arrived in Baltimore in 1833 and was licensed as a dentist by the Medical and Chirurgical Faculty. In 1839 he joined with Dr. Hayden and others in petitioning the Legislature for the right to incorporate as a school of dentistry. The Legislature granted the petition and the Baltimore College of Dental Surgery was chartered on February 1, 1840. By this act it became the first dental college in the world.

Dr. Hayden and Dr. Harris also collaborated in forming in 1840 the American Society of Dental Surgeons, the first national association of dentists. Unfortunately the world was not large enough to hold these two heroic figures. Bad feeling developed between them and reached a culmination when Harris established the *American Journal of Dental Science* over the opposition of Hayden. The college which they founded continues to flourish as the dental school of the University of Maryland. If, unlike the people of Europe, Americans do not assume that false teeth are as inevitable as death and taxes; and, through regular and scientific care, hold on to their God-given teeth, they have to thank Horace Hayden and Chapin Harris.

Thus when, in 1867, Johns Hopkins got his medical school and hospital incorporated Baltimore already had an old and respected medical tradition. Its physicians and surgeons bore a more than favorable comparison with those in other parts of the country. It is well to bear this fact in mind if a full understanding is to be had of the manner in which the proponents of the new medical school rode roughshod over the leaders of the old. Very likely the conflict was inevitable and perhaps Gilman was right in making little pretense at appeasement.

Johns Hopkins himself selected the site for the hospital on Broadway in East Baltimore and bought the land. There is evidence that he had in mind the laying out of a wide boulevard to connect the hospital with the university which he pictured as being at Clifton. Actual establishment of the hospital and the medical school awaited his death and the bequest set forth in his will. The school of arts and sciences began work in 1876, but the hospital did not open until the spring of 1889 and the medical school not until October, 1893.

Gilman was a rank outsider with no local loyalties. As in the case of the school of arts and sciences his object was to create an institution not of buildings, but of men. Likewise as in the case of the school of arts and sciences he proposed to make the whole world his recruiting ground. The new medical school did make a gesture in the direction of the local medical hierarchy by naming an advisory committee that included a number of the older men. But it never was called on for advice and eventually went out of existence.

Several times Gilman attempted to attract to the faculty of the new school men of established reputation in Europe but he failed. His much greater success lay in choosing brilliant young men eager to have a part in this bold experiment. Again, as in the case of the school of arts and sciences, Gilman displayed his genius at choosing the right ones. From the outset the hospital and the university were intimately associated. The boards of the two institutions were almost identical. Very early in the proceedings a joint committee was established to coordinate the programs of the two institutions and it has continued to function throughout their history. Thus Gilman had as much of a hand in establishing the hospital as the university.

His first step was to enlist the help of five authorities on hospital construction. Each was requested to submit a paper setting forth his idea of what a hospital should be. The most acceptable response came from Lieutenant Colonel John Shaw Billings, who had had both experience and success in designing military hospitals during the Civil War. Billings then was working in the library of the Surgeon of the Army but he found time to apply himself to the Hopkins problem. He traveled extensively abroad studying hospitals. He also worked closely with Gilman in the search for men to head the departments in the new medical school and contributed valuable suggestions for the program of training. He and Gilman agreed that candidates for admission should have premedical courses with special emphasis on the biological sciences. This view, unique at the time, had the approval of Thomas Huxley. The result of intensive search for the men to carry out the program was the assembling of a wealth of genius seldom encountered on a single medical faculty.

The first find was William H. Welch, whom Dr. Gilman discovered working in a pathological laboratory in Germany. Welch was another indefatigable New Englander, educated at Yale and Columbia. He had left Germany and returned to this country to practice medicine in New York City when Gilman offered him the chair of pathology at the new school.

Next on the list of acquisitions was William Osler, a Canadian who at the time was professor of medicine at the University of Pennsylvania. Several years before he took up residence in Baltimore Osler was offering suggestions to Gilman for the hospital and the school. While the plans were taking shape Gilman invited Welch and Osler to go with him on a trip to New York and there the three of them made an intensive study of one of its leading hostelries, the Fifth Avenue Hotel. For, explained Dr. Gilman with practical wisdom somewhat rare among scholars, "There is no difference between a hospital and a hotel. This is really the hospital and we shall model ours upon it."

Osler, it appeared, had himself made a discovery at the University of Pennsylvania which he promptly passed on to Gilman. It was a promising young surgeon in the person of Howard A.

Kelly, a native of New Jersey. So impressed was Osler with Kelly's work that he unhesitatingly recommended him for the professorship of gynecology. Welch, too, had a protege to recommend. This was William S. Halsted, a New Yorker and, like Welch, a graduate of Yale and Columbia. Halsted, along with several other young doctors, had been making an exhaustive study of anesthetics. They became so absorbed in their work that they took the dangerous course of experimenting on themselves with the unfortunate result that all became addicted to the cocaine habit.

Halsted was undergoing treatment at a sanatorium when Welch, confident of his great ability, boldly recommended him for the important post of professor of surgery. The Hopkins trustees, stolid business men, were naturally reluctant to accept so grave a risk. Welch nevertheless persisted and he got wholehearted support from Osler. The upshot was that the trustees agreed to a compromise under which Halsted was to be given a year's trial as associate professor of surgery. The risk proved highly advantageous. At the end of the year Halsted gave no indication of returning to his old habit and he then was promoted to full professor. The Hopkins profited from Halsted's genius which soon brought world-wide fame to the new school.

In such manner was completed the group of "The Four Doctors" whom John Singer Sargent immortalized on his canvas. Yet without the great artist's help they won an even greater immortality through their own work in the wards and laboratories of the hospital and the medical school. One can imagine the skepticism of the mature members of the medical profession in Baltimore when they saw the new institution being abandoned to the caprices of these striplings. For, when they entered upon their careers at the Hopkins, Osler, the eldest of the four, was forty years old, Welch was thirty nine, Halsted was thirty seven and Kelly, the infant of the lot, was but thirty one.

Of the four doctors Welch was the great administrator. It did not take him long to organize his pathological laboratory on standards equal to those in Europe. Bacteriology then was a comparatively new discovery. People were just then abandoning the theory that disease was spread through foul air and learning there were such things as germs. In the laboratories young research workers were busy with slides and microscopes identifying and classifying. Welch was a pioneer in this country. But his tastes were catholic. No sooner was one school firmly established than he was off to start another. He was largely instrumental in founding the School of Hygiene and Public Health in 1918 and became its first director. The Johns Hopkins was the first medical institution in the United States to have such a school. It soon was attracting students from all parts of the world who were seeking training as public health officers.

In his old age Dr. Welch was the prime mover in the establishment of the Institute of the History of Medicine, another subject in which he was greatly interested. This, too, was the first of its kind in this country. As a crowning honor he was made professor of the history of medicine and assigned the congenial task of going to Europe in search of books for the library. More than forty years before Welch had been given a similiar mission. He then was sent to Europe with $2,000 to buy books and equipment for his laboratory. On his return he calmly announced that he had overspent his allowance by $500. But he got the money. In fact one of his strongest points was getting money for objects in which he was interested.

This incident was negligible compared with his operations on his second trip as a buyer in 1927. The Johns Hopkins gave him $5,000 to spend and the General Education Board added $7,500 to it. Again on his return home Dr. Welch confessed he had overspent his allowance. This time he estimated his total outlay at $100,000! The Rockefeller Foundation promptly footed the bill.

Dr. Welch has been described as "a medical statesman." A man of natural cultivation and profound scholarship he could hold his own in any learned company. His frequent trips abroad gave him an acquaintance with the leading lights of the medical profession in many countries. His opinion and advice were constantly being sought on the subjects in which he was expert.

Dr. Welch never married. As time went on his short rotund body and his twinkling eyes gave him more and more the appearance of a Santa Claus. He kept bachelor quarters and spent much of his leisure time in the Maryland and University Clubs. For many years he was president of the latter. To his students he was affectionately known as Popsy. His secretive habits inspired one of them to compose a ditty which gained wide popularity:

> Nobody knows where Popsy eats,
> Nobody knows where Popsy sleeps,
> Nobody knows whom Popsy keeps,
>   But Popsy.

Dr. Welch never bothered with a secretary and in consequence his correspondence suffered. As letters arrived he piled them on a table, then when the pile reached unsightly proportions he spread a newspaper over them and began a new layer. Dr. Hugh Young once undertook to remedy the situation by presenting him with a dictaphone. At first Dr. Welch delighted in the novelty. But he made only one record. This was the beginning of a letter which, after a few stumbling sentences, ended abruptly: "Hugh, I can't use this machine. Send your boy around and get it."

Even when he was editor of the *Journal of Experimental Medicine*, which he founded in 1896, Dr. Welch refused secretarial help. As a consequence many of the manuscripts submitted for publication were neither acknowledged nor returned to their authors. Distinguished members of the profession knowing Dr. Welch's failing implored help from Dr. Henry M. Hurd, Superintendent of the hospital. So, when Dr. Welch was out, Dr. Hurd would slip into his apartment, steal the manuscripts and forward them to their owners. Dr. Welch lived to a ripe old age and died universally lamented.

William Osler spent sixteen years with the Johns Hopkins. Welch said they were the most fruitful in Osler's life, for it was during that time that he established the first medical clinic worthy of the name in an English-speaking country. It was when he was in Baltimore that he also brought out his famous textbook on medicine. Like Welch, Osler was a man of exceptional cultivation. He was a philosophical essayist of no little distinction in addition to being a physician, and his pen was constantly at work turning out treatises on many subjects. Notable among them was his essay on "Immortality."

To students and hospital staff Osler was known as "the Chief," a title granted to no other member of the faculty in the entire history of the medical school. His daily visits to the wards of the hospital, on which he was accompanied by members of the staff, nurses and students, assumed the nature of a royal progress. Those who accompanied him never forgot the brilliance with which he described each interesting case encountered.

Dr. and Mrs. Osler lived in a cheerful and commodius house at 1 West Franklin Street, in the center of town. There on Saturday evenings members of the graduating class of the medical school assembled regularly on the invitation of Dr. Osler. On the bare dining-room table the butler had set out beer, pretzels and cigars. Dr. Osler sat at the head. Each man was called on in turn to describe the case he was attending, after which Dr. Osler would lead the discussion and conclude with his own comments.

There was still another favored group composed of young unmarried doctors who had studied under Osler and were just entering practice. Each was given a key to the Osler house and privileged to come in at leisure, browse in the library or sit down to tea with Mrs. Osler. They got to be known as "the latch-keyers." The Oslers had one child, a son named Revere, who spent his early years in this house. In keeping with the local custom of the day he was attended by a colored "mammy." All went well until one day the Oslers heard Revere give an order to "Heist dat winder." Forthwith the mammy was tactfully eased out and replaced by a Scotch governess with an authentic burr.

Though popularly regarded as a man of saintly quality, Osler had a strange sense of humor that sometimes bordered on the sadistic. Fortunately, his wife was understanding and made allowances for what could be described only as an eccentricity. For example, he once told her with a straight face of a mutual acquaintance fifty years of age who, he said, was going to have a baby and took childish delight in her surprise at a story he had made up out of the whole cloth.

On another occasion Dr. Osler brought a man home to dinner and, in advance, warned Mrs. Osler that he was deaf. Then before introducing the guest to Mrs. Osler he cautioned him to speak loud, explaining that Mrs. Osler was deaf. After that he sat throughout the meal with a beatific smile while Mrs. Osler and the guest, neither of whom was deaf, shouted at each other.

Even less pardonable was a trick he played on a young probationer. She had just completed the measuring of a tray of drugs for the night when Dr. Osler chanced to pass by her in a hospital corridor. Yielding to a sudden mischievous impulse the great physician began to pour the doses into each other. The probationer eventually completed her training and became the wife of a distinguished surgeon. Needless to say, after her experience, all praise of Osler left her cold and unimpressed. Another time he met in the corridor a nurse who was carrying a bowl of soup on a tray, seized a napkin that also was on the tray and stuck it into the soup. The nurse did not hesitate to express her indignation. That evening Mrs. Osler made a special trip across town to the hospital to offer an apology.

Yet, like most practical jokers, Dr. Osler could not take it when the joke was on him. For all the sins he had committed in this respect fate had arranged a cruel and more than adequate retribution. The occasion was the university's Commemoration Day, February 22, 1905. Osler had just accepted the invitation of Oxford University to become its Regius Professor of Medicine. He was delivering his valedictory address before the trustees, faculty and friends of the university. He evidently had taken great pains to prepare it and it sparkled with the best of his humor.

In the course of his address he alluded to a novel by Anthony Trollope in which the plot hinges on the scheme for a college into which at the age of sixty years men were to retire for a year of contemplation before a peaceful death by chloroform. Osler went on to say, "That incalcuable benefits might follow such a scheme is apparent to anyone who, like myself, is nearing the limit (he was 55) and who has made a careful study of the calamities which may befall man during the seventh and eighth decades." He concluded that he was a little dubious whether Trollope's proposal should be carried out "as my own time is getting so short."

The statement caused no more than a ripple of laughter in the audience. But it so happened a newspaper reporter was present and he was on the lookout for a feature. The allusion to Trollope and the chloroform struck his fancy. So next day when Baltimoreans picked up their newspapers their eyes fell on a headline which read "Osler Recommends Chloroform at Sixty." This from the greatest physician of the day!

Editors immediately saw the human-interest and news value of the story and invited comments. Press associations grabbed it and broadcast it to the nation. Men approaching sixty wrote indignant letters to the press. The question was discussed in editorials. Entertainers in musical comedy and vaudeville could be assured of a laugh by coming on the stage wearing a doctor's conventional frock coat, long black whiskers like Osler's and carrying a gallon bottle marked "Chloroform." There was to be no other public furore like it until somebody wrote the song "Everybody Works But Father." Of course Osler had not really recommended "chloroform at sixty." But no explanations could possibly erase the damage done by that headline. Osler "the Great Physician" stood before the world as an enemy of old age.

Now at last Osler learned the suffering that can be induced by a practical joke. Referring to the incident he remarked to a friend, "It's not pleasant to wake up in the morning and find yourself not famous, but infamous." Thereafter he never wanted to hear the incident mentioned.

Most impressive was the admiration and affection between Welch and Osler, a relationship entirely free from jealousy. Welch declared publicly that Osler was, in his opinion, the greatest clinician in the English-speaking world. Osler, for his part, once said of Welch that "He has the greatest mind, the greatest soul and the greatest heart of any man I know."

Osler is credited with using his charm and great gift for friendship in easing the somewhat strained relationship between the youthful Hopkins group and their elders of the University of Maryland. On coming to Baltimore he immediately plunged into the organized medicine in the city as it already existed. He was directly responsible for bringing the two groups together by enlivening the meetings of the Baltimore City Medical Society and the Medical and Chirurgical Faculty. He was active also in the construction of the Faculty building on Cathedral Street and the assembly of its excellent library.

Halsted was altogether different from his three other colleagues. He lacked the warmth and human touch of Welch, Osler and Kelly. The theory has been offered that he kept a tight rein on his emotions for fear of falling back into his old habit. He also was fastidious and had a private fortune that permitted him to indulge his expensive tastes. He delighted in good food and kept a stock of terrapin in his cellar. His house was filled with rare antiques and his table set with the finest silver and porcelain. The story is told of him that, having been particularly pleased with the way his stiff shirts were laundered during a trip to Paris, he thereafter sent them across the Atlantic to be done up.

As a lecturer Halsted was considered dull by some of his students to whom he was known as "the Professor." Others protested that he was dull only to dullards and neophytes. Those who knew him well contend that his greatest contribution was instilling in younger competent minds the concept of what surgery could be rather than what it had been. They claim further that, shadowy, reserved and aloof though he may have been in life, his figure thirty years after his death has accumulated much more substance and his ideal of surgery has become the stepping stone to further advances made by men whom he trained and by men who, even though without direct contact, have been imbued with his investigative spirit.

Halsted was a perfectionist whose every operation was a work of art. He refused to let himself be hurried. It was said of his operations that he removed so much of the patient with his refinements that sometimes there was serious doubt after an operation which part should go back to the ward. In the famous portrait of "The Four Doctors," Halsted's face is now less distinct than that of the other three men. This has given rise to the legend that Halsted, with his brusque manner, offended Sargent who got revenge by painting him in colors that would fade. It is a good story but lacks authentication.

Halsted however contradicted his reputation for frigidity by falling in love with one of his nurses, Miss Caroline Hampton, whom he married. The romance was responsible for an important new departure in surgical practice. In preparing for an operation it then was customary for doctors and nurses to make their hands sterile by prolonged scrubbing with germicidal soap and soaking them in a strong antiseptic solution. Miss Hampton's hands were delicate and the effect of the antiseptic on them most painful. As the romance progressed her suffering became increasingly painful to Dr. Halsted. He put his mind to the problem and came up with specifications for thin rubber gloves which Miss Hampton could wear in the operating room. The experiment was a success.

The thought then occurred that, if the gloves were practicable for a nurse, they might be used by the surgeon, too. Thus, thanks to a romance of the operating room, the wearing of rubber gloves by surgeons during their operations has become universal practice.

Youngest of the four doctors was Kelly. Not only was he young in years but also in looks. This sometimes led to misunderstandings. Patients who had learned of Kelly's fame from afar would not believe that one so immature in appearance actually was the great man. Dr. Tom Cullen, who was Kelly's assistant, once argued in vain after introducing Dr. Kelly to a patient who insisted: "You can't fool me, young man. That boy's not Dr. Kelly!"

Osler was quick to make use of the circumstances for one of his practical jokes. He delighted to hang about the dispensary where Kelly's patients were waiting to see him and warn them that Kelly was a very old man, in fact almost too old to be operating because his hands trembled. After that he would assure them there really was nothing to worry about. For, said he, as soon as Kelly got into the operating room the trembling disappeared and he was as steady as a rock.

That part of Osler's tale at least was true. Kelly's manual dexterity was phenomenal. Men who saw him operate spoke of his fingers "twinkling" and of his swift, clocklike precision. Osler, Welch and Kelly were all natural showmen and altogether conscious of their unique position in the world of medicine. In this quality Kelly was by no means the least. An operating clinic as he conducted it was a dramatic affair. First the patient was anesthetized and rolled into the well of the amphitheater. Then the instruments were sterilized and laid out while subordinate aides and nurses took their stations. When all was in readiness there was a moment of silence and suspense. Then Kelly made a dramatic entrance accompanied by a couple of lieutenants and the show was on.

On one such occasion, according to report, Kelly entered with his customary speed, seized a knife, stepped up to the operating table and with one deft stroke made an incision from the patient's navel upward to the breastbone. At this point one of his assistants tugged at the master's sleeve and whispered in his ear. Kelly nodded his head in acknowledgment. Then with another equally deft stroke he made an incision in the opposite direction from the patient's navel to the crotch.

In the 1890's because of a surgeon's exalted position it was considered essential that he always appear professionally in a frock coat. This was the badge of his rank. When he performed an operation he departed from formality only to the extent of rolling up his sleeves. But the great doctors at the Hopkins changed all that. They adopted a common-sense operating uniform consisting of a white cotton shirt, trousers and skullcap. On their feet they wore white tennis shoes. This was a shock to old fashioned patients. Dr. Kelly once called on one of them without waiting to get out of his operating uniform. No sooner was he out of sight that she summoned a nurse.

"This certainly is a queer hospital," she complained. "The cook has just been here and he has been asking me the most impertinent questions."

Dr. Kelly had a deep religious faith that was fundamental in nature. It was his custom to say a prayer before every operation. In his later years he was a prohibitionist and active in the Lord's Day Alliance. With other members he toured the Maryland counties urging observance of the Sabbath and looking out for infractions of the blue laws. He was interested in politics and once ran for Governor of Maryland, though his candidacy was not taken very seriously by the public and he won only a handful of votes.

Dr. Kelly felt a deep sympathy with the down-and-out. On occasion he enlisted the help of a newspaper reporter who could guide him through the city's flop houses where men paid a nickel a night for the privilege of sleeping on the floor. He also was an ardent herpetologist and sheltered a sizable collection of snakes in his house on Eutaw Street. In the early days of his professorship it was his custom to ride a bicycle from his home all the way across town to the medical school. He was distinguished also as a sire. He and Mrs. Kelly produced five sons and four daughters. For some ten years there was hardly any age group among the young people of the town that was without a Kelly.

Interestingly enough a warm friendship existed between Dr. Kelly and H. L. Mencken. Diametrically opposed as they were in so many ways each found much to admire in the other's genius.

The work of the Four Doctors might have gone unnoticed had it not been for Dr. Hurd, superintendent of the hospital. He was a methodical man and prodded them without mercy until they wrote up their most interesting cases and the results of their experiments. These reports were widely distributed and, within a very few years, the important things being done at the Hopkins were known in every medical clinic in Europe. As in the case of the graduate school, the Hopkins brought the fame of Baltimore to parts of the world that had never before heard of the place.

A major share of the genius of the Four Doctors lay in their gift for imparting their methods and techniques to their pupils, inspiring them with the same enthusiasm for research and discovery. They established a tradition which was taken up by the next generation of doctors who became masters in their own right. Outstanding among these pupils was Dr. John M. T. Finney who came to the Hopkins as assistant to Dr. Halsted. Dr. Finney went to Princeton for his academic degree and to Harvard for his medicine. He starred on the Princeton football team and, when he entered the Harvard medical school, continued his athletic career there. He had the unique distinction of winning both a "P" and an "H."

After serving his apprenticeship under Halsted, Dr. Finney achieved a nation-wide reputation as the leading surgeon of his day. During the administration of Theodore Roosevelt he included the White House on his professional rounds. Dr. Finney eventually shifted the major part of his work to the Union Protestant Infirmary, an old Baltimore institution. This was moved to a new site, housed in a new building and rechristened the Union Memorial Hospital. During his lifetime this hospital reflected the bigheartedness that was a Finney characteristic. The buoyancy passed from him to his assistants, the residents, and nurses and was caught by the patients themselves.

At the outbreak of World War I Dr. Finney volunteered with the Johns Hopkins unit and went to France with it. But his reputation already was too great to permit his being limited to a local post. He had been in France only a short time when he was named consulting surgeon for the whole American Expeditionary Force. He intrigued the French who couldn't understand how a man could be named "*J'ai fini*." Interestingly enough, Dr. William S. Thayer, who then was associate professor of medicine at the Johns Hopkins Medical School, was assigned to the companion office of consultant in medicine to the A.E.F. On returning from the war Dr. Finney was very active in community affairs, serving on numerous important committees and boards.

Dr. Thayer, at the close of the war, returned to Baltimore where he rounded out his career as professor of medicine at the Johns Hopkins. A dapper and cultivated Bostonian he was long a familiar figure both at social and professional gatherings. He was never seen without a nosegay in his buttonhole, which led to the popular belief that he wore one on his pajamas.

Two young Canadians who followed Osler to Baltimore were Lewellys F. Barker and Thomas S. Cullen, classmates at the University of Toronto. Barker studied under Osler and succeeded him as professor of medicine. Cullen became the assistant to Kelly and followed him as professor of gynecology. Like Dr. Finney, Dr. Cullen also has found time to work for the community. His important contribution has been as president of the Board of Trustees of the Pratt Library.

A student of Halsted's who attained nationwide distinction was Hugh Hampton Young, who already has been mentioned in connection with the acquisition of the portraits of the Lords Baltimore and the gift of the dictaphone to Dr. Welch. Hugh Young was a native of Texas, though his paternal grandfather and his mother were Virginians. His father, William Hugh Young, was a brigadier general in the Confederate Army.

Young Hugh attended the University of Virginia where he got both a bachelor of arts and a medical degree. In 1894, at the age of twenty four years, he arrived in Baltimore and started in with Dr. Finney in the surgical dispensary. He was privileged also to come under the influence of Halsted. Dr. Young made genito-urinary surgery his speciality. He had a knack for inventing new instruments and he also developed a new technique for the removal of the prostate gland. This apparently required great physical strength, for the doctor once remarked to an acquaintance that he did not go in for golf or other strenuous sports since performing his operation was all the physical exercise he needed.

The Young specialty once was the subject of an encounter

between Dr. Young and Baltimore's outstanding stateswoman, Mrs. Marie Bauernschmidt. They met in the lobby of the Lyric and Mrs. B. accused Dr. Young of failing to speak to her. "Don't think you can high-hat me, Dr. Young!" she warned. "One thing I know, I'll never need *your* operation." Mrs. B. was fortunate. The shadow of the Young specialty has hung over many an elderly man. The operation itself has been dreaded even less than the Rabelaisian jokes of the heartless "G.U.Men" made at the expense of their patients.

Dr. Young was blessed with abounding self-confidence. This quality stood him in good stead when he set out to serve his country in World War I. Though he was forty seven years old at the time and a married man with a large family he volunteered his services and was commissioned a colonel with orders to sail for France. His first thought was getting himself a uniform. He and the several doctors who were to go with him moved heaven and earth to persuade a tailor to make them before sailing time. Dr. Young always succeeded when he wanted something badly enough. So the completed uniforms were delivered and Dr. Young and his aides were in them when they set out in a tender to board the liner which was to take them to France. They made a fine military appearance.

On the tender also was a rather drab party in ill-fitting civilian clothes. The Young party wondered what such an unmilitary-looking group of people was doing going to Europe. But the mystery soon was cleared up when one of them approached Dr. Young and informed him that the civilians were none other than General Pershing and his Staff who were departing in deepest secrecy.

The disclosure left Dr. Young unruffled. Within a few hours he had met the generalissimo and created such a favorable impression that Pershing at once named him head advisor to the Expeditionary Force on the vital subject of venereal disease. It was a wise choice for, thanks to Dr. Young's common-sense approach to the problem and the establishment of prophylaxis stations, venereal disease among American soldiers was reduced to a minimum.

Of all the various benefactions in which Dr. Young had a hand the richest was that brought to the Johns Hopkins Hospital by a grateful patient, "Diamond Jim" Brady. James Buchanan Brady was born a poor boy on the East Side of New York. He had unlimited energy and developed phenomenal gifts as a salesman. Railway cars were his speciality and, in his prime, he sold an average of 100 steel cars a day for the Mellons of Pittsburgh. He did it by making the acquaintance of railroad executives, inviting them to New York, wining and dining them and showering them with handsome gifts. Diamond Jim derived his name from his passion for jewelry. He would wear as much as $250,000 worth on his person at one time. Diamonds adorned his necktie, waistcoat, watch chain, cuff links and the head of his cane. He is said to have owned twenty five complete sets of personal jewels.

It was in April, 1912, that the customary serenity of the Johns Hopkins Hospital was broken by the arrival of Diamond Jim, who came as a patient of Dr. Young. Hospital routine and discipline went by the boards when word spread that the new patient was repaying small services rendered by the nurses with diamonds. Brady was delighted when Dr. Young assured him the operation he needed could be performed under a local anesthetic. The job was done, the patient suffered no pain and got relief. His gratitude was unbounded. He set out to repay the surgeon by treating him as though he were a railroad president in need of rolling stock.

But Dr. Young preferred another sort of payment. He too had some of Diamond Jim's genius as a salesman. With a little skillful maneuvering he soon convinced Diamond Jim that the most valuable return he could make for what the Hopkins had done for him was to finance the construction of a department of the hospital for genito-urinary ailments. As a further inducement Dr. Young assured him the institution would bear his name for all time. Such was the story behind the establishment of the James Buchanan Brady Institute. It opened for patients in 1915.

Yet another distinguished pupil of Halsted was Harvey Cushing, who came to Hopkins from the Harvard Medical School. While at the Hopkins Dr. Cushing founded the Hunterian Laboratory, where experiments are made on dogs before the methods which prove successful are applied to human beings. Cushing, probably carrying out the ideas of Halsted, laid down the rule that dogs hospitalized there should receive exactly the same standard of care as that set for human beings. Suffering was to be relieved by the use of anesthetics and dogs were to be prepared for operations just as people are. Yet these humane provisions have not stifled the outcry of the anti-vivisectionists. Almost continually the Hopkins scientists are waging a battle to presereve the right to experiment on animals through which progress is made in relieving human suffering. Dr. Cushing eventually returned to New England. He won fame as one of the nation's greatest brain surgeons.

Another Halsted pupil who stayed on at the Hopkins and became famous as a brain surgeon was Walter Dandy. It was he who was flown across country to California to perform an emergency operation for a brain tumor on George Gershwin, the composer. But Gershwin was beyond the help of any surgeon. It was Dandy, too, who invented the operation for removing a disc from between the vertebrae which has relieved so many people suffering with bad backs.

The Hopkins Hospital and the Medical School at the time of their foundation set a new standard in this country for medical education, research and practice. They served as models for other hospitals and schools in many parts of the country. They did the job so well that they no longer have the field to themselves. Other schools of equally high standards and much larger endowments now exist. Nevertheless in spite of strong competition and financial problems the Hopkins institutions continue from time to time to announce valuable and spectacular finds from the laboratories and clinics.

Thus, for example, it was Dr. Perrin Long and Dr. Eleanor Bliss, of the department of medicine, who were the first Americans to grasp the potentiality of the sulfa drugs. Their relentless work in the laboratories of the Hopkins established the sulfa group as a remedy for innumerable infections.

Spectacular also has been the development of the technique for the now famous "blue baby" operation. This is attributed to Dr. Alfred Blalock, professor of surgery, and Dr. Helen B. Taussig of the department of pediatrics. The sulfa drugs and the blue baby operations are the sort of things that make the headlines. The Hopkins laboratories have been and continue to be the scene of other activities that are less spectacular but equally important to the advancement of medical knowledge. Such for example has been the work of John Jacob Abel and E. Kennerly Marshall in pharmacology. Other Hopkins contributions have taken a variety of forms, from the pioneer work of J. Staige Davis in plastic surgery to the marvelous drawings of Max Broedel, a find of Dr. Kelly's in Germany who held the chair of professor of medical art.

Throughout its history the Hopkins medical school has set its face firmly against sensationalism and false claims. If the Hopkins announces officially that it has found a cure then it may be reasonably assumed that a cure has been found. Its men do not rush into print and arouse the hopes of sufferers that later end in disappointment.

As the heads of the departments have reached the retirement age in recent years the committees of selection of successors have returned to the method adopted by Gilman with great success. That is to say, they have not gone after great names but have scoured the nation for young men whose records give promise of future accomplishment. Such a choice was Blalock in surgery. A. McGehee Harvey in medicine and Francis Schwentker in pediatrics, William W. Scott in urology and Russell H. Morgan in radiology—recent acquisitions—are still very young men. Isaiah Bowman, in whose administration they arrived, used to say that the greatest thrill that came to a college president was giving such people a place to work and then waiting to see what they would turn out.

Back in the early days Osler once remarked to Welch that it was just as well they had come to the Hopkins as members of the faculty since neither could have made the grade as students. So conscientiously has the institution stuck to its standards that the same remark would probably apply as well today.

Chapter 17

SPEAKING OF THE WEATHER

IN CALIFORNIA it is said to be a high crime to criticize the weather. Not so in Baltimore. The local weather is a constant source of criticism and complaint. Baltimoreans will tell you they have the worst climate in the world. They boast about it. It is a popular belief that the success of the city as a great medical center rests chiefly upon the large amount of clinical material obtained through the devastating effect of the vagaries of Baltimore's climate on the respiratory organs.

Now and then there comes a day so perfect that even Baltimoreans have to confess that it can't be beat. In such instances they do not hail it as their own. They call it a "typical New England day."

The local newspapers, by way of appealing to the public taste, make a feature of the eccentricities and unexpected behavior of the weather. One of the first things that strikes a stranger after a few days in Baltimore is the lengths to which the newspapers, with the assistance of the local weather bureau, will go to achieve the breaking of a record.

It makes little difference what the record is just so long as the announcement can be made that one has been broken. If an April 4th is not the hottest April 4th in the bureau's history it can be proclaimed as "the second hottest." A January 1st may not be the coldest in history, but it can be the "coldest in 51 years." Whatever sort of day shows up can be compared with the corresponding day in some other year with respect to heat, cold, rainfall, drought, fog or snow. A weatherman could not hope to make good in Baltimore if, among the wide choice of meteorological phenomena, he did not dig up something that at least sounds like the breaking of a record. Perhaps the finest example of co-operation between the weather bureau and the press in this worthy field of endeavor was a solemn announcement to the effect that February 14th of a certain year was the warmest day since January 9th of the same year.

Where, it may be asked, would a reporter in California have found himself had he described a day there as a Baltimore reporter did a day in his own city, calling it "a filthy, unspeakably, damp, dank and miserable day"?

Another reporter on an especially hot and humid day obviously was playing to the local gallery when he recorded a conversation allegedly overheard in a Baltimore bar. It was started by a man who was said to have remarked that Baltimore was "just like Poona in the monsoon season." This brought the rejoinder from another man present that it reminded him "more of the climate of Dutch Guiana or northern Brazil." A third chimed in that to his way of thinking it resembled even more closely the Belgian Congo, while a fourth closed the discussion by declaring that all these comparisons were far too mild. There was no question about it that it was infinitely worse than the Persian Gulf.

Baltimoreans also take a sadistic delight in calling attention to the destructive power of the local elements. They seem never so happy as when they are announcing in glaring headlines that a late frost has killed the peach crop, rains have caused damage to farms "estimated at $5,000,000," or that a windstorm has smashed plateglass windows, uprooted trees, torn off tin roofs, downed television aerials and powerlines and left half the city in darkness. They like to speak of a thunder storm as "a twister."

In Baltimore hail invariably stimulates the imagination. Hailstones "as big as goose eggs" are commonplace. If the public is really to be impressed they must be described as being "as big as a man's fist" or "as big as baseballs." Baltimore seldom has plain "heat." It has "scorching heat." Some conception of the true Baltimorean's attitude toward his weather may also be found in a summary for 1947 which appeared in a local newspaper shortly after New Year's Day of 1948. It noted that during the year there had been "fierce winter storms of snow and ice, a fruit-killing frost in May, a gale, a drought, several periods of protracted heat and humidity and a violent thunder storm in November." The chronicler concluded cheerfully: "Notwithstanding the weather for the most part was seasonable and rather mild."

Associated with every locality is some weather phenomenon of unusual violence which gives the locality special flavor and notoriety. Kansas and Nebraska have their tornadoes; Florida and the

Gulf Coast are distinguished for their hurricanes; the basins of the great rivers of the Middle West for their floods; Texas and Oklahoma for droughts and dust storms; Minnesota and the Dakotas for subzero weather. Baltimore, too, has such a weather specialty. It is its two-inch snows.

On the day when one of these momentous events is about to occur the town awakens and looks out on a leaden sky. There is an unusual sharpness in the air which reduces chronic sniffles and clears up ailing sinuses. Baltimoreans meeting each other on the street remark forebodingly that "It looks like snow." But since snow is rare in Baltimore nobody really believes it.

Nevertheless soon after the noon hour a few flakes float down. They increase in number until the air is thick with them. Baltimoreans look out of their windows and cringe. So it is snow after all. Once convinced that it is snowing they are seized by a sudden panic. Parents ring up schools and urge that the children be let out immediately. Business establishments, fearful of having their office forces marooned all night, close down and speed their employes homeward.

Persons who have engagements call their hosts and announce that of course they do not dare to come. Concerts and lectures are out of the question. Housewives look at their pantry shelves to decide whether they are prepared for a siege. They conclude they are not and rush to the corner grocery to stock up on canned goods, bread, eggs, milk, butter and green vegetables. Primitive instinct leads them also to lay in matches and candles.

Yet, in spite of all these timely precautions the town is soon demoralized. There is just enough snow to make hills slippery and just enough hills to stall cars and create traffic jams on all the main arteries leading from the center of the city.

The more resourceful drivers direct their passengers to get out and push and so get their cars to the top of the hill. Many take flight, leaving cars parked at the side of the road for the night. The vast majority somehow manage to get home and for weeks boast about their hair-raising experiences. The newspapers rush photographers out to get pictures of the snow before it has time to melt. From then on everybody speaks of it as "the blizzard." Interestingly enough visitors from the northwest and from Canada who are accustomed to snows that are six feet deep confess that

Baltimore's two-inchers frighten them out of several years' growth.

A popular explanation of the peculiarity of Baltimore weather has to do with the unending war between the cold front from the north and the low-pressure area from the south. The former is based on Winnipeg and Medicine Hat in Canada, the latter upon the Gulf Coast and the sultry waters of the Carribean. In this eternal conflict, as in that in 1861-1865, Baltimore is the chief city of a border state. Being equidistant from the Canadian steppes and the Gulf Coast tropics the Baltimore area constitues a veritable no man's land while overhead the cold front and the warm air currents are engaged in a titanic struggle.

Baltimore also is described by the scientists as holding a central position in what is known as "the storm track area." This is a zone on the Atlantic Coast bounded by Boston on the north and Washington, D.C. on the south. The official figures show that in this area sudden weather changes occur 200 times in a year. In these changes the temperature may shift as much as 50 degrees in a day.

During a sudden rise in temperature, due to Baltimore being in the storm-track area, in order to throw off heat a human being's blood vessels dilate. This sends blood to the surface and more blood has to be made in a hurry. Scientists tell us that the extra work required in the blood-making process results in a feeling of exhaustion. This is known under the familiar name of "spring fever."

Newcomers, exposed to a suddenly rising temperature and becoming exhausted, wonder what has happened to them. They struggle to keep going and getting things done. The old Baltimore hand, on the contrary, knows there is no use trying to contend with the local climate. He admits defeat, accepting the situation without a struggle. He fortifies himself with cooling drinks and undertakes no serious work until he can find refuge in an air-conditioned office or until the first invigorating chill of September arrives.

Scientists also say that Baltimore lies just south of the 75-degree isotherm. This 75-degree isotherm is a line on the map drawn through all places which have an average temperature of 75 degrees in the summer months. North of the line, so the scientists say, lies North America's "area of high intelligence." Below it civilization begins to crumble. So here again Baltimoreans are seriously handicapped by the climate's unfavorable influence on their intellects.

Under the circumstances Baltimoreans naturally have the weather constantly on their minds and take precautions against it. For example, when they leave home in the morning they know they can never foretell what changes in the weather may occur in the course of the day. They realize that if they are to be fully prepared for anything that may happen they should carry with them everthing from a tropical worsted to a fur-lined parka. If this is impractical at least they can keep a sweater, umbrella, raincoat and rubbers at both ends of any regular beat they cover daily.

Baltimoreans—and particularly the female element of the population—take pains to keep abreast of what is going on or about to go on by reading or listening to the weather reports. Everyone has a favorite source. Some praise the weatherman of the *News-Post* while others insist that the *Sunpapers'* weatherman is more reliable! The weather reports over particular radio or television stations also have their personal followings. Still another appreciable group will declare that the most reliable service is the weather lady employed by the telephone company to repeat the forecast when dialed. They can cite any number of instances in which their favorite weather medium gave the correct forecast while the others failed. If anyone suggests that all forecasts have a common origin in the local U. S. Weather Bureau they just smile an incredulous smile.

The telephone company's weather lady, whose voice and message come from a recording, did not please one distinguished Baltimorean. This gentleman's wife told him he could get a weather report simply by dialing WE-2222. The gentleman did as he was instructed. Later his wife inquired if he had got the forecast. He replied that he had; but he didn't like the way it was done. For, said he, the woman kept on talking and he couldn't get a word in edgewise.

In Baltimore the court of highest appeal on weather issues is the Hagerstown Almanack. This historical publication has been going since 1797. It undertakes the astonishing feat of forecasting the weather for a whole year in advance. Its system is to group the days of the month in threes and give the same forecast for all three. For example, the forecast for June 1st, 2nd and 3rd might be "rain," and that for June 4th, 5th and 6th might be "fair." No true Baltimore woman would dream of selecting a day for some great event such as a debutante party, a wedding or baptism without first consulting the *Almanack*. In order to make assurance doubly sure, where the prediction of "fair" is made for three days in a row, the invariable custom is to choose the in-between day.

A Baltimore weather phenomenon equal in importance to the two-inch snow is one that occurs when the wind is from the south. If the conditions are right, Baltimore as far north as the fashionable suburb of Guilford gets what old residents call "the breeze from the Bay" and which newcomers describe irreverently as "that smell." It is associated with a portion of the harbor known as Curtis Bay, which is the center of the fertilizer industry for which Baltimore has long been famous.

But the fertilizer industry is not alone to blame. Newcomers whose sensory organs have not yet been deadened by long subjection to the local atmosphere have made a painstaking study of the smell and come up with a careful analysis. Their conclusion is that it is a composite odor of decayed fish, tankage, decomposed animal matter, sulphuric acid, sludge, rendered bones, molasses waste, oil waste, cocoa-bean hulls and so-called "trace odors." These last include among other things nitrogen, phosphates and potash.

When a new arrival in town encounters this strange phenomenon for the first time he is certain to inquire of an old resident what the smell is. To this question the conventional reply is: "Smell, did you say? What smell?" In the course of time later arrivals will accost the former newcomer and put the same question. When the former newcomer finds himself replying automatically, "Smell, did you say? What smell?" it's a sure sign he is well on the way to becoming a real Baltimorean.

Chapter 18

THE FIELD OF SPORTS

THE EARLIEST DESCRIPTIONS of Maryland tell of the Chesapeake Bay teeming with fish, the skies black with wildfowl and the forests alive with game. Fish and game have declined considerably in recent years in spite of the valiant efforts of conservationists to convince the natives that the dwindling supply is not an act of God but merely the result of their own failure to use restraint in what they catch and kill. Nevertheless something is still left and the ancient urge to fish and hunt is as strong among a large part of the male population of the city as it ever was.

Your true Baltimore sportsman never allows business to interfere with sport. If the issue comes up he settles it by inviting his prize customers to go along with him. Since he hasn't far to go he frequently can work in his sport merely by announcing that he will be "a little late" getting to the office in the morning or by "slipping out a little early" in the afternoon.

Squirrels and rabbits are to be had in abundance in season in the counties adjoining the city. It is usually customary to go to Southern Maryland for quail and to Western Maryland for wild turkeys and deer. But these sports are nothing like so important or as generally indulged in as those afforded by Chesapeake Bay. There are good fishing grounds within an hour or two by automobile from Baltimore. Parties go to Kent Island, Solomon's and other points where they hire a "captain" and his motorboat and troll for rock and bluefish. A favorite spot for shad is the shallow waters of the Susquehanna River just below Conowingo Dam.

During the few weeks of the open season in December and January duck hunters shoot from the flats at the mouth of the Susquehanna near the head of the Bay or journey to various ducking areas on the Eastern Shore. There are any number of duck clubs to which Baltimoreans belong with fairly elaborate club houses, guides, flat boats, decoys and other equipment. On both the eastern and western shores there also are State-owned ducking areas open to the general public on payment of a fee.

A sport peculiar to Baltimore is gudgeon fishing. The gudgeon is a member of the carp family, about five inches long with a back of iridescent blue and a silver belly and fins. In the spring gudgeons appear in streams in great number, coming in from the bay to fresh water to spawn. Gudgeon fishing is strictly a family affair. Many a Baltimore sportsman will tell you that his career began in quest of the lowly gudgeon. On such adventures he would be armed with a tiny fly hook baited with a worm, a spool of cotton for a line and a switch cut from the nearest sapling for a rod.

When word goes out that the gudgeon are "running" the fishermen—father, son and often mother, too—hurry off to enjoy the sport. Favorite spots for snaring gudgeon are the Patapsco River at Relay, several miles to the south of the city; the Gunpowder Falls below the B. & O. bridge some ten or fifteen miles to the north, and Winter's Run in the same general vicinity. If a fisherman's luck is good he may catch as many as 80 or 100 of the little fellows. Frequently they are cleaned, rolled in cornmeal, and fried in bacon fat right on the bank of the stream where they are caught. Gudgeon enthusiasts say this is a feast for the gods.

Next in age to hunting and fishing are sports associated with the horse. Baltimore is surrounded by gently rolling open country that is perfect for riding. As in Virginia and Kentucky its natural blue grass and temperate climate (when not indulging in phenomena) are peculiarly suited to horse breeding. Fox hunting was a popular sport among the planters in pre-Revolutionary days and horse racing was a regular fixture during terms of court at the various county seats as early as the middle of the 18th century. Annapolis, capital of the colony had a racing season which attracted sportsmen from Virginia as well as from Maryland. Among the attendants was George Washington who left behind him a record of bets made—and lost. The Maryland Jockey Club traces its origin to the races in Annapolis in 1745.

As Baltimore grew in size and importance it was inevitable that this popular sport should be taken up in the new settlement. Before the Revolution races were run on a track to the west of the town on property belonging to John Eager Howard, near the present Lexington Market. After the Revolution the scene shifted to Govans, several miles to the northeast of the town. Mention already has been made that it was at the races there that, among other places, tradition fixed the first meeting between Betsy Patterson and Jerome Bonaparte. Thereafter the race course moved successively to the Old Frederick Road, to Timonium in Baltimore County and then to Herring Run.

In 1823 a racing association was organized for the conduct of the sport. Six years later it was merged with the Maryland Jockey Club which continued in charge until the Civil War. That conflict temporarily put an end to the sport in Baltimore. Immediately after the war Maryland was blessed with a sportsman of the first water in the person of Governor Oden Bowie. In 1868 Governor Bowie journeyed to Saratoga Springs for the racing season. One evening while he was dining with friends the conversation turned to the revival of racing in Maryland, a subject dear to the Governor's heart. Before the party broke up it was tentatively agreed, under the Governor's leadership, to put horse racing in Maryland back on a sound footing. The primary factor in accomplishing this end was to be the establishment of a track near Baltimore. Plans were made for a fall meeting and, to insure its being a success, a special feature race for three-year-olds was proposed. Significant of the occasion which saw the birth of the idea this race was to be called the Dinner Party Stakes.

Pursuant to this program a tract of land was purchased well out in the country to the west of the city. It was part of an estate owned by an Englishman who had given it the name of Pimlico, a famous quarter of London. Here a track was laid out and a grandstand and clubhouse erected. The first meeting was held according to schedule in the fall of 1870. The initial feature race, worth $18,500, was won by a bay colt named Preakness, owned by Mr. M. H. Sanford and ridden by Billy Hayward. The Dinner Party Stakes was continued as a feature of the Pimlico meetings until 1873 when its name was changed to the Dixie Handicap. That same year a new race for three-year-olds was established and named the Preakness Stakes in honor of Mr. Sanford's colt that won the first Dinner Party Stakes. Thus was born the great race that today constitutes one tier of the triple crown for three-year-olds, whose other tiers are the Kentucky Derby and the Belmont.

Famous, too, in the annals of the old track was a race on October 24, 1877, for which the United States Congress adjourned. This was a triangular sweepstakes whose entries were F. B. Harper's Ten Broeck, George L. Lorillard's Tom Ochiltree and Pierre Lorillard's Parole. These had earned thousands of dollars for their owners. Ten Broeck, the Western entry was making his first invasion of the East. So great was public interest in the event that sportsmen from all parts of the country assembled in Baltimore.

The distance of the race was 2½ miles. When the three champions were called to the post a crowd of 20,000 persons was on hand. Conspicuous among the spectators were senators and representatives who made the trip from Washington by special train. In the betting interest was fairly divided between Ten Broeck and Tom Ochiltree. Parole was pretty generally overlooked. But when the race had been run and the dust cleared from the track it was the forgotten Parole who was declared the winner.

The Dixie Stakes, which replaced the Dinner Party, was run continuously until 1888 and the Preakness until 1889. Then racing in Maryland again entered a dark age. Pimlico suffered from competition with other out-of-state tracks and the sport got into bad hands. This situation continued until 1898 when a group of sportsmen headed by William P. Riggs came to the rescue very much as Governor Bowie had done following the Civil War. They organized the Maryland Steeplechase Association; then, having organized, they obtained the charter of the old Maryland Jockey Club. Under the new management spring and autumn meetings were resumed at Pimlico.

In 1909 the Preakness was renewed in all its glory and has been run annually ever since. In 1924 the Dixie Handicap also was renewed. The Preakness customarily follows the Kentucky Derby by one week. Almost invariably the winner of the Derby is entered, seeking a second victory before going on to the Belmont Stakes in New York. The Preakness field is small, averaging around eight horses. Never in its history has there been a walkover, though on three occasions the contest has been reduced to two horses. The largest field was that of 1926 when eighteen horses went to the post. The race is limited to three-year-olds and the distance is 1 3/16 miles.

Pimlico on Preakness Day presents a picturesque spectacle. The quaint mid-Victorian clubhouse, with its broad spacious porches and pagoda-like appearance testifies to the age of the establishment. There members of the Jockey Club and those lucky enough to get an invitation for the day gather for lunch. By the time the bugle blows for the first race clubhouse, boxes, grandstand and inclosures are comfortably filled and the crowd is still growing. A half hour before the feature every vantage point is occupied, and all but a fortunate few have to stand on tiptoe to see at all.

An impressive spectacle is the parade of the horses from the paddock past the grandstand to the barrier, the thoroughbreds on edge with excitement and their jockeys sporting the colors of the nation's great racing stables. Then comes the ticklish business of maneuvering the horses into the starting stalls followed by the cry of "They're off!" as the field breaks and battles for position.

The horses flash by grandstand and clubhouse. On Preakness Day the midfield is packed, too. There once was a rise inside the track which gave Pimlico the popular name of Old Hilltop. One looks in vain for the hill today. The horses round the course and make a final spurt as they come into the home stretch. In less than two minutes after the start the winner has crossed the finish and another Preakness has passed into history.

The winner pulls up and returns for the weighing in before the grandstand, the horseshoe of "Black-eyed Susans" goes over his head, the jockey is congratulated and the owner presented with the Woodlawn Vase. The Governor of Maryland is always on hand to make the presentation.

The Woodlawn Vase, which usually is displayed in a silversmith's window on Charles Street the week before the race, stands some four feet high and is surmounted by a horse and jockey. It looks not unlike a wedding cake wrought in silver. The vase has quite a history. It was designed and fashioned by Tiffany back in 1860 for Col. R. A. Alexander of Kentucky, put up for a race and won just once before the outbreak of the Civil War. The winner, a Southern sympathizer, buried it along with the rest of the family plate to keep it out of the hands of the Yankees.

When the war was over and peace once more restored the vase was dug up and put back into circulation. It served as a trophy at various tracks, finally being won by Mr. Thomas Clyde who, in 1917, presented it to the Maryland Jockey Club to be an added feature of the Preakness. The owner of the winning horse becomes the custodian of the vase for a year. It then is customary for him to offer it for the next running. He gets a small model of it for his permanent property.

Among the great three-year-olds who have won the Preakness are Sir Barton, Man O' War, Gallant Fox, Omaha, War Admiral, Challedon, Whirlaway, Count Fleet, Assault, and Citation. Kentucky-bred horses have predominated. Among the 61 winners through 1951, 45 have been Kentucky bred; 5 have claimed Pennsylvania as their native state, 3 have hailed from Maryland, 3 from Virginia and one each from England, Tennessee, New York, Texas and California. War Cloud, imported from England, is the only foreign-bred horse ever to win the race.

Yet for all its national importance in the field of racing Preakness Day creates scarcely more than a ripple of excitement on the surface of Baltimore. It passes almost unnoticed save in the newspapers and at Pimlico and among race followers. Space at hotels is, of course, at a premium. There are overflow crowds also at the popular bars. Otherwise a visitor might arrive in the city that day and never guess that a great sporting event is taking place. Baltimoreans distribute their sporting interests widely, and for every one found at Pimlico on Preakness Day there will be a half dozen engaged in some other favorite pastime.

An annual sporting event of primary importance is the Johns Hopkins Hospital's Turtle Derby. This is a delightful burlesque of the Preakness staged by the doctors, nurses, internes and convalescents of the hospital. A large circle is drawn in one of the hospital's court yards and the competing turtles dumped in the center. The turtle that crawls out of the circle first is declared the winner.

Each department, designated as a "stable," makes its entries which bear such intriguing names as Cataract, Adenoids, Panic, Coma, Ophthalmia, Calomel, and Athlete's Foot. There are "bookmakers" "judges," "trainers" and other track officials. Betting is brisk and excitement keen while the race is on. The Turtle Derby has been going on now since the early 1930's, always gets a prominent place in the newspapers and rivals the real event at Pimlico in public interest.

A striking proof of Baltimore's British origin are the point-to-point races run annually in the spring in Baltimore County. These are strictly amateur events in contrast to the professional flat racing at Pimlico. They are the outgrowth of fox hunting which has gone on continuously around Baltimore since colonial times. In England it was customary for fox hunters to pick out a church steeple in the distance and challenge each other to a race around it and back to the starting point. The sport came to be known as a steeplechase and also as a point-to-point race. Sometimes, too, at the end of a day's run, riders would test the speed and stamina of their mounts by racing back to the kennels. These contests were called pounding races. Both kinds of races were brought to this country from England and perpetuated by the squirearchy of Baltimore County.

The races are run over what is described as "natural hunting country." The jumps, which are numerous, are either plank or post-and-rail fences. The events take place on three successive Saturdays in April. The first is run at My Lady's Manor; the second, known as the Grand National, in lovely Deep Run Valley in Baltimore County. The climax is reached in the Maryland Hunt Cup which is the classic event in this particular sport.

In the spring of 1894 a member of the Elkridge Hunt Club proposed a cross-country race for hunters to test their endurance, speed and jumping ability. It was proposed further that a $100 cup be donated to the winner and that, in consequence, the race should be known as the Maryland Hunt Cup. This met with general approval, conditions were drawn up and it was agreed also to invite members of the Green Spring Valley Hunt Club to take part.

The conditions set forth were that the race should be for a distance of about four miles and that the course be flagged at intervals. There were to be no artificial jumps and the race was to be run over natural hunting country. Riders must be members of either of the two clubs and the horses ridden the property of the members. Racing colors were to be worn. These same fundamental conditions prevail today.

The first running took place at 4 P.M. on May 22, 1894, near Stevenson Station in the Green Spring Valley. There were nine starters, the riders all sons of old Baltimore families. The race was won by a horse named Johnny Miller, ridden by John McHenry, a descendant of George Washington's Secretary of War for whom Fort McHenry was named. It was hardly over when Ross W. Whistler and Jacob A. Ulman, members of the Elkridge Club set to work to establish the race as an annual fixture. They invited Redmond C. Stewart, master of the Green Spring Valley Hunt Club, to join in the organization with them.

Jake Ulman was a keen sportsman of Jewish blood who entered the exclusive valley circle through his vivacious personality and his marriage to a daughter of Wilson Miles Cary. An intimate friend of Redmond Stewart, he was one of the gay party that traveled in a special car to York, Pennsylvania, for the marriage of Mr. Stewart and the lovely Katherine Small. Another member of the party was Basil Gordon, a cripple from his youth, who was distinguished for his wit.

As the train drew into the station at York, Ulman called Gordon aside and whispered to him, "Basil, will you do me a favor? Don't tell these people up here I'm a Jew."

"Indeed, I won't," replied Basil. "And, Jake, will you do me a favor? Don't tell these people I'm a hunchback."

As time went on the Hunt Cup elegibility rules were broadened to include members and horses of any recognized hunt club in Maryland, and then to include those of any recognized club in the United States or Canada. In 1898 the Committee decided to standardize the cup. They selected a silver tankard of Georgian design 12¾ inches high. A cup of exactly the same style and proportions has been offered for each race since.

The year 1900 was outstanding in that it saw the appearance of John H. O'Donovan's Garry Owen and his rider Jervis Spencer, Jr. In earlier years all the entries were half-breds, technically horses that are not registered as thoroughbreds. But the half-breds had plenty of thoroughbred blood and, as time went on, only the thoroughbred had much of a chance to win. Jervis Spencer was the first rider to cover the course at top speed and Garry Owen the first horse to take the jumps in stride.

Another distinguished contender in these days was Princeton, owned and ridden by the Watters brothers, W. J. H., Jr., and Sidney. Garry Owen and Princeton were the first horses to win the Hunt Cup three times. Princeton was the winner in 1903, 1905 and 1906. Garry Owen turned the trick in 1901, 1902 and finally in 1907 at the ripe age of seventeen years. Jervis Spencer long had the reputation for being Maryland's greatest amateur steeplechase rider. He rode in the Hunt Cup twenty times, won five of them, finished second five times and third twice.

A more recent claimant for the honor is Frank A. Bonsal, better known to his friends and the public as "Downey," who won the Hunt Cup twice and, before he stopped counting, rode in 138 timber races, winning 40, finishing second in 28, and third in 20. Persistent, yet less successful was Redmond Stewart who rode in 16 Hunt Cup races but won only one of them. Still another distinguished rider of a more recent vintage was W. Stuart Janney, Jr., four times winner of the Hunt Cup and three times winner, respectively in 1942, 1946 and 1947 on his horse Winton.

The course in use since 1915 is in the Worthington Valley and spreads over the estates of G. Bernard Fenwick, J. W. Y. Martin and C. Wilbur Miller. The four miles are laid out from east to west in two elongated loops. There are 22 jumps, including 4 board fences and 18 post-and-rail fences, not to mention one small brook. They vary in height from 2 feet 8 inches at the brook to 5 feet.

To the north of the course is a steep hill on top of which is perched Mr. Martin's gracious old red brick mansion. The hillside makes a natural grandstand on which several thousand people find room and from which they can get an unbroken view of the race from start to finish. On a Maryland Hunt Cup day, if the weather is fine, the spectacle is a charming one. Early comers bring their lunch with them and spread a tablecloth on the bank of one of the brooks which run near the course. A luncheon also is held at the Green Spring Valley kennels, within walking distance of the race, for members and their guests. Many private luncheons are given in Baltimore's suburbs. This is a great time for entertaining friends from out of town and repaying social obligations. Every group has its sweepstakes, each person chipping in a dollar or two and drawing a horse's name, or a blank.

The Maryland Hunt Cup is a grueling race; only the best horses in top condition have a chance. It costs no small sum to buy and train a horse for the race. There is no purse; the race is run for glory and glory alone. A wit once remarked that winning the Hunt Cup calls for three P's—Patience, Perseverance and Pocketbook. In consequence the field is small. Perhaps from six to eight horses will go to the post.

In pioneer days when good highways were rare the journey by automobile from the city out to Worthington Valley was something of an adventure. Not infrequently a shower made the dirt roads slippery and created a traffic jam. State police to handle the traffic were still years in the future and volunteers had to step in to do the job. Old racegoers recall a spring in the early 1920's when the late Representative Nick Longworth, Alice Roosevelt's husband, stood in spats at a crossroads and, waving hands clad in yellow chamois gloves, skillfully untangled what seemed to be a hopeless snarl.

The Maryland Hunt Cup is generally recognized as the greatest timber race in the United States. It has been compared with England's classic jumping race, the Grand National, which is run at Aintree. But horsemen will tell you there is no more basis for comparison than there would be between baseball and cricket. The two races represent two entirely different tests. No English horse that has run at Aintree has ever attempted the Maryland Hunt Cup. On the other hand, two winners of the Maryland Hunt Cup have run in England's Grand National. The horses were Mr. Howard Bruce's Billy Barton and Mr. B. Leslie Behr's Burgoright. The year was 1928.

Billy Barton began his career as a flat racer, turned out to be a rogue and was ruled off the track. Mr. Bruce bought him, had him gelded and hunted him regularly with the Elkridge hounds of which he was master. Then he decided to try him at timber racing and got Albert G. Ober, Jr. to ride him. The combination proved a brilliant success reminiscent of the team of Garry Owen and Jervis Spencer. In 1926 Billy, ridden by Mr. Ober, won Maryland's Grand National point-to-point, the Maryland Hunt Cup and the Gold Cup, run at Warrenton, Virginia. In 1927 he won the Maryland Grand National again, the Meadow Brook Cup, the Pennsylvania Hunt Cup and the New Jersey Hunt Cup.

By this time Mr. Bruce's faith in Billy Barton was so great that he felt it proper to give the horse a try at the oldest and most famous of all races—the English Grand National. So Billy was shipped to England and, with Mr. Ober, started training there. A few weeks before the race, however, Mr. Ober was replaced by a professional Irish jockey. Excitement over the race ran high in Baltimore not only in hunting circles but among the general public. A large Baltimore delegation made the trip to England for the race and the Baltimore *Sunpapers*, with commendable initiative, arranged to have an eyewitness account of the running reported by overseas telephone direct from Aintree to Sun Square in Baltimore where a large crowd assembled on the great day.

Billy lived up fully to expectations. He was in the race from the very beginning and leading all the way. He took the novel English hedges and brooks as calmly as though he were in familiar Maryland hunting country. Baltimoreans in the stands at Aintree and in Sun Square at home were spellbound at his performance. Then, at the very last fence, he had a collision with another horse and went down. Before his rider could remount and continue, the race was lost. Nevertheless Billy had demonstrated he could hold his own with the best jumpers in the world.

Burgoright's performance was disappointing. He failed to take to the English climate and was in the worst possible physical shape for the race. Ridden by Downey Bonsal he got into a jam at the Canal Turn and failed to finish.

So determined has been the effort to keep the point-to-point races on a strictly amateur basis that even the suggestion of installing a loud-speaker system for the convenience of the public was promptly voted down a few years ago. Gloomy prophets have warned that if the Hunt Cup is to continue either the race will have to be made easier or a cash stake offered to the winner. Neither inducement has been added and still the race goes on.

For a brief period Baltimore also was a great baseball town. Though the ranks are fast dwindling there still are a few old timers who recall vividly the Golden Age when the Baltimore Orioles were making baseball history. The town had a professional baseball team as early as 1869. The 1880's witnessed a fresh impetus to the game when Harry Vanderhorst, a local brewer, established a Baltimore team in the six-club American Association, with the primary object of selling beer at the ball park on Huntington Avenue. Three years later the team first assumed the name of "The Orioles."

In 1887 a Baltimore pitcher named Mat Kilroy performed a feat unheard of in modern baseball. He pitched sixty-nine complete games without being relieved. The year 1891 also was a momentous one. For in that season a stocky snubnosed and pugnacious youngster of eighteen years, from Truxton, New York, joined the team as a right fielder. He was John McGraw, destined to become famous in later years as manager of the New York Giants.

But the Golden Age did not really dawn until 1892. That year the National League decided to increase its membership from eight clubs to twelve and took Baltimore in. In midsummer of the same year there arrived in Baltimore one Edward Hanlon who had been engaged as field manager. Hanlon was another in the long and distinguished line of New Englanders who have left their imprint on the city. He was born in Montville, Connecticut, and got the finishing touches on his baseball education as an outfielder for Detroit. When he reached Baltimore the Orioles were in last place in the league. He set to work at once buying new players and improving the team. In 1893 he became the owner. By the time of the winter training period in the South in 1894 things were going in dead earnest. This was when Hanlon got the nickname of "Foxy Ned." He directed his genius toward developing a scientific game, teaching his players to use their heads as well as their hands. Under his tutelage the Orioles became famous for their originality and daring.

Hanlon figured that the object of professional baseball was to win games, and adopted every play that led to that end. It was before foul balls counted as strikes. Hanlon taught his players to hit fouls until the opposing pitcher was worn out. Every morning the Orioles would go out to the ball park and work on the plays to be used in the afternoon. They are credited with having invented the hit-and-run play, sacrifice hits, bunts, base stealing and place hitting. They have been charged also with grading the foul line on the home grounds so that bunts rolled inside instead of outside, of sliding into bases with their spikes up and of tripping base runners of the opposing team. Legend has it that facilities at the ball park were so arranged that the visitors had to pass by the Orioles' bench. When they did so they always found the Orioles with files in hand apparently hard at work sharpening their spikes.

These tactics, sporting or otherwise, brought results. Nothing could touch the Old Orioles with their tough ways and handlebar mustaches. They won their first pennant in 1894, and repeated the performance in 1895 and 1896. They placed second in 1897 and 1898. For a time Baltimore went baseball mad. The last game of the 1894 season was with Washington and hundreds of Baltimoreans journeyed to the capital to see the game. When the team returned home with its first pennant the town turned out at Camden Station to welcome the players home. Of course Baltimore had to have a parade. It formed at the station and marched to the 5th Regiment Armory and is said to have been five miles long. The community celebration ended with a great banquet at the Rennert Hotel where the players, looking miserable in tuxedos, stiff shirts and high collars, heard their praises sung.

Among the great players that Hanlon produced were Dan Brouthers, Hugh Jennings, John McGraw, Steve Brodie, Wee Willie Keeler, Wilbert Robinson and John J. (Sadie) McMahon. In 1894 the Orioles had a team batting average of .328, the highest ever made by a pennant-winning team.

But even while the team was winning pennants decay was setting in. Though it was the best team in the nation—some say the greatest team of all time—the fickle Baltimore public wearied of supporting it. The first great season of 1894 netted Owner Hanlon $50,000. Next year the profit dropped to $25,000. The third pennant-winning year and the following year the Orioles actually lost money at home and, with the profit made on the road, did little more than break even.

Hanlon, being a business man, picked up the cream of his Oriole flock and carried it to Brooklyn where gate receipts were better. John McGraw and Wilbert Robinson remained in Baltimore for reasons that shortly will be made apparent. McGraw took over the job of manager of the Orioles and soon demonstrated the ability that was to win him fame in the same capacity with the New York Giants.

So Baltimore has the distinction of having been the birthplace of scientific baseball. Years passed and baseball fashion completed a full cycle. The public demanded, not scientific victories, but slugging matches. Again Baltimore rose to the occasion. For it was a Baltimore boy, George Herman Ruth, who became the greatest exponent of the new style of play. Babe Ruth, at the age of twenty years, came out of St. Mary's Industrial School and got his first tryout with the Orioles. The owner at that time was Jack Dunn, who had a genius for developing and selling players. Dunn sold the Babe to the Boston Red Sox, and from Boston the Babe went on to the New York Yankees and ever-lasting fame.

Baltimore had a team in the American League in 1901 and 1902. Then it dropped to the minors and there it has been ever since. There was a flash of the old brilliance in the 1920's when the Orioles, under the ownership and management of Dunn, won seven pennants in a row in the International League. Dunn's team has been described as the greatest minor league team in baseball history and the period in which it performed the Silver Age of baseball in Baltimore.

The city lays claim to three of the great players who occupy places in baseball's Hall of Fame. They are John McGraw, Babe Ruth and Wee Willie Keeler. Keeler led the National League in batting in the triumphant days of the old Orioles. He is the author of the immortal advice "Hit 'em where they ain't." And Keeler did just that. McGraw once said of him that in his thirty years of baseball he never saw another player who could get from the home plate to first base as fast as Wee Willie.

It has been mentioned that when Hanlon took most of the

old Orioles to Brooklyn, McGraw and Robinson stayed in Baltimore. One reason for their reluctance to leave the city was that they had a valuable property which demanded their presence. It was a sports establishment on North Howard Street bearing the name of "The Diamond," and combining a billiard parlor, bowling alleys and a bar. It is to The Diamond and its owners that Baltimore is indebted for another of its popular and characteristic sports.

During the winter The Diamond did very well indeed. But with the coming of summer proceeds from the bowling alleys declined. Baltimoreans, chronic labor savers even in matters of sports, just couldn't see any good reason for swinging those great, heavy balls in hot weather. Besides, many of the patrons of The Diamond were baseball players and were afraid bowling might hurt their throwing arms. There is another story to the effect that a lot of old and much-battered tenpins and balls accumulated around the alleys and the proprietors were looking for a way to salvage them. Whatever the true motive McGraw and Robinson called in a woodworker named John Dittmar, who had a shop at Pratt Street and the Fallsway, and got him to cut down both the pins and the balls, until their size was more in keeping with the reduced energy of Baltimoreans in hot weather. The smaller pins and balls were tried out and proved popular.

Some say it is because the pins look like wooden decoys. Others say it is because the pins scatter when they are fired at just the way wild ducks do. At any rate Wilbert Robinson called them "Duckpins" and a new game was born.

That was some fifty years ago. Duckpins has grown steadily in popularity in Baltimore ever since. It has virtually driven out the old game of tenpins. No less than 30,000 Baltimoreans are members of organized leagues. Nearly every business house and industrial plant has its team. Besides the members of the leagues there are the casual players who stop in for a friendly game on the way home from work in the afternoon. All in all it is estimated that the bowling population of Baltimore numbers anywhere from 80,000 to 90,000 persons.

This Baltimore-born game also is proving popular in other parts of the country. There is a national duckpin association whose activities cover the eastern seaboard from Maine to Georgia. The duckpin alley is the same as that for tenpins except for a minor difference in the slope of the gutter. The duckpin is approximately 9½ inches high as compared with the tenpin's 15 inches. The tenpin ball weighs 12 to 16 pounds and has finger holes drilled into it. The duckpin ball may not exceed 3 pounds. It is a solid ball which is palmed by the bowler, who uses his wrist and fingertip action to produce the desired hook, curve or "English." Perfect 300 games (they require 12 consecutive strikes) are by no means uncommon in tenpins; in duckpins a score of 300 has never been rolled. The world duckpin record is 239. A topnotch tenpin bowler will average between 200 and 210, while the best duckpin averages in the nation are around 130. As in tenpins and other organized sports there are national rankings. In spite of growing competition from outside, Baltimore, the birthplace of the game, continues to hold its own. In 1950, for example, of the 30 women and 30 men ranked nationally, 15 women and 11 men were Baltimoreans.

Visitors to Baltimore may be surprised to see schoolboys carrying, in place of baseball mitts or gloves, long sticks with what appear to be loose nets at the end. These are lacrosse sticks. Lacrosse, an Indian game that was made the national sport in Canada in 1867, took root in Baltimore in the late 1870's and has flourished ever since. Accounts agree that it arrived in 1877 but vary as to who brought it. One version credits the importation to the Penniman boys—Bill, Henry and Nick. They are said to have seen it played in Canada and learned to handle a stick during a summer vacation there. The other version states authoritatively that it was introduced to the community by J. Harry Lee, Jesse Tyson and Alexander Brown who discovered it at Newport, Rhode Island. They are described as having become fascinated by the game and to have invested $35 in sticks and other equipment.

J. Harry Lee was at the time president of the Baltimore Athletic Club and there seems to be no question that the first lacrosse team in Baltimore was sponsored by the club. A field in Druid Hill Park was set aside for the sport and the players thereafter called themselves "the Druids." They chose an oak leaf as insignia and green and gold as their colors. Meanwhile a group of City College boys, too young to join the B.A.C., oragnized their own team and played under the name of "the Monumentals." These youngsters were the sons of doctors, lawyers, and business men and bore familiar Baltimore names. Among them were Gerald T. Hopkins, Frank L. Perry, Howell Carroll, N. Winslow Williams, Richard C. Johnson, William Cator, R. Brooke Hopkins, Harry Pennington, Nathan Ryno Smith and Charles Frick.

The records tell of a practice game with six-a-side that was played September 20, 1878, on the grounds of the Mt. Washington Cricket Club. November 23, 1878, is recorded as the date of the first game between 12-man teams. This was played at a place called Newington Park before a crowd of 4,000 persons. Some of the Monumentals eventually moved up from City College to the Johns Hopkins where the game was introduced in 1882. In 1891 the Hopkins team won the national collegiate championship, a distinction it has earned many times since. At that time lacrosse was taken up by athletic clubs in many cities and also by a number of colleges. A collegiate association was formed which included Yale, Princeton and Harvard. They ultimately withdrew, but lacrosse continued at the Hopkins, Lehigh and Stevens. In the early days it was impossible to arrange a whole season's schedule with college teams; the Hopkins had to fill in with athletic clubs and teams from Canada.

In those pioneering days players wore neither helmets nor gloves nor padding. There still are to be seen in Baltimore elderly men with scarred faces and broken noses which identify them as old lacrosse players. At the outset coaches were imported from Canada but eventually Baltimore devoloped its own experts. Prominent among them was William C. Schmeisser, "Father Bill," an old Hopkins player who gave his services to his university up until his death in 1941, and turned out a number of championship teams.

On the only two occasions when lacrosse has figured in the Olympic Games the United States has been represented by teams from the Johns Hopkins. That was in the years 1928 and 1932. It is not at all unusual for the Hopkins to go through a whole year undefeated by a college team. Equally distinguished in the post-graduate field is Baltimore's Mt. Washington Club, composed of former college players. Mt. Washington generally holds the open title. One of the classic games of the year is the meeting between Mt. Washington and the Hopkins.

In Baltimore, boys grow up with lacrosse. Training begins as soon as a boy is old enough to hold a stick. Public, parochial and private schools all have lacrosse teams and it is estimated that more than 1,000 Baltimore boys are regularly engaged in the sport. Not to be outdone by their brothers Baltimore girls too have taken up lacrosse with great enthusiasm and no little success. They learn to play it at school and have carried the art with them and transplanted it as far north as Smith and as far south as Sweet-briar. Baltimore girls also are conspicuous on regional and all-American teams that occasionally are organized and battle it out among themselves for the greater glory. Meanwhile old-fashioned parents agonize for fear the darlings will get their teeth knocked out and lose their looks.

In recent years lacrosse has taken hold in many colleges in the East. Teams now are found all the way from Maine to Georgia. It also now is being played in such well-known New England schools as Andover, Exeter and Deerfield. Wherever it appears you are reasonably sure to find that the coaches or the star players learned the game in Balitmore.

Baltimore institutions of higher learning are not distinguished for their football teams with the exception of Morgan College, which is outstanding among the Negro colleges. The annual contest with Virginia Union takes on the proportions of a miniature Rose Bowl. Morgan usually wins. Morgan, too, in recent years has had the best mile relay in the country.

Baltimore's white football players who have won fame usually have done so by way of Princeton. Every once in a while a Baltimore boy stars for the Tigers. Such have been Pepper Constable and Jake Slagle, both All-American players. But long before either of them was born Princeton football history was made by Trip Haxall, the Poes and the Riggses.

It was back in 1882 that J. Triplett Haxall, a Baltimore boy, executed his famous placement kick in the game with Yale at the Polo Grounds, New York. The distance was 65 yards, more than half the length of the field. This record has never been equaled. The distressing part of it was that, in spite of "Haxall's Kick," Yale won the game. The Poes and the Riggses were distinguished both for quantity and quality. There were six Poe brothers and eight Riggs brothers. Their era was the 1890's. While they were performing for Princeton the Yale bulldog didn't have a chance. Edgar Allan Poe and John Prentiss Poe were chosen for Walter Camp's all-time All-Americans. Edgar Allan captained Princeton successively in 1889 and 1890. Out of 23 starts he led the Tigers to 21 victories and one tie. Baltimore's most recent outstanding contribution to the game has been Bob (Robert A.) Williams, Notre Dame's phenomenal quarterback.

Yet when all is said and done perhaps Baltimore's greatest achievement in the field of good clean sports was the famous roll of George Howell Parr. Hindu Yogi are said to have achieved prodigious feats in the matter of rolling. There may be other outstanding instances of prowess in this line in other out of the way parts of the world. But it is an indisputable fact that a Baltimorean holds the record for the longest consecutive roll ever achieved in the United States.

The roll in question was made on May 18-19, 1914. Mr. Parr was then thirty four years old, in the prime of life and the pink of condition. It all began in February of the same year as the result of a friendly argument at the Maryland Club. Mr. Parr was a member of a congenial party there one evening when another person got up to leave. Asked what his hurry was he said he had to catch a train at the Pennsylvania station at a certain hour. "Why," said Mr. Parr, "I could roll to the station in that time."

The claim did not go unchallenged. Mr. Parr was invited to prove his ability at rolling. Before the meeting broke up he agreed to the test. The conditions provided that it should take place over a course extending from the Elkridge Kennels south of Charles Street Avenue to University Parkway, a distance of approximately 15,580 feet, or about three miles. The roll had to be finished not later than June 1st. Mr. Parr could take as much time as he pleased, but once he had started rolling he could not leave off until he had completed the distance. The proposed contest aroused tremendous interest among younger members of the club. Thousands of dollars were wagered on both sides. Mr. Parr's personal stake was said to have been in the neighborhood of $1,000.

Mr. Parr found a stout backer in his brother Ral who volunteered as trainer. Every day he repaired to the Baltimore Athletic Club to practice rolls, increasing the number daily. Trainer Ral figured that his brother would never make it if, in rolling, he breathed the impurities along the highway. He therefore contrived a fancy roll in which the roller's head would always be high off the ground. Football pads were proposed to protect elbows, knees and other vulnerable spots.

On the evening of May 18 Parr, accompanied by his trainer and retinue of attendants, proceeded to the start. He wore khaki football pants, a woolen sweater and a plaid golf cap. His hands were bandaged. One attendant, D. Harry Mordecai, carried a small mattress on which the roller might take an occasional rest. Promptly at 8 P.M. the rolling began.

Throughout the night brothers Ral and Harry A., Jr. walked by the roller's side to cheer him on. Others in the brave little group were Harry Mordecai, with the mattress, Spalding Lowe Jenkins and Douglas H. Thomas, Jr. When day broke the principal was still hard at it. From time to time he took sips of water but did not swallow it. He neither smoked nor ate during the entire roll.

At 8 A.M. a laborer passing in a wagon commented: "If I did that they'd give me seven months for disorderly conduct."

At 9 A.M. the contender was considerably cheered by the arrival of his wife and Mrs. Eugene Levering, Jr., and Miss Frances Gilmor. As the sun was well up and it was beginning to get warm, brother Ral raised an umbrella and held it over the roller.

At 11:10 A.M. sharp Mr. Parr rolled triumphantly over the finish line. Including the intermissions for rest it had taken him just 15 hours 10 minutes. None the worse for wear he climbed into a waiting automobile and was driven to his home in the Latrobe Apartments. There he had a bath and a brief rest. In the afternoon he was at the Pimlico Race Track to collect his bets. So far as is known nobody in this country has ever rolled that far. Certainly ever since 1914 the Charles Street Avenue course has been free of rollers.

Chapter 19

CITIZENS OF COLOR

I T IS ESTIMATED that Negroes make up 20 per cent of the total population of Baltimore, forming one of the largest Negro communities in the country. On the one hand they have contributed generously to the support of those amenities of life which characterize a civilized community; on the other hand their presence poses a social problem of formidable proportions.

Since Negro slavery was an institution of the Maryland colony it is to be presumed that Negroes were in Baltimore from the town's beginning. Though a century was to pass before slavery was abolished, protests against the institution began early in Baltimore. The first one of which there is record was made at the eighth Methodist conference meeting in Baltimore in April, 1780.

It is significant perhaps that this particular conference was attended only by Northern preachers, who therefore may have been legislating rather more for their Southern brethren than for themselves. However that may be, they declared officially that keeping slaves was contrary to the laws of God, of man and of nature, and resolved that all traveling preachers of the Baltimore Conference who owned slaves should be required to set them free.

Eight years later, on September 8, 1788, there was established in Baltimore "The Maryland Society for Promoting the Abolition of Slavery and the Relief of Free Negroes and Others Unlawfully Held in Bondage." This was the first antislavery society to be formed in Maryland, the fourth in the United States and the sixth in the world. Conspicuous among its founders were members of the Society of Friends, but other leading citizens took part.

On July 4, 1791, the society at a public meeting listened to an oration delivered by Dr. George Buchanan, a member of one of Baltimore's oldest families and a physician of national distinction. "God," said Dr. Buchanan, "hath created mankind after his own image and granted them liberty and independence, and if varieties may be found in their structure and color, these are only to be attributed to the nature of their diet and habits, as also to the soil and the climate they may inhabit, and serve as flimsy pretexts for enslaving them." He went on to mention by name several Negroes who had achieved high position in various fields and remarked, "These are sufficient to show that the Africans whom you despise, whom you inhumanly treat as brutes and whom you unlawfully subject to slavery, are equally capable of improvement with yourselves."

In a slave-holding community it was indeed bold thus frankly and publicly to argue equality of the races. Yet apparently Dr. Buchanan's thesis provoked no objection. On the contrary the minutes show that the president of the society was directed to thank Dr. Buchanan "for the excellent oration." The president at that time was Samuel Sterett and the vice-president Alex McKim, both like Dr. Buchanan members of Baltimore's oldest and most influential families.

Baltimore, too, was exceptionally active in the movement in the 1820's to transport free Negroes in the United States back to Africa and establish a colony there. Liberia was the result. Many prominent persons were enthusiastic supporters of this scheme for righting the wrong of slavery. They did not realize that the Negro population in this country had grown to such proportions that an attempt to return any appreciable part of it to Africa was altogether impracticable. John Eager Howard and Isaac McKim were vice-presidents of "The American Society for Colonizing the Free People of Colour of the United States." In the second annual report of the society issued in Washington in 1819 reference was made to "the generosity of the city of Baltimore" in the matter of money contributed toward the operations of the society. Other Baltimoreans active in putting through the program were General Robert Goodloe Harper and J. H. B. Latrobe. General Harper is credited with having suggested the name Liberia for the colony while Mr. Latrobe proposed Monrovia as the name of the capital. In recognition of Maryland's contribution, which largely was that of Baltimore, a part of the colony situated at Cape Palmas was given the name of Maryland which it still bears.

Shortly after the establishment of the colony its first governor, John B. Russwurm, a Negro, arrived in Baltimore on a visit. The

Board of Directors of the local chapter of the society tendered him a handsome dinner and drank his health. As auspicious as the occasion may have seemed with respect to racial relations something like a century was to pass before whites and Negroes would again sit down at the same table at a public dinner in Baltimore.

Slaves were property. It is understandable that persons whose wealth depended upon the institution were reluctant to surrender it. Yet there can be no doubt that owning slaves was on the conscience of many Marylanders. They showed it by manumitting them in their wills. Among those taking this course was Charles Ridgely, former Governor of the State and master of Hampton. The liberation of all Negro slaves in Baltimore of course came only with the Civil War. It is interesting to note that at the time of the riot in April, 1861, attending the march of the 6th Massachusetts Infantry through the city, some 300 of the most respectable Negro residents tendered their services to the city authorities. Mayor Brown thanked them for their offer and asked them to hold themselves in readiness in case they should be needed.

But emancipation did not prove to be a complete solution of the Negro problem. Some members of the race prospered while others found it hard to make a living in their new-found freedom. In Baltimore as in other large cities the Negroes comprise the poorest element in the community. It has been said that, in hard times, the Negroes are the first to lose their jobs, and, as times improve, the last to be re-employed. The racial problem is accentuated by the constant movement of Negroes from Virginia, the Carolinas and other Southern states who are attracted to the Balimore labor market. Unlike the Baltimore-born Negroes they are not adapted to the local environment, and through the working of the old law of supply and demand the influx of newcomers depresses the labor market. It also adds to the already crowded conditions in those sections of the city which have been taken over by the Negroes.

In Baltimore segregation is the general rule. When Negroes enter a neighborhood the whites moved out. Consequently as the increasing Negro population seeks more room and tries to spread out into hitherto white neighborhoods it meets opposition. Nevertheless expansion has continued, but not at a rate sufficient to prevent heavy congestion in the Negro sections. Here the population is more than 58,000 to the square mile compared with 9,000 to the square mile in the white neighborhoods.

Even when the Negroes take over a neighborhood they inherit the oldest houses in the city. In short what they get is a blighted area. It has been estimated that while only 27.3 per cent of the white population lives in blighted areas, no less than 92.6 per cent of the Negro population does. The effect of this crowding is reflected in the unfavorable figures on health and crime. For example a few years ago the life expectancy of a Negro child in Baltimore was put at 53.9 years as compared with 65 years for a white child. Serious crimes committed by Negroes are far out of proportion to their population in the community.

There are three large Negro neighborhoods in the city. One is in northeast Baltimore in the vicinity of Johns Hopkins Hospital, another is in South Baltimore convenient to the harbor and the third is in northwest Baltimore. The last named is by far the largest and the most important. Pennsylvania Avenue, from Dolphin to Laurens Street, is its "Great White Way." Here are found its night clubs, its theaters, its beauty shops and fortune tellers. Here the sporting element congregates on Saturday nights and here on Easter Sunday the Negroes have their own fashion parade.

As was true of other Southern cities, the large Negro population once afforded an abundant supply of domestic help. At the turn of the century, before the exodus to the suburbs, Baltimore's fashionable residential area lay in the blocks adjacent to and north of Mt. Vernon Place. It embraced Mt. Vernon Place itself, and Park Avenue, Cathedral Street, North Charles, St. Paul and Calvert. Most of the houses ran to four stories and, in addition, had their kitchens in the basement. They were extravagant to run and, as a rule, required the care of five servants. There was a cook, a downstairs maid and an upstairs maid on continual duty. There was in addition a laundress and also a man who looked after the furnace and washed the front steps.

These were the houses of the wealthy and the well to do. But families of modest means supported at least one servant. They wondered how people in the North and in the West got along with no servant at all. This happy existence continued pretty well up to the outbreak of World War II. Baltimoreans caught a glimpse of the realities of life only on occasions when sickness or a death in a domestic's family kept her at home. In the 1920's and 1930's it was estimated that the domestic servant industry in Baltimore, almost entirely controlled by Negroes, amounted to $19,000,000 annually.

Then, with the advent of World War II and a demand for labor in the factories turning out war goods, the domestic servants vanished from their accustomed places. Men who were making good wages wanted their wives at home to cook for them. Unmarried women had no difficulty finding jobs in the war plants. Housewives found it hopeless to persuade them to stick to domestic labor. They couldn't be convinced that it was any easier.

So, with considerable distress, Baltimoreans in the middle-income brackets found themselves in the same boat with their opposite numbers in the North and West. They had to go without. They learned to cook. At least there was consolation in not having to feed and pay a servant. Money saved on those items was used for labor-saving devices in the kitchen. In Baltimore as elsewhere the profession of baby sitting was born.

An agency that has been active in attacking the problems arising from the proximity of the two races is the Baltimore Urban League, one of a number of such leagues found in other cities with large Negro populations. Its membership is composed both of white and Negro citizens. It was established in 1924 "to improve conditions under which Negro citizens of Baltimore live and work" and "to build a better climate of racial understanding." The individual generally identified as founder of the League was John R. Cary, a member of the Society of Friends. Thus was maintained the Baltimore tradition of Quaker interest in the welfare of the Negro which was manifested more than a century earlier in the antislavery society.

At the time of the founding of the league the city's outstanding scandal was a congested square in the Negro quarter of northwest Baltimore known as "Lung Block." It was bounded by Pennsylvania Avenue, Druid Hill Avenue, Biddle and Preston Streets. Negroes are notoriously susceptible to tuberculosis. In

"Lung Block" the death rate for the disease was 958 per 100,000 of population as compared with a citywide rate of 131. 9. The League seized upon the cleaning up of "Lung Block" as its first project. By dint of hard labor and pitiless publicity it aroused the community to the shame and disgrace of conditions. Eventually the block, with its tumble-down and germ-infested houses, was razed and a modern housing development erected on its site.

On the occasion of its twenty fifth anniversary in 1950 the League published a survey of the progress that had been made and was being made toward the realization by Baltimore Negroes of those rights set forth in 1947 by President Truman's Committee on Civil Rights. The survey reported that in Baltimore the threat of widespread violence or mob action was virtually nonexistent. That is interesting in view of Baltimore's earlier unsavory reputation as Mobtown.

Under the heading of safety and security of person the chief complaint was that the police handle Negro prisoners more severely than whites. Note was made also that in the courts punishment meted out tended to be less for Negroes who committed crimes against each other than those who committed crimes against whites, and in some instances, punishment of whites was less than that for Negroes for the same crime.

The survey noted that it was customary for Negroes to be represented on juries and public boards. It called attention to the fact that segregation was practiced generally. But while white and Negro children were educated separately in the public schools, some progress had been made in getting professional courses in local colleges opened to Negroes. Reference was made to Negroes in the graduate schools of the University of Maryland. There were individual instances also of a Negro at St. John's College, Annapolis, and of Negro students in the engineering school of Johns Hopkins University, Loyola College and the Peabody Institute. The survey went on to point out that while Negroes had been taken on the Baltimore police force, they were excluded from driving buses of the Baltimore Transit Company and that certain job restrictions were in effect with the Telephone Company and the Gas and Electric Company. It was pointed out that Negroes found a barrier raised against them in trade unions.

A source of irritation in recent years has been use of the public parks and their recreational facilities. Negroes also complain over being excluded from theaters, restaurants and hotels and of receiving differential treatment in the stores.

Baltimoreans looking back over the past fifty years are impressed with the progress that has been made in the recognition of rights of the Negro citizens. There is no question that there will be further recognition as the years go by. The question is how rapid the progress should be. Thus far the white population has yielded with surprising calm to the demands for change. Constant agitation thus far has achieved such gratifying results from the standpoint of the Negro that there is a tendency for the more radical element to increase its demand with the end to wiping out all racial distinction. That is not likely for many years to come.

Striking evidence of the progress that has been made by Baltimore Negroes is to be found in the several institutions run by them. Conspicuous among these are the Provident Hospital, Morgan College and the Baltimore Institute of Musical Arts.

The Provident Hospital is housed in the old buildings of what once was the Union Protestant Infirmary, now Union Memorial Hospital. It is strategically located in the Negro neighborhood in northwest Baltimore and serves the Negro population. White physicians act in an advisory capacity. Aside from that the medical and surgical staffs, nurses, orderlies and administrative staffs are all composed of Negroes. Associated with the hospital is a nursing school conducted entirely for and by Negroes.

Morgan College is attractively located in the northern suburbs in what otherwise is a white neighborhood. It offers courses in the cultural arts and the sciences including domestic science. Morgan is coeducational and has a student body of several thousand.

The Baltimore Institute of Musical Arts is a new agency. It owes its creation to the fact that, as a general rule, Negro students have not been accepted by the Peabody Conservatory of Music. It is too soon to evaluate the instruction it offers in vocal and instrumental music. In view of the natural musical endowment of the Negro the Institute of Musical Arts offers great promise of achievement.

The growth of Baltimore's Negro community has produced a

demand for special services presented by Negroes. The weekly newspaper, the *Afro-American*, is an outstanding example. The demand has led also to the development of a professional class including lawyers, doctors, dentists, teachers, insurance men, real estate men and merchants.

For many years catering for the city's leading social events has been in the hands of Negroes. Two names which stand out in this field are those of Charles Shipley and T. Henry Waters.

Until shortly before his death in 1943 the cream of the business went to Shipley. Shipley came originally from Howard County. An older brother, William, held the important post of butler to General John Gill of R., a bon vivant of his day. Charles entered the Gill household as second man. In that capacity he had the opportunity to put his special talents to work learning how the best food was prepared and served.

For years Shipley regularly served the suppers for the Bachelors Cotillon and for the Assembly. Whenever distinguished visitors came to Baltimore Shipley was called in to prepare the menus for them. And when he was in charge it could be taken for granted that the food would be the very best and that it would be served with exquisite taste. On the visit of Cardinal Mercier of Belgium, hero of the German occupation of his country in World War I, to Cardinal Gibbons, it was Shipley who had charge of the food. He acted in a similiar capacity during the visits of Queen Marie of Rumania, Prince Paul of Greece and the Duke and Duchess of Windsor.

Shipley's men on formal occasions were attired in plum-colored livery and his equipment was the finest. He owned several after-dinner silver services whose value ran into hundreds of dollars. An admirer once said of him: "It was the achievement of Shipley that he and his men could come into any house, or any apartment, and turn it for an evening into a sort of ducal palace." One lady said she never enjoyed her own parties until she discovered Shipley. After that she could turn everything over to him confident that there would never be a slip.

Shipley made a speciality of old Maryland country-cured ham and terrapin. Once King Prajadhikop of Siam came to the Johns Hopkins Hospital as a patient. Among other things his doctor prescribed Maryland terrapin. Of course the only person in Baltimore regarded as fit to prepare terrapin for a king was Shipley. Prajadhikop was so delighted with the dish that, after his return to Siam, he several times had orders of Shipley's terrapin sent halfway round the world to him.

Shipley went out of business several years before his death in 1943 at the age of sixty four years. He was a born epicure and in his later years confessed that he could not acclimate himself to what he called the "gin, jazz, hot dog and blues days." Fortunately he confided the secret of preparing terrapin to his son who still carries on the Shipley tradition at the Maryland Club.

Following Shipley's death Waters, who had already been pressing him hard in general popularity, took over most of the entertainments. Waters got his start as a butler to Hugh Bond another prominent Baltimorean who belonged to an age when good living was a fine art. His service has shown the results of that early training.

Another Negro associated with Baltimore's entertainments, both public and private, is Rivers Chambers. His catering is done for those who want, not food, but music. When an invitation says Rivers Chambers will be present it is put there to draw a crowd. For Rivers Chambers is a surefire attraction. Sometimes Rivers Chambers is an individual, sometimes he is three people, sometimes he is an orchestra of twenty pieces, sometimes he is in several places at once. However many he may be Rivers Chambers is synonymous with gay music and general good cheer.

It all began back in 1930 at the beginning of the great depression. Chambers then was playing the organ in a movie house in New York City. At the same time one Charles (Buster) Brown was playing in a jazz band in Albany, New York, and one Leroy (Tee) Loggins was making music in a traveling musical show in Louisiana. When times got hard all three headed for Baltimore. They formed the nucleus of an orchestra which played for seven years as a pit band in the Royal Theater on Pennsylania Avenue. Rivers Chambers was the leader and the general inspiration behind the venture.

Around 1937 Chambers, Brown and Loggins, forming a musical trio, extended their operations to include outside parties. It did not take them long to achieve fame throughout the city and to build up an extensive clientèle. Success was speeded by an accident. One night in a beer garden on Wilkens Avenue Buster Brown had his accordian going and was in the middle of a hill billy song entitled "They Cut Down the Old Pine Tree," when he forgot the words and had to improvise. He found himself singing and then repeating "Oh, cut it down, oh cut it down, and they hauled it away to the mill." The tune was catchy and in a few minutes everybody in the place had joined in. No telling how many times since the old pine tree has been cut down. The song requires no voice. It isn't sung, it is shouted. It never ends. And it makes a party go.

Rivers Chambers and his fellow musicians are almost invariably present at alumni dinners, lodge smokers, convention banquets, anniversary parties, wedding receptions, debutante parties and wherever more than two or three are gathered together to have a good time. The orchestra plays for the fashionable dancing classes, too. Chambers thinks he must have appeared in virtually every house in the Green Spring Valley. He has played also for various Governors of Maryland, Mayors of Baltimore, U. S. Senators and lesser statesmen.

An incident Chambers likes to recall is when the Duke of Windsor joined his band for an evening. The occasion was an exclusive dinner given by an old Baltimore friend of the Duchess during one of the visits of the Windsors. Chambers was engaged to sing spirituals. But, being an experienced showman, he prepared for any eventuality by tossing his drums and other noisemaking instruments in the back of his car. Sure enough, after a round of spirituals, the Duke approached Chambers and remarked that he knew something about playing the traps. He supposed Chambers hadn't brought his along. But Chambers had and soon the Duke was having the time of his life as a member of the orchestra.

It is not unusual for a stranger at a party to find Buster Brown before him, playing an accordian and singing some song appropriate to the stranger's home, college club or profession. Brown has been put up to it by some other guest. There isn't any song he doesn't know or can't learn in a couple of minutes after somebody has hummed the air to him. If a guest from Patagonia were to appear at a Baltimore party Brown could be counted on to produce a Patagonian folksong or its national anthem, if Patagonia has one.

On Sunday, January 7, 1933, the *Sunpapers* announced the death of William Paine, hat-check man at the Merchants' Club, after a service of thirty years. The interesting thing about Paine was that he was a hat-check man who used no checks. Though he handled hundreds of hats and coats at one time he could remember every person to whom a hat and coat belonged. The announcement went on to say that it was expected that from then on checks would be used. It seemed unlikely that anybody could duplicate this remarkable feat of memory.

However, apprenticed to Paine for nine years was a young man named William Gilbert. In the course of those nine years Gilbert had learned the secret from the master. When he first replaced Paine, old members of the club were skeptical. But not for long. Soon Gilbert was taking care of hats and coats on the memory system as confidently as Paine had ever done. At a Christmas party at the club he once handled as many as 550 hats and coats without making a mistake. How he does it is Gilbert's secret, as it was Paine's. When questioned he replies that he "just trusts to mother wit."

In the course of years Baltimore has sheltered or produced other individual Negroes of unusual distinction for a variety of reasons. The town was still young when, around 1796, there appeared on the local scene one Joshua Johnston. Information about him is fragmentary. There is reason to believe he came from the West Indies as a slave. Local tradition has made him a bondsman of General Sam Smith, of General John Stricker and of Hugh McCurdy. It is based on the fact that he painted portraits of the families of all three of these gentlemen, for he was a portrait painter of no little talent. Somewhere along the line Johnston, if he actually had been a slave, must have been manumitted, for in the city directory for thirty years between 1796 and 1824 he is listed as a "free Negro householder." Some twenty one existing oil portraits are known to have been his work. He evidently was influenced by the Peale family which also was producing portraits at that time. Critics give Johnston serious consideration as an "American primitive."

More famous throughout the nations than Joshua Johnston, and for quite another reason, was Joe Gans, a native Baltimorean. Joe was born on November 25, 1874. He grew up around the fish market. In 1890, at the age of sixteen years, he took part in his first prize fight at the Avon Club, knocked out another Negro boy and won $4 out of a $5 purse. His official career, however, dates from 1894. From then on he was continually in the ring and for eight years spent his time working his way up to the top. On May 21, 1902, he became the lightweight champion of the world. Joe held the title until he was knocked out by Battling Nelson at San Francisco in the 17th round of a fight on July 4, 1908. Many said that it was not Battling Nelson but tuberculosis that dethroned Joe. At San Francisco he already was a sick man; two years later he died of the disease.

Old sports writers have said that Joe Gans was the greatest fighter of all time. In addition to his skill he had the reputation for being a good sportsman and a clean fighter. He was idolized in his home town by white and black alike.

Joe's last losing battle was fought in Arizona where he had gone in the hope of regaining his health. Realizing that the end was near he was rushed back home to die. After his death his body lay in state in Whatcoat Methodist Episcopal Church and crowds passed by to pay "The Old Master" their last respects. Joe was buried in Mount Auburn Cemetery, in Westport, a southwest Baltimore neighborhood. People still come from distant parts of the country to visit his grave.

Nearly thirty years later Baltimore witnessed the state funeral of another distinguished son. It was that of Chick Webb, known nationally and internationally as "Harlem's King of Drums." William Henry Webb, to give him his full name, was born in East Baltimore. He was one year old when respects were being paid to the mortal remains of Joe Gans. At an early age Chick was crippled by tuberculosis of the spine. While making a living as a newsboy he got into the habit of drumming out tunes on fences, boxes and on the wooden steps of row houses which abound in Baltimore.

Drumming was in Chick's soul. At fifteen years he played in a Negro orchestra. At sixteen he left for New York and showed so much ability that shortly he was organizing his own band. His style of drum playing came to be known as the "power drive." Soon the connoisseurs were saying that Chick Webb's was the "hottest" swing band in the country. It got a contract to play at the New York World's Fair in 1939. Chick was a composer as well as a band leader and the author of several song hits. His band had the distinction of being the only swing band ever to perform at the Metropolitan Opera House. It took part in a benefit concert and accompanied Lily Pons, Helen Jepson and Grace Moore in a complex arrangement of "Minnie the Moocher."

The old and deadliest enemy of the Baltimore Negro caught up with Chick as it had done with Joe Gans. He died of tuberculosis in Johns Hopkins Hospital in June, 1939. His body was taken to the humble home of his grandparents at 1313 Ashland Avenue. There, and later at Waters African M. E. Church, his frail form, clad in his white tuxedo, lay in state in a silver casket. It was estimated that 15,000 persons of all races passed by his bier to pay him final honors. Among the mourners were Duke Ellington, Cab Calloway and other great names in the world of swing. In East Baltimore, which the musician knew well in his youth, his name has been immortalized in the Chick Webb Memorial Center, an athletic club for poor Negro boys.

A Baltimore prophet "not without honor" is Father Divine. Around the turn of the century this native son was known as George Baker, who earned a modest living as a hedge trimmer and odd jobs man. That was before he went onto New York and Harlem, experienced a rebirth and came out as Father Divine. Another bull's-eye for Baltimore. "Peace, it's wonderful!"

The Negro race produced still another rare man in Emanuel Chambers. For thirty years he was known affectionately to hundreds of members of the Baltimore Club and the Maryland Club. Emanuel was born on a farm in Harford County and came as a boy to live in Baltimore. In 1907 he commenced his distinguished career as a club servant. The Baltimore Club then was situated at Charles and Madison Streets and Emanuel entered its employ. There he remained until it merged with the Maryland Club in

1933. Emanuel was part of the merger. In the course of the thirty years he served the two clubs he earned a reputation for solving the problems of the club members which became legendary. In fact it was generally believed there was nothing Emanuel couldn't do.

A club member wanted seats to grand opera at the Lyric which had been sold out for six months. He appealed to Emanuel who produced the seats. A club member sought in vain for a Pullman reservation to Chicago; Emanuel came up with a whole section. Once he is said to have arranged for an express train to stop at Laurel Race Track to pick up two friends of members of the club who wanted an afternoon at the races before returning to their home in New York.

White ties, shirt studs and collar buttons were no trouble at all. In an emergency Emanuel could always provide them. Once he is said to have reminded a forgetful club member that it was his wedding day. There was a time when the District of Columbia required a District license for all cars coming into the area from Maryland. A club member who had business in Washington and wished to use his car once appealed to Emanuel, and Emanuel produced the District license. He cautioned the borrower, however, to return it before 4 P.M. that same day. For, he explained, there was a funeral at that hour and the license belonged to the hearse.

The late Chief Judge Carroll Bond of the Maryland Court of Appeals once was visiting in London and was entertained by friends at a London club. The conversation turned to the subject of servants. In the company was a much-traveled Englishman who was unacquainted with Judge Bond's background. He remarked in the judge's hearing that in his travels he had run up with many excellent servants but, in his opinion, by far the best he had ever known was a man named Emanuel at the Maryland Club in Baltimore.

Emanuel never married. During the course of his service at the clubs he lived on his salary and saved his tips. These he turned over to his friend Ellicott H. Worthington for investment. Regularly dividends were plowed back into the capital amount. In 1937 Emanuel retired at the age of seventy-six years. He lived to be eighty-four. Thanks to his frugality and the skill of his financial advisor, his estate had by that time grown to more than $154,000. In his will Emanuel provided for the establishment of the Emanuel Chambers Foundation, Inc., naming Mr. Worthington and four other members of the Maryland Club as trustees. The testator expressed the wish that income from the estate be allocated to nonprofit charities "regardless of race, color or creed." The trustees have faithfully carried out Emanuel's wishes. A recent audit revealed that since Emanuel's death in 1945 the corpus had increased to $180,000 and yielded income to the amount of $6,000 a year. Out of that income $26,625 already has been contributed to local charities.

In a discussion of the contribution of members of the Negro race to Baltimore, the life and character of Emanuel Chambers is an appropriate and inspiring note on which to end.

Chapter 20

SOCIETY, CAPITAL "S"

A BOSTON FAMILY of high social position some years ago came to live in Baltimore where the father had accepted the presidency of one of the city's large trust companies. Having been carefully briefed on local custom they took a house in the Green Spring Valley. A daughter of the family arrived at the age to be presented to society and the parents made the facts known. Yet in spite of their living in the right place and having all the proper credentials, their daughter received few invitations to debutante parties.

The mother suspected some mistake had been made. But what? In her perplexity she laid her troubles before a friend. "Did you register her at Downs'?" asked the friend. Then for the first time the Boston-bred mother learned that, in order to be on the official list of debutantes in Baltimore, it is essential to make the fact known at a stationer's shop on Charles Street.

The incident gives some idea of the informality of Baltimore society which defies exact definition. For, though it is informal, it is at the same time also both subtle and complex. There is no State law or city ordinance to prevent anybody claiming to be in Baltimore society. There is no authority vested with power to say who is in society or who is not. In the opinion of some people it is sufficient to have one's name in The Blue Book (a local publication) or in the Baltimore edition of the Social Register. Frequent appearance of one's name in the society columns of the local press might be accepted as evidence.

In Baltimore, social position is a mysterious compound of family, money, occupation, residence, membership in exclusive organizations and friends. Yet there are many fine people who possess many of these qualifications and are not considered to be in society because they have not bothered to take part in purely social activities. On the other hand, there are persons whose names appear frequently in the public prints in connection with social activities, but whose claim to being in society could be subject to question.

It has been said that being in society in Baltimore is a process that extends from the cradle to the grave. It begins at birth with having the right parents, it ends with being buried by that most fashionable of undertakers--Jenkins. For those who are not born into it another popular way is to marry into it. To be in Baltimore society now it usually is regarded as essential to live in that segment of the city bounded by University Parkway on the south, York Road on the east, Reisterstown Road to the west and as far north as the Pennsylvania line. Add to this a few "cave dwellers" around Mt. Vernon Place or living "up on the hill" in the territory ruled by the Mt. Royal Improvement Association.

Newcomers from the North and West are shocked also to discover that a place in society demands attendance at a private, not a public, school. Among the occupations to which social prestige obtains are the standard professions, wholesale but not retail trade; and, above all, that of gentleman of leisure. The extent of the prestige is of course in proportion to the size of the income. However, in obtaining social preferment in Baltimore, family position is still the equivalent of many thousand dollars in cash.

A story illustrative of the great importance of family is told of the late Rebecca Shippen. Mrs. Shippen was born a Nicholson and descended also from the Lloyds of Wye House in whose veins flows the bluest blood in Maryland. She was sitting one afternoon with a friend over a cup of tea. "Rebecca," inquired the friend, "did it ever occur to you that if Our Lord had come to Baltimore we wouldn't have met him, since his father was a carpenter?" "But, my Dear," replied Mrs. Shippen, "you forget. He was well connected on his mother's side." In Baltimore it is essential to be "well connected" on one side or the other, if not on both.

The first important step in ascending the social ladder comes around the age of six years when the campaign starts to get a child into the right dancing class. These classes usually are run by select committees of mothers. Committee members are overwhelmed with personal appeals. Friends of committee members, too, are corralled and asked to write letters of recommendation for little John and little Mary. Eligibility for a particular dancing class depends also upon age. The date of birth in consequence becomes a prime factor. November 1st is by long tradition selected as the deadline. A child who is so unlucky as to have been born on November 2nd must wait another year no matter how many of her friends are born before the vital day. Dancing classes are chronically hard up for boys so their chance of getting into the right dancing class is considerably better than that of their sisters.

When little girls in the private schools reach their early teens one fine day one of them will announce proudly to her fellow classmates that she is going to be presented to society at the Bachelors Cotillon. Others in the class may retort that they are too. The rest will go home that evening to ask their parents just what the Bachelors Cotillon is and what is the meaning of coming out. If a father is not a member the moment will have arrived that many Baltimore parents have dreaded.

Although many racial strains are found among its people Baltimore is fundamentally a city with a British background and British social customs. Therefore from the time it ceased to be an outpost it has had some sort of exclusive assembly or ball, or series of balls, corresponding to the county balls in England. A conspicuous architectural feature of the city that rose shortly before 1800 was the Assembly Room on the northeast corner of Fayette and Holliday Streets, especially designed for balls and similar fashionable gatherings.

The Cotillon frequently is compared with the Philadelphia Assembly which claims to go back to 1744, and Charleston's St. Cecelia Ball, which puts the date of its founding in 1747. Were the Cotillon to regard itself as a continuation of earlier social organizations it might trace its origin to 1796 when a similar ball is known to have been held. The unbroken record is believed to go back no farther than the middle 1850's, while the present name of the "Bachelors Cotillon" appears to be no older than 1870. In the beginning a series of balls was given. But, as time went on, these were dropped one by one until there remains only the one which takes place the first Monday in December at which the debutantes of the year are presented.

The Board of Governors is a self-perpetuating body, whose

members invariably are selected from old Baltimore families. Wives of subscribers are included under the subscription, but widows and maiden ladies are invited as guests of the organization. If a debutante receives an invitation her mother is invited also to come as her chaperon, even though her father is not a subscriber and receives no invitation.

While little girls boast of their connection with the Cotillon not so their fathers. They are afraid that if it gets noised abroad in the business world that they are engaged in any such frivolity their careers will suffer. In consequence they preserve a discreet silence and, though half-dead from sitting up most of the night, make a point of being at their desks bright and early on the day after the Cotillon just as though they had never been there or heard of it.

Grim stories are told of girls whose lives have been ruined and who have carried the scar to the grave because they were not invited to the Cotillon. If such is the case then only a very small part of the city's female population has escaped this sad fate. For the facilities are limited and not more than from sixty to eighty Baltimore girls in the eighteen-year-old group can be invited each year, in addition to a few from out of town with Baltimore connections. Spokesmen for the Cotillon are emphatic that its governors have no authority to say who shall or shall not be debutantes. All it does is to invite certain girls to a dance. So great is the prestige of the Cotillon, however, that the town usually regards as debutantes only the girls who are invited.

Though it may be hard for a girl to get an invitation, it is even harder for a man. Relatively few young bachelors or other new subscribers are added to the list each year. It might fairly be said of the membership of the Cotillon that few die, none resign and those removed for bad behavior are insignificant in number. The average age of those attending is high, and bachelors are far outnumbered by fathers and grandfathers. Bald heads, gray hair and the well-rounded figures of middle age predominate. So often have the trousers to their dress suits been let out that it is said few members of the Cotillon would dare lift their tails and show the gussets that have been let in the waistline.

Once a girl has received an invitation the next problem is to find partners. Only fortunate ones can expect to have escorts who are young: the majority have to make out as best they can with fathers, uncles and friends of fathers. Most of the girls go with three or more partners since the typical Cotillon partner hasn't the wind and stamina to go the whole evening alone. If there are several partners they can spell each other. Three is the ideal number. This provides one for active operations, one in support, and one, so to speak, in dry dock for refitting and repairs.

The Cotillon is preceded by many dinners in private homes, clubs and hotels. For many years it has been held in the Lyric Theater. For this occasion a dance floor is erected over the orchestra seats and the orchestra pit is concealed by carpeted stairs which lead up to the stage. The stage is arranged for supper which is substantial. There, too, champagne is served.

The only really elaborate feature of the Cotillon is the profusion of flowers sent the debutantes by escorts, relatives and family friends. A single debutante may receive as many as fifty or sixty bouquets. Every seat in the boxes which flank the Lyric auditorium is assigned to the chaperon of a debutante. The fronts of the boxes are decorated with southern smilax held in place by wire mesh. In this mesh are entwined the flowers of the debutantes so that by the time the ball begins there is an unbroken border of flowers running the whole length of each side of the dance floor. The ballroom is further adorned with massive gold candelabra, and pillows and draperies of gold brocade which have been the property of the Cotillon for many decades.

In comparison with balls in some other cities the Bachelors Cotillon is an exceedingly modest affair. There is no Queen, no Veiled Prophet; there are no maids of honor, courtiers or pages. The debutantes and their mothers and other ladies attending merely wear their best gala dresses. It is customary for the debutantes to come in white. Among the older women the dresses they wear often get to be as familiar a sight as the women themselves.

Promptly at 11 P.M. the orchestra stops, a whistle is blown and the debutante figure is announced. The floor is cleared except for the debutantes and their partners. One of the governors then leads the couples through a simple figure, or march, which maintains the tradition of the "german" so popular with an earlier generation. The chief purpose of the figure is to give the old people a chance to see the debutantes—rather like show horses being put through their paces. It is an altogether simple, unpretending but dignified ceremony and it is over in less than ten minutes. A girl who has looked forward to it for years might well ask, "Is this all?"

And it is, save for one more figure later in the evening and dancing—or trying to dance—with elderly gentlemen old enough to be one's father and wondering what to say to them. In fact because of the many blood relationships among members of Baltimore society the cotillon takes on the aspect of a sort of glorified family reunion. This quality was charmingly emphasized a few years ago when D. Stewart Ridgely, a governor of long standing, led the debutante figure with his eighteen-year old daughter, Dorothy.

Despite the lowering of standards in most human enterprises during the past two decades the Cotillon has been remarkably successful in keeping its own up. Save during war years white tie and tails have been compulsory. And, after World War I, the Cotillon returned to the convention long before New York and other cities. It was at this time that two dapper young men, Yale graduates both, came to live in Baltimore temporarily and received guest cards to the Cotillon. They duly arrived at the Lyric and presented the cards to the doorkeeper. He looked at the cards, then looked at them.

"I'm sorry," he said, "But you can't come in. You are wearing black ties."

"Why," replied one of the young men, "I never heard of wearing a white tie with a tuxedo."

"Oh," said the doorkeeper, "so you have on tuxedos? Then you certainly can't come in. You must wear a dress suit to get in here." So they went away disappointed.

The dapper young men were just then completing plans to go on to New York and start a magazine. The magazine was *Time*. The young men were Henry R. Luce and the late Briton Hadden.

A surprising fact about the Cotillon is that while it has not lowered its standards at the same time it has not in the course of the last thirty years raised its dues. It must be unique in that respect among all organizations in all classes of society. Baltimore is unique also in that a girl, assuming she has the proper connections, may be formally presented to society at no more cost to herself than a ball dress and a tip for the maid in the dressing room. No wonder girls from other cities who have any claim on Baltimore flock back to "come out."

Another social hurdle of formidable proportions is the Assembly. This is sponsored by a committee of some thirty women and it is a smart affair indeed. It cannot boast great age, having been established as recently as 1905. It was suspended during both World Wars and also during the depression years of 1931–1933 when its funds were turned over to charity. The Assembly is definitely a party of grownups. Only a handful of debutantes is included on its invitation lists and in at least one year not a debutante was invited. Emphasis is laid on the fact that it is a ball, including a seated supper. In some years it has been held at the Sheraton-Belvedere Hotel and in others at the Alcazar. This latter establishment, owned and operated by the Knights of Columbus, provides a spacious ballroom with a stage and balcony and two supper rooms.

The feminine touch is everywhere apparent at the Assembly. It shows up in the elaborate flower arrangements in the ballroom and at the supper tables, and in the originality of the decorations, particularly in the supper rooms. Great pains are taken to have good music, and some nationally famous orchestra is imported for the occasion. At midnight the supper march is played and the entire company repairs to the supper rooms for terrapin, champagne, and a few embellishments. Since almost everybody has just got up from a sumptuous dinner only a couple of hours before this extra test of gastronomic capacity is somewhat appalling. Yet no true Baltimorean could refuse terrapin and champagne, especially after he has paid good money for it.

The third top-flight social institution is the Supper Club. It is a dinner dance and was originally sponsored by a smart and gay young married set. It also is redolent of the Green Spring

Valley. It meets twice a year. One feature of the Supper Club parties which suggests their gaiety and exuberance as contrasted with the dignity of the Cotillon and the Assembly is that guests are assured that on every table will be found a bottle of Scotch and a bottle of rye.

The Cotillon, the Assembly and the Supper Club represent the triple crown of Baltimore society. An aspirant for social distinction who is received into all three no doubt feels something like a man that has won a hurdle race or a horse that has captured the Kentucky Derby, the Preakness and the Belmont.

The existence of society has, of course, called for society editors to report the doings of the smart set. With only one exception the editors in Baltimore have been women. Their chief qualification has been that they themselves belong and know who is who. Yet of all Baltimore's society editors the most famous was a man. He was Dr. Frederick Taylor, member of an old Virginia family and a real doctor of medicine with an M.D. degree as his father had been before him. But he was never interested in the profession and, as he explained it, took the M.D. degree only to please his father. His true interest lay in the social world at a time when society was taken very seriously in this country and the doings of its members made first page news as do those of Hollywood celebrities today. Most of Dr. Taylor's career was spent on the *Baltimore News,* but after its sale to Hearst, he moved to the *Sun.*

Dr. Taylor was a man of short stature and of marked refinement. He was an ardent Anglophile and never so happy as when he was in England. If a fog descended over Baltimore he would rush out into the street and take long breaths exclaiming in delight that it reminded him of London.

When Dr. Taylor edited a society column it bore all the dignity and solemnity of England's Court Circular which obviously was its model. Nobody ever got in who didn't belong there. It was the popular belief that he enjoyed the confidence and friendship of several powerful social leaders and that a small item in his column, exactly phrased and perfectly timed, played an important part in the strategy of the rival forces.

For the general Baltimore public Dr. Taylor served as an

arbiter elegantiorum. These were the days before Emily Post, Dorothy Dix and Beatrice Fairfax. When a question of etiquette came to the office it was referred to Dr. Taylor. His answers were brutally frank. If some poor fellow called to say he was going to be married at 4 o'clock in the afternoon and asked if it would be proper to wear a tuxedo at that hour, Dr. Taylor in a scathing tone would reply over the telephone, "You would be as suitably dressed in your pajamas!"

On one occasion a higher up conceived the notion that Dr. Taylor's column needed jazzing up and gave orders to that effect. The Doctor had no other course but to obey. Next day he started it off by commenting that "Anybody who lives in the Green Spring Valley has either to be a Stewart or a Horse." After that Dr. Taylor was told he might return to his court circular style.

Yet there was much truth in the good doctor's description of the Valley. Very tersely it presented the two outstanding characteristics of that social paradise, which are its function as a stronghold of old families and the worship of horseflesh.

The Valley tradition may be traced to the post-Revolution period in Baltimore when the sudden growth of the city brought great prosperity to the merchants and led to the amassing of many fortunes. The majority of these merchants were of British extraction with a Briton's love of the soil. They had their town houses to which they repaired in winter, but their hearts were in the country estates which they purchased and on which they erected handsome houses. With their horses, cows, sheep, pigs, poultry and gardens they delighted in playing at gentlemen farmers. These estates, long since absorbed by the city, survive in such familiar place names in modern Baltimore as Belvedere, Mt. Royal, Bolton, Greenmount, Druid Hill, Auchentoroly, Homewood, Mt. Clare, Guilford, Homeland, Evergreen, Clifton and Montebello.

This custom among Baltimore's well to do of having a town house and a country estate within a few miles of each other survived through the generations. As the city grew and streetcar and railway lines brought new areas within reach the country estates moved farther out into the counties. From a social standpoint the Green Spring Valley takes precedence over all other localities. Social life centers around its hospitable homes, the Green Spring Valley Club and the Green Spring Valley Hunt. Old St. Thomas's Episcopal Church at Garrison Forest takes care of the religious requirements of a fashionable congregation. The graveyard connected with the church is the most exclusive in the Baltimore area. The head of one family which recently succeeded in getting hold of a lot there remarked that though his family might not have made Valley society in life at least they would enjoy the privilege of joining it in death. Many of the fox hunters now have moved farther afield to the picturesque Worthington Valley and Western Run Valley and to the hunting country around My Lady's Manor. Nevertheless enough of the old guard is left in the Green Spring Valley to insure its continued prestige.

Through most of its existence Baltimore society has been ruled by a hierarchy so subtle in its control that nobody quite knows just where the power lies or, in fact, if there actually is any central power. The person who comes closest to having been an individual leader of society was the late Mrs. Henry Barton Jacobs. Born Mary Frick, the member of an old Baltimore family, her first husband was Robert Garrett, a son of John W. Garrett, the Civil War president of the B. & O. Railroad. Robert Garrett, too, was for a time president of the road.

The Garrett mansion on Mt. Vernon Place came as close to approaching a palace as any house in Baltimore. Its width was the equivalent of several ordinary Baltimore dwellings. Conspicuous inside features were spacious drawing rooms, a large central court in which exotic plants flourished under glass, a gallery housing a large and impressive collection of paintings and a ballroom. Mr. Garrett had as well a handsome country estate on the western outskirts of the city.

Early in his career Mr. Garrett suffered a breakdown from which he never recovered. He required a physician in constant attendance. Called to fill the position was Dr. Henry Barton Jacobs, then a handsome young man with all the polish of a Harvard graduate and the physical vigor of an athlete. He had rowed on the Harvard crew. It was not altogether surprising that, upon the death of Mr. Garrett, the intimate friendship that had existed between Mrs. Garrett and the Doctor ripened into romance and they were married. Mrs. Jacobs was impudently referred to behind her back as "Mame."

Three other prominent figures on the stage were Mrs. H. Irvine Keyser, born Mary Washington of Virginia and one of the real Washingtons; Mrs. John Gill, popularly known as "Almighty Lou," and Mrs. Alexander (Allie) Brown. Gossip writers in the early 1900's had it that a bitter battle for supremacy was waged between "Mame" Jacobs and "Almighty Lou." If such was the case the conflict couldn't have lasted long. For all her forceful personality Mrs. Gill could not hope to contend successfully against Mrs. Jacobs, her palace on Mt. Vernon Place, her country estate and her villa at Newport. Certain it is that there was never a conflict between Mrs. Keyser and Mrs. Jacobs who saw eye to eye on social matters and whose mutual aim was to keep Baltimore society pure and undefiled. Mrs. Jacobs had two other faithful lieutenants in Mrs. Josias Pennington (Margaret Pleasants) and Mrs. Miles White (Jenny Bonsal).

Persons invited to Mrs. Jacobs' house or who were honored by her presence in their houses needed no other evidence that they belonged. In manner Mrs. Jacobs was gracious and she was loyal to her small coterie of intimate friends and their children. When she appeared at a reception in her sable coat and attended by Dr. Jacobs, if it was only for a few minutes, the party was made.

In striking contrast to the staid Jacobs-Keyser faction was one led by the Allie Browns. Mr. Brown, of the banking family, was an ardent fox hunter and a sportsman of the first water. Mrs. Allie was another Virginia Montague and a woman of striking beauty and vivacity. The Browns' impressive mansion, with ballroom adjoining, on Cathedral Street was the scene of continuous gaiety and hospitality. The Browns also were the owners of Mondawmin, a "country estate" of no less than sixty acres set down among row houses in the west end. The Allie Browns and their following looked upon the conservative element as dull company indeed. So different in character were the two groups that it could hardly be said there was rivalry between them. Baltimore was big enough to hold both.

Other members of the Garrett family who have had every right to social leadership are the John Garretts and the Robert Garretts, John and Robert being sons of T. Harrison Garrett and nephews of the Robert Garrett who was Mrs. Jacobs' first husband. John Garrett had a distinguished diplomatic career and, consequently, Baltimore saw little of him. It was not until the twilight of his life that he came back with his charming wife, the former Alice Warder of Washington, to open Evergreen House on North Charles Street. With a retinue of Italian servants they entertained Baltimore friends and visiting dignitaries lavishly.

A delightful feature of Evergreen House is a little theater, in an annex, designed by Bakst, the Russian artist. Here Mrs. Garrett occasionally displayed her talent as an actress in private theatricals. Here, too, twice a year, lucky music lovers were invited to attend a series of concerts by the Musical Arts Quartet for which the Garretts acted as patrons. Mrs. Garrett at the height of her career had an exotic beauty to which Bakst paid full justice in a portrait. On a visit to Evergreen House, Arthur Balfour, the English statesman, saw the painting before he saw the subject. Seizing it in both hands and gazing at it in admiration he exclaimed, "Now, there's a wicked woman!" Mrs. Garrett, it is said, was delighted.

Following Mr. Garrett's death Evergreen House, its rare collection of books and its expansive garden and lawns were bequeathed to Johns Hopkins University, though Mrs. Garrett continues to live there.

The Robert Garretts live at "Attica," just across the way. While the John Garretts were without children the Robert Garretts have an impressive family of three sons and four daughters. While the John Garretts were living a cosmopolitan life in foreign capitals the Robert Garretts were attending conscientiously to their civic duties at home.

Mrs. Robert Garrett was, before her marriage, Katharine Johnson, whose finely cut features and red-gold hair marked her out for special notice among her contemporaries. In spite of her exacting role as mother of a houseful of children and her keen interest in promoting public playgrounds she has found time also to live up to her social obligations by serving on numerous committees having to do with strictly social activities. Mr. Garrett throughout his useful life has been a devout Presbyterian. It happens that his dressing room at Attica is inclosed in glass. This circumstance and his always circumspect behavior once led a wit to remark: "So God can see him on all sides."

Since Mrs. Jacobs' death nobody has quite filled her place. Baltimore society has had to worry along without a single conspicuous head, trusting to little groups to maintain in a fashion the practice of favors and exclusiveness without which no society in the narrow sense can live. One wonders how she would feel were she to know that her house on Mt. Vernon Place now is occupied by the local temple of the Order of the Mystic Shrine.

A familiar and picturesque figure in Baltimore society during the first and second decades of the century was Walter de Curzon Poultney, a bachelor of ancient and honorable lineage who lived alone in a house in the heart of the city, stocked with family heirlooms and bric-a-brac. He was known to the town as Sir Walter. No social occasion was complete without his presence. He was diminutive in size, in his old age had white hair and a goatee, carried a cane and delighted in gay shirts and neckties. When he walked down Charles Street he was so light on his feet he gave the impression of skipping. Sometimes known as "The White Rabbit" he once came to a fancy-dress ball costumed as one.

Even after he was well up in years "Sir Walter" never failed to appear at dances and to dance throughout the evening with the abandon of the youngest persons present. It was an unforgettable experience to see him with a partner several times his size, flitting like a butterfly around a flower.

Baltimore's most famous contribution to society was a native son who seldom appeared on his home ground but performed under the spotlights of Newport. He was Harry Lehr. His activities took place when great fortunes were being amassed and the nouveaux riches, in their garish mansions in New York and Newport, were looking for diversion and willing to pay a good price to those clever enough to provide it. Lehr knew how to amuse them.

The stunt that gave him a national reputation was the dinner at Newport to which the guests were invited to meet "Prince de Drago." On arrival at the dinner they discovered that "the

Prince" was a monkey in full evening dress who sat at Mrs. Lehr's right. The story was played up in the press and delighted a nation that derived infinite pleasure in reading about the depravity of the rich. It made Harry Lehr almost as famous as Ward McAllister.

Generally speaking Baltimore society is sedate and astonishingly well behaved. Scandals are few and far between. But on the rare occasions when they occur society assumes a tolerant attitude. In one such instance this attitude was well illustrated by a comment made about the lady in the case: "Well, after all, she is just a poor Southern gentlewoman in very seduced circumstances."

In the whole of its long history nothing shocked Baltimore society so much as the incidents associated with the Munnikhuysen Ball. This event took place at the handsome brownstone-front residence of Mrs. William Munnikhuysen on North Charles Street in the early 1900's. The basement was transformed for the evening into "Hell" with demons running about in scarlet tights. Through an unfortunate error in judgment the champagne was allowed to flow too freely and the party got out of hand. Everyone said it was too bad it had happened at Mrs. Munnikhuysen's because she was such a dear soul and hadn't planned it that way.

For weeks the town rang with gossip over what had gone on. Children cocked an ear and listened to the whispered conversations of the grownups. Before long the teen-age boys and girls in the private schools were chanting the limerick:

> There was a young lady named Nance
> Who attended the Munnikhuysen dance
> She went down the cellar
> With a handsome young feller
> And now all her sisters are aunts.

The idea underlying formal society is, of course, that a girl who belongs enjoys the privilege of meeting eligible young men among whom she will find a husband. But it does not by any means work out that way. In fact Baltimore boys and girls seem instinctively to develop a distaste for the prospective mates their parents pick out for them. If Baltimore marriages depended upon acquaintances made at dancing classes or the Cotillon there would not be many of them. Actually the worldly wise think the Johns Hopkins Medical School, with its embryo specialists, offers more brilliant opportunities. However the fallacy is a pleasing one and many people derive much enjoyment from it. So, until a guillotine is set up in Mt. Vernon Place and the tumbrels begin to roll, the system will probably go on.

Chapter 21

BALTIMORE "FIRSTS"

IT IS INEVITABLE that a city of Baltimore's size and antiquity should have been the scene of the origin of a number of inventions and other human endeavors. Many already have been mentioned under separate headings. Still there are a few miscellaneous ones of sufficient interest to be gathered together and treated in one group.

Tradition has it that in the year 1772 a merchantman put into Baltimore harbor and tied up at a dock. In its cargo was an umbrella fashioned of coarse oiled linen and rattan sticks. Umbrellas then were rare also in western Europe. Doctors, ministers and other persons subject to call in all kinds of weather protected themselves with an oiled linen cape hooked around the shoulders.

Some bold innovator, seeing the umbrella in the ship's cargo bought it, opened it and proceeded to march up the street with the umbrella over his head. Women screamed at sight of the strange contraption, horses took fright and ran away. On the other hand, children are said to have delighted in the novelty and followed behind the umbrella carrier. Even in those early days Baltimoreans were suspicious of innovators. So they stoned the man, took his umbrella from him and tore it in shreds.

Such is the tale that has been passed down through the years, though definite proof is lacking. Since no other city has disputed it, Baltimore takes the credit for being the first place in the United States where the umbrella was used. The claim also has been made that Baltimore was the scene of the first umbrella manufacture. That no doubt stems from the fact that for years it was the center of the umbrella trade. Even today it is second only to New York in production and is the home of the largest individual manufacturer. The only factual evidence is that as early as June 4, 1794, one William Cummins was advertising in the local press as a maker and repairer of umbrellas. There may have been others before him.

Baltimore too was in at the birth of aeronautics in this country. The year 1783 was an important one, for it was the year the French pioneers, Joseph and Étienne Montgolfier, fabricated the balloon which gave them credit for being the inventors of this particular form of flight. In the same year Pilatre de Rozier, another Frenchman, made the first ascent by man in a captive balloon. This was followed swiftly, before the year was out, by a flight of twenty-seven miles in a free balloon accomplished by the Robert brothers and a Professor Charles.

These exciting experiments across the sea had their repercussions in Baltimore. Peter Carnes, a local attorney, was inspired to emulate the Frenchmen. He constructed a balloon out of what was described as "beautiful, costly and variegated silks." It was thirty-five feet in diameter and thirty feet high, and equipped with a cylindrical iron stove to heat the air which filled the bag. Suspended from the bottom was a chariot large enough to hold two people. When the balloon was completed Carnes put an advertisement in the newspaper announcing that he would give a public demonstration. The cost of admission was set at $2 for the best seats and 10 shillings for second choice. The site of the demonstration was Howard's Woods, where the Washington Monument now stands.

The ascension took place as advertised on June 3, 1784. The following day an account of Carnes's "curious AEROSTATIC EXPERIMENTS" was carried in the *Maryland Journal and Baltimore Advertiser*. A large crowd assembled to witness what was described as "the awful Grandeur of so novel a scene, as a large Globe making repeated voyages in the airy Regions, which Mr. Carnes's Machine actually performed, in a Manner that reflected Honor on his Character as a Man of Genius, and could not fail to inspire solemn and exalted Ideas in every reflecting Mind."

The unexpected high light came at the close of the demonstration. For, as preparation was being made for the last flight, a youth named Edward Warren volunteered to embark as a passenger. As the balloon rose the lad, says the contemporary account, "behaved with the steady Fortitude of an *Old Voyager*." The gazing multitude below wafted to him their loud applause which he graciously acknowledged by a significant wave of his hat. When Edward reached terra firma again the admiring crowd took up a cash collection and presented it to him. Who Edward Warren was and what became of him afterward is not recorded. This is unfortunate since he may have been the first human being in the United States to fly.

Though the event was duly recorded in a newspaper of the day Baltimore's claim has never received official confirmation. The credit for the first ascent in this country has instead been given to Jean Pierre François Blanchard, who made his ascent in Philadelphia in 1793 in the presence of President George Washington. Baltimore's claim, based on its local flight nine years before, has been disallowed on the ground that the ascent was made in a captive, not a free, balloon.

There appears to be no question, however, that Baltimore was the scene of the first use of illuminating gas. The generally accepted story is that the place of the demonstration was Peale's Museum on Holliday Street and the date June, 1816. The medium used for lighting the building was described as "carboretted hydrogen gas" and for several nights running crowds came to marvel at this novel illumination. Rembrandt Peale had his own gas-making plant on the premises. There appears to have been a very practical purpose behind this public demonstration. For on June 14, 1816, the *Baltimore American* carried a story to the effect that Mr. Peale had made a proposition to the Mayor to light the streets of the city with "the very brilliant and pleasing light."

The offer was accepted and the Baltimore Gas Company was inaugurated in the same year. It was the first company in the United States organized for producing and selling gas for illuminating purposes. The original incorporators in addition to Mr. Peale were William Lorman, James Mosher, William Gwynn and Robert Cary Long. Boston did not have such a company until 1821 and New York's was not incorporated until 1823. A year after the incorporation of the gas company a gas lamp went up at the corner of Baltimore and Holliday Streets, a few blocks from the museum. This public gas lamp has the distinction of being the first in the nation.

No outsider has ever attempted to steal Rembrandt Peale's thunder as a pioneer in illuminating gas. But the claim is challenged by another Baltimorean. This second man was Benjamin Henfrey. The *Federal Gazette* of February 26, 1802, carried an announcement that the "New Light Exhibition will commence on Monday, March 1st, at Mr. Robardett's ball room." In the *Federal Gazette* of March 11th a "Subscriber" contributed a paragraph in which he gave an eye-witness account of the illumination. In the face of the evidence it is hard to deny that a successful demonstration was made in Baltimore fourteen years ahead of that of Mr. Peale. But it did not culminate in a gas company. Besides, when for years the glory has gone to Peale it is awkward to transfer it to somebody else.

Impressive evidence of the progressive spirit of Baltimore in antebellum days, and in particular of the Baltimore & Ohio Railroad, was their conduct toward Professor Samuel F. B. Morse. Morse was a native of Charlestown, Massachusetts, who set out to become an artist. However, while on a trip to England in 1832, he conceived the notion of sending messages by electric telegraph. For twelve years he worked to perfect a machine. He first applied to a railroad in New Jersey for permission to string a wire along its right of way, but the officials of the line turned him down. They took the eminently practical position that if Professor Morse's invention proved a success people would do business by telegraph instead of traveling over the railroad.

Morse then set out for Baltimore and sought the advice of J.H.B. Latrobe. He could not have appealed to a better person for Mr. Latrobe was without doubt the most versatile Baltimorean of his day, and probably of all time. And he did not share the typical Baltimorean's prejudice against innovation. He had been educated first as a soldier and an engineer at West Point. But he abandoned these professions for the law and became a leader at the local bar. In addition to these attributes he displayed exceptional gifts as a poet, painter, writer, philanthropist, and inventor. At the time of Morse's visit he was counsel for the B. & O. After hearing the professor out Latrobe sent him off with a letter of introduction to Louis McLane who recently had been made president of the railroad.

Following the interview McLane remarked to Latrobe that he had had a visit from a crazy man. Latrobe replied: "The day when you and I are dead and forgotten this man will be remembered." Latrobe's prophecy must have had its effect since Morse obtained complete co-operation from the railroad in stringing his wire. In 1837 he applied for a patent on what he called "the American Electro-magnetic telegraph."

Morse received help from another important source. He needed funds to keep his experiment going and asked Congress for an appropriation. It so happened that at this time Maryland was represented in Congress by, among others, John P. Kennedy of Baltimore. Kennedy was an intimate friend of Latrobe and a man of equal imagination. It is highly probable that Morse was passed on to Kennedy by Latrobe. At any rate it was Kennedy who got Morse's bill referred to a committee of which he was chairman. The bill was reported out favorably by the committee and passed by Congress. It granted Morse a salary of $2,500 a year and an appropriation of $30,000 for the erection of an experimental line between Washington and Baltimore. Latrobe, acting in the absence of President McLane, put the Mount Clare Shops of the B. & O. at the disposal of the inventor.

Thus it came about that on May 24, 1844, the telegraph line between Washington and Baltimore was completed and ready for business. So, too, was Professor Morse's machine. Sitting at it as the sending operator in the old Supreme Court Chamber in Washington was Morse. Arrangements had been made to receive the message in Baltimore at the B. & O. passenger station, which at the time was located at Light and Pratt Streets.

On Miss Anne Ellsworth, daughter of the Commissioner of Patents, Professor Morse bestowed the honor of choosing the first message. She took from the Old Testament the now memorable words: "What hath God wrought!"

The message was successfully dispatched and received. It was followed by a solicitous message from Dolly Madison, widow of the fourth President of the United States, to her friend Mrs. John Wethered, wife of a Baltimore congressman. Baltimore in 1844 was still riding high, for there was taking place probably the most momentous event of the whole 19th century. Yet so blind were contemporaries to its significance that the *Sun* dismissed the story in a few lines on page 2 in a column headed "Local Matters."

A few years later still another incident illustrated the progressive spirit of Baltimoreans of the day. And this time the person chiefly responsible for it was Mr. A. S. Abell, publisher of the *Sun*. At Catskill, New York, there lived a man named James Bogardus, a watchmaker. He turned to invention and conceived novel notions on construction. Hitherto buildings had been supported by their brick walls. Bogardus's idea was to erect a frame structure of iron and bolt it together. The walls were not to serve as supports but merely as screens to keep out the weather. Provision, of course, had to be made for the expansion and contraction of the metal.

Around 1850 Bogardus offered his plans to persons in New York but they were skeptical and turned them down. He then submitted them to Abell, who at the time was considering a new building to house his growing newspaper. Abell was impressed by the plans and convinced of the soundness of the principle. He engaged an architect, R. G. Hatfield of New York, to try them out. The result was the famous Sun Iron Building which was completed and opened for business on September 13, 1851. It rose to a height of five stories and was regarded as the wonder of the age. Two other cast-iron structures were envisioned simultaneously with the Sun building. They were the dome of the Capitol at Washington and the famous Crystal Palace outside of London which was designed by Sir Joseph Paxton. The significance of the Sun Iron Building was that it embodied the principle of construction which, by substituting steel for iron, made possible the modern skyscraper. The building served its purpose nobly until it was destroyed in the Great Fire of 1904. A century after the occupation of the Iron Building, lacking a few months, the *Sun* in the last week of December, 1950, moved into its latest home which, for its size, treatment of mass and general appointments is as impressive today as was the Iron Building when it first rose almost a century before.

Baltimore achieved two more outstanding "Firsts" within a year of each other in the 1880's. One was the invention of the linotype by a Baltimorean, Ottmar Mergenthaler. In 1876 Mergenthaler, a German, emigrated to the United States and settled in Baltimore. He interested himself in typewriters and printing machinery and set to work to invent a machine which would make typesetting obsolete. By 1884 he succeeded and took out a patent on his invention. The *Sun* might have tried out the machine but, contrary to its earlier adventurous spirit, it declined the offer. It is said this was not due to the lack of initiative on the part of the Abells. Rather it was because the *Sun* had in its composing room a staff of printers who had been with it for years and the management didn't want to see them lose their jobs. So Mergenthaler took his patent to New

York where the *Herald* adopted the machine and got the glory for being the first newspaper to use it.

In the following year, 1885, Baltimore saw on its streets the first commercially operated electric cars in the United States. The line ran by way of Huntington Avenue to Hampden, a few miles outside the city limits. It replaced horsecars. In fact the same cars were used, being propelled by electric locomotives instead of drawn by horses. Power was conducted by a third rail except at street crossings where an overhead trolley was used. The innovation inspired the popular song which advertised Baltimore through the East and whose words, set to the tune of "Ta-ra-ra-Boom-de-ay," were:

> I've got a girl in Baltimore
> Street car runs right by her door
> Brussels carpet on the floor
> I've got a girl in Baltimore.

But electric streetcars were ahead of their time. The line failed to pay and, after eighteen months, the horses were put back on the job.

In December, 1897 members of the press got a thrill out of a trip around the Patapsco in a submarine. This was the *Argonaut*, designed and built in Baltimore by Simon Lake. From his boyhood when he read Jules Verne's *Twenty Thousand Leagues Under the Sea* Lake had an ambition to build a submarine. He made his first set of drawings when he was fourteen years old. In 1888, at the age of twenty-two years, he left his native New Jersey, settled in Baltimore and married a Baltimore girl.

At that time the United States Navy was beginning to show an interest in submarines and Lake submitted his plans to it. Though the Navy preferred those of John P. Holland, nevertheless Lake proceeded with the construction of his ship. The *Argonaut* made successful trial runs in August. She was an unimpressive craft 33 feet long and 9 feet in diameter. When she lay in the Patapsco off Ferry Bar little could be seen save her conning tower amidship and two masts about 15 feet tall. These were hollow and through them fresh air was pumped into the ship when she was submerged.

The December demonstration was the first Lake had arranged for the press and the public. Ten members of the press, including one woman, accepted Lake's invitation to cruise on the bottom of the river. One practical city editor delivered brief instructions to the reporter covering the story. "If Lake succeeds," he said, "give him two columns. If he fails make it an obit."

The guests went below and seated themselves in a cigar-shaped cabin lit by electricity. Lake closed the conning tower and the Argonaut got under way. Shortly thereafter Lake announced that they were under water. The *Argonaut* was equipped with wheels with the idea that she could roll along the bottom. But several feet of mud prevented this. However she cruised about the harbor for an hour before again rising to the surface. Lake's submarine is credited with having been the first to be equipped with a combustion engine and the first to make a successful cruise in the open sea.

A number of less spectacular "Firsts" also are claimed. Proof can be presented to show that Baltimore saw the birth of the first metallic pen. P. Williamson's "Celebrated Elastic Three Slit Pen" was first made in 1806 and patented in 1810. The year 1784 which saw the first balloon ascension saw also the first calico printed in the United States, the first silk woven in this country and the first sugar refined—all in Baltimore.

In Baltimore, according to the record, the first silk ribbon was made from American silk (1829), the first steamboat made wholly of iron was constructed (1838-1839), the first revolving cylinder press was used (1853) and the first Y.M.C.A. building was erected in 1859. In 1892 a Baltimorean, William Painter, invented and began the manufacture of the first crown cork stoppers for bottles that ushered in the era of bottled beer and soft drinks.

Most important of all in the eyes of many people both young and old is Baltimore's claim to being the home of the first ice-cream factory. This plant, which pioneered the making of ice cream commercially, was located at the present site of the Western Maryland's Hillen Station. It opened for business in 1851. A tablet has been placed on the spot to mark the 100th anniversary of this great humanitarian achievement which has culminated in the "Take Home A Block" habit and the merry jingles of the bells of the Good Humor truck.

No doubt other important "Firsts" have originated in Baltimore in recent years. But, like the magnetic telegraph, their importance may not be recognized by contemporary observers. Perhaps they are now waiting to be brought to light and mightily evaluated by future generations. Certainly those whose responsibility it is to keep the records have failed to list any "First" of importance for a considerable time.

Back in the 1920's it looked as though Baltimore might have something really worth while. Those were the days when automobile traffic was beginning to expand and create problems. It was not at all unusual for two cars to meet at an intersection and this raised a question of which one was to have the right of way.

An ingenious Baltimorean found a solution. He invented a box with a mechanism sensitive to sound and connected it with a traffic light. When a motorist approached a red light and sought a right of way he had only to sound his horn, the light automatically turned green and he went ahead.

No telling how far this device might have gone had there not been a dog with a husky voice in the neighborhood where it was tried out. When the dog barked the light turned from red to green as automatically as though he had been the siren on an ambulance. That just about ended the chronicle of Baltimore Firsts.

Chapter 22

THE FOURTH ESTATE

BALTIMORE has three daily newspapers—the *Sun*, the *Evening Sun* and the *Baltimore News-Post*. There also is the *Sunday Sun* and there is the *Sunday American* which is the Sunday edition of the *News-Post*. Then there is the *Afro-American*, a Negro newspaper which appears semi-weekly and circulates among the Negro population of Baltimore and several other cities.

These are the sole survivors of dozens of Baltimore newspapers of all sizes and descriptions which experienced various vicissitudes of fortune before passing out of existence. Some died after their first issue or two; others flourished for thirty or forty years. Most of them are forgotten now save for their names and a few brief notes about them and their editors embalmed in Mr. Scharf's Chronicles. The *Baltimore Telegraph*, the *Patriot*, the *Republican*, the *Whig*, the *Morning Post*, the *Morning Chronicle*, the *Jefferson Reformer*, the *Daily Transcript*, the *Public Ledger*, the *Star*, the *Baltimore Messenger*—all are brave names suggesting the ambitious dreams and hopes of their founders. There also are *Der Deutsche Correspondent* and the *Baltimore Wecker*, reminiscent of the time not so long ago when Baltimore had a large German-speaking population.

Of the few survivors the *American* boasts the longest pedigree, for it claims descent from the town's first newspaper, the *Maryland Journal and Baltimore Advertiser*. This newspaper was founded by William Goddard, a Rhode Islander, and the first number appeared on August 20, 1773. It was Goddard who, it will be recalled, offended The Whig Club by publishing criticisms of General Washington and whose office was invaded by the patriots. However, after the close of the Revolution he made his peace with the community. He was on good terms with everybody when in 1793 he sold out his interests, penned a cheerful valedictory and departed for his old home in Rhode Island.

The newspaper first appeared as a daily in 1794. Then followed several confusing mergers and changes of name that leave the lineage a trifle obscure. There finally emerged on May 11, 1799, a newspaper bearing the name of the *Baltimore American and Daily Advertiser*. Whether or not this is a direct descendant of Goddard's *Maryland Journal and Baltimore Advertiser,* in any event it has the distinction of having been published continuously as a daily from 1799 to 1928, with but one important exception. That was in September, 1814, when its editor and owner, William Pechin, shut up shop while he went off to lead the 6th Maryland Infantry Regiment in battle against the British at North Point. The *American* also is credited with the great distinction of having been the first newspaper to publish Francis Scott Key's "Star Spangled Banner."

In 1815 Editor Pechin took several partners into business with him and from then until 1853 the *American* appeared under the proprietorship of Pechin, Dobbin, Murphy and Bose. In the course of those years a new and formidable competitor appeared on the scene. This was the *Sun* which was founded by Arunah S. Abell in 1837. Abell came of an old New England Puritan family and began his journalistic career as a printer's apprentice in Providence, Rhode Island. It seems as though Providence's function was to provide Baltimore with publishers for it was from there that Goddard also came.

At the age of twenty-one years Abell moved to Boston to take a job as foreman in a large printing shop. Soon thereafter he turned up in New York where he made the acquaintance of two other printers, Benjamin H. Day and William M. Swain. At that time newspapers were published primarily for the merchants who advertised in them. Frequently also they were the official organs of political parties and confined their columns to affairs of state, foreign dispatches, and material of a literary and educational nature. They sold for 6 cents a copy and annual subscriptions ran to $8 and more a year. The general public could not have afforded to subscribe even if it had had any desire to partake of this stodgy fare. In consequence newspapers depended for their support on advertising rather than on a large circulation.

Day, however, had a novel idea. He envisioned a newspaper devoting its columns chiefly to local news of popular interest. It would give attention to fires, cases of assault and battery, and reports of which citizens had been drunk and disorderly over a week end. His newspaper would be designed to be of interest not only to the merchant but to his wife, his children and the household servants. In order to make it available to the general public he proposed to cut the price from the prevailing 6 cents to one cent the copy.

Abell was skeptical, but Day went ahead just the same. On September 4, 1833, his dream became a reality with the first issue of a newspaper after this popular model. He called it the *New York Sun*. Contrary to Abell's fears the venture prospered. So did another one like it established by James Gordon Bennett who called his paper the *Herald*. Sedate old timers looked on with disgust at the rise of what they called the "Penny Dreadfuls." But they could not deny that the "Penny Dreadfuls" brought in excellent profits.

With these successes before him Abell hesitated no longer. In 1836 he signed agreements with Swain and Azariah H. Simmons to establish a penny paper in Philadelphia. The agreement was duly carried out and the paper that resulted was the *Public Ledger*. But Abell did not stay in Philadelphia. Leaving his interests there in the care of his partners he repaired to Baltimore, then the second largest city in the nation. It was in this promising field that he determined to apply his major effort. The first issue of the *Sun* appear on May 17, 1837.

Baltimore at that time already had six dailies. In addition to Pechin's *American* there were Nelson Poe's *Chronicle*, William Gwynn's *Gazette*, Isaac Monroe's *Patriot*, Samuel Harker's *Republican* and the *Transcript* which was published by Skinner and Tenney. Besides these dailies there were also nine weeklies and two monthlies, so that from the very outset Abell was up against the stiffest sort of competition. But his innovation of covering the local news and printing it in a straightforward manner—at least for those days—immediately met with popular approval. Three years after its founding the *Sun* boasted: "We have a circulation equal to all the daily morning papers of this city combined and our sheet is read by all classes, from the Hall of Congress to the humble dwelling of the poor." Already its readers were beginning to speak of it familiarly as "the *Sunpaper*."

From the outset Mr. Abell realized the importance of speed in bringing news before the public. The *Sun* was only a few months old when its first correspondent was posted at the seat of government in Washington. The *Sun* also promptly made use of the telegraph after Morse's successful demonstration. It kept carrier pigeons in London to help speed its European news and it helped to organize a courier service from Halifax, Nova Scotia, to transmit to the States as quickly as possible the foreign dispatches landed by boats newly arrived from abroad. During the Mexican War the *Sun* established a pony express over those stretches of country between New Orleans and the North which were not covered either by train or by telegraph.

During its long career the *Sun* has earned recognition not only through its own columns but also by the many men it has trained who have gone on to achieve success on other newspapers. As a school of journalism it began early. One of its first graduates was Charles C. Fulton. Fulton was a native of New Jersey who came to the *Sun* as a printer shortly after its founding. He soon showed marked ability and moved from the job of compositor to that of reporter. By 1841 he had reached the exalted position of managing editor and there he remained until 1853. In that year he had the opportunity to buy a half-interest in the *American*. As soon as Fulton moved to his new property he introduced the methods he had learned under Abell on the *Sun*. They proved equally advantageous to the *American* and very soon Fulton's paper became the *Sun's* most dangerous competitor.

The Civil War was a trying period for all Baltimore newspapers. After the attack of the mob on the 6th Massachusetts Regiment the North cried out for vengeance and thereafter Baltimore was treated as a captive enemy city. The writ of habeas corpus was suspended and on the slightest provocation Southern sympathizers clapped into jail. In spite of his New England background Abell's sympathies were with the South. Yet his native shrewdness warned him against committing the same indiscretions that were bringing disaster to his journalistic colleagues. To ardent adherents of the Southern cause Abell's course no doubt seemed ignominious. Be that as it may, by observing a strictly correct attitude Abell remained free and held onto his property.

The *American*, chief rival of the *Sun*, labored under no such handicap. Mr. Fulton was well known as a vigorous supporter of the Union cause. In fact, because of family connections with the Navy, he made the *American* virtually the official organ of that branch of the Federal service. Yet, amusingly enough, it was Fulton and not Abell who suffered arrest and imprisonment for publishing news the Federal authorities didn't like. It took all of Mr. Fulton's exceptional resources to establish his identity as a loyalist and to convince the authorities that publication of the objectionable matter had been a mistake.

At the close of the Civil War there became associated with the *American* a colorful individual who was to guide its destinies for many years. He was Felix Agnus. Born in Lyons, France, in 1839, of French parents, he showed a taste for the military early in life and found ample opportunity to gratify it in the various conflicts which then disturbed Europe.

Young Agnus then determined to try his fortune in the United States and reached this country in 1860 just in time to encounter the storm that was then brewing. He signed up as a sergeant with the picturesque New York Zouaves, saw very active service, was wounded several times, won successive promotions and in the last year of the war crowned his career by being brevetted a brigadier general. For the rest of his life he carried the title of General Agnus.

In the course of his wanderings General Agnus found his way to Baltimore. Because of the part he had played in the Federal Army he proved congenial company for Mr. Fulton of the *American,* whose paper so staunchly supported the Northern cause. The result of this acquaintance was that the General met, wooed and won the hand of Annie E. Fulton, a daughter of the publisher. Mr. Fulton made his son-in-law business manager of the *American* and, on the death of Mr. Fulton in 1883, General Agnus succeeded him as publisher and general manager.

With his fierce mustachios and ebullient Gallic temperament the general cut quite a figure in Baltimore. As he grew older the young men on his staff tired of his reminiscences, and spread the story that the general's service had been performed in nothing more heroic than the Quartermaster Corps. Still another popular story had it that, as a matter of fact, he had started his career as a barber. Consequently in local journalistic circles his newspaper was disrespectfully referred to as "The Hot Towel." The General lived in style in the Green Spring Valley on an estate he called Nacirema, which is not the name of some fair oriental damsel encountered on the General's extensive travels, but "American" spelled backward.

The *Sun* emerged from its postwar lethargy in 1882. Maryland at that time had been taken over by a corrupt political ring controlled by Arthur Pue Gorman and I. Freeman Rasin, and in which at that time William Pinkney Whyte also had a part. The bosses became so bold that they dared to put their men in the judiciary. This met with strong opposition from the better element in the community and an independent ticket was chosen to contest the election with the machine. This ticket was backed by the *Sun* and it won a decisive victory at the polls. Never since "The Judges' Fight" have political bosses touched the Baltimore Bench.

Another newspaper that came into prominence in the last decade of the century was the *Evening News*. It was founded in 1872 by James R. Brewer, an Annapolitan. In 1892 Charles S. Grasty, who hailed from the Valley of Virginia, formed a syndicate and bought it. Members of his group were Julian Le Roy White, Douglas H. Gordon, Thomas K. Worthington and General Lawrason Riggs, all high-minded citizens whose primary purpose was to establish an independent paper that would be a power for good in the community.

While the Gorman-Rasin machine had taken a licking on the issue of the judges it had not been knocked out and, in fact, was going its wicked way as cockily as ever. An organization known as The Reform League was formed to do battle with it. The League was headed by Charles J. Bonaparte, grandson of the Prince Jerome whose romance with Betsy Patterson thrilled Baltimore a century before. Under Mr. Grasty's direction the *Evening News* backed the League in its attack on the machine. It was joined in battle by the *Sun*.

These combined forces won a sweeping victory in the election of 1895. Lloyd Lowndes, a Republican, was elected Governor of Maryland, the first member of his party to hold that office. Alcaeus Hooper, another Republican, was elected Mayor of Baltimore. The State Legislature was wrested from the control of Gorman and the City Council from that of Rasin. The *Evening News* was connected with no political party so that its role in the fight did not involve a departure from tradition. But the *Sun's* abandonment of the Democrats, who it had hitherto supported, was a shock to the people of the State.

In the Great Fire of 1904 the plants of Baltimore's four leading newspapers—the *Sun*, the *Evening News*, the *American* and the *Herald*—were victims of the flames. The staffs stuck at their posts until the buildings caught fire and they were ordered out. Those who were the last to leave were heroes for the rest of their lives. The fire afforded an opportunity for the lavish display of that loyalty and devotion which entitles members of the newspaper profession to a place of honor somewhere between the Boy on the Burning Deck and St. Bernard dogs. Newspapers in Washington and Philadelphia offered the Baltimoreans the use of their facilities.

Yet even the tragedy of the fire—the greatest news story in Baltimore since the invasion of the British in 1814—failed to shake the *Sun* out of its traditional sense of decorum. Throughout the first day of the fire it issued not a single extra. Instead, accurate down to every detail, including of course the proper spelling of names, it appeared at its usual time on Monday morning.

In 1908 the *News* was sold for $1,500,000 to Frank A. Munsey, the successful New York magazine publisher, who had turned his interest in the direction of newspapers and was buying them up in various cities. Mr. Grasty at first accepted a position as assistant to Mr. Munsey in the management of his publications. But their temperaments clashed and he retired from the field to resume his newspaper career in the Middle West. He was succeeded on the *News* by another Virginian, Stuart Olivier, to whom Munsey had taken a liking. Charles M. Harwood, who had been Grasty's managing editor, stayed on as editor of the paper.

It was not long before the office of the *News* began to discover the eccentricities of the newcomer. Mr. Munsey continued to make his home in New York, periodically visiting his Baltimore properties. He objected strenuously to the use of tobacco and the order went out that smoking was absolutely to be forbidden in the news rooms of all his papers. Dick Steuart, the universally beloved city editor of the *News* who never as a rule raised his voice to correct a subordinate, startled the newsroom now and then by shouting, "Mr.——, put out that cigarette!" When he did it meant that Mr. Munsey was down from New York and in the building.

The owner was as downright in his prejudices against people. On one of his inspections his eye fell on an employe whose looks he didn't like. Without further inquiry he ordered that the man be fired. The man in question happened to hold a key position and his dismissal would have caused keen embarrassment to the local management. So the order wasn't carried out. Thereafter on Mr. Munsey's visits the poor executive, along with the cigarettes and pipes, had to be hidden from view.

When Munsey bought the *News* it had only been a few years in the building constructed for it after the fire. In his customarily extravagant manner Mr. Munsey had this practically brand-new building torn down and raised in its place a skyscraper which was given his name. Nearly half a century has passed and it still is known as the Munsey Building though probably few of the present generation of Baltimoreans know why.

Shortly before the close of 1920 Mr. Munsey rounded out his newspaper properties in Baltimore by buying the *American* from General Agnus, moved it over to the *News* and continued it as a daily morning newspaper. Meanwhile the *Evening Sun*, founded in 1910, had become firmly established. The *News* and the *American* soon began to feel the effect of the competition of the *Sunpapers*. Word got around that Mr. Munsey wanted to dispose of his Baltimore newspaper properties. It was followed shortly by the rumor that a possible purchaser was William Randolph Hearst.

At the time the Hearst papers were regarded by conservative business men as highly radical. The rumor that Hearst might enter Baltimore sent shivers down the spines of local capitalists. They had visions of tumbrels rattling over the city's cobblestones with their loads of bankers, brokers, merchants and captains of industry, on the way to a guillotine set up in Mt. Vernon Place.

There was one ray of hope. After all, Mr. Munsey was a conservative business man. Naturally, he was a Republican. Surely he would not be a party to letting Mr. Hearst into Baltimore. Mr. Munsey was approached and apprised of the alarm of the merchants. The encouraging report went out that he showed a sympathetic attitude. While these matters were in the air Mr. Olivier came out with an impressive valedictory announcing his retirement from the newspaper field, and the business men set to work to see if they could form a syndicate to buy the *News* as Grasty had done many years before. But times were different and Mr. Munsey put a high estimate on the value of his property. The necessary capital could not be raised in a day. Then, like a bombshell, the news burst over the city. Munsey had sold out to Hearst! Suspicion grew that his encouragement of the Baltimore group was given merely to bid up Mr. Hearst.

While the city was still trembling under the shock, the advance guard of Hearst's army entered the city and took over the *News* and the *American*. They let it be known that the people of the city would be treated in a humane manner. Nobody would be hanged and no throats would be cut. They gave assurance that Mr. Hearst was a good and kindly man. By way of proof the *News* began to print a text from the Bible, selected daily by a different local divine, across the front page.

When the *News* was published seven days a week it had been Mr. Harwood's custom to appear in his office for a short time every Sunday in a cutaway. Such was the dignity of the high command in the days of Grasty and Munsey. For the time being Mr. Harwood remained at his desk but he referred all inquiries to an emissary of Mr. Hearst. This young man, wearing matching necktie, handkerchief and socks, sat on a table in Mr. Harwood's old office, dangling his legs, and urged everybody not to worry. For, said he, under Mr. Hearst things were going to be just the same!

The scene in the newsroom was less assuring. Departments were shifted about and turned upside down. A task force had been sent in to instruct the local staff on the new technique. Contrary to other statements the *News* got its face lifted and came out looking just like Hearst papers in other cities.

The most noticeable difference in the newsroom was that the heads of the copy desks now worked in their hats and were addressed as "Chief." The old employes of the Munsey-Olivier regime quickly adapted themselves to the new order. One veteran consoled himself with the thought that Mr. Hearst would have to keep somebody who knew where the City Hall was. The most melancholy picture of all was two venerable gentlemen—one a classical scholar with a Harvard background—who were ousted from the copy desk where they had labored for years and put to work sorting great piles of comics.

As time went on events proved that the city's worst fears were groundless. Local laborers were not encouraged to rise in revolt against their masters. Many members of the old staff of the *News* stayed and, in spite of the typical makeup of Hearst papers, continued to give this one a special Baltimore flavor. Among them were Dick Steuart, who was retired from his position as city editor to write a column dealing with old Baltimore under the name of Carroll Dulaney; Louis Azrael who conducted another column and during World War II did a fine job as war correspondent in France, and Norman Clark and Pinkney McLean who stuck to their old posts respectively as dramatic critic and financial editor. Warren Wilmer Brown, music critic and a picturesque figure at all Lyric concerts with his flowing black tie and inevitable pipe, remained at his post for a time. He then resigned to edit *Gardens, Houses and People*, a sprightly magazine mirroring the lives of dwellers in "the District," which is to say the northern suburbs of Guilford, Roland Park and Homeland. Incidentally at his death he was succeeded by R. P. Harriss, a former associate editor of the *Evening Sun* whose varied talents both as writer and artist fit him nicely for the job.

Robert Garland, dramatic critic of the *Baltimore American*, was promoted to the same position on the *New York American*. But before that happened he got a bad scare. Things were in a state of flux. Nobody could be sure of his job. A man might suddenly discover he was no longer wanted. So one morning Garland walked in and discovered a stranger at his desk. He immediately assumed that this was his successor. So he approached the stranger, said he was sorry to disturb him, but there were some personal belongings in a drawer he would like to retrieve before he left. The stranger looked surprised. "Haven't you come to take my place?" asked Garland. It turned out that the man merely needed a typewriter and found Garland's unlocked.

Not only did Mr. Hearst live down the reputation for radicalism; when he began to berate Franklin D. Roosevelt, the New Deal and then Truman, he followed a line that was welcomed by the most conservative people in the city. In fact about the only instance in which he caused the town real concern was his advocacy of antivivisection which threatened seriously to handicap research at the medical schools of the Johns Hopkins and of the University of Maryland. Fortunately the public listened to the doctors and voted down the antivivisectionists by about seven to one.

Soon after he began operations in Baltimore Mr. Hearst bought a Scripps-Howard tabloid called the *Post* and merged it with the News, thus creating the present *Baltimore News-Post*.

Now to return to the *Sun*. Arunah Abell, the founder, died in 1888. Even before that he had turned over the running of the paper to his sons. George Abell, Edwin and Edwin's son Walter succeeded each other as publisher.

A distinguished member of the postwar staff of the *Sun* was Francis A. Richardson, son of the proprietor of the *Republican*. During the Civil War he had been sent South and later arrested when he tried to return home and confined for the duration in a prison camp. Mr. Richardson had a long and distinguished career as the *Sun's* Washington correspondent. A handsome man with great personal charm and rare professional talent he was said to have enjoyed the personal friendship of all the Presidents who served during his days at the capital.

In 1900 a young nephew and namesake who joined the *Sun* and also was to have a distinguished career as correspondent, executive and columnist was Frank Richardson Kent. Six years later the staff received formidable reinforcement in the persons of H. L. Mencken and Folger McKinsey. Mencken took over as editor of the *Sunday Sun*. McKinsey filled the post of exchange editor, but his fame was to rest on his contribution as staff poet and columnist writing under the pseudonym of The Bentztown Bard.

The reticence of the management passed all understanding. Mencken had been in office for a while when he became curious to know what progress he was making with his public. So he went to Walter W. Abell, who then was the publisher, and asked him what the circulation of the *Sunday Sun* was. Mr. Abell looked at him in shocked surprise. When he had recovered his composure he explained that the *Sun* never revealed its circulation figures!

In 1909 Walter Abell retired from the presidency of the A. S. Abell Company and dissension over the management arose among various members of the family. Charles S. Grasty, who then was in the Middle West, was informed of the situation and hurriedly returned to Baltimore. As he had done in 1891 when he took over the *Evening News,* he organized a syndicate and made an offer to purchase a controlling interest in the *Sun.* The offer was accepted and Mr. Grasty assumed the position of publisher. Members of the syndicate were H. Crawford Black, R. Brent Keyser, Robert Garrett and John Campbell White. Of these gentlemen, Mr. Black held the controlling shares. It was their policy, however, to leave the actual running of the paper to Mr. Grasty. Mr. Black was known to have appeared at the *Sun* office only once during his ownership.

Sale of the *Sunpapers* was approved in January, 1910. A few months later Mr. Grasty founded the *Evening Sun.* He at once set to work to demonstrate his ideas of an independent newspaper. His outstanding achievement was to throw the weight of the *Sun* behind Woodrow Wilson as nominee of the Democratic Party for President of the United States. A large share of the credit for the defeat of Champ Clark and for Wilson's victory went to Mr. Grasty's campaign.

A feud with James H. Preston, Mayor of Baltimore, had a less satisfactory ending. In fact Mr. Preston succeeding in arraying the city bosses against the *Sunpapers* and in creating disaffection among the advertisers. Just at the time, the *Evening Sun* was slow in getting on a sound financial basis. In consequence the *Sunpapers* found themselves in the red; in 1914 Mr. Grasty resigned and Van Lear Black, elder son of Crawford Black, tackled the job of putting the *Sunpapers* back on their feet. Frank Kent, who had spent a brief period in Washington as correspondent was called back to act as managing editor both of the *Sun* and the *Evening Sun.*

Mr. Kent was keenly interested in local politics and under his management of the *Sunpapers* emphasis was laid on that department. Two star reporters John W. Owens and Harry E. West were put to work describing the political scene and the public was kept informed in a delightful manner of every move made by the bosses. Our entry into World War I, however, widened the *Sunpapers'* horizon. Raymond S. Tompkins was sent to France to report in particular the activities of the 29th and of the 79th Divisions in which there were many Marylanders. Mr. Kent dropped his duties as managing editor to cover the Peace Conference in Paris. He was the first correspondent to break the news of the bitterness of feeling among the Allies which up to that time had been kept carefully concealed from the American public.

After Mr. Grasty's resignation in 1914, as president of the A. S. Abell Company, which publishes the *Sunpapers*, the post remained vacant until Armistice Day, November 11, 1919, when Paul Patterson was elected to it by the Board. Mr. Patterson then had been with the organization eight years. Most of his time had been spent as business manager though he had had much previous experience as an editorial man both in Chicago and in Washington before coming to Baltimore.

As in the days of Grasty the owners took deliberate pains to leave the editorial direction to the professional staff. Much of the underlying philosophy on which operations were based was evolved in nightly discussions in which Mr. Patterson, Mencken and Harry C. Black took part. Mr. Black was a son of H. Crawford Black and a younger brother of Van Lear Black.

The *Evening Sun* now entered a novel and interesting phase. Its managing editor was J. Edwin Murphy, an excitable Irishman and, to his staff, the beau ideal of a newspaper man. An outstanding quality was his bold defiance of the advertisers. Let a suggestion on policy come to him from an advertiser by way of the business office and it was as good as dead when it reached him. His guiding principle was the inviolability of the news columns.

The *Evening Sun's* right bower was Mencken, just then rising to national distinction. His first contribution was a column bearing the title "The Free Lance" which ran from May, 1911, to October, 1915. In it he plugged away at all the pious frauds in the town and invariably closed with the warning "Swat the fly" and "Boil your drinking water." He also carried as a feature "The Typhoid League" in which he ranked the large cities of the country according to the prevalence of the disease. Baltimore then stood high on the list.

As Mencken became more absorbed with his work as editor of *The Smart Set* and in writing numerous books he abandoned his daily column and in place of it wrote a weekly essay. It appeared on the editorial page of the *Evening Sun* and seldom failed to shock the local public with its damning frankness. Mencken had a way of putting into print the things that most people confine to conversations among their intimates. It was in these essays that he introduced the South as "The Sahara of the Bozart" and raised a storm below the Potomac. He took especial delight in lampooning the Anti-Saloon League and its leaders. In these essays, too, appeared gibes at the Fundamentalists. William Jennings Bryan was a favorite target and even death did not give him immunity. As his body lay in state and publicists praised his virtues Mencken compared him to a rooster on a dunghill.

In the 1920's Harry Black took special interest in the editorial page of the *Evening Sun*. Hamilton Owens, then in his early thirties, had been recently hired as editor and his associates for the most part were even younger. The editorial page was definitely a young man's production with all the vices of inexperience and the virtues of youthful exuberance. It was outrageously frivolous. Its editorials were short and pithy. They, too, were frequently leveled at the dry leaders. An active campaign was waged also on the growing army of Federal jobholders. They were laid end to end and the distance they would cover across the continent carefully calculated. They were weighed and their total weight converted into so many dead-weight tons of battleships. The lesson was brought home with appropriate illustrations showing the battleships or the jobholders stretched out across the map. Famous, too, were the *Evening Sun's* editorials putting candidates on the spot with the direct questions: "Mr.——, are you Wet or are you Dry?"

When the Hearst press adopted green and pink newsprint for some of its editions the *Evening Sun* editorial page solemnly debated what shade of newsprint it should use and decided to make it "Paris nude." It discovered that the birthday of the *Evening Sun* coincided with that of Dick Turpin, the English highwayman, and celebrated the event annually by inviting criticism. It chose the bitterest which came in and printed them under the headline "A Shower of Brickbats." It made fun of the Ku-Klux Klan and derided the suckers who were willing to pay $10 for a nightshirt.

The *Evening Sun* editorial page first introduced "Oswald" who each day addressed an impudent question to some public figure. It also began printing a spicy morsel under the heading of "Gob Humor." These gems, true to their name, were culled from the ships' newspapers of the United States Navy. Sometimes they were so raw that hesitant editors submitted them to Paul Patterson for final judgment. Invariably he gave them his "O.K." For, he argued, if they appeared in a ship's paper they had been passed by the chaplain. They also had gone through the United States mails. So what right had the *Sunpapers* to question their propriety?

Another popular feature was the *Evening Sun* Forum in which the letters to the editor appeared. One regular contributor signed herself "American Mother" and invariably took a highly moral attitude on all the current sins. She was, of course, a "Dry." Pretty much everything shocked her. In The Forum the question "Is Baltimore a Hick Town?" was argued at great length.

Mr. Black's daily visits to the newsrooms aroused the curiosity of a copy boy, who couldn't figure his connection with the paper. Finally he inquired of a member of the staff: "Who is that guy who walks through here every day as though he owned the place?"

Those were the days when Edmund Duffy was drawing cartoons daily for the *Sun*. He won the Pulitzer Prize two years running. Folger McKinsey, also on the *Sun*, was busily at work on his "Good Morning" column which for length of run probably broke all records. It began in April, 1906, and continued every weekday until the Bard's retirement in 1949, a total of forty-three years. The Bard was a prolific writer of verse. He not only wrote several poems a day for his column but also others which appeared in the *Evening Sun*. He was fortunate in that he did not have to wait long for inspiration. Once when he was about to leave the office with a friend he suddenly remembered that he had not written a poem for the day. Asking the friend to wait a minute he sat down at the nearest desk and typed one as rapidly as though he were taking dictation from Apollo.

Other giants of the period were Frank Kent, whose "Great Game of Politics" has been mentioned, and John W. Owens, for a time editor-in-chief of the *Sunpapers* whose editorials won a Pulitzer award. And there was Gerald W. Johnson who wrote editorials for and also contributed a weekly essay to the *Evening Sun* while on the side he penned biographies and miscellaneous volumes. This age saw also the development of A. Aubrey Bodine, newspaper photographer of rare genius, whose pictures have won practically every important photographic competition in this country and abroad. Unromantic but most essential were Clark S. Hobbs' series of articles in the *Evening Sun* revealing to the public the shame of Baltimore's slums.

Quite as prolific as Gerald Johnson was Neil H. Swanson, a Minnesotan, who came to the *Evening Sun* as assistant managing editor to Murphy. As though playing up to Murphy's volatile temperament eight hours a day was not enough, he dashed off historical novels in the evening at the rate of about one a year. On the death of Mr. Murphy, Swanson became managing editor of the *Evening Sun* and eventually emerged as executive editor in charge of the news columns of the *Sun*, the *Evening Sun* and the *Sunday Sun*.

World War II was a challenge to the imagination of Paul Patterson and Neil Swanson. *Sunpaper* correspondents were dispatched to all theaters of the conflict. They went to the Southwest Pacific as casually as in the old days *Sunpaper* reporters went to the southwest Police District. They were present as MacArthur's strategy gradually moved our forces closer and closer to Japan. They were at Cassino, Anzio and the Normandy beaches and followed with the American armies to Berlin.

Not the least of the more recent ambitious programs of the *Sunpapers* was its plan for covering the decline of the British Empire. To this end Price Day was sent to South Africa and India, Philip Potter to the Far East, Lee McCardell to the British Isles proper and Tom O'Neill to Canada. Their reports were duly published and Price Day's won a Pulitzer Prize. Still another Pulitzer Prize winner was Mark S. Watson a veteran of World War I who, when most men his age were content to stay by the fireside at home, insisted on going to the front and giving readers of the *Sun* a running explanation of the significance of each military operation.

In fact the *Sunpapers* had a stableful of star correspondents ready at a moment's notice to pack a bag and take passage on a plane to cover any story that might break from Cape Horn to Iceland or anywhere east or west of Greenwich. These stalwarts were popularly known as "The Household Cavalry." After a while current history ran out of enough important events to keep them occupied.

Another important department of the *Sunpapers* is the Washington Bureau which, since the days of Francis Richardson, have attracted some of the staff's best talent. The Washington Bureau, too, has had its Pulitzer Prize winner in the person of Paul Ward who got it for the excellence of his reports on international affairs.

Several years ago Edmund Duffy severed his connection with the *Sun* to go as cartoonist to *The Saturday Evening Post*. Since his departure the post has been capably filled by Richard Q. Yardley. He started as an illustrator for the *Sunday Sun* with a romping sense of humor, caricaturing the familiar Baltimore scene. He also made a specialty of local politics and no political boss felt that he had arrived unless he had been done by Yardley. Since Duffy's departure he has applied his talent with good effect both to national and international matters.

Of the "Penny Dreadfuls" that appeared simultaneously in the 1830's the Philadelphia *Public Ledger* has long since vanished. The *New York Sun* and the *New York Herald* have lost something of their original character through mergers. The only one that has survived as it was founded is the *Sun* of Baltimore. In 1937 the *Sunpapers* celebrated their 100th birthday and started out boldly on their second century. They have kept up with the times by adding to the establishment a television broadcasting station. And they have recently moved into a handsome new building of mammoth proportions that gives every impression of having been constructed for permanency. If civilization survives the atomic bomb and other terrifying agents it looks as though in Baltimore they will say, not newspaper, but *Sunpaper* for sometime to come.

Chapter 23

NOTE ON POLITICS

A LOCAL COLUMNIST, on the day after a recently bitterly contested election in Baltimore, described a visit to the polls with his daughter to cast their votes. They were greeted cordially by the election officials and felicitations were exchanged. It was like a social gathering in a private house. He summed it up in the one word "respectability." He ventured the opinion that respectability is what the world needs most and is searching for today.

In Baltimore, elections were not always like that. The respectability Baltimore voters now enjoy has literally been bought with the blood of their ancestors. No doubt politics played a part in the life of the town from the beginning, but it was the wars and the events leading up to them which bred the liveliest animosities. At the time of the American Revolution the line was sharply drawn between Patriot and Tory and, as soon as hostilities commenced, most of the Tories were driven out. We have seen also how the Whig Club visited its wrath on William Goddard, the publisher.

Violence arising out of opposing political creeds was in large part responsible for Baltimore's unsavory reputation as "Mobtown." It was the mutual hatred between the Jeffersonian Republicans and the Federalists that inspired the brutal attack on editor Hanson and his friends at the outbreak of the War of 1812.

This same uncompromising spirit showed up in Baltimore several decades later in the Know-Nothing movement, which stemmed from the fear of the old inhabitants for the hordes of newly arriving immigrants from Germany and Ireland. In many ways Know-Nothingism resembled the more recent activities of the Ku-Klux Klan. The name derived from the fact that those taking part in it organized themselves into secret clubs and, when questioned, invariably replied that they "knew nothing." Because Baltimore received so many immigrants through its port the Know-Nothing movement was particularly virulent there. As we already have noted, Baltimore on election day was like a battlefield.

What is most surprising is that the Know-Nothing movement

was not confined to the irresponsible riffraff but that respectable people were identified with it. Thus, for example, Thomas Swann was twice elected mayor on the Know-Nothing ticket and ignored a request of Governor Ligon to join with him in breaking up the lawlessness attending elections. Yet Mayor Swann was a native Virginian of the highest social position and presumably a model of integrity. Henry Winter Davis, another Baltimorean who in his day was regarded as a high-minded statesman, was not above garnering votes through association with the Know-Nothing element.

The public at last revolted against the excesses of the Know-Nothings and their corrupt political allies. A reform party put up George William Brown as their candidate for Mayor and elected him. He was the same plucky little man who tried so valiantly to control the mob when it attacked the 6th Massachusetts Infantry in 1861.

The period following the Civil War witnessed an unceasing struggle for political power in the city, and the rise and fall of a succession of bosses. A giant in those days was William Pinkney Whyte whose public career extended over a period of nearly sixty years. It began when, as a young man, he ran for Congress in 1851 and it continued right up to his death at the age of eighty-four years in 1908. In the course of his career he served three separate times as United States Senator, besides being Governor of Maryland, Mayor of Baltimore, State Comptroller, Attorney General and City Solicitor. He was regarded as the first real leader of the Democratic party the State ever had.

Yet even when Mr. Whyte was serving his first term in the Senate and appeared to be at the height of his power he was successfully challenged by another man destined to rule Baltimore city and the whole State as no other boss has ever ruled it. This was Arthur Pue Gorman. While Senator Whyte was enjoying official life in Washington and supposing himself secure, Gorman was quietly at work getting control of the State Legislature which, in those days, elected the United States Senators and wielded great political power in other matters.

Senator Whyte turned down a request of Gorman's and won his undying enmity. Before he realized what was happening he had lost his political control and Gorman had seized it. Out of the

Senate went Whyte. In Baltimore Gorman's chief lieutenant was I. Freeman Rasin; and, for years, the two ran the town to suit themselves. The skill with which these men handled their machine was phenomenal. One of their greatest feats of political legerdemain was the election of Elihu E. Jackson as Governor in 1888. A year and a half before his nomination Jackson had been picked as their candidate. Yet neither Jackson nor his opponents was aware of this arrangement. Both sides set to work to conduct a heated campaign and the fight was carried into the Democratic convention. It was not until the sixth ballot that an apparent deadlock was broken and Jackson was named. Yet Gorman and Rasin had enough strength to nominate Jackson on the first ballot if they had chosen to use it. They preferred to sit back quietly pulling the strings and make it look like a real fight. So, too, in spite of personal enemity Gorman had a part in the election of Whyte as Mayor, yet was careful that the latter did not get back too much of his earlier power.

At last, as in the corrupt days of the Know-Nothings, reform caught up with Gorman and Rasin. With the help of the *Sun* and the *Baltimore News* the reformers in 1895 won an overwhelming victory in which an entire Republican slate was elected and at least temporarily Gorman and Rasin were shorn of their power. This was a most unusual situation since fundamentally Baltimore is an overwhelmingly Democratic city.

As Baltimore is temperate in other things so is it temperate in its politics. While it is Democratic, it is not so in the sense that the States below the Potomac are Democratic. For example, it is not at all uncommon for a Baltimorean to register as a Democrat, vote Democratic in local elections, and later vote the Republican ticket in the national election. Occasionally, too, when the Democratic jobholders overstep the mark Baltimoreans retaliate by throwing them ignominiously out of office. But such revolts do not generally last long. Before the next election rolls around the Republicans, demoralized by their unaccustomed good fortune, can be counted on to have behaved so badly that they in turn are thrown out and the Democrats restored to power.

Around the turn of the century "Free" Rasin departed this life. William Pinkney Whyte by this time had attained the stature of a statesman. He had come to be affectionately known and revered as Maryland's "Grand Old Man." He was back in the United States Senate, holding by appointment the seat vacated through death by his old political rival Gorman. He was in far too exalted a position to be considered when the question arose as to who was to succeed Rasin as Boss of Baltimore city. That distinction fell upon John J. (Sonny) Mahon, an Irishman who had long been Rasin's loyal lieutenant.

For the next twenty years in Baltimore politics Mahon's name was law. His intimate associates were Frank Kelly, Bob Padgett and Daniel J. (Danny) Loden. They were popularly known as "The Royal Family" and were so immortalized in a cartoon by McKee Barclay, the *Sun's* political cartoonist. Mahon and his minions controlled both the Baltimore City Council and the State Legislature. Little could be accomplished without their consent. Like lawyers or doctors with their clients those old-fashioned bosses considered that they were entitled to a fee when they got a bill safely through the legislative mill and on the statute books. While Mahon, Kelly and Padgett stuck seriously to business Danny Loden provided the comic relief. In Barclay's cartoon he figured as the Crown Prince. A short, round man with a closely cropped mustache and hair worn in bangs, he presented a droll appearance. And he had an Irish wit to match it. As president of the Democratic Concord Club he engaged in a feud with another club, and claimed that he had hidden a dictaphone in the enemy's territory. The disclosures, which became as regular a feature of the newspapers as the comics, delighted the public while they set Danny's opponents wild. Though officers of the club suspected everybody they never found the leak.

Danny no doubt developed a technique out of his own experiences as an informer earlier in his career. This was when he was acting as political adviser to Mayor Thomas G. Hayes. Hayes was elected as a Rasin man but broke away from the boss's influence on assuming office. While Loden was acting as adviser to Hayes he was going nightly to Rasin's house and reporting what was going on in the Hayes camp.

Among the men who have served Baltimore as its mayor Edward Johnson and Ferdinand Latrobe are outstanding. Johnson was a practicing physician who gave up his profession for public life. He was six times elected to office. It was during his tenure that the British attacked the town; and, in his official capacity, Johnson collaborated with General Sam Smith in planning the defense. His medical experience also stood him in good stead during a yellow-fever epidemic which struck the city in 1820. His conduct on that occasion was described as heroic.

Ferdinand Latrobe made and still holds the record for length of tenure. He was elected Mayor no less than seven times, serving intermittently over a period of twenty years, from 1875 to 1895. Mayor Latrobe came of a distinguished family. His grandfather was Benjamin Latrobe, the architect. His father was J. H. B. Latrobe, lawyer, literary man, inventor and civic leader. His uncle, another Benjamin, was the engineer who built a large part of the B. & O. Railroad including the famous viaduct at the Relay.

Mayor Latrobe knew and was beloved by practically everybody in the city. He rarely failed to show up at a public gathering. Mencken, in his volume of reminiscences entitled *Happy Days*, has presented a homely picture of the Mayor as he recalled him at the annual picnics of Knapp's School. The Mayor, according to Mencken, never failed to appear, always praised the Germans for their inventive genius and other skills and, in spite of his French name, claimed German descent. After Mencken had left school and was working as a reporter the Mayor was still attending public gatherings and claiming blood relationship with whatever racial stock was present. The list was extended, says Mencken, until the only races left out were the Afro-Americans and the Chinese. Ferdinand Latrobe died in 1911 at the age of seventy-eight years, universally lamented.

Baltimore, in its heyday, was called Mobtown and the Monumental City. Strangely enough it did not get a name it richly deserved—that of the Convention City. The national party conventions originated in Baltimore. The first Democratic convention, and the first of any political party, met there in 1832. Previous to that time candidates had been nominated in legislative caucuses. In fact even in 1832 Andrew Jackson had been so nominated; the convention in Baltimore merely "indorsed" his candidacy. The only candidate nominated was Martin Van Buren as vice president. Incidentally it was at the first convention in Baltimore that the Democrats adopted two-thirds rule to which they adhered for so many years.

The second Democratic Convention also was held in Baltimore. This time Van Buren was nominated for the presidency and Richard W. Johnson of Kentucky for the vice-presidency. In the convention the two-thirds rule adopted at the previous convention was first applied. As at the previous convention there was neither friction nor oratory. It was actually nothing more than a public mass meeting to exhibit to the nation the solidarity of the ticket. The opposition in fact denounced it as an office holders' assemblage. Not only was there no speaking but there was a rule against speeches for, argued the chairman, *"They might be productive of much evil and the rule against them is intended to prevent any violent, angry and unnecessary discussion that might otherwise arise."*

Democratic conventions succeeded each other in Baltimore every four years until six had been held. On the occasion of the seventh in 1856 the scene was shifted to Cincinnati. In 1860 Charleston, South Carolina, witnessed the abortive convention which split on the subject of slavery and failed to agree on a candidate. After ten days of fruitless discussion it adjourned to meet in Baltimore on June 18. It was the Baltimore convention that nominated Stephen A. Douglas for President and Herschel V. Johnson of Georgia for Vice-President. It was in Baltimore also that several more of the Southern States, led by Virginia, bolted the convention, adopted their own platform on slavery and nominated John C. Breckinridge of Kentucky and Joseph Lane of Ohio respectively as President and Vice-President.

This convention met in the old Front Street Theater. The sloping parquet of the theater was leveled by laying a floor on struts. In the heat of the discussion part of the floor gave way. Fortunately the drop was only a few feet and nobody was hurt. Once the scare was over the incident was treated as a joke. One delegate, addressing the chair, exclaimed: "Mr. President, the platform has not broken down, only one of the planks." Considerable fun was made of New York and Pennsylvania "going down together."

Baltimore was not the scene of Democratic conventions alone. Here also was held in the Athenaeum the National Republican Convention of 1831 which nominated Henry Clay for President and John Sergeant for Vice-President. Here, too, in 1856 the "Old Line Whigs" met in National Convention at the Maryland Institute to indorse Millard Fillmore for President and Andrew Jackson Donelson for Vice-President. In 1860 Baltimore also saw the Constitutional Union Convention. This was a combination of the Old Line Whigs and the American, or Know-Nothing, Party and represented the last gasp of both. It nominated, for President, John Bell of Tennessee; for Vice-President, Edward Everett of Massachusetts.

A still more important convention was that of the Union Party which met in June, 1864. It was composed of Republicans, pro-War Democrats and others and it renominated Abraham Lincoln for President and chose Andrew Johnson as his running mate. Actually the proceedings were cut and dried yet President Lincoln himself was greatly concerned over the outcome. The war had not been going too well, the President had made enemies and the radical Republicans were clamoring and scheming for a change. Although assured by his political lieutenants that his nomination was secure Lincoln could not forget that he had first been nominated in a convention in which at the outset two-thirds of the delegates favored his opponent.

Following the Civil War Baltimore was not again chosen for a convention until 1872. This was a convention of Democrats who nominated Horace Greeley of New York and B. Gratz Brown of Missouri, respectively as candidates for the presidency and the vice-presidency. Meanwhile Baltimore was being outstripped in population by New York and Philadelphia in the East and by Chicago and the other great cities of the Middle West and of the West. It ceased to have an appeal as an assembling place for politicians. It was destined to figure only once more as the scene of a presidential nomination. That occasion was the Democratic Convention of June, 1912, which nominated Woodrow Wilson.

Old timers who had attended many Democratic conventions declared that, beyond a doubt, the 1912 convention was the most dramatic of all. The central figure was William Jennings Bryan, "The Great Commoner." Bryan had been nominated for President by the party in 1896, 1900 and 1908 and each time had gone down to defeat. He now announced that he would not again be a candidate, but would "continue to fight in the ranks for the progressive cause."

At the outset the convention was in control of the reactionary element, which was to say the delegates pledged to Representative Champ Clark of Missouri, Senator Oscar Underwood of Alabama and Governor Judson Harmon of Ohio. Woodrow Wilson was the candidate of the independent Democrats; but, as Governor of New Jersey, he had kicked over the traces and the bosses were against him. Wilson clubs had been formed throughout the country and the men who ran his campaign made skillful use of telegrams which, at critical moments, poured in from all parts of the country and fairly deluged the delegates.

The first objective of the Clark-Harmon-Underwood group was to separate Bryan from Wilson. In an effort to accomplish this they made use of a letter of Wilson's in which he had remarked that he hoped Bryan would be "knocked into a cocked hat." But Bryan refused to take offense. There were rumors that what he really hoped was that the convention would be deadlocked and again turn to him.

When the name of Judge Alton B. Parker, candidate of the reactionaries, was proposed for temporary chairman, Bryan rose to oppose him. His presence in the center of the platform caused an uproar. There were some cheers but they were almost drowned out by hisses, catcalls, and curses. Bryan had faced many a political crowd before and he stood calmly waiting for the storm to die down. Then he made the convention listen to him. In the end Bryan also was put in nomination. When the vote of the convention was taken it showed 579 for Parker and only 508 for Bryan. So the reactionaries drew the first blood.

Nevertheless the Clark-Harmon-Underwood group by now had become alarmed. It tried to win Bryan over by offering him the permanent chairmanship of the convention. But Bryan was too clever to fall into the trap. Throughout the convention Wilson had the loyal support of the *Sun*. Soon after the opening there arrived on the scene Thomas Fortune Ryan, a New York millionaire, as a delegate from Virginia, his native state. The *Sun* at once made political capital out of it by printing Mr. Ryan's picture on the front page. Meanwhile Bryan's attack on Judge Parker brought a flood of telegrams. Bryan alone received more than a thousand.

Soon thereafter the balloting began. On the first ballot Clark led with 440½ to Wilson's 324. As one ballot followed another Clark's total grew until, on the 10th, he had more than a majority.

His followers were jubilant. Only once before in the history of the Democratic Party had a candidate for the presidential nomination won more than a majority and failed of nomination. At this crucial moment Champ Clark's pretty daughter Genevieve tried to start a stampede by mounting the platform and waving a flag.

Bryan sat through it all, imperturbable. He refused to give up hope. Again the telegrams poured in. The Wilson managers, throughout the country were playing their parts superbly. On the 14th ballot Bryan broke away from his Nebraska instruction and voted for Wilson. It soon became apparent that Clark had passed his peak. On the other hand Wilson's vote was growing. On the 43rd ballot Wilson got a majority and on the 46th he came through with the necessary two-thirds and the victory was his. From that day to this Baltimore has never again been the scene of such a spectacle. The Democratic convention of 1912 was the last to be held there.

After the death of Sonny Mahon in 1928 no politician of sufficient stature rose up to take his place as undisputed boss of Baltimore city. For years the Irish dominated city politics, their stronghold being the 10th Ward in East Baltimore. But the Irish no longer stick together in one neighborhood. They have long since spread out all over the city and, through intermarriage, have contributed their blood to the polygot individual who goes by the name of Baltimorean. The strong political racial groups of today are the Italians, the Poles, the Czechs and the Lithuanians. The Italians got their first mayor in the election of Thomas J. D'Alesandro, the present incumbent, who has done a good job. He was recently re-elected by a handsome majority in spite of a scurrilous attack on the eve of the election.

Though there is no boss there are a number of "bosslets," conspicuous among whom are D'Alesandro, Billy Curran and Jack Pollack. They control a few wards and members in the City Council and the Legislature. But they no longer name their candidates and dominate elections as Whyte, Gorman, Rasin and Sonny Mahon used to do. They would be known only to a small part of the community were it not for Yardley's cartoons in the *Sun* where they are regularly given space.

The most prominent figure in Baltimore politics during the past thirty years has been a woman—Marie Bauernschmidt, also known to the public as "Mrs. B." She comes of a German family in South Baltimore and her maiden name was Mary Oehl von Hattersheim. In 1896, she married William Bauernschmidt, the youngest son of one of Baltimore's wealthiest brewers, George Bauernschmidt. Her first introduction to community affairs was as a charity worker. She also got some experience of the city when, on the death of her father-in-law, she had an important part in distributing his benefactions among worthy institutions. Her shift to politics followed.

According to her own story she was in the yard of the Bauernschmidt brewery when she came on two men in conversation and heard one of them remark: "That there man Van Sickle has got to go." She later identified the speaker as Frank Kelly, Sonny Mahon's chief lieutenant. "That there man" he was planning to get rid of was none other than the Superintendent of the Baltimore public schools.

Mrs. Bauernschmidt had heard enough of such talk to know that the political bosses ran the schools for their own benefit. The School Board was dominated by politicians, and appointments and promotions of teachers were made to suit the whims of the bosses. The bosses also got their slice out of repairs, construction and purchases of supplies.

Mrs. B. set to work to do what she could to change it. She stirred up the parents to such good effect that word went around to the teachers that if they wanted promotions they had better steer clear of Marie. She got wind of that and went to the board with the result that there was quite a shakeup on the board and in the school administration.

In 1919, during the administration of Mayor Broening, the Women's Civic League, of which Mrs. Bauernschmidt was a member, formed the Public School Improvement Association, and the following year Mrs. B. became the executive secretary. This was the beginning of a stormy career that took her before the City Council, to the Mayor's office, the Governor's office, to meetings of the Board of Estimates and to committee rooms of the Legislature. At home and when moving in social circles Mrs. Bauernschmidt displayed good breeding and charm. But when "Marie" went after the politicians she could be as hard-boiled as the best of them. Her sharp, piercing rejoinders have been collected and treasured.

"Look here, big boy," she is credited with having told one political boss, "bigger boys than you have tried to stop me and they have never succeeded." In another frank moment she charged that "Many schoolhouses built out of the old $10,000,000 loan stand as monuments to the colossal stupidity of city officials." After one particularly bitter political fight she commented: "There's only one word to describe the whole primary. It stinks."

The old-time political bosses hated her. But they could not help but admire the skill with which she played their game. Alarmed by her growing power Mahon and Kelly once tried to win her over by flattery, offering to make her the first woman State Senator. But Mrs. B. would have none of it. Not once did she seek an elective office.

Mrs. Bauernschmidt's most effective way of reaching the Baltimore public has been through the radio. On the eve of an election she has made a practice of appearing on a program entitled, "Mrs. B. Speaks Her Mind." In the course of half an hour she presents a thumbnail sketch of the candidates and the issues and says what she thinks of them in no uncertain terms.

Where one side is black and the other white Mrs. B. has carried the public with her. But there have been times when both sides presented an almost indistinguishable gray. Consequently sometimes she has seemed to penalize a reasonably good candidate and at others throw her weight to one who did not deserve it. But no one will deny that she has performed a noble task in bringing corruption into the open where it can be properly dealt with.

Whether it is due to the occasional conscientious public citizens like Mrs. Bauernschmidt, or the inherent independence of the average Baltimore voter, the city is fortunate in its freedom from corruption. There is dubious dealing in municipal jobs and there may be petty graft but seldom, if ever, are there major scandals such as one almost comes to expect in municipalities of comparable size. Baltimore enjoyed its fling early in its history. As the columnist intimated, it now has settled down to a state of eminent political respectability.

Chapter 24

FIRE FIGHTING AND FIGHTING FIREMEN

VISITORS to Baltimore will see on many houses a rectangular plaque painted black and, superimposed on it, clasped hands and the figures 1794 in gold. The plaques make a quaint decoration and signify that the house is insured against fire by the Baltimore Equitable Society.

The date 1794 indicates the year in which Baltimore Equitable was incorporated by the General Assembly of Maryland "for insuring houses from loss of fire." The company has been in active operation ever since. A somewhat surprising provision of the policy is that persons insured pay a lump sum when they take it out and this covers their property indefinitely. If at any time they dispose of the house that has been insured they get back the money they originally paid in. A similar but less common symbol is an iron disk displaying in outline the early model of a fire engine and the letters "F.I.Co." This was got out by the rival Firemen's Insurance Company which was incorporated in 1826. But the great fire of 1904 put it out of business; the disk now is merely a picturesque antique.

Soon after Baltimore Town was founded plans were set forth for the organization of bucket brigades to put out fires. Scientific fire fighting, however, dates from 1769 when the town took up a general subscription for an engine, the first machine of the kind in Baltimore. Local fire fighters proudly organized themselves around this impressive contraption as "The Mechanical Company." It was soon followed by what the old chroniclers described as "kindred associations who devoted themselves to a truly benevolent object with a gallantry amounting to heroism." In 1787 mention is made of four such companies meeting and adopting uniform regulations for fighting fires.

It was in the 1840's that the volunteer fire companies reached the peak of their activity. By then they had established that great national institution—the firemen's parade. Indicating the growth of the companies was the long list of those taking part. It included the ancient Mechanical Company, the Union, Friendship, Deptford, Liberty, Independent, Vigilant, New Market, Columbian, First Baltimore, United, Franklin, Washington, Patapsco, Howard and Watchman.

Those were rowdy days in Baltimore and the fire companies served as excellent instruments for working off the local blood lust. They neglected fighting fires to fight among themselves. Rivalry degenerated into armed conflict. There were innumerable instances in which fires were deliberately set for the purpose of starting a race to the scene, resulting in a collison of the rival organizations and a battle royal.

The brick sidewalks and streets paved with cobblestones supplied unlimited ammunition. The firemen's picks, axes, and hooks made formidable weapons and pistols also were used freely. Some of the fights lasted for several hours; men were killed and many others were wounded. The press and public protested the shameful conduct of the firemen but with little success. In fact battles between rival companies went on until 1858 when at last the volunteer companies gave place to a paid fire department.

Even then some of the old spirit of rivalry was carried on in the new organization until well after the turn of the century. There still are Baltimoreans who can remember as boys the undeviating loyalty they displayed toward a neighborhood company. The choice was proudly announced in reply to the question: "What company do you go for?"

The new paid fire company went on public display for the first time in 1858 in a gala parade. This civic ceremony was arranged in honor of the visit to the city of the first Japanese mission to this country following Commodore Perry's famous trip to Japan. History has not recorded the reaction of the delegation to Baltimore's firemen.

Of the many Baltimore fires, both naturally and artificially started, the first of appreciable size was one which broke out at 10:15 A.M. on Friday, July 25, 1873. It began legitimately enough in the shaving box of a sash-and-blind factory then located at Park Avenue and Clay Street. Whipped by a strong wind it spread quickly until eighteen houses were on fire in the block bounded by Park Avenue, Clay, Mulberry and Saratoga

Streets. From there it moved toward Lexington Street on the south, Howard on the west and Mulberry on the north.

There were times when the tall spire of St. Alphonsus Catholic Church at Park Avenue and Saratoga Street was completely hidden by smoke, but the edifice miraculously escaped the flames. A block to the north a group of volunteers climbed out on the great dome of the cathedral and spread wet blankets to protect it from sparks. The Washington Fire Department offered help which was accepted and a special train on the B. & O. brought engines and other equipment the 40-odd miles from the capital to Camden Station in the record time of 39 minutes. By evening the fire at last was under control and the weary firemen returned to their stations. Baltimoreans boasted they now had a fire that compared favorably even with great conflagrations in Chicago and Boston.

For more than thirty years the fire of 1873 held a conspicuous place in the annals of Baltimore catastrophes. Then in 1904, within a matter of hours, it was erased from memory by the fire which dwarfed all others and assumed the title of "The Fire." No Baltimorean since has had to ask which one.

February 7, 1904, was a quiet Sunday morning. Between 10 and 11 A.M., while people were on their way to church, fire broke out in the large and inflammable dry-goods warehouse of the John E. Hurst Company at Hopkins Place. Popular belief was that a lighted cigarette was tossed through a grating on the sidewalk and from there found its way to the basement of the building. The fire set off an automatic alarm which brought an engine company promptly to the scene, but a succession of explosions spread the flames throughout the whole structure. A strong southwest wind served also to whip up the fire and soon many other buildings were burning. By this time the city's fire department realized that it had a monster conflagration on its hands and virtually the entire force of twenty four engines was called out to try to bring it under control.

But the fire had gained too much headway and was sweeping eastward and northeastward, leaping across streets as though they were not there. Thousands of people were attracted to the scene and pushed and shoved to get a better view, but there was no serious disorder. In the early afternoon the firemen, realizing that pouring water on the fire was doing no good, tried to stop it by blowing up buildings. This expedient added to the excitement but failed to be of help. As the fire progressed it developed an intense heat which even the supposedly "fireproof" buildings could not withstand. By night several of the city's new skyscrapers were aflame and from a distance looked like giant blazing torches against the skyline. The reflection rose so high in the air that it could be seen in Washington and the northern counties of Virginia fifty miles away.

Appeals for help were sent to Washington, Wilmington and Philadelphia and, as in the fire of 1873, apparatus was rushed to Baltimore by special train. But all man-made efforts to stem the fire were unavailing. It continued throughout Sunday night and part of Monday and did not stop until it reached Jones Falls. By then the heart of the downtown business district looked like a desert. One could stand at Hopkins Place, where the fire began and get an unobstructed view of the inner basin. Ashes, bricks and débris wiped out all traces of sidewalks and streets and scarcely a building was left standing. The burned district extended as far south as Lombard Street, east to the Falls and north to Fayette Street. A survey later revealed that, in the space of 40 hours, the fire had burned over 140 acres of commercial property, including 1,343 separate buildings, putting 2,500 firms temporarily out of business. By the evening of the 7th there was hardly a man of means in Baltimore who knew whether he had any property left. During the fire an effort was made to save valuable records but transportation was at a premium. Owners of vehicles demanded exorbitant pay to carry ledgers and papers a few blocks out of the fire zone.

In the midst of the disaster Baltimoreans of the older generation behaved in a characteristically proud and defiant manner. They looked upon the fire as sheer impudence and an affront to their dignity, and regarded it as cowardly to give in. As the fire approached within a few feet of O'Neill's store, at the corner of Charles and Lexington Streets, a proposal was made to blow up the building. Mr. Thomas O'Neill, a redheaded Irishman and owner of the establishment, protested vehemently. He took his stand on the first floor and announced in no uncertain terms that he had no intention of moving, and that if his store was blown up then he would be blown up with it. The authorities did not dare dispute him and the idea was abandoned.

In the Centre Street neighborhood, a few blocks from the fire, there dwelt elderly ladies who had held onto their houses in defiance of the popular move northward and westward. Children, alarmed for the safety of their parents, set off to move them but met with stolid resistance. Typical was the case of Mrs. Thomas H. Morris who occupied the old Morris house at Charles and Centre Streets. Her son-in-law, Mr. Hollins McKim, had his spanking team of horses harnessed and set out posthaste in his carriage to rescue her from the flames. But Mrs. Morris objected strenuously to being rescued. She took the attitude that the house had been the property of the Morris family for generations, that it was in a sense a sacred trust, and that she saw no reason to allow herself to be panicked and dispossessed because of a fire several blocks away. Like a horse under similar circumstances she practically had to be blindfolded before she could be coaxed out of her home.

Even closer to the fire, at Charles and Mulberry Streets, was the home of the William DeFords. Two quiet but determined ladies were Mrs. DeFord and her mother, Mrs. Frank Howard. Neither arguments nor entreaties could persuade them to move. The official version was that a shift of the wind in the nick of time saved this part of the town. Nancy and Lydia DeFord, who then were little girls, took no stock in that. They grew up in the firm belief that the fire stopped because their mother and grandmother forbade it to come closer.

When news of the Baltimore disaster spread throughout the country there was great public sympathy and a fund of $200,000 was raised by popular subscription for relief of the sufferers. But Baltimoreans are proud of standing on their own feet. And, since the fire was confined to the business district, no persons were made homeless. So the relief fund, untouched, was returned to the donors with thanks.

Many of the local insurance companies were bankrupted by the disaster, the total damage from which was estimated at between $125,000,000 and $150,000,000. But the city faced the future with magnificent courage, and confidence was soon restored. A Burnt District Commission was appointed with Sherlock Swann as its chairman. It proceeded at once to laying plans for rebuilding and seized the opportunity to widen streets, enlarge the docks and introduce many other much-needed improvements. It was not long before the disaster was being looked upon as a blessing in disguise, since it gave the city a brand-new business district with far less congestion. It did away with many of the old glorified "cowpaths" in the downtown area that had served as streets.

Baltimore has been fortunate in escaping the disasters so common to great cities. The only one in any way comparable to the Great Fire was the explosion of the *Alum Chine* in Baltimore harbor on March 7, 1913. She was a British tramp steamer which put into Baltimore to load a cargo of 350 tons of dynamite at Wagner's Point. According to the subsequent investigation by the city coroner the explosion was caused by a stevedore sticking a bale hook into a box of dynamite which was being loaded from a scow.

With a flare and a crash the vessel was blown into a thousand pieces. Huge fragments of steel and iron were hurled to the new collier *Jason* that was tied up near by, killing a number of men aboard her. The rumble following the explosion resembled an earthquake and windows were shattered throughout East Baltimore. Earth tremors from the shock were felt as far away as Atlantic City and Philadelphia. At Dover, Delaware the Legislature paused in its deliberations, the speaker remarking that there must have been an earthquake somewhere. A count of the victims revealed thirty three men killed and sixty injured. In contrast, not a single human life was lost in the Great Fire.

In Baltimore ask a person what he knows about "the Fire" or "the *Alum Chine*" and the answer he gives will determine his status with respect to age and his right to be classed as a true Baltimorean.

Chapter 25

GASTRONOMICAL REFLECTIONS

IN THE YEAR 1859 the "Autocrat of the Breakfast Table" was at the peak of his popularity. It was then that Oliver Wendell Holmes in his column acclaimed Baltimore as "the gastronomic metropolis of the Union." "Why don't you," he asked, "put a canvas back duck on top of the Washington column? Why don't you get that lady off from the Battle Monument and plant a terrapin in her place?"

This was not just a fulsome compliment. There was considerable basis for the reputation. As evidence one could do no better than call attention to the famous railroad dinner of July 15, 1857, only two years before Dr. Holmes wrote his column. The Baltimore & Ohio reached St. Louis that year. To signalize the achievement a special train loaded with dignitaries journeyed to St. Louis. Shortly thereafter an equally distinguished party of St. Louisians arrived in Baltimore to return the visit, and the municipality prepared a banquet in their honor at the Maryland Institute, which then overlooked Marsh Market.

As soon as the guests were seated they were given a choice of two soups, of four kinds of fish and eight relishes. Their appetites having been thus whetted they attacked a course of "boiled dishes," which included boiled ham, boiled lamb and boiled spring chicken.

Next came a pick of eleven entrées. This was followed by a so-called "Maryland course," featuring saddle of mutton, soft crabs, hard crabs, summer ducks, green goose and roast ham, each with an appropriate sauce. The menu then listed eight vegetables and, after them, eleven "cold and ornamental dishes." The dinner wound up with 24 desserts, including seven flavors of ice cream, and after them eight kinds of fruit.

Private entertainment was on quite as lavish a scale. In a surviving account book of the Ridgely family, whose country seat was Hampton a few miles north of the city in Baltimore County, there appears a detailed statement of the food provided for a reception given there on March 4, 1851. The occasion for it is not mentioned. The provisions included 24 chickens for salad, 29 partridges, 5 pheasants, 10 turkeys and a round of spiced beef weighing 25 pounds. There were as well two boxes of mushrooms, 12 sweetbreads, 12 gallons of opened oysters for stewing, 4 bushels of oysters for pickling, 5 dozen terrapins, 20 dozen rolls, 4 dozen loaves of bread, 4 salted tongues, 3 boiled hams and 12 heads of lettuce.

The parched throats of the guests were slaked with 7 dozen bottles of champagne, 6 bottles of madeira, 6 of brandy and 6 of whisky. Dessert consisted of 4 "Charlottes," 2 Russian creams, 2 "Swans," 6 dozen meringues, 24 quarts of ice cream and water ice, 5 gallons of punch, 12 pounds of cakes, 8 pounds of grapes, 1 box of oranges and 1 box of lemons. Cost of the food and drink, plus payment of the servants reached a grand total of $329.96.

The hard times which followed the Civil War saw a decline in the quantity of food deemed essential to a Baltimorean's subsistence. Yet meals still were gargantuan compared with present-day standards. Aunt Priscilla, who for years counseled *Sunpapers* readers on matters of food, once described a Christmas Day repast that might have been served in the eighties or nineties of the last century. The day began with a breakfast of fruit, oatmeal, boiled guinea, French fried potatoes, waffles, hot rolls, Sally Lunn, cold bread, coffee and milk.

In the middle of the day came the Christmas dinner. The assembled company were given a choice of roast or boiled turkey with baked ham as an appetizer. Along with the turkey and ham were presented scalloped oysters and five vegetables, sauerkraut, two jellies, celery, cranberry sauce, plum pudding, mince pie, wine jelly, ice cream, fruit cake, nuts and coffee.

After such a breakfast and dinner one might assume that everybody would have had enough food to last at least until next day. But no, the housekeeper foresaw that after the young people had spent the afternoon outside in the crisp December air they would be in the humor for more nourishment. She therefore got ready for a "pick-up" supper including turkey salad, cold ham, pickled oysters, beaten biscuit, cold rolls, loaf bread, tea, coffee, milk, nuts, fruit cake and cookies.

Eating on such a scale was possible because food was cheap and servants were plentiful. Most large households also treasured a maiden sister who earned her bed and board by acting as house-keeper. The married sister or sister-in-law, had as much as she could do bearing the long succession of children characteristic of the families of those burgeoning times. Food now is dear. Domestic servants are emancipated. So too are maiden sisters who hold well-paying jobs in business, live independently in their own little apartments and can snap their fingers at their erstwhile oppressors. In addition to this social revolution Baltimore, like other parts of the country, has felt the baneful effects of nationally advertised foods that have standarized eating throughout the country.

Yet a tradition for good food such as Baltimore once enjoyed dies hard. For all the standardization there is a vestigial remainder. Some famous local dishes are still to be had, though usually they are saved for special occasions, and there are a few of common occurrence that may fairly be described as typical of the place. Were Dr. Holmes to pay a return visit to Baltimore today he might be so fortunate as to renew his acquaintance with canvasback duck and terrapin, though he would find neither so plentiful as they were in Baltimore a hundred years ago. Though in recent years the price has declined along with the demand diamondback terrapin is still expensive. Preparation of the meat is a tedious business which finds few volunteers. Terrapin, therefore, is not for the masses who probably wouldn't appreciate it even if they could afford it. Even persons who like it find it hard to explain its subtle and seductive charm. Very likely a taste for it is based on a child's recollection of never hearing the word mentioned by its elders except with a smacking of the lips.

The only terrapin whose flavor meets the exacting specifications of the connoisseurs is the diamondback. Local restaurants occasionally offer lesser breeds to their patrons; the diamondback is seldom met outside the Maryland Club, or the supper which is a feature of The Assembly, or the private homes of the wealthy. The Maryland Club has long enjoyed distinction for its terrapin. The secret is said to lie in the fact that it is cooked with sweet butter. Usually sherry is added just before serving, and a cruet of sherry also accompanies the terrapin to the table. According to well-authenticated reports Mrs. Miles White personally inspects and chooses every terrapin that is to appear at the Assembly as carefully as the committee on invitations scrutinizes the list of potential guests before sending out bids to the ball.

Philadelphia, too, is a terrapin city. But, to the horror of Baltimoreans, Philadelphians serve their terrapin with a cream sauce! At least such is the scandalous report in Baltimore.

On occasion terrapin appears at debutante parties, to the great distress of older guests who hate to see it wasted. At one such party two elderly gentlemen barely escaped apoplexy when they heard a youth inquiring of a waiter, "Have you got any more of that soup?" There wasn't any more. It was all gone because the youth and others like him had eaten it all up thinking it was bouillon.

Twenty-five years or so ago, because the open season for ducks was longer and the permitted daily bag larger than at present, duck hunters frequently returned with more ducks than they could possibly use themselves. These surplus ducks made welcome gifts to friends who delight in eating duck but lack the moral courage to sit exposed in a ducking blind on a cold winter's day. Or, better still, the hunters invited friends in to eat the ducks. Wild duck, too, in those halcyon days, was found along with terrapin on the bill of fare at the Maryland Club. With the passing of years, however, the ducks have grown scarcer. To reverse the trend the season has been shortened, the legal bag limited and sportsmen have contributed generously to improving conditions on the breeding grounds in Canada. These heroic efforts seem to be having the desired effect, though progress is gradual. So today in Baltimore the highest compliment one person can pay another is to make a gift of wild duck or invite him to come and eat it.

Local tradition calls for a vastly different treatment of wild duck from that accorded the ordinary barnyard duck which appears on menus as "Long Island duckling." The barnyard duck is stuffed with bread and roasted until well done. It then is served with thick gravy, apple sauce and very likely mashed potatoes to soak up the gravy.

The story is told of a Baltimore bride who received a gift of a pair of wild ducks and seized the opportunity to entertain an elderly friend she knew would appreciate them. Looking in her cookbook she came upon a recipe for duck and gave instructions to the cook she had hired for the occasion. She went to a nearby golf course for a bit of relaxation before time for dinner.

The little bride ran into her prospective guest on the course. "Hope you are not cooking those ducks too long," he remarked, as he passed her. "Have you got currant jelly?" he inquired on their second meeting. Piece by piece he let her know that wild ducks should not be stuffed, that they should "fly through the oven," that currant jelly and not apple sauce should be served with them, and that wild rice or creamed hominy, not mashed potatoes, are the preferred vegetable. The bride did not wait to finish her match but rushed home to countermand the orders given and rescue the ducks from the tragic fate she unwittingly had prepared for them.

Because of its proximity to Cheasapeake Bay Baltimore has always enjoyed a reputation for seafood and, in particular, for oysters. Poor conservation practice and the tendency of oyster-men to ignore the advice of the scientists and to blame God for a dwindling supply have played havoc with the industry. The bay now produces virtually no oysters. So "Baltimore on the Chesapeake" is forced to the ignominious practice of importing its oysters from rivers contiguous to the bay, from Chincoteague, Lynnhaven Bay and other alien waters.

Baltimore observes the custom of eating oysters only in those months which have an R in their names. Ships reach the local market on September 1st with the season's first oysters and the gourmets lose no time sampling them and expressing expert opinion on the flavor and quality of the new crop. From then on oysters appear regularly on local menus. They are to be had raw on the half shell at oyster bars where patrons sit on high stools. They are to be had in soup, in stews, broiled on toast, panned and in fritters. Most popular of all are oysters dipped in egg, rolled in cracker crumbs and fried.

A fine old local custom is the oyster roast. A popular time for it is a moonlight night in October or November. It can be held at any house with an acre or more of land around it; if the property looks out over a body of water so much the better. Guests come in warm sweaters, tweeds and other sports clothes because a good deal of time is spent out of doors. Inside the house of the persons giving the party an open fire and a choice of drinks help to get things going.

At a convenient spot outside a pit will have been dug and a hot wood fire started. The oysters make their appearance in gunnysacks holding a bushel each. A metal grill is placed over the fire and on it the oysters are roasted in their shells. Oyster knives are provided for opening the shells and each guest has also a saucer of melted butter in which the roasted oysters are dipped before eating. An oyster bar also is rigged up where guests may eat their fill of raw oysters out of the shell before beginning on the roasted oysters. Bottled beer too is on hand.

When the guests have eaten all the oysters they want, they return to the house for a spread of cold cuts, sandwiches, potato salad, cheese and crackers, doughnuts, pie and hot coffee.

In her description of a Christmas dinner in the 1880's and 1890's Aunt Priscilla mentioned sauerkraut with the turkey. This combination is still found in many Baltimore households though the origin of it is obscure. It is natural to suppose that, since sauerkraut is a German dish, the custom was borrowed from local Germans or the Pennsylvania Dutch. But the Germans and the Pennsylvania Dutch disclaim it. And the surprising fact is that the practice prevails among families of Southern background. Despite disclaimers surely the Baltimore Germans must in some manner have been responsible, if only by providing the sauerkraut.

At Christmas and on New Year's Day friends still are invited in for a glass of eggnog. This is a rich concotion of sugar, eggs, milk or cream, whisky, brandy and Jamaica rum. The eggnog itself has become little more than a symbol. A few guests can be persuaded to sample it and to eat a piece of fruit cake, but the vast majority make their excuses and run for a drink that is more of a drink and less of a meal.

An altogether characteristic item of food is the Maryland biscuit which today is all but obsolete. When it does appear it is as an accompaniment to terrapin or Smithfield ham. The Maryland biscuit, as a matter of fact, is nothing more than the beaten biscuit of the entire South from which it differs only in size and shape. The beaten biscuit is round and flat with a diameter of from two to three inches. The Maryland biscuit on the other hand is about the size and shape of a pullet egg. The recipe calls for nothing more than flour, salt, lard, milk and water worked into a dough and dumped on a floured biscuit board.

Then begins the pounding of the dough with a rolling pin for a solid half hour which gives the biscuit its unique quality. Nothing less, say the experts, will do. They scorn short cuts such as passing the dough through a meat grinder. In the old days it is said that one could tell the hour before breakfast by the sound of cooks beating biscuits all the way down the block. One no longer finds cooks who will take that much trouble. There are a few people in Baltimore who turn out Maryland biscuits wholesale for the market, but the biscuits have passed out of the ken of the ordinary family kitchen.

Oyster experts say there is no valid physical reason for removing oysters from the menu after April. It stems from the fact that, in Europe, oysters in the summer months carry their embryo young on their lobes and the beginnings of the shells are responsible for an unpleasant gritty taste. Our ancestors brought the custom to this country and have followed it for some three centuries though our oysters do not carry their embryos in the same manner. But there is a compelling practical reason in that in spring other choice foods are coming on the market. For the sake of variety it is high time to give the oysters a rest.

Favorite among Baltimore's spring dishes is baked shad. There is no sweeter nor more delicate meat than that of the shad. But it is cursed with bones as forbidding as the spines of a hedgehog. Chefs in hotels and restaurants know the secret of boning a shad so as to rid it of its greatest drawback, but few people in private homes are trained to do it. In consequence those who tackle home-baked shad are in imminent peril of death by strangulation and do so at their own risk. Shad roe, on the other hand, is harmless and altogether delightful. Broiled and served with crisp bacon it is appropriate at breakfast, lunch or dinner. Spring, too, ushers in young spring lamb with mint sauce and new potatoes.

Mention of mint sauce reminds that spring in Baltimore sees the opening of the mint-julep season. For Maryland, along with Virginia and Kentucky, is in the mint-julep belt. Frank Van Wyck Mason, the Baltimore novelist, has called attention to the interesting phenomenon that, in the northern suburbs where the julep-drinking population is thickest, the best mint was until very recently found growing in the cinders along the right of way of the Northern Central Railroad. Go out to the tracks on a Saturday afternoon, see who was there and you knew who would shortly be refreshing friends with juleps. But conversion from coal-burning engines to oil-burning Diesels eliminated the cinders and with them the mint. It was just another painful sacrifice to progress. Fortunately, enough "brood stock" was saved to start hundreds of mint beds convenient to family dwellings in Baltimore County. Though the mint may have lost some of its old flavor it does reasonably well.

Baltimore's largest contingent of displaced persons from Virginia is responsible for a continuous and acrimonious controversy over the proper making of a mint julep. Virginians regard it as a sacrilege to crush the mint. They bruise it ever so gently to bring out its aromatic smell. Their object is to drink the whisky while merely smelling the mint. Baltimoreans, on the other hand, form the base of their julep by crushing mint leaves in sugar and water in the bottom of a tall glass and blending it with the whisky. They then fill the glass with crushed ice and stir with a spoon until frost forms on the outside of the glass. Sprigs of mint are used to garnish the drink. Strict constructionists insist that the julep be made of Maryland rye. Distressingly enough Kentucky bourbon in recent years has been insinuating itself into juleps within sight and sound of the Washington Monument. Is there no longer such a thing as provincial patriotism?

Spring in Baltimore also is the season for strawberry shortcake. The Baltimore version calls, not for cake, but for shortbread about the consistency of biscuit dough. A large flat biscuit is baked and split in half crosswise. Crushed strawberries sweetened with sugar are put between the two biscuit halves which absorb the juice. On top are piled whole strawberries, after which shortbread and berries are smothered in blankets of whipped cream.

A once popular all-the-year-round dish that is on its way out is kidney stew. There was a time when no true Baltimore family would have thought of facing the rigors of Sunday without being fortified by a breakfast of kidney stew and waffles. This was the ideal means of putting oneself in a receptive mood for an hour-long sermon. But family breakfasts on Sunday morning are a thing of the past in most households. The young people prefer to sleep. If they eat any breakfast at all, it is most likely to be no more than orange juice, toast and coffee.

Most important of all, spring bears witness to the arrival of a new crab season. When all is said and done nothing is so characteristic of Baltimore as the omnipresence of the crab. With modern methods of refrigeration crab meat is to be had the year round. Hardly a week goes by that crab is not served in some form in most households. Unlike terrapin and wild duck it is available to all. It is to Baltimore what baked beans and codfish cakes are to Boston. Seldom does a menu appear in a hotel or restaurant which does not feature crab in some form.

Early in the season soft crabs make their appearance. They are merely cleaned, sprinkled with flour and broiled. In this stage the shell is so soft that all of it can be eaten. Soft-shell crabs are to be had measuring as much as five inches across, but small ones are preferred because they are more delicate. Broiled tomatoes go nicely with them. There was a golden age when soft crabs were to be had in abundance at a few cents a dozen. Now a dozen commands from $3.00 to $4.00 and one person can eat three crabs comfortably. Obviously at such a price they are not a staple food.

As the days go by the soft shells harden. Crabs grow by shedding their hard shells and returning to the soft stage, becoming larger with each change. It is the meat of the hard crab that is used in many different ways. The most primitive method of attacking hard crabs is to steam them and serve them "as is." The fingers are used to break up the crab and get the meat out. The crab is then washed down with beer. It is messy but that consideration is of small moment to the epicure.

Crabs may be broken up and tossed into water with green peppers, butter, onion, rice, tomatoes, okra and fish broth and cooked until they evolve into what is known as "crab soup shore style." Flaky crab meat combined with crisp lettuce and mayonnaise, makes a perfect salad. A universal favorite is crab imperial. Selected crab flakes are seasoned with onion, butter, salt and pepper. To this is added cream sauce, Worcestershire sauce, mustard, chives, egg yolks, green peppers, red peppers and bread crumbs. The mixture is then packed into crab shells and put in an oven and baked until well browned on top. A delicious dish, too, is crab well seasoned and baked with breadcrumbs. And creamed crab flakes are popular the year round.

Summer is the season for that most famous of Baltimore dishes—fried chicken á la Maryland. No other local dish has enjoyed quite the same publicity and exploitation. Whenever a local newspaper columnist or editorial writer is in need of an idea he falls back on fried chicken á la Maryland. He compares its virtues with the lesser virtues of other sorts of fried chicken. He enlarges upon its succulence, flavor and delicacy. A public movement once was started to erect a monument in honor of fried chicken á la Maryland. Prizes were offered for the discovery and identification of its inventor.

Yet, in spite of all the enthusiastic praise of chicken á la Maryland, the scandal is that few persons even in Baltimore actually know what it is.

An authoritative book on Maryland cooking is Mrs. Ben Howard's *The Queen of the Kitchen*. The first edition of this classic was published in Baltimore in 1870. Not once does Mrs. Howard use the term "fried chicken á la Maryland." A reasonable conclusion is that the name is a comparatively recent one coined by some clever advertising man for use in hotels or railway and steamboat diners.

However, Mrs. Howard does present a recipe for fried chicken whose outstanding qualities are those attributed by other high authorities to the so-called chicken á la Maryland. That is to say the chickens, after being jointed, are sprinkled with pepper and salt and a little flour and fried in boiling fat. The drippings of the frying pan are then mixed with cream to make a cream gravy, which is poured over the chicken. Mrs. Howard adds that mush cut into thin slices and fried "are an improvement if added to the dish when served."

Yet there are some fully authenticated Baltimoreans with generations of Maryland lineage behind them who will tell you that the cream gravy is no part of true chicken á la Maryland. Well, all that can be said in reply is that they have against them the weight of the combined authority of Aunt Priscilla, the Duchess of Windsor and Fred P. (*Eat, Drink and Be Merry in Maryland,*) Stieff as well as of Mrs. Howard.

No dissertation on characteristic Baltimore food should omit mention of that most delectable of desserts—the Kossuth cake. Local tradition holds that it was created by an East Baltimore Street confectioner on the occasion of the visit of Louis Kossuth, Hungarian patriot, in 1851, and named in honor of him. Kossuth was the leader in his country of a revolt against Austrian rule that was part of the wave of revolutions which swept over Europe in 1848. For a time Hungary achieved its independence and Kossuth was its governor but, with the aid of imperial Russia, Austria regained control. Kossuth was imprisoned temporarily and, upon his release, accepted an invitation to visit the United States. Here for a time he was hailed as a popular hero and champion of freedom. Kossuth's hope was to raise money for a new revolt.

Baltimore gave him a cordial reception and made him the chief figure in a grand parade. But when it came to contributing hard cash the Baltimore public held back. Kossuth's total take was a trifling $25.00. Even the dedication of so sublime a dessert as Kossuth cake could hardly have assuaged his disappointment. Ironically enough anyone who has partaken of this food feels in anything but a revolutionary mood. Nothing could be more conducive to complete acquiescence to the status quo.

The Kossuth cake is a particularly proud member of the Charlotte Russe family. A sponge cake about three inches in diameter and two inches high is hollowed out and filled with thick whipped cream. On top of the whipped cream is a thick cap of bitter chocolate or strawberry icing. Each Kossuth cake sits in a pleated paper cup. It is served slightly chilled. No local cookbooks mention Kossuth cakes which obviously have been the monopoly of confectioners and caterers. There still are one or two old establishments which make them, but an order has to be given in advance. A pseudo-Kossuth cake sometimes finds its way on to a local bill of fare. In this spurious version a dip of vanilla ice cream is substituted for whipped cream. It is inevitable that in so fraudulent a concoction the sponge cake should be stale and the chocolate cover thin and anemic. The true Kossuth cake must be made of the very best ingredients and you must be prepared to pay for them.

The complete disappearance of domestic servants save in the more ambitious households has revolutionized the Baltimore ménage during the past decade. Now that most housewives do their own cooking meals have been greatly simplified and full advantage is taken of such labor-savers as ice-box biscuits and rolls and the vast array of pastry and cake mixes. One sees less and less corn-bread muffins, corn-bread sticks, spoon bread and other homemade hot breads once associated with Southern cooking.

Newcomers to Baltimore too in recent years have led the natives along strange paths in the direction of startling culinary adventures. Ten or so years ago a Baltimorean invited to dinner with Baltimoreans could be reasonably sure of being offered a soup (with a dip of whipped cream floating on top), roast meat or fowl, potatoes and a green vegetable, a salad and dessert. Today he would not be surprised to be confronted with a casserole, French bread and a bottle of wine, or something equally unconventional and Bohemian, served on a checked tablecloth.

If a Baltimorean wants wine with his meals he can now get a good wine made within the sound of the bell on the City Hall (when the wind is right) from grapes grown in the same radius. It is the produce of Boordy Vineyard, J. & P. Wagner, Proprietors, at Riderwood in Baltimore County. Other wine is made in the State from imported grapes, but Boordy winery is the only one which makes wine from grapes produced on Maryland soil.

Philip Wagner is a grape grower and wine maker by avocation. He is also editor of *the Sun*. Experiments in wine making began during Prohibition, but his interest continued and resulted in successful experiments in finding suitable wine grapes for the Maryland soil and climate. Mr. Wagner made his selection from French hybrids, which is to say grape varieties bred in France by crossing the classic European varieties with certain of the wild American species. He has proved that it is possible to make both red and white wine of good quality from grapes grown on Maryland soil, and to make the business pay into the bargain. His production amounts to several thousand gallons a year. Because it is native the wine is served at many local banquets and carried as a speciality by a number of Baltimore restaurants. Thanks to Mr. Wagner, Baltimore is probably the only city of the East Coast that has its own *vin du pays*.

Nevertheless, while Baltimoreans are patient and docile, there are certain lengths to which they cannot be made to go. For example, there is the incident of a newcomer who, unlike many others of his kind, instead of introducing innovations undertook to adopt local customs. On an evening in June he invited his guests to dinner. His spacious porch provided a charming view of the countryside and in that altogether congenial setting he had his butler serve mint juleps. The butler knew his business and the juleps were perfect. The old Baltimoreans present congratulated themselves that a foreigner could so quickly and successfully adjust himself to the amenities of a civilized society. In due course the butler announced dinner. What was the chagrin of old Baltimoreans when plates of terrapin were set before them! The newcomer did not know that terrapin in June is as much of an anachronism as turkey and plum pudding on July 4th.

Under the new social system in which the housewife does all the work it has become customary to give the cook at least one day of rest a week by rescuing her from the kitchen and repairing to a restaurant. In consequence Baltimore's public eating places have taken a new lease on life and are well patronized. Such establishments are legion; yet, at risk of making glaring omissions, a few of them may be mentioned.

From the days when persons of German blood first found their way to Baltimore they began to play an important part in providing food and drink for the public, and they continue to predominate in the field. At the luncheon and dinner hours there is almost always a queue in front of Miller Brothers, on Fayette Street in the center of the downtown area. Other popular establishments with German backgrounds are Baum's, Walker-Hasslinger's, Harry L. Hasslinger's, Schellhase's and Haussner's. The last named place is unusual in that it is situated in an altogether unlikely spot far off the beaten path in that eastern section of the city known as Highlandtown. Yet Baltimoreans journey there from all directions to enjoy excellent food and also to view the proprietor's remarkable collection of paintings which adorn the walls and his objets d'art. So many familiar pictures are exhibited that a diner has a sense of viewing New York's Metropolitan, London's National Art Gallery and the Louvre rolled into one.

An Italian restaurant with a distinct New York flavor is Marconi's, on Saratoga Street. Those who like Italian cooking also feel well repaid if they make a special visit to that portion of the town centering on Albemarle Street, set picturesquely near the harbor, inhabited by the Italian-born colony and popularly known as "Little Italy." In that quarter bright neon lights advertise the presence of a number of Italian restaurants the best known of which is Maria's, where excellent Italian food and wine are served. There, one will run into Tommy D'Alesandro, Baltimore's first mayor of Italian blood. He lives across the way.

Good food and local color also are to be had at The House of Welsh, a quaint structure tucked away on Guilford avenue in the shadow of loftier neighbors and looking as though it were a part of the London of Charles Dickens. Good food without quite so much local color is also to be had at Marty's, on Fayette Street, a restaurant run by Martin J. Welsh, Jr., a brother of the proprietor of the House of Welsh. And of course there are numerous Chinese houses.

Less ambitious than these establishments but a conspicuous part of the local scene is the chain of Hooper's restaurants. The proprietor comes of an Eastern Shore family, where good living is classed among the higher virtues. The Hooper clan is closely associated with sea food. The restaurants advertise a substantial dinner for an exceedingly modest sum. High chairs are conspicuous. Here will be found young fathers and mothers with their several children taking an evening out.

In addition to these facilities there also are the various hotel dining rooms and the taverns and restaurants along the highways which entice the traveler entering Baltimore as well as provide gustatory diversion for the Baltimore resident. On the whole it may be said that ample provision is made against the possibility of anybody starving.

No Baltimorean today would be so bold as to claim that his city is the gastronomic metropolis of the Union. But, as food goes these days, Baltimore does pretty well.

Chapter 26
LITERARY INTERLUDE

IF BALTIMORE can be said to have had a golden age of literature the best claim is held by the period between 1820 and 1850. Peace with the outside world followed the close of the War of 1812 while the disappearance of the Federalist Party brought a momentary calm to the domestic scene. President Monroe succeeded Madison in the White House and the country entered upon what was known all too briefly as "the Era of Good Feeling."

Having successfully defended their city from the British the Baltimoreans sheathed their swords and directed their attention toward the arts. Conspicuous in this literary renaissance was the Delphian Club. It was organized in the summer of 1816 and, save for two years when yellow-fever epidemics interfered, continued its activities until 1825. The Delphian followed the pattern of the social and literary clubs that flourished somewhat earlier in Annapolis and were a holdover from the coffeehouse era. Its declared purposes were, first, to "foster the interest of members in literary and scientific pursuits"; and, secondly, "to amuse." The club met every Saturday evening at the home of a member and was presided over by an officer who bore the title of Tripod. He was supposed to be the representative of Apollo. There were nine regular members to each of whom was assigned a muse as a consort. Meetings were given over to exchanges of witticisms, humorous stories and epitaphs, many of which later were printed in a magazine named *The Portico*.

The literary production of the members was impressive. From sixteen of them during the period of the club's activity there came forty-eight books of fiction, history and travel, nine volumes of poetry, one play, and nineteen speeches. Twelve newspapers and magazines were edited by members. However, many professions other than journalism were represented. William H. Winder, for example, was a military man and lawyer, John Howard Payne was an actor, Horace Haden was founder of the nation's first dental school and Rembrandt Peale was a painter. There also was a generous sprinkling of doctors. John Pierpont then was distinguished as a poet; today his chief claim to fame is that he was the grandfather of J. Pierpont Morgan.

These various achievements, however, are insignificant compared with the fact that three Delphian members were the authors of three of this country's most popular songs. The members were Francis Scott Key, Samuel Woodworth and John Howard Payne; and the songs are respectively "The Star Spangled Banner," "The Old Oaken Bucket" and "Home Sweet Home."

Included in the membership also were William Wirt and John P. Kennedy. Wirt was an accomplished lawyer and Attorney-General under President Monroe. The duties of his office brought him frequently before the Baltimore courts and to Baltimore he came after his retirement to spend his declining years. Wirt had a facile pen and was the author of several volumes of essays. He also was biographer of Patrick Henry. When Edgar Allan Poe came to Baltimore as a young man in 1831 he was referred to Mr. Wirt and submitted some of his poems to him. Wirt, however, returned them with the comment that he was not qualified to pass judgment on "modern poetry."

In this literary renaissance Kennedy was a prominent figure. He too was a lawyer. His service in the United States House of Representatives already has been mentioned in connection with Morse's telegraph. At the close of his public career, he was Secretary of the Navy. In his youth Kennedy was a founder and editor of a serial of light prose and verse known as *The Red Book* which ran for several years. He also found time to turn out three novels which were *Swallow Barn*, *Horseshoe Robinson* and *Rob of the Bowl*, and to write a two-volume biography of Wirt. The novels have long since passed into oblivion; what is still remembered is Kennedy's kindness and encouragement to Poe.

Poe came to Baltimore from Richmond, Virginia, to visit his Poe relations. He was a grandson of David Poe, Washington's deputy Commissary General in the Revolution. His grandmother was the Mrs. Poe who, it will be recalled, won the gratitude of Lafayette by making "garments" for his soldiers. She now was a paralyzed old woman living in poverty with a daughter Maria Clemm. Other members of this drab household on Milk Street were Maria Clemm's seven-year-old daughter, Virginia, her son Henry who lay dying of tuberculosis, and Edgar's older brother, William Henry Leonard Poe whose weakness was drink.

The poem which Poe submitted to Wirt was "Al Aaraaf."

After several rejections this poem, "Tamerlane," and some minor poems were accepted for publication by the Baltimore publishing firm of Hatch and Dunning and appeared in December, 1829. This was Poe's second published volume, "Tamerlane" having previously appeared in Boston. After his brief career as a cadet at West Point in the session of 1830-1831 Poe returned to Baltimore and again lived with his Aunt Maria Clemm. In 1832 the household moved to No. 3 Amity Street where it remained until 1835 when Poe became editor of the *Southern Literary Messenger*. The house still stands and is preserved as a Poe Shrine.

In these years Poe wrote short stories and also his *Tales of the Folio Club*, a satire incidentally on literary clubs like the Delphian. He haunted E. J. Coale's bookstore on Calvert street and also became a familiar figure at the Widow Meagle's Oyster Parlor down by the harbor on Pratt Street. There he startled the lady by reciting his poems. She called him "the Bard." By way of further diversion he carried on a handkerchief flirtation with a Miss Mary Devereaux who lived across the way from the Clemms, and immortalized her in an eight-verse poem entitled "To Mary."

In July, 1833, the *Baltimore Saturday Visitor*, a weekly, offered a $50 prize for a short story and $25 for a poem. The judges of the contest were Mr. Kennedy, Dr. James H. Miller and J. H. B. Latrobe. Poe submitted several short stories and was awarded the prize for "A Ms Found in a Bottle." The judges also liked his "Descent Into the Maelstrom." The award was announced and the prize story published in the October 19, 1833, edition of the magazine. Thus Kennedy and Latrobe collaborated in helping Poe as they had done in helping Morse.

After this Kennedy became Poe's patron, entertaining him at dinner and supplying him with clothes. He not only introduced him to Latrobe but also to the editor of the *Southern Literary Messenger*. This second introduction was especially useful since thereafter Poe became a regular contributor to the magazine and, two years later, its editor. Kennedy was one of the few people who stuck by the poet until the very end.

It was in St. Paul's Church that Poe was married to his cousin Virginia Clemm who at the time was only thirteen years old. With her and his mother-in-law he then moved to Richmond. Old Mrs. Poe had meanwhile died. This marked the end of his residence in

Baltimore. On September 29, 1849, he returned on his final journey, having come from Richmond by boat. He then was a very ill man. He eventually was found in a tavern on Front Street and recognized. Henry Herring, a cousin by marriage, was notified and the then dying poet was carried to the Washington Hospital, now the Church Home and Hospital, on North Broadway. There four days later he breathed his last. He was buried in the yard of Westminster Presbyterian Church, where his body still lies. His wife Virginia had died in 1847 and been buried in Fordham, New York. Her body later was moved to Baltimore and now rests beside that of the poet.

Reference already has been made to J. H. B. Latrobe's many varied talents. He and Kennedy occupied adjoining offices in the Athenaeum and, though Latrobe was eight years junior to Kennedy, the two were lifelong friends. After the death of his father Benjamin Latrobe, the architect, the family was left virtually destitute. While studying law Latrobe made money by rewriting such classic children's stories as "Jack the Giant Killer." He also wrote a life of Charles Carroll of Carrollton.

The children's stories were done for another interesting Baltimorean of the period—Fielding Lucas, Jr. Lucas was a bookseller and a publisher. Moreover he was a cartographer of no little ability. He was the author of atlases of the world, the United States, and the West Indies, obtaining much information on foreign lands from the ships' captains who came into Baltimore harbor. Lucas produced a progressive drawing book which was standard in its day. He also got out an illustrated book on flowers written by Mrs. William Wirt and called *Flora's Dictionary*. It was a great favorite and passed through eight editions. Lucas was withal a raconteur and bon vivant, a member of the Delphian Club and an intimate of Latrobe. His business was continued by his descendants and gradually evolved into an office supply and stationery concern under the name of Lucas Brothers. It continues to this day on Baltimore Street only a block from the site of the original establishment of Fielding Lucas, Jr. But it is no longer in the hands of the Lucas family.

A landmark in the intellectual life of the city was the founding in 1844 of the Maryland Historical Society. Latrobe was active in this endeavor as also were Lucas and Brantz Mayer, one of the

Baltimore Germans, an author, lawyer and editor of the *Baltimore American*. Ever since its founding the society has interested itself in local history and has become the repository of many various heirlooms. Judge Samuel K. Dennis, a member of its governing council, once remarked jokingly that what the Salvation Army refuses to take Baltimoreans offer to the Historical Society. Nevertheless the society has done very well. It boasts a rare collection of portraits of Marylanders. It has also many valuable Washington letters; old papers, literally dug up in England, having to do with the Calverts, Benjamin Latrobe's original sketches of the proposed national Capitol at Washington and countless other items associated with Baltimore history including acquisitions as up-to-date as a manuscript of Mencken's.

The Civil War had its paralyzing effect on the literary life of the city as on its other activities. Yet it was a native Baltimorean, James Rider Randall, who contributed the most stirring song of the period—"Maryland, My Maryland." There was a hiatus until 1873 when there appeared another luminary in the person of Sidney Lanier. He came from Georgia with his wife and four sons determined to devote his life to his two passions, poetry and music, which he maintained were closely allied. He became the flutist of the Peabody Orchestra then being directed by the Dane, Asger Hamerik, who was director also of the Conservatory of Music. Dr. Gilman, always on the lookout for genius, offered him employment as lecturer in English literature at the Hopkins. His career was cut short by death from tuberculosis at the age of thirty-nine years. "The Marshes of Glynn" and "The Song of the Chattahoochee" were among the numerous poems turned out during his residence in Baltimore.

The city boasted no other national literary figure until the advent of H. L. Mencken, who since 1910 has dominated the local literary scene. His dynamic personality as revealed in his newspaper work, his treatises and his reminiscences has given him a predominant place in the community among his contemporaries. This very immediate importance has tended to obscure those qualities which, in the end, are likely to give him more lasting fame. The opinion seems to be growing that his contributions to native speech contained in *The American Language* and its *Supplements* and in *A New Dictionary of Quotations* will long survive his other works. And if the birth of a true American Literature, as distinguished from the long years of following the English model, is definitely assigned to the 1920's, then Mencken surely will be remembered as one who was foremost in helping it along.

Baltimoreans have a peculiar flair for poetry which is manifested in many odd ways. It might fairly be said of them, as Alexander Pope said of himself, that they "lisp in numbers." It will be recalled that when Mencken started out on his literary career he instinctively turned first to poetry. This later distressed him and he has made valiant efforts to suppress his own work. Where might he not have ended had he stuck to it! When he wrote poetry he was responding to an overwhelming local urge.

If a gift is to be bestowed upon a member of the family or guests are to be bidden to a party a Baltimorean's first thought is to invite the muse. The obituary columns of the *Sunpapers* are embellished every day by memorial verses to the dead. On the rare occasions when inspiration is lacking the *Sunpapers* offer their patrons a choice selection of ready-made memorial poems after the manner of singing telegrams.

The readiness with which Baltimoreans fall into verse is in part attributable to the fact that Baltimore verse is "free." Local convention usually demands that the first two lines rhyme and scan. After that the poem is permitted, so to speak, to reach its own level. If after four or five lines a poem continues both to rhyme and scan the suspicion is strong that the Baltimorean has filched it from a book.

As a rule, Baltimore poetry runs to quantity, rather than quality, but there have been some notable exceptions. Conspicuous among them is the work of the local schoolma'm, the late Lizette Woodworth Reese. Miss Reese's verses are crisp and cool, having to do largely with springtime, curling woodsmoke and the delicate blossoms of the hawthorne. But once she struck fire and commanded the attention of the whole literary world with her sonnet "Tears." Those fourteen lines may be expected to endure.

Could it be an accident that Carl Shapiro, the most promising of the young poets to come out of World War II, is a native Baltimorean and a product of City College and the Hopkins? He recently left for Chicago to assume the editorship of *Poetry*.

Baltimore is probably unique among American cities for having had two official poets laureate. The first was the late Alexander Geddes who assumed office on June 17, 1912. The appointment was made by Mayor James H. Preston. Even before that Alex, a graduate of vaudeville, had been distributing his broadsides through the offices of the municipal jobholders in the City Hall. Mayor Preston concluded that Alex's zeal deserved official recognition. Hence the office and title of poet laureate. The installation, according to the record, took place at the City Hall "with appropriate ceremony." At its conclusion the Mayor's secretary Bob Lee took the new laureate to a restaurant nearby and treated him to a chicken dinner washed down with six steins of beer.

Geddes, as is customary with laureates, specialized in verses of occasion, signalizing the marriages of friends and the births of their children. His Christmas and Easter verses were said to have been awaited by the Baltimore public with keen anticipation. But the laureate was not allowed to enjoy his office without challenge. One seeker after the job identified himself as Andrew Jackson Cummings, pastor of Shiloh African American Baptist Church, of Red Springs, Arkansas, who wrote: "I know the salary is small but the thought of having an office in City Hall and wearing a crown is everything." The name may have been A. J. Cummings, but the voice sounded suspiciously like that of "the Sage of Hollins Street," H. L. Mencken.

Baltimore's second poet laureat was Max Rubin, who owed his appointment to Mayor Theodore Roosevelt McKeldin. Mr. Rubin, a native of Bessarabia, came to Baltimore in 1914 to follow a career as philosopher, poet and pants maker. When he took office Mayor McKeldin enjoined him, "Max, make Baltimore poetry conscious." As though Baltimore needed that! However, Max sat down and, under the inspiration of his newly acquired honor, dashed off a seven-verse poem in ten minutes entitled "Baltimore, I'm Grateful." This seems to bear out the opinion of one literary critic who remarked that Max "writes easily and rapidly."

But Baltimore's poetical *cause célèbre* occurred in the winter of 1925. *The Nation*, according to its annual custom, had offered a poetry prize of $100 and the poets responded with more than 4,000 entries. One day in February the news was flashed across the country that the winner was one Eli Siegel, of Baltimore. The winning poem bore the intriguing title, "Hot Afternoons Have

Been In Montana." *The Nation* also published the poem which brought howls of derision and resentment from all directions. Amos W. W. Woodcock, then the local U. S. District Attorney, declared that: "If a magazine of the standing of *The Nation* could select such an outburst as 'Hot Afternoons' as the best the literature of this country can produce, then I am skeptical of the future of the country." Even the liberal Upton Sinclair, who generally could be counted on to champion lost causes, wrote, "This poem seems to us the climax of futility." What appeared to annoy the critics most was that Siegel admittedly had never been in Montana. It did no good to remind them that Coleridge had never visited Xanadu nor Milton Paradise when they wrote about them.

After "Hot Afternoons" Siegel shook the dust of Baltimore from his feet and proceeded to Greenwich Village, New York. When last heard from he was teaching others how to write poetry and also working on a book defining his philosophy which, it seems, was enshrined in "Hot Afternoons."

A chapter on literature should not omit mention that Ogden Nash, the poet, married a Baltimore girl; and, when not at work in New York or Hollywood, makes his home there. Scott Fitzgerald, the novelist, passed his last sad, lonely years in Baltimore. In recent years the town seems to have experienced a marked literary revival. Certainly there has been considerable increase in the number of volumes published by natives. Hardly a week now goes by that a show window at the Pratt Library is not heralding the publication of a book by some local author.

In Baltimore, as in other parts of the world, a number of doctors have "gone literary" and written their memoirs. Baltimore boasts two historical novelists in Neil H. Swanson and Frank Van Wyck Mason. The sales of Mason's romances with their intrepid heroes and warm-blooded heroines run into the hundreds of thousands. Gerald W. Johnson, a free-lance author, is good for a volume or two of history or biography every year. Holmes Alexander, a native son, has led a busy literary life as biographer, novelist, playwright and columnist.

On the whole it may fairly be said that, for a town that makes no great boast of being bookish or exceptionally intellectual, in the field of literature Baltimore hasn't done so badly.

Chapter 27
RALLYING OF THE CLANS

In the early days of the Gay Nineties a child of the late General James A. Gary was about to alight from a streetcar at Linden Avenue and Dolphin Street when she heard a fellow passenger remark: "That's General Gary's house there. He'd be a rich man if he didn't have so many daughters." Rather than cause embarrassment by revealing that she was one of the blameworthy daughters she rode on for another block.

Yet the comment, as it applied to Baltimoreans in the eighties and nineties of the last century, contained much truth. They produced offspring wholesale with utter disregard for its effect on the dissipation of fortunes to say nothing of the cost of upkeep. The Gary family consisted of one son and seven daughters. Just across the street and affording a neat balance was the family of Major William Stuart Symington, C.S.A., consisting of one daughter and seven sons. This was the Mid-Victorian era and the Queen of England was setting the fashion for the English-speaking world. Large families were as much in order as peacock fans, wax flowers under glass and anti-Macassars.

Impressive as were the Gary and Symington households there were others which outnumbered them. The Charles K. Harrisons, for example, boasted nine sons and three daughters. Running the Harrisons a close race was the family of Richard Cromwell, Sr., the first of the Cromwells to break away from the family stronghold in Anne Arundel County and come to seek his fortune in Baltimore. Richard Cromwell, who was twice married, had seven sons and three daughters. But the record was just about reached by the C. Morton Stewarts and their household which overflowed with fourteen children—seven sons and seven daughters.

Still another Baltimore family which came to flower in the Mid-Victorian age was that of the Slingluffs. The first to arrive in the town was Jesse Slingluff, a man of Pennsylvania Dutch origin, who came from Germantown, Pennsylvania, around 1812. He had a son Jesse who married a Frances Cross, from Southern Maryland, and raised a family of five sons and two daughters which for that time was not exceptional. But these grandchildren of the first Jesse went in for production in a big way. By their combined efforts they produced a new generation of more than fifty children. Even the Slingluff family historians are in doubt as to the exact number, some fixing it at fifty-four and others claiming fifty-seven.

Nor most certainly would Baltimore be recognized without its ample quota of Leverings. The local branch of this prolific family owes its origin to Enoch and Mary Levering who came from the neighborhood of Philadelphia in 1773 to make their home in Baltimore. Enoch and Mary had seven sons who produced numerous offspring, and thereafter city directories regularly featured the Levering name. One member of the family commanded a company of the 5th Regiment and played a conspicuous part in the Battle of North Point, in 1814.

The Levering who made his mark as a merchant prince of the town was Eugene, grandson of Enoch. Arrived at manhood he formed a partnership with his brother Frederick A. in the wholesale grocery business which continued until Frederick's death in 1866. Mr. Levering then took into partnership three of his sons— William T., Eugene and Joshua—and changed the name of the firm to E. Levering & Company. As time went on the company specialized in coffee.

Eugene Levering, Sr., and his wife Mary Walker had eight sons and two daughters who lived to maturity. Especially prominent were the twin brothers Eugene and Joshua. Like most Leverings they were devout Baptists and their lives were dedicated to good works. Joshua was distinguished as a leader of the "Dry" forces. He was candidate of the Prohibition Party both for Governor of Maryland and for President of the United States. He went down in defeat, of course, but in the campaign for governor polled a flattering testimonial vote.

Leonard Levering, a nephew of Joshua, was married to Mary Donnell Tilghman, a daughter of one of Maryland's old planter families of the Eastern Shore. At the reception following the wedding, in keeping with the Shore's immutable laws of hospitality, champagne flowed freely. When the party was at its height a shrill voice was raised above the tumult crying out in anguish, "Is there no place in this house where a man may get a drink of water?" It was that of Uncle Josh.

The Levering Coffee Company is still in business though no

members of the Levering family are connected with its management. In the days when it was being run by the sons of Eugene,
Sr., the City Collector once received a letter that must have surprised him. It read: "We think that the volume of our business last
year justifies us in requesting you to add another $50,000 to the
assessment of the firm of E. Levering & Co. for taxable purposes."
In other words, the Leverings were asking the municipality to put
an extra $1,000 on their tax bill. Such was their rare sense of
responsibility to the community.

On the broad plateau of Pikesville, dominating the northwest-
ern approaches to the city, were arrayed the formidable forces of
the Randolph Bartons and the A. Adgate Duers. The Duers were
blessed with four sons and five daughters, and the Bartons with
seven sons and two daughters. The Barton establishment was all
the more remarkable because Major Barton was not a merchant
prince but a lawyer. Supporting so large a household on a lawyer's
practice must have been a problem of considerable proportions.
But, having served for four years in the famous Stonewall Brigade
of the Confederate Army Major Barton was schooled in audacity;
and, consequently, was ready to meet the responsibilities of head
of a large family that would have terrified an ordinary man. He
was also a lawyer of unusual talent so the task was competently
performed.

The Bartons and Duers were loyal members of the congregation
of the Protestant Episcopal Church of St. Mark's-on-the-Hill in
Pikesville. At morning prayer the two families occupied so large a
part of the church that an observer once suggested that the name
be changed to "St. Barton's and All Duers."

Two old Baltimore families invariably linked together are the
Poes and the Riggses because of their genius for turning out ath-
letes. Mention already has been made of the signal contribution of
the Poes and Riggses to Princeton's football team. The six sons of
the John Prentiss Poes were Edgar Allan, Neilson, Arthur, Gres-
ham, S. Johnson and John P. There were also three daughters for
good measure. The Lawrason Riggses confined themselves to sons
—eight in number—who were Jesse B., Lawrason, Clinton, William P., Barry, Frank, Alfred and Dudley. There were as well
other and smaller branches of these families which swelled the
number of Baltimoreans bearing the names of Riggs and Poe.

A name prominent in Baltimore, as it is throughout Maryland, is Dorsey. In the old days when the *Maryland Historical Society Magazine* laid emphasis on genealogical notes, the Dorsey family used to take up most of the available space. Yet even with this help it is doubtful if much was accomplished in untangling the many lines. In fact Dorseys in Baltimore are numbered by the score. There may be three or more Dorsey families living within a stone's throw of each other, yet none of them claiming relationship. The same also is true of Fishers. Yet one group of Fishers has achieved special prominence in the business and social life of the city. These are the descendants of William Fisher who came to Baltimore from Carroll County. William Fisher had six sons who were J. Harmanus, William A., Parks, Harry, Charles and Frank and one daughter who became Mrs. Alexander Robertson. J. Harmanus was a banker, William A. a distinguished lawyer and judge and Charles one of the city's leading capitalists. The two sons of Judge Fisher, the four sons of his brother Frank, and the Judge's six grandsons—all prominent in the life of the city—carry on this branch of the family.

Names which once were as frequently heard in Baltimore as those of the Leverings and Fishers today are the Moales, Howards, Carters, Buchanans, Gilmors, McKims, McLanes and Perines. These old and large families have run to the distaff side so consistently that many surnames have been lost or now are carried only by a few individuals. For example, the descendants of General John Eager Howard once were legion, but members of the family bearing the Howard name now are relatively few. Yet interestingly enough there still are two John Eager Howards. By way of distinguishing himself from his cousin one of them has followed the old Baltimore custom of adding the initial of his father's first name to his own, calling himself John Eager Howard of B, or son of Benjamin Howard. The late John Fife (Jack) Symington was known as John Symington of W (son of William) to distinguish him from an uncle who also bore the name of John. Other Baltimoreans who follow the custom are John E. Hurst of W., Lawrason Riggs of J., John Merryman of J., John Ridgely of H. and J. William Middendorf of H.

In the eighties and nineties the homes of these large families were the centers of social life. Each child was encouraged to bring in its friends and, of course, when the girls grew up they attracted beaux. It was never known in advance how many would sit down to dinner and places were set indiscriminately. Most of the well-to-do families maintained both city houses and country estates. On the latter they raised much of the food that supplied their tables. Since there was so much running back and forth between households the entertaining evened up in the long run. After all, there were a certain number of persons to be fed each day; it therefore mattered little where each one was fed.

The Gary household with its seven attractive daughters was endlessly full of young men coming and going. "1200 Linden Avenue," as the town residence was popularly known, shared equal honors with "The Summit" which was the General's country home near Catonsville. "Cliffholme" the estate of C. Morton Stewart in the Green Spring Valley also was a scene of constant informal entertaining. All seven of the Gary daughters married, though not to the seven Symington sons who lived so conveniently across the way.

Naturally in this intimate society there was much intermarriage and the blending of many of Baltimore's various strains. Conspicuous, not so much for its numbers as for the extent to which its blood has been diffused among other leading families, is the Whitridge clan. The Whitridges stemmed from William Whitridge and his wife Mary Cushing, of Tiverton, Rhode Island. Two sons, Dr. John Whitridge and Thomas Whitridge came to live in Baltimore. So did a grandson Horatio L. Whitridge. Dr. John had a distinguished medical career and the medical tradition was carried on in the family by a son William and a grandson, J. Whitridge Williams.

Brother Thomas entered the shipping business under the firm name of Thomas Whitridge & Co., became the owner of a fleet of ships and made a fortune in the Rio trade. Horatio L. Whitridge came to Baltimore at the age of fourteen years and entered the shipping business of his uncle Thomas. He eventually left his uncle to establish his own firm under his own name and later under that of Horatio L. Whitridge and Son and achieved much the same success his uncle had done. Not only have the Whitridges kept their own name alive but they also have married into other prominent Baltimore families. Whitridge blood is found among the

Garretts, Shoemakers, Williamses, Douglas Thomases, Turnbulls, Blackfords, Bruces and Igleharts.

A particularly potent blend is that of the Symingtons and Charles Harrisons. This was brought about by the marriage of Emily Harrison to W. Stuart Symington. As in the case of the proverbial MacGregor, where a Symington sits is the head of the table, and the Harrisons too are quite capable of holding their own in any company. A conspicuous product of this union is W. Stuart Symington, Jr., who in recent years has played such a prominent part in Washington in the program of national defense.

Mr. Symington might have inherited self-confidence on both sides of his family. That his father had it in abundance is illustrated by a single incident. On the occasion of the inauguration of A. Lawrence Lowell as president of Harvard, sister universities throughout the land were invited to send representatives. Mr. Symington attended as representative of his alma mater, Johns Hopkins. At the luncheon which followed most of the guests were overawed by the assemblage of Harvard men, surrendered to their inferiority complexes and hardly dared open their mouths. Not so Stuart Symington. When he was called on he rose and delivered an entire speech in Negro dialect. It brought down the house.

A blend which has produced even more startling results is that of the Fishers and Bruces. The origin of the Fisher family in Carroll County already has been mentioned. The first of the Virginia Bruces to arrive in Baltimore was William Cabell Bruce. He was a son of Charles Bruce of "Staunton Hill" in Halifax County. Situated just north of the Carolina border this castellated mansion stands out defiantly on the heights above the Staunton River, protecting the Old Dominion from roving Carolinians much as the strongholds of the Marcher lords used to protect England from the Welsh.

Cabell Bruce had brains, blood and looks, but the Civil War had made his family land-poor. He had very recently been graduated from the law school at the University of Virginia where he crowned his career by beating another promising young man in the annual oratorical contest. His unsuccessful opponent was Woodrow Wilson. Describing the incident in later years Mr. Bruce used to conclude by remarking that "Wilson didn't behave very well about it either."

Shortly after his arrival in Baltimore Mr. Bruce won the heart of Louise Este Fisher, daughter of Judge William A. Fisher and a person of unusually forceful character. Mr. Bruce entered into a partnership with his brother-in-law Este Fisher in the practice of law. At the same time he began a public career as a political reformer which took him to the State Legislature and, later, to the United States Senate. In addition he gave further evidence of his scholarship by writing definitive biographies of John Randolph of Roanoke and of Benjamin Franklin. For the Franklin biography he was awarded the Pulitzer Prize.

The combined talents of William Cabell Bruce and of his wife were inherited by their sons James and David. James won the hand of Ellen Keyser whose beauty, charm and family background combined to make the match a brilliant one. At a comparatively early age James reached the peak of his profession as president of the Baltimore Trust Company which had just taken occupancy of its 35 story skyscraper in downtown Baltimore.

Unfortunately the expansion of the Baltimore Trust coincided with the boom which followed World War I and ended with the crash of 1929. The Baltimore Trust was one of the first victims. When the institution closed its doors Baltimore experienced a shock hardly less than the one which followed the Baltimore Fire. A less determined man than Mr. Bruce might have closed his career then and there. On the contrary no phoenix ever rose more majestically from its ashes than did James Bruce from those of the Baltimore Trust. He left Baltimore to pursue his fortune in New York and prospered greatly as one of the leading lights in National Dairy Products. Then the old diplomatic urge overtook him. When, in 1948, even the most discerning imagined that President Truman's goose was cooked, James stuck by him loyally and actually raised more hard cash for the campaign than did Louis A. Johnson. So when Mr. Truman resumed his new lease on the White House it was not surprising that James Bruce was named United States Ambassador to Argentina. He was credited with handling his mission effectively and returned home with his reputation greater than ever. Indeed he was slated for the post of United States Ambassador to the Court of St. James's had not President Truman at the last minute been forced by his advisers to change his mind.

Had Mr. Truman not reneged Baltimore would have the rare distinction of seeing two of its sons, and themselves brothers, respectively as ambassadors in London and Paris. For David Bruce already was occupying the United States Embassy in the French capital. Having served in the Maryland Legislature, the Virginia Legislature and various important Federal posts, David's career has been as distinguished as that of James.

Leading citizens of Baltimore also are Howard Bruce and Albert Bruce, nephews of the late Senator, and first cousins of James and David. Howard and Albert started as poor relations but forged ahead by the sweat of their brows. Howard first made his mark with the Bartlett-Hayward Company but he has been engaged in many other enterprises. No citizen of Baltimore enjoys greater respect. It is significant that when disaster descended upon the Baltimore Trust Company it was Cousin Howard who was called in to do what he could to restore confidence. He too has held important posts in the Federal Government as well as being a political power in the State. He married Mary Graham Bowdoin, member of an old Baltimore family. Their country estate "Belmont," a few miles to the south of the city, is one of the showplaces of Howard County. Albert also has made his mark as an industrialist. And he, too, allied himself with another old Baltimore family by his marriage with Helen Whitridge.

After the turn of the century large families began to disappear from the upper reaches of Baltimore society. Among the last to carry on this fine old tradition were the Gustavus Obers with six sons and three daughters, the Isaac Dixons with six daughters and two sons, the Blanchard Randalls with four daughters and three sons, the Ferdinand Chatard Dugans with a grand total of seven sons and five daughters, the Key Comptons with seven sons, the Robert Garretts with four daughters and three sons, and the Arthur Barksdale Kinsolvings with five daughters and two sons. These figures are exclusive of children who died in infancy.

A major addition to the life of the city were the Kinsolvings who took up their residence when in 1906 Dr. Kinsolving accepted a call as rector to Old St. Paul's Church. Both Dr. Kinsolving and Mrs. Kinsolving were born Virginians. Mrs. Kinsolving brought in more of the Bruce blood, being a daughter of Seddon

Bruce of Richmond, a niece of William Cabell and a first cousin of Howard, Albert, James and David.

Dr. Kinsolving served as rector of St. Paul's for the impressive span of thirty-six years before being retired as rector emeritus in 1942. During the early years of his incumbency the old rectory at Liberty and Saratoga Streets was a cheerful and hospitable place with its household of children. Very soon the four attractive older girls—Bruce, Sally, Eleanor and Anne—were entertaining a succession of beaux, while Lucinda Lee was still in school. All five married. The most brilliant match according to wordly standards was that of Anne to John Nicholas Brown of Providence, Rhode Island, a young man of large fortune.

Dr. Kinsolving was blessed with keen wit and a delightful sense of humor that have endeared him to countless people and made him the life of every party he has attended. Before their marriage John Nicholas Brown asked Anne what she thought would be an appropriate fee to give her father for performing the ceremony. The amount he suggested ran into five figures. Anne protested, declaring that her father would not consider accepting anything. Afterward when he recited the story, the Doctor's terse comment was: "The dear girl spoke too soon." Late in life Mrs. Kinsolving went over to the Roman Catholic Church and soon thereafter Sally married a member of the Jewish faith. Dr. Kinsolving resigned himself to the situation with the philosophical conclusion that it was evident God intended him to be the connecting link between Abraham and the Pope. The Doctor is now in his ninety-first year and his wit is still nimble. He and Mrs. Kinsolving continue the idyllic existence that began when they were first married. Once Mrs. Kinsolving paid her husband the highest compliment a wife could give when, at a parish meeting in his honor, she testified that "Dr. Kinsolving never preaches from the pulpit anything he doesn't practice at home."

Something very much worth while went out of the life of Baltimore when the big families passed from the picture. The memory of them lingers on, refreshed by portraits, mahogany, silver and china that have been distributed widely among the many descendants and which once were part of the great establishments they called home. These are the sole remains of fortunes profligately dissipated through cheerful production of children unlimited.

Chapter 28

ODDMENTS AND REMAINDERS

IN COMPOSING a dissertation on Baltimore the great difficulty is finding a place to stop. For, when the picture appears fairly complete, one is reminded of some vital individual or institution that has been overlooked.

Surely it is inexcusable to wait until the end of the book to remark on the row houses with their white steps, which usually are singled out as the most obvious characteristic of the city. They are still there, stretched out like the keys on a piano. But, in the vast amount of building which has taken place since World War II the design has been streamlined and modernized. Baltimore's new houses now give the impression of being welded into a single whole. Steps and porches are subordinated while attention is directed rather toward surfaces of rich, warm Baltimore brick. That local brick, by the way, is another feature of the town that warrants special mention.

There is no valid defense for having gone thus far without more than a brief reference to the Baltimore Symphony Orchestra. It is the most conspicuous feature of the musical life of the city. It has the distinction also of having been the first symphonic orchestra in the United States to be organized by a municipality. The order was issued by Mayor James H. Preston in the winter of 1915-1916; Frederick R. Huber was named Municipal Director of Music and assigned to do the job. Gustave Strube, of the faculty of the Peabody Conservatory, became the first conductor. The orchestra continued as a municipal responsibility until 1942 when labor troubles forced its discontinuance. Almost immediately however an orchestra association took over the management, while the city still helps with a sizable appropriation. The series of midweek subscription concerts, the popular Sunday concerts at reduced prices and the concerts for school children on Saturday morning provide the Baltimore public with liberal doses of the best music. The orchestra also tours Maryland towns, sometimes journeys to the south and also has been as far north as Canada, from which came its present conductor Reginald Stewart. Several of the original members of the orchestra are still with it. An "original" recently retired was Bart Wirtz, veteran cellist, one of the city's best-known and most beloved musicians.

Peale's Museum has previously been mentioned in connection with the early demonstration of illuminating gas. It exists today under the same name and on the original site. It was in the early 1800's that Rembrandt Peale, a son of Charles Willson Peale the artist, came to Baltimore to exhibit the skeleton of a mammoth. The enterprise must have been a success for, in 1813, he returned to stay and set up a museum on North Holliday Street. Here he offered for the edification of the populace a collection of stuffed birds and animals, wax figures and a gallery of paintings. Eventually the museum was moved to the northwest corner of Market and Calvert Streets. This second home is conspicuous in early prints. The original building was turned over to the municipality and served as the City Hall from 1830 to 1876. After that it was left in neglect until 1931 when plans were made to restore it as nearly as possible to its original condition under the painstaking supervision of the architect, John H. Scarff. It was opened again as a museum, housing collections of paintings, drawings and other objects, and putting on exhibits having to do primarily with the city and its people. Typical of these was an exhibit a year or two ago of original water colors of the Indian country made by Alfred J. Miller, a Baltimorean who was a member of an expedition to the Far West in the 1840's. Miller's sketches of Indians, if somewhat dramatized, are nevertheless regarded as one of the most valuable examples of early American art.

There ought to have been mention long before of Druid Hill Park, a tract of several hundred acres in northwest Baltimore, comprising extensive groves of trees, lawns, walks, driveways, bandstands, a boat lake, a botanical garden and a zoo. Druid Hill Park came into being in October, 1860. The individual most responsible for it was that versatile citizen J. H. B. Latrobe. He headed the commission that purchased the land from Lloyd Rogers, whose estate it was. A crowd of men, women and children, to the estimate number of 30,000, took part in the dedication ceremonies at which the school children of the city sang an ode composed for the occasion by Mr. Latrobe.

Since J. H. B. Latrobe has again come into the picture, now is an appropriate time to speak of his invention, the Latrobe stove, which carried Baltimore's fame to the outside world almost as effectively as the Johns Hopkins University has since done. This was an ingenious device for heating two rooms at one time. A coal grate, inclosed in isinglass, heated a downstairs room while a flue carried warm air to the room above. Herein lay the crude principle of central heating. Until the turn of the last century many of the humbler homes of Baltimore, as well as of other cities, knew no other heating than a Latrobe stove.

Public parks bring to mind another of their promoters, Major Richard M. Venable. A Virginian and a Confederate veteran, the Major came to Baltimore in 1871 and engaged in the practice of law. Appointed president of the Park Board in 1904 he is credited with tripling Patterson Park in East Baltimore, enlarging Carroll Park and in creating Wyman and Gwynns Falls Parks. At his death, in 1910, in accordance with his wishes, his ashes were strewn over Druid Hill Park. Major Venable was a bachelor, kept house on Calvert Street and was waited on by an impressive staff of Negro servants. It is said that he boasted he never had servant trouble. His secret was to keep a close watch on the market and pay his servants a dollar a week more than the prevailing wage.

There should have been at least a passing word or two about Greenmount Cemetery, Baltimore's Valhalla. There are other cemeteries within the city limits, but Greenmount has held a preferred position because of the distinguished company it has attracted. The site was the country estate of Robert Oliver, one of the city's leading merchants. When Greenmount was dedicated in 1839, John P. Kennedy delivered an oration in which he grew ecstatic over its trees and meadows and streams which made it a sylvan paradise. That description draws a smile from those who know it today as a bleak hillside in the heart of the city from which all but a few trees have been removed to make room for the graves. The cemetery now contains some 54,000 of the city's dead. Madam Bonaparte and the Booths already have been mentioned as occupying spaces in Greenmount. Other celebrated persons whose bodies rest there are J. H. B. Latrobe; his brother Benjamin H. Latrobe, the engineer; and Ferdinand C. Latrobe, the longtime city mayor; Enoch Pratt, General Joseph E. Johnston of the Confederate Army; Sidney Lanier the poet, William

T. Walters and Henry Walters the art collectors. A more recent arrival is Albert Cabell Ritchie, for fifteen years Governor of Maryland.

Distinguished company of an earlier age also is found in the graveyard adjoining Westminister Presbyterian Church and that of Old St. Paul's which stands by itself west of the downtown business district.

Ross Winans is among those who rest in Greenmount. He will be recalled as the inventor who pioneered the designing of railway equipment for the B. & O. His fame spread to Russia where Czar Nicholas I had plans for building a railroad and invited Winans to do the job. Mr. Winans declined and instead sent his sons, William and Thomas DeKay Winans. Tradition has it that when the route was discussed the Czar took a ruler and drew a straight line from Moscow to St. Petersburg and ordered the right of way to follow it.

Thomas DeKay Winans returned to Baltimore with a French wife and there built a fabulous mansion at Baltimore Street and Fremont Avenue in the midst of an extensive park, which he ornamented with the reproductions of classical sculpture. He called the place Alexandroffsky. The nude figures caused a hue and cry from the neighbors. Most vociferous were said to have been the protests of the ladies of the bordellos then situated not many blocks away. They were horrified at the gross immorality of the spectacle. So Mr. Winans had to appease local opinion by hiding the statues behind a high stone wall.

Alexandroffsky was inherited by Winans' only daughter, Marie Celeste, who became Mrs. Gaun M. Hutton. The Huttons had three daughters and a son and a few carefully selected children were invited to play with them. The guests brought home spectacular stories of the largest Christmas tree they had ever seen, and of holes bored in the hardwood floors through which warm air passed to heat the rooms. This invention of Thomas Winans was a forerunner of radiant heat. The mansion at Alexandroffsky was set off by a tall ornamented chimney, another invention of the builder designed to carry away the fumes from the gas lights. Also an impressive feature of the mansion was a grand stairway with a mahogany rail supported by sixteen brackets of solid silver.

And there was an aviary for Mrs. Hutton's collection of more than a hundred song birds from all parts of the world. It was a great day for Baltimore in the 1930's when the Huttons had departed and a sale was arranged by the estate, and Alexandroffsky was thrown open to the public for the first time.

Nor should the Charcoal Club be overlooked. It was incorporated in 1885 by a group of artists and still holds meetings in a converted stable on Eutaw Place. Its prize possession is a beer growler of hammered brass lined with silver and ornamented with a female nude on the rim. This was designed by the artist A. J. Volck, an early member of the club who is best known for his series of beautifully etched satirical cartoons of Abraham Lincoln. The club used to sponsor a Bal des Arts, a wild costume party, which rivaled its namesake in Paris. It has grown sedate with the years and now its regular meetings are devoted to talks on art by such distinguished club members as Stanislav Rembski, the portraitist, and R. McGill Mackall who is known for his portraits and also for his murals and stained glass. Gala occasions of the club are the Halloween Party, the New Year's Eve Party and the Ignatius L. Glutz dinner on April 1st. This last event celebrates an imaginary character who is supposed to have invented modern art.

No treatise on Baltimore surely should omit the Flag House on Pratt Street. It was in this quaint little dwelling down near the harbor that Mary Pickersgill pieced together the original "Star Spangled Banner" that flew over Fort McHenry and inspired the National Anthem. It might not have been the National Anthem had it not been for the indefatigable labors of another picturesque Baltimorean, Mrs. Reuben Ross Holloway. Mrs. Holloway was the driving force behind Congressman J. Charles Linthicum who introduced the bill which eventually was enacted into law making "Star Spangled Banner" the official choice.

Thereafter Mrs. Holloway regarded the flag as her personal charge, handing out certificates of merit to business houses and other institutions which displayed it in the proper manner. Mrs. Holloway also was famous for her hats. She was short of stature and to accentuate her height always wore a hat that went straight up a distance of at least a foot. The color and trimming might change but the shape was invariably the same.

A contemporary of Mrs. Holloway, who also was prominent for years in the life of the city, was Elizabeth Gilman, daughter of President Gilman of the Hopkins. "Miss Lizzie," as she was popularly known, developed into a leading liberal. Her sympathies were always with the downtrodden. She sent food and supplies to striking miners and raised funds for striking seamen. She was the first woman in Maryland to be a candidate for Governor, running on the Socialist ticket. Other elections found her as candidate of the same party successively for United States Senator, Mayor of Baltimore and even Sheriff of Baltimore City. An apparently shy, mild-mannered person she would have been lost in a crowd save for the chow dog which invariably accompanied her on her trips downtown. Yet in her time she terrified the conservative element with her socialistic doctrine about as effectively as the Communists terrify today.

It would be appropriate to include the Gilmors. First to arrive was Robert Gilmor, a Scotchman, who entered the mercantile business and made a fortune. He is credited with having opened American trade with Russia. His son Robert continued in the business and was, as well, one of Baltimore's most cultivated men. He traveled extensively abroad, was a collector of books and art and had his portrait painted both by Sir Thomas Lawrence and Gilbert Stewart. Robert Gilmor, 2nd, kept a fine cellar and was generous with his wines. But he abhorred waste. His motto was "Fill what you please, but drink what you fill." The next famous Gilmor was Captain Harry, dashing cavalryman of the Confederate Army. He led the raid on Baltimore in 1864 in which Governor Bradford's house was burned.

The list of persons and things deserving mention could be carried on almost indefinitely. But practical considerations demand that the work be brought to a close at risk (even with the knowledge) of having made glaring and inexcusable omissions. It will have to be left to writers who follow to make amends.

For there will be other writers to carry on the story, assuming always that man does not succeed in destroying himself as, at the present moment, he seems so determined to do. Since the invention of the atomic bomb we can no longer speak with complete confidence of the future of our cities. Considerations of defense may eventually call for a dispersion which either will dissolve the cities or else transform them into something very different from what they now are.

Barring such disaster Baltimore's future is as promising as her past has been distinguished. Her natural facilities and her strategic location give every guarantee of continued prosperity. Her leaders still show enterprise. Her growth and progress may not be spectacular but they should be steady. Whatever the future holds in store and whatever the world may become, something tells us that there will always be a Baltimore full of amiable people, going its leisurely and contented way.

BIBLIOGRAPHY

A History of the City of Baltimore. Published by the *Baltimore American*. Baltimore, 1902.

A History of the University Founded by Johns Hopkins. By John C. French. Baltimore, 1946.

American Notes. By Charles Dickens. New York, 1842.

A Surgeon's Autobiography. By Hugh H. Young. New York, 1946.

Aunt Priscilla in the Kitchen. By "Aunt Priscilla." Baltimore, 1929.

Baltimore and the 19th of April, 1861. By George William Brown. Baltimore, 1887.

Baltimore, A Not Too Serious History. By Letitia Stockett. Baltimore, 1928.

Baltimore, A Pioneer in Organized Baseball. By John A. Lancaster. Maryland Historical Society Magazine. March, 1940.

Baltimore in the '80s and '90s. By Meredith Janvier. Baltimore, 1931.

Baltimore Health News. December, 1943.

Baltimore on the Chesapeake. By Hamilton Owens. New York, 1941.

Chronicles of Baltimore. By J. Thomas Scharf. Baltimore, 1874.

Charles Street. Yesterday, Today and Tomorrow. Published by the Charles Street Association. Baltimore, 1932.

Eat, Drink and Be Merry in Maryland. By Frederick Philip Stieff. New York, 1932.

Enoch Pratt. By Richard Hart. Baltimore, 1935.

Fads and Fancies. By Charles C. Bombaugh. Philadelphia, 1905.

Fountain Inn Diary. By Matthew Page Andrews. New York, 1948.

Francis Asbury, A Methodist Saint. By Herbert Asbury. New York, 1927.

Green Mount Cemetery. By Gerald W. Johnson. Baltimore, 1938.

Henrietta Szold. By Marvin Lowenthal. New York, 1942.

Highlights of Baltimore Jewry. Published by the Jewish Educational Alliance. Baltimore, 1945.

History of Baltimore City and Baltimore County. By J. Thomas Scharf. Philadelphia, 1881.

Iron Men and Their Dogs. By Ferdinand C. Latrobe. Baltimore, 1941.

Israfel. By Hervey Allen. New York, 1934.

J. H. B. Latrobe and His Times. By John E. Semmes. Baltimore, 1917.

Johns Hopkins. By Helen Hopkins Thom. Baltimore, 1929.

Joshua Johnston. By J. Hall Pleasants. Maryland Historical Society Magazine. June, 1942.

King Lehr and the Gilded Age. By Elizabeth Drexel Lehr. Philadelphia, 1935.

BIBLIOGRAPHY

LETTERS OF CHARLES DICKENS. London, 1882.

LEVERING FAMILY HISTORY AND GENEALOGY. By John Levering. Indianapolis, 1897.

LIFE OF GEORGE PEABODY. By Phebe A. Hanaford. Boston, 1870.

LIFE OF JAMES CARDINAL GIBBONS. By Allen S. Will. Baltimore, 1911.

MARYLAND AND THE THOROUGHBRED. By D. Sterett Gittings. Baltimore, 1932.

MAY'S HISTORY OF THE THEATER IN BALTIMORE. Maryland Historical Society Manuscript.

MONUMENTS AND MEMORIALS. By William Sener Rusk, M.A. Baltimore, 1929.

OLD BALTIMORE. By Annie Leakin Sioussat. New York, 1931.

RECOLLECTIONS GRAVE AND GAY. By Mrs. Burton Harrison. New York, 1911.

REMINISCENCES OF BALTIMORE. By Jacob Frey. Baltimore, 1893.

SECOND ANNUAL REPORT OF THE AMERICAN SOCIETY FOR COLONIZING THE FREE PEOPLE, OF COLOUR OF THE UNITED STATES. Washington, 1819.

THE DELPHIAN CLUB. By John Earle Uhler. Maryland Historical Society Magazine. December, 1925.

THE DEMOCRATIC PARTY. By Frank R. Kent. New York, 1928.

THE FIRST FORTY YEARS OF WASHINGTON SOCIETY. Portrayed by Family Letters of Mrs. Samuel Harrison Smith. Margaret Bayard. New York, 1906.

THE GREAT PHYSICIAN (WILLIAM OSLER) by Edith Gittings Reid. New York, 1931.

THE JEWS OF BALTIMORE. By Isidor Blum. Baltimore 1910.

THE JOHNS HOPKINS HOSPITAL AND THE JOHNS HOPKINS MEDICAL SCHOOL. By Alan M. Chesney. Baltimore, 1943.

THE LORDS BALTIMORE. By James W. Foster and Beta K. Manakee. Enoch Pratt Free Library Publication. Baltimore. 1942.

THE MARYLAND GERMANS. By Dieter Cunz. Princeton, N.J., 1948.

THE MARYLAND HUNT CUP. By Stuart Rose. New York, 1931.

THE MARYLAND JOCKEY CLUB. By C. Edward Sparrow. Baltimore, 1924.

THE MAYORS OF BALTIMORE. By Wilbur F. Coyle. Baltimore, 1919.

THE MEDICAL ANNALS OF MARYLAND. By Eugene F. Cordell. Baltimore, 1903.

THE STORY OF AVIATION IN BALTIMORE. Magazine Baltimore. November, 1941.

THE STORY OF MARYLAND POLITICS. By Frank Richardson Kent. Baltimore, 1911.

BIBLIOGRAPHY

THE STORY OF THE BALTIMORE AND OHIO RAILROAD. By Edward Hungerford. New York, 1928.

THE STORY OF THE JOHNS HOPKINS. By Bertram M. Bernheim. New York, 1948.

THE SUNPAPERS OF BALTIMORE. By Gerald W. Johnson, Frank R. Kent, H. L. Mencken and Hamilton Owens. New York, 1937.

THE TRUE STORY OF THE MARYLAND FLAG. By Francis Barnum Culver. Baltimore, 1934.

THE VAGABONDS. By G. H. Pouder. Gardens, Houses and People. November, 1946.

TOM CULLEN OF BALTIMORE. By Judith Robinson. New York, 1949.

WHEN THE HOPKINS CAME TO BALTIMORE. By Allen Kerr Bond. Baltimore, 1927.

FILES OF THE SUN, *The Sunday Sun* and *The Evening Sun*.

INDEX

[383]